STUDIES IN THE HISTORY OF THE NEAR EAST

Studies in the History of the Near East

P. M. HOLT

Professor in Arab History in the University of London

FRANK CASS : LONDON

This collection first published 1973 in Great Britain by
FRANK CASS & COMPANY LIMITED
67 Great Russell Street, London WC1B 3BT, England

and in United States of America by
FRANK CASS AND COMPANY LIMITED
c/o International Scholarly Book Services, Inc.
P.O. Box 4347, Portland, Oregon 97208

ISBN 0 7146 2984 7

Library of Congress Catalog Card No. 72-92964

Printed in Great Britain by
The Camelot Press Ltd, London and Southampton

Contents

INTRODUCTION

THIS volume brings together a number of studies concerned with the Near East and its history from the sixteenth century. They fall into three groups. The first is concerned with English Arabists of the seventeenth and early eighteenth centuries, and particularly with Edward Pococke, whose researches marked the emancipation of scholarship from bigotry, and who, with the other great orientalists of his time, laid the foundations of the modern understanding of Islam, its history and its culture. The papers in the second group deal with the history of the Nilotic Sudan, and especially attempt to exploit the sparse source-materials available on the Funj Sultanate and to throw some light on developments between the sixteenth and the nineteenth century. Another "dark age" in modern Near Eastern history is the subject of the third group of papers—the period of Egyptian history from the Ottoman conquest in 1517 to the French occupation in 1798. Here the difficulty is not lack of documentation; the source-materials, both chronicles and archives in Arabic and Turkish, are abundant, but so far they have attracted few scholars to research.

With the exception of the first, all the studies in this volume have previously appeared in learned journals and elsewhere over a number of years. I have taken the opportunity of their re-publication to revise and correct them in matters of detail, and, in one instance, to combine two related papers into a single article. Here it is my duty and my pleasure to thank those responsible for the original publication of these papers for permitting me to re-publish them; these are:

Cambridge University Press and the Editors of *The Journal of African History* ("The Coming of the Funj"; originally "Funj Origins: a Critiquc and New Evidence", *JAH*, IV, 1963, 39–55, and "Sultan Selim I and the Sudan", *JAH*, VIII, 1967, 19–23).

The University of Chicago Press ("Modernization and Reaction in the Nineteenth-Century Sudan" from William R. Polk and Richard L. Chambers (edd.), *Beginnings of modernization in the Middle East: the nineteenth century*, Chicago and London, 1968, 401–15. © 1968 by The University of Chicago).

Princeton University ("Holy Families and Islam in the Sudan". Princeton Near East Papers, Number 4, 1967).

The Editor, *Sudan Notes and Records* ("Four Funj Land-Charters". *SNR*, L, 1969, 2–14).

The Publications Committee, School of Oriental and African Studies, University of London ("The Treatment of Arab History by Prideaux, Ockley and Sale" from Bernard Lewis and P. M. Holt (edd.), *Historians of the Middle East*, London, 1962, 290–302; "Ottoman Egypt (1517–1798): an Account of Arabic Historical Sources" from P. M. Holt (ed.), *Political and social change in modern Egypt*, London, 1968, 3–12).

The Editorial Board, *Bulletin of the School of Oriental and African Studies* ("The Study of Arabic Historians in Seventeenth-Century England", *BSOAS*, XIX, 1957, 444–55; "The Sons of Jābir and their Kin: a Clan of Sudanese Religious Notables", *BSOAS*, XXX, 1967, 142–57; "Al-Jabartī's Introduction to the History of Ottoman Egypt", *BSOAS*, XXV, 1962, 38–51; "The Beylicate in Ottoman Egypt during the Seventeenth Century", *BSOAS*, XXIV, 1961, 214–48; "The Exalted Lineage of Riḍwān Bey: some Observations on a Seventeenth-Century Mamluk Genealogy", *BSOAS*, XXII, 1959, 221–30; "The Career of Küçük Muḥammad (1676–94)", *BSOAS*, XXVI, 1963, 269–87).

My thanks are also due to those who advised me generally or on specific points when these studies were first prepared; particularly my colleague, Professor Bernard Lewis, the Rev. Dr A. J. Arkell, Professor J. W. Fück and Sayed Mohamed Omer Beshir.

P. M. HOLT

Short References

Brockelmann, *GAL*; *S*: C. Brockelmann, *Geschichte der arabischen Literatur* (2nd edn., Leiden, 1943–9); *Supplementband* (Leiden, 1937–42).

Bruce, *Travels*: James Bruce, *Travels to discover the source of the Nile, in the years 1768, 1769, 1770, 1771, 1772, and 1773* (2nd edn., Edinburgh, 1805).

BSOAS: *Bulletin of the School of Oriental and African Studies* (London).

BSOS: *Bulletin of the School of Oriental Studies* (London).

Crawford, *Fung kingdom*: O. G. S. Crawford, *The Fung kingdom of Sennar* (Gloucester, 1951).

DNB: *Dictionary of national biography* (London, 1908–9).

*EI*²: *The encyclopaedia of Islam* (2nd edn., Leiden and London, 1960–).

FC: The Funj Chronicle, published as al-Shāṭir Buṣaylī ʻAbd al-Jalīl (ed.), *Makhṭūṭat Kātib al-Shūna* (n.p., n.d. [? Cairo, c. 1961]).

Fück, *Die arabischen Studien*: J. Fück, *Die arabischen Studien in Europa bis in den Anfang des 20. Jahrhunderts* (Leipzig, 1955).

Ghazawāt/Barq: Quṭb al-Dīn Muḥammad b. Aḥmad al-Nahrawālī al-Makkī, *al-Barq al-Yamānī fi'l-fatḥ al-ʻUthmānī*, published as *Ghazawāt al-Jarākisa wa'l-Atrāk fī janūb al-Jazīra* (al-Riyāḍ, 1387/1967).

Hill, *Biographical dictionary*: Richard [L.] Hill, *A biographical dictionary of the Sudan* (2nd edn., London, 1967).

Ibn Iyās: Mohamed Mostafa (ed.), *Die Chronik des Ibn Ijās* [Muḥammad b. Aḥmad b. Iyās al-Ḥanafī, *Badā'iʻ al-zuhūr fī waqā'iʻ al-duhūr*], V (2nd edn., Cairo, 1380/1961).

al-Jabartī: ʻAbd al-Raḥmān b. Ḥasan al-Jabartī, *ʻAjā'ib al-āthār fi'l-tarājim wa'l-akhbār* (Būlāq, 1297).

JAH: *The Journal of African History* (Cambridge).

JESHO: *Journal of the Economic and Social History of the Orient* (Leiden).

JRAS: *Journal of the Royal Asiatic Society* (London).

MacMichael, *Arabs*: H. A. MacMichael, *A history of the Arabs in the Sudan* (Cambridge, 1922).

Shaw, *Ottoman Egypt*: Stanford J. Shaw, *The financial and administrative organization and development of Ottoman Egypt 1517–1789* (Princeton, N.J., 1962).

Shuqayr, *Ta'rīkh:* Naʻūm Shuqayr, *Ta'rīkh al-Sūdān al-qadīm wa'l-ḥadīth wa-jughrafiyyatuh* (Cairo, n.d. [1903]).

SNR: *Sudan Notes and Records* (Khartoum).

T: Yūsuf Faḍl Ḥasan (ed.), Muḥammad al-Nūr b. Ḍayfallāh, *Kitāb al-ṭabaqāt fī khuṣūṣ al-awliyā' wa'l-ṣāliḥīn wa'l-ʻulamā' wa'l-shuʻarā' fi'l-Sūdān* (Khartoum, 1971).

Twells, *Works*: Leonard Twells, *The theological works of the learned Dr. Pocock* (London, 1740).

I

EARLY STUDENTS OF ARAB HISTORY IN ENGLAND

1

AN OXFORD ARABIST: EDWARD POCOCKE (1604–91)

THE long life of Edward Pococke covers nearly the whole of the seventeenth century and his career illustrates the early history of Arabic studies at Oxford.[1] His father, also named Edward, was vicar of Chieveley in Berkshire. He was born in Oxford and christened on 11 November 1604, at the church of St. Peter-in-the-East. His early education was at the grammar school of Thame, some fourteen miles from Oxford, which had been opened in 1570 by the executors of Lord Williams of Thame, an ambitious politician who died in 1559, president of the Council of the Marches. The headmaster in Pococke's time was Richard Boucher or Butcher (1561-1627), an Oxfordshire man who had been educated at Winchester and New College, with which foundations the school at Thame was connected. Pococke's memories of his teacher were kindly; Twells describes him as "a Man of great Accuracy in Grammatical Learning, whose Skill and Industry the Doctor, even in his old Age, would often very gratefully remember".[2] The function of the school was mainly the teaching of Latin, in which the master was advised by the statutes to "follow as nearly as he can, the method of teaching which he will know to be served at Winchester in the School founded by Wykeham".[3] Pococke may also have learnt Greek at school, although that language does not seem to have been prescribed by the statutes.

In the spring of 1619 Pococke matriculated at Magdalen Hall in Oxford, and was admitted as a scholar of Corpus Christi on 11 December 1620. He graduated as Bachelor of Arts on 28 November 1622, and as Master on 28 March 1626. He became a probationer-fellow of Corpus on 24 July 1628, and on 20 December 1629 he was ordained. His interest in oriental studies had already appeared. Between 1626 and 1629, a refugee German scholar, Matthias Pasor,[4] who had been professor of philosophy and mathematics at Heidelberg, but had fled when the city was sacked in 1622, lectured in Hebrew, Aramaic, Syriac and Arabic at Oxford. His inaugural lecture, delivered on 25 October 1626, was published as *Oratio pro linguae Arabicae professione* (Oxford, 1627). It deals very fully with the reasons for the study of Arabic which weighed with European scholars of the period, and was a prototype of many similar disquisitions. Before Pasor left to take up the chair of philosophy at Groningen, he had taught Pococke the rudiments of Arabic.

Pococke continued his study under the pioneer English Arabist, William Bedwell (c. 1562–1632),[5] one of the company of translators who produced the Authorized Version of the Bible, and, from 1607, vicar of Tottenham High Cross. In 1612, Bedwell published an Arabic version of St. John's epistles, the Preface to which contains a defence of Arabic studies.[6] Unusually in writings of this type, Bedwell suggests the importance of Arabic to diplomats and merchants, but he passes on quickly to speak of its value as a language of learning, and as an aid to Hebrew studies. Pococke's own first work was an edition of the Syriac version of II Peter, II and III John and Jude, accompanied by the Greek version, a Latin translation and notes. He was encouraged to publish it by the Dutch scholar, Gerard John Vossius (who visited England in 1629, and was presented by William Laud to a canonry at Canterbury), and it was printed by Ludovicus de Dieu at Leiden.

The opening of the next stages in Pococke's career may be told in the words of the Court Book of the Levant Company. At "a Generall Court holden at the Governor's House on Thursday the 25th. of March 1630", the Governor informed those present "that the speciall occasion of somoning this Court at this tyme was to make choice of a Preacher to resyde at Aleppo to goe over in the next shipps, and did first move to knowe whether they would send a Preacher or noe, wch being considered of as a matter tending to the Glory of God the reputacion of the Companie, and the benefitt of the English Nation there resident, was wth free and full consent approved of and resolved by the whole vote of this Assembly; And then the Governor made knowne unto them a gent who was desirous to be entertained in that employment: namely one Mr. Pocock a Mr of Arts of whom both himselfe and others of the Company had received very good testymony and recommendacions both for his abilitie in Learninge, Soundness in the Studdy of Devynitie, conformitie to the constitucions of the Church and integritie of Lyfe and conversacion, who being heere present and expresseing his desire to be entertained, was made acquainted with the anuall stypend the Company have formerly and doe allow to Men of his qualitie if hee was willing to accept of if hee should bee chosen to that employmt: but for that the Company have usually (before they have made choice of such as they have heretofore sent over) heard them Preach and upon approbacion have made choice of them, They have therefore desired that Mr. Pocock would give them a Sermon on Wensday next in th'afternoone at the Parish of St. Andrewes Undershaft wch he willingly condiscended unto And at the next Court they will proceed to their choice accordingly."[7]

Pocock duly preached his sermon and a General Court was held "on Wensday the Last of March 1630". The record of its proceedings is as follows:

"*Mr. Edw. Pocock chosen to be Preacher at Aleppo*
This Court being espetially and duly appointed for the choosing of a Preacher to resyde at Aleppo, Mr. Edw: Pocock recommended to the Company at the last Court being a Mr. of Arts, and fellowe of Corpus Christie Colledg in Oxford and having made a sermon to the Companie this afternoone according to their desire and custome, Was by free consent of this Court chosen for supply of that place, who is to reside there for the space of 4 yeares, upon the Salary or Stypend of 50£ per an to begin at the tyme of his arrivall at Aleppo, to be paid ether heere in Sterling monie or there by 200 dollars per ann . . . and the Court doe thinke fitt of their respect unto him to allow him 20£ towards the furnishing himselfe wth Bookes and other necessaryes for his voyage. All wch hee being made acquainted did most thankfully accept of; And to take his passage upon the next shipps bound for that place."[8]

Pococke arrived at Alexandretta, the port of Aleppo, on 14 October 1630, and reached Aleppo itself three days later. During the years he spent there he took great pains to improve his knowledge of Arabic. He had first a Jewish teacher but later an Arab named Fatḥallāh (Phatallah).[9] Visible evidence of his Arabic studies at Aleppo is afforded by his great manuscript transcription of al-Maydānī's collection of six thousand Arabic proverbs, accompanied by Pococke's Latin translation and commentary. This was completed on 12 September 1635. It is still preserved in the Bodleian Library, never having reached publication.[10] In 1636 Pococke returned to England, having acquired a considerable mastery of Arabic. Fatḥallāh gave him the parting assurance that he understood Arabic as well as the *muftī* of Aleppo—who may indeed have been a Turk.

While at Aleppo, Pococke had been in correspondence with William Laud who had been chancellor of Oxford university since 1629, and in 1633 became archbishop of Canterbury. He had heard of Pococke from Bedwell, and wrote in 1631 asking him to bring back Greek and oriental coins and manuscripts when he returned to England. Laud planned the establishment of a chair of Arabic, with a stipend of £40 annually, and in 1634 he wrote to tell Pococke that the new chair was intended for him.[11] On Pococke's return to Oxford, he took his B.D. on 8 July 1636, preaching on that occasion a Latin sermon before the body of royal commissioners who had come to Oxford for the confirmation of the new Laudian statutes of the university.

On 10 August he gave his inaugural lecture, which is lost apart from a passage concerning the Arabs' esteem of poetry.[12] He followed this up with a course of lectures upon the proverbs ascribed to the Caliph 'Alī, using as a textbook a recent publication by the Dutch scholar, Golius (1596–1667), the professor of Arabic at Leiden.[13] "Upon this Book, observing the Directions of the *Archbishop*, in the Statutes he had provided, he spent an Hour every *Wednesday* in *Vacation-time*, and also in *Lent*, explaining the Sense of the Author, and the Things relating to the *Grammar* and *Propriety* of the *Language*; and also showing the Agreement it hath with the *Hebrew* and *Syriack*, as often as there was Occasion. The *Lecture* being ended, he usually tarried for some Time in the publick School, to resolve the Questions of his Hearers, and satisfy them in their Doubts; and always, the Afternoon, gave Admittance in his *Chamber*, from One a-Clock till Four, to all that would come to him for further Conference and Direction."[14]

Among the Pococke manuscripts in the Bodleian Library, two throw some light on the way in which he handled Golius's *Proverbia Alis*. One is a fragment of his own lecture-notes upon the grammar of these proverbs.[15] The second manuscript has all the appearance of being the notebook of one of Pococke's pupils.[16] The writing, which at the start is small and reasonably clear, becomes larger and cruder as we turn the pages. The notes, full at first, become thinner with the passage of time. Contractions abound, and either the course of lectures was never finished or the writer fell off in his attendance. It is possible that the notes are not of the course to which the previous manuscript belongs as they appear to contain rather more elementary material, but unfortunately the student's notes have become so rough by the time that the fragment of the professor's notes begins that comparison is not easy. The student's notes contain frequent page-references on grammatical points. These make possible the identification of the Arabic grammar used in connection with this course, namely Erpenius's *Rudimenta linguae Arabicae*.[17] Pococke's own notes do not include these references but there is a reference in his manuscript to the *Libellus centum regentium* which forms part of another of Erpenius's publications, his *Grammatica Arabica dicta Gjarumia, et libellus centum regentium cum versione Latina et commentariis* (Leiden, 1617), an edition of the Arabic grammatical work usually called *al-Ājurrūmiyya* by Ibn Ājurrūm al-Ṣanhājī (d. 723/1323). The *Libellus centum regentium* is a treatise by al-Jurjānī.

When Golius reissued the large *Grammatic Arabica* of Erpenius in 1656, under the title of *Linguae Arabicae tyrocinium*, he added a certain amount of fresh reading matter. Among this was the first *Maqāma* of al-Ḥarīrī. Pococke used this also as material for his lectures and part of his lecture-notes survives.[18] These notes are also largely grammatical but are intended for a more advanced audience than the lectures on the proverbs. They begin with an account of al-Ḥarīrī and his work. Golius's own text-book contains, besides the proverbs of 'Alī, an Arabic poem, *Lāmiyyat al-'Ajam*, generally known by Pococke and his contemporaries as *Carmen Tograi* from the name of its author, Abū Ismā'īl Ḥusayn b. 'Alī al-Ṭughrā'ī (d. 514/1120). Pococke used to lecture on this poem, and in 1661 he republished it.

Pococke was not, however, satisfied with the materials available in Oxford for pursuing his studies, and sought to make another journey to the East. The arrangements in this connection illuminate a complicated web of patronage, interest and personal relations. Among his friends at this time was John Greaves (1602–52) one of the talented sons of the rector of Colemore in Hampshire.[19] Greaves had some acquaintance with Arabic and Persian, which were germane to his studies in mathematics and astronomy. He was a fellow of Merton, and since 1630 had also held the chair of Geometry at Gresham College in London, where his predecessor had been Dr. Peter Turner (1586–1652).[20] Turner, also a fellow of Merton and Savilian Professor of Geometry at Oxford, belonged to Laud's circle, and on 10 February 1637 Greaves wrote to seek his good offices on Pococke's behalf and his own. Pococke desires, he says,

> "once more to goe into those Parts, and to get further light for the perfit edition of that same excellent authour, with which he is in hand, and for the printing of some others not yet extant, which he likewise intends. It was not possible for him, during his stay at Aleppo, to bring these his intentions to perfection, his College calling upon him continually to returne home, and thereby disquieting him, and the Merchants tying him to too strict termes of preaching, besides the performing of other Ministerial offices. Yet doth he not desire by this journey to draw any greater Expense upon his Grace [Laud], then what his Grace hath already beene pleased to bestowe upon him; or els in situ of this the addition, if it might be, of some Prebendary, or some good living sine cura: So that his purpose is the labour shall be his owne, and the honour my Lords. To whome I conceive it will be a greater honour, to employ a man of such eminent parts in forrein Countries, under the title of procuring bookes, . . . then it can be in staying at home, and making Profession of a bare language."

John Greaves goes on to suggest that his younger brother, Thomas, recently made a fellow of Corpus Christi, could act as Pococke's deputy during his absence abroad, "without any further reward, then that my Lord will graciously protect him in his right to the next Living in the Charter-House gift". He then mentions his own project of making a journey to Constantinople and Alexandria, to obtain antiques as well as to "improve those studies which I had begun in the Orientall languages, and make some Astronomicall observations, a thing that hath beene much desired by the Astronomers of this age, but never undertaken by any". He had discussed this with the Earl of Arundel's agent in Rome, who offered him his master's patronage, but finally decided to finance himself:

> "I intend to lay out 250£ of my owne, in making the fairest and largest instruments of brasse that I can procure, and if I had more, more I would expend. For my maintenance abroad for 3 or 4 yeares for myselfe, and a man to assist me, I thinke my stipend here [i.e. at Gresham College], my allowance from Merton College a little enlarged, and 20£ a year that I shall receive from my mother, with that frugality I have used, may in a reasonable manner be sufficient."

He fears, however, that his stipend at Gresham College will not be paid during his absence, and therefore seeks Laud's influence to obtain a dispensation from the king.[21]

In the summer of 1637, Pococke duly made his way to Istanbul, leaving Thomas Greaves to act as his deputy at Oxford. John Greaves, after spending some months in Istanbul went on to search for manuscripts in Egypt.[22] While at Istanbul, Pococke made the acquaintance of the Orthodox patriarch, Cyril Lucaris. The patriarch had other friends among the English community, amongst them Sir Peter Wyche, the English ambassador, who had named his son Cyril after the patriarch. These foreign connections were no doubt partly responsible for the ultimate fate of the patriarch, who was put to death by order of Sultan Murad IV during Pococke's visit. On his return to England, Pococke passed through Paris where he met the Maronite scholar, Gabriel Sionita[23] and also Hugo Grotius.

When Pococke returned to England in 1641, he found that great changes had occurred. The Long Parliament was in session, and his patron, Laud, had been committed to the Tower. To him went Pococke with a message from Grotius, urging the archbishop to escape. Laud admitted that the scheme was feasible, perhaps even desired by his gaolers, but he rejected it, since it would gratify his enemies and expose him to contempt. "No," said he, "I am resolved not to think of Flight; but, continuing where I am, patiently to expect and bear, what a good and wise Providence hath provided for me, of what Kind soever it shall be."[24] Lest Pococke's own livelihood should be imperilled in the general ruin of the archbishop's fortunes, Laud had secured the endowments of the chair on land in Berkshire.[25]

Laud's fall placed Pococke, and indeed the continuance of Arabic studies at Oxford, in a precarious position. Of Pococke's religious and political opinions, and of his personal loyalties, there was never any doubt, but he lived as withdrawn as possible from public and even academic life, except when entry therein was unavoidable. In 1643 he was presented to the Corpus Christi living of Childrey, near Wantage, which he held during the rest of his life. During the early years of his incumbency, when he spent most of his time in the village, "he showed the greatest Diligence and Faithfulness, preaching twice every Lord's Day, and catechizing likewise, when the Length of Days would permit him. Nor was he less exact in discharging the private duties of his Function, such as visiting sick and ancient People, and the like."[26] Yet he made no attempt to dazzle the villagers with his erudition: "One of his *Oxford Friends*, as he travel'd through *Childry*, enquiring, for his Diversion, of some People, who was their Minister? And how they liked him? Receiv'd from them this Answer: *Our Parson is one Mr.* Pocock, *a plain, honest Man; but, Master*, said they, *he is no Latiner*."[27] During the Civil Wars, probably in 1646, Pococke married Mary, the daughter of Thomas Burdett of West Worldham in Hampshire, not far from the home of the Greaves family. In due course six sons and three daughters were born. The eldest son, a third Edward Pococke, also became an Arabic scholar. Mary Pococke outlived her husband and set up the memorial to him in Christ Church.

At this critical juncture in his life, Pococke was fortunate to find a new and influential patron in place of Archbishop Laud. This was the eminent jurist, John Selden, who in his time had also a considerable reputation as a Hebraist and orientalist. His scholarship subserved his polemical interests, and the current bitter controversy over church order attracted his attention to *Naẓm al-jawhar*, the chronicle of Sa'īd b. al-Biṭrīq (d. 939), alias the Patriarch Eutychius of Alexandria. Pococke, while not sharing Selden's opposition to episcopacy, had assisted him in editing a portion of this work, which was published in 1642. Since the beginning of the Long Parliament in 1640, Selden had sat for the university of Oxford, and when the split developed between the Parliament and Charles I, Selden remained, although with reservations, with the former. A moderate in a faction increasingly swayed by extremists, he was able for some years to exert his influence on behalf of his university and of individuals, such as Pococke, who might otherwise have been obnoxious to the Parliamentary regime.

After Laud's execution in 1645, Pococke's salary was detained from him. John Greaves, Pococke's intermediary as previously, thereupon solicited Selden to obtain its restoration.[28] This was not achieved until the middle of 1647. Greaves's intercession with Fairfax at the end of the year also obtained for Pococke the protection of the Parliamentary general against plunder, violence or excessive quarter.

Meanwhile another problem was arising. In 1647 the Parliamentary visitation of Oxford took place, "in which the earl of Pembroke had been contented to be employed as chancellor of the university, who had taken an oath to defend the rights and privileges of the university: notwithstanding which, out of the extreme weakness of his understanding, and the miserable compliance of his nature, he suffered himself to be made a property in joining with Brent, Pryn, and two or three other Presbyterian ministers, as commissioners for the parliament to reform the discipline and erroneous doctrine of that famous university, by the rule of the covenant; which was the standard of all men's learning, and ability to govern; all persons of what quality soever being required to subscribe that test."[29] Pococke's parish was a sufficient reason for his keeping away from the university during these critical times. He did not appear in Oxford until the Parliamentary commissioners appointed him professor of Hebrew on 30 March 1648. He had already been nominated to the chair by King Charles I, a rare example of agreement between the two parties. On the advice of John Greaves and Selden (who was a member of the Parliamentary commission) Pococke continued to keep out of Oxford as much as possible.

Greaves, who was now professor of astronomy, soon found his own position untenable under the new dispensation. He gave up his chair, having first ensured an adequate successor in the person of Seth Ward, later bishop of Salisbury, and retired to London in November 1648. Even in retirement he was not left in peace. A letter from Pococke to Selden, dated 11 February 1652 describes the loss of a copy of a work by Albumasar (Abu'l-Ma'shar al-Balkhī) which had been given to Greaves by a London merchant and which was probably destroyed when Greaves's room at Gresham College was ransacked.[30]

The power of the Presbyterians crumbled rapidly in these years. The purging of Parliament, followed by the trial and execution of the king, marked the triumph of the Army and the Independents. The establishment of the Commonwealth was followed by the imposition of a new engagement, "the substance whereof was, that every man should swear, that he would be true and faithful to the government established without king or house of peers, and that he would never consent to the readmitting either of them again, or words to that effect: and that whoever refused to take that engagement should be incapable of holding any place or office in church or state".[31] The engagement was to be subscribed by 20 March 1649. Pococke seems deliberately to have allowed the time to lapse. In consequence, the

Parliamentary commissioners deprived him of the canonry at Christ Church which had been annexed by Laud to the chair of Hebrew. This was wanted for a brother-in-law of Oliver Cromwell, Peter French, who died in 1655. Pococke was subsequently deprived of his two professorships, probably in December 1650, but the Arabic chair was soon restored to him since nobody could be found to take his place. Greaves and Selden, amongst others, were working on his behalf at this time.

During this period, Pococke published a work of major importance for the future of Arabic and Islamic studies in the West. This was *Specimen historiae Arabum*, a long excerpt from the Arabic chronicle *al-Mukhtaṣar fi'l-duwal* of Abu'l-Faraj b. al-'Ibrī, alias Bar Hebraeus (d. 1286), with a Latin translation and over three hundred pages of notes, many of which are little monographs on topics in Arab and Islamic history. Profoundly erudite in content and uncontroversial in tone, Pococke's notes show the emergence of the scholarly study of Islam from the distortions of medieval polemic. They contain, however, an occasional reflection of his opinons on the troubles of his own time and country. An excursus on the Islamic science of jurisprudence develops by implication into a defence of kingly government. Commenting elsewhere on the condemnation of the Caliph al-Ma'mūn for encouraging the study of philosophy, he remarks:

> "No-one will be astonished at this sentiment . . . who has heard petty creatures amongst us boldly asserting that all human letters and sciences are hostile to religion, and should be entirely rooted out from Christian commonwealths, that everyone's vernacular tongue is enough for him, and that whatever time is spent on others is wasted. It is truly wonderful that what seemed to Julian the shortest way to get rid of the Christian religion should now be the sole means of promoting it."[32]

The death of John Greaves in October 1652, followed by that of Selden in November 1654, deprived Pococke of his closest friend and his patron at a critical time. The traditional structure of authority and web of relationships in the university had been destroyed, while even withdrawal to Childrey did not secure Pococke from disturbance. His path was crossed by a fiery sectarian, John Pendarves (1622–56), who had been parish lecturer at Wantage before becoming the pastor of the Baptist congegation at Abingdon. According to Anthony Wood, Pendarves, "having got a numerous multitude of disciples, made himself head of them, defied all authority, contradicted and opposed all orthodox ministers in their respective offices and employments, challenged them to prove their calling, and spared not many times to interrupt them in their pulpits, and to urge them to disputes".[33] Pendarves tried to obtain permission to preach at Childrey but Pococke, who had little taste for polemic, refused him. Pococke corresponded early in 1656 with John Tombes who was a leading Baptist preacher yet lived to be on good terms with Bishops Sanderson and Ward, and to maintain a furious doctrinal controversy with Richard Baxter.

In August 1655, Cromwell as protector promulgated an ordinance appointing commissioners in each county for the ejecting of ignorant, scandalous, insufficient and negligent ministers. In the following year, some of Pococke's parishioners cited him before the commissioners at Wantage for scandalous living, one of the articles exhibited against him being his refusal to allow Pendarves to preach in his church. In this crisis he found strong supporters in the family of Fettiplace, which had held Rampayns manor in Childrey since early Tudor times. One member of the family, perhaps Charles Fettiplace, had become a Turkey merchant and was in Aleppo during the early part of Pococke's residence there, while during Pococke's visit to Istanbul, his stipend was transmitted to him by Fettiplace. When Pococke was brought before the county commissioners on 27 March 1655, four Fettiplaces witnessed on his behalf. The charge of scandal failed but was followed by an attempt to prove ignorance and insufficiency. The absurdity of this provoked strong representations from the university of Oxford, supported by the Puritan vice-chancellor, Dr. John Owen, and the attempt failed. The support which Pococke was able to gain in these difficult times from men such as Selden and Owen, whose political and religious views differed from his own, bears witness to the respect in which his scholarship and integrity were held.

In spite of personal and political distractions, Pococke pursued his studies and writing at Childrey through the Interregnum. In 1655 he published *Porta Mosis*, an edition, with a Latin translation and notes, of six discourses of Maimonides upon the Mishna. It was intended to serve as an introduction to rabbinical studies, and also to Arabic written in Hebrew characters. As he gave a Latin translation of the Arabic texts in the *Specimen*, for the benefit of students of history, so did he here for those whose interest was confined to the theological and philosophical ideas of Maimonides. To the text and translation are appended nine long notes, the purpose of which was "to shew . . . how much the Knowledge of *Arabick* and *Rabbinical Learning*, will contribute towards the finding out the genuine Sense of many difficult Places of Holy Scripture".[34] The part of this work which is chiefly of interest in connection with Arabic studies is the seventh note concerning Islamic eschatology. Like the notes in the *Specimen*, this monograph is important for the stress it lays on the study of the Arabic authors themselves in order to find out what Muslims really believe. Translated into English, Pococke's essay provided the substance of Sale's account of Muslim eschatology in the Preliminary Discourse to his translation of the Qur'ān.[35]

In 1652, at Selden's request, Pococke had begun a translation of the whole of Ibn al-Biṭrīq's *Naẓm al-jawhar*. He continued to work on this after Selden's death, and ultimately published an edition of the Arabic text with a Latin translation and some introductory and supplementary material. Published as *Contextio gemmarum*, which is an exact rendering of the Arabic title, the second volume was the first to appear, in 1654, and was followed by the first volume in 1656. The complete work was reissued in two quarto volumes in 1658.[36] In the preface Pococke states that the duty of editing the work was laid upon him by Selden, and he goes on to explain the principles he has followed in making the translation. This is followed by two accounts of the life of Sa'īd b. al-Biṭrīq, one taken from Ibn Abī Uṣaybi'a, and the other reprinted from Selden's book, published in 1642. The text and translation are accompanied by chronological tables and indexes of topics, places, rivers, mountains and persons.

In describing his principles of translation, Pococke says that he has not attempted to give a word-for-word rendering, "which often brings more obscurity than light to authors translated from one language to another", but to give the sense of the writer. This, he thinks, will be approved by those acquainted with Arabic and oriental subjects. He has given various renderings to the same word where he thought that by so doing he could better express the meaning. He gives several examples of Arabic words which have a number of meanings, among them *mawlā* and *wazīr*. Of *mawlā* he says that it has several meanings, and he has sometimes translated it "slave" (*servus*), at other times "freedman", while some might prefer to render it "follower" (*assecla*). His note on *wazīr* is interesting as showing that the word was beginning to be naturalized in English: "although I had very often rendered it 'adviser' (*consiliarius*), which is the meaning of the noun, afterwards, having altered my mind, I changed it to 'vizier' (*vizierus*), because our countrymen are accustomed to this title when they have to do with Mohammedan and Turkish matters". On Selden's advice, errors of syntax in the text have not been corrected, "since Arabic syntax is so certain and easy that the faults may be corrected by anyone having some skill in grammar". Three manuscripts were supplied for the work, two by Selden and one from the Cottonian Library, "of which however he wished me to follow one during the work of editing, and not to confound several together".[37]

In 1659 Pococke published anonymously a translation of a short Arabic work on coffee.[38] Twells, his biographer, has an alarming story of the effect of coffee-drinking on Pococke's health: "Writing became exceedingly troublesome to him through a Palsy in his Hand, which drinking of Coffee, to which he had used himself ever since his residence in the East, first brought upon him and which increased as he advanced in years."[39] Pococke was one of the first coffee-drinkers in England.

A more remarkable production of these years is Pococke's English translation of *Risālat Ḥayy b. Yaqẓān*, the philosophical romance of Ibn Ṭufayl (d. 581/1185). Of this only a fragment remains, among Pococke's papers in the Bodleian.[40] The first page is dated "Jul: 10. 1645", showing that it was made while Pococke was living withdrawn at Childrey. He seems never to have disclosed this translation to anyone. It is not mentioned in Twells's biography, and when his son, the younger Edward Pococke, published an edition of the complete Arabic text together with a Latin translation in 1671, no reference was made to this earlier English version, even though the elder Pococke wrote a preface to his son's book, saying that it had been undertaken and published with his persuasion and encouragement. The first English translation of the *Risāla* to be published was made by Simon Ockley in 1708, and was dedicated to the younger Edward Pococke. Again, there is no mention of the elder Pococke's version, and a comparison of Ockley's translation with the fragment shows them to have been quite independent of each other. The nature of the work probably explains why it remained unpublished in the middle of the seventeenth century, and why, on the other hand, it became popular towards the end of that century. It is concerned with the self-improvement of man in the state of nature, a topic congenial to western European thought in the late seventeenth and eighteenth centuries. It would appeal to those who were coming to believe in a natural religion, independent of all ecclesiastical organizations, and hence, in different ways, to Deists, Socinians and Quakers. It has also been regarded as a parent of *Robinson Crusoe* and hence of the whole subsequent literature of desert islands.

An important scholarly project in which Pococke collaborated during the Protectorate was the preparation of the English Polyglot Bible. This was the latest in a series published in western Europe. Like its predecessors, the Complutensian (1514–17), Antwerp (1569–72) and Paris Polygots (1628–45), the English Polyglot was a product of the biblical humanism of the Renaissance; unlike them, it was the work of Protestant scholars. Its promoter was Bryan Walton, like Pococke a Laudian and a royalist, and nearly all of those who supported or assisted the project were deprived episcopalian divines. Walton's proposal to edit a polyglot, made in 1652, had the backing of Selden and his friend, Archbishop Ussher—both of them men whose influence and acquaintanceship crossed factional lines. With these sponsors, the project received a modest degree of encouragement from the Council of State and the protector, and Walton's *Biblia polyglotta* was published in six volumes between 1654 and 1657. Pococke lent three manuscripts from his collection and gave assistance with the Arabic text of the Pentateuch, while his advice was sought on many matters.

The production of Walton's Polyglot stimulated work on other tools of scholarship. Walton himself wrote a brief introduction to oriental languages in 1655[41] but a much more serious and important publication was the *Lexicon heptaglotton* of Edmund Castell, a Cambridge scholar who had been one of Walton's principal assistants. The preparation of a dictionary of the oriental languages (i.e. those of importance to biblical studies) was discussed late in 1657 and early in 1658 in correspondence between Castell and other scholars.[42] The *Lexicon heptaglotton*, which was produced largely at Castell's own expense, appeared in 1669.

The Restoration of the monarchy in May 1660 brought some benefits to Pococke. By letters patent of Charles II, dated 20 June 1660, he was at last formally constituted Regius Professor of Hebrew and canon of Christ Church. On 20 September 1660, Pococke proceeded Doctor of Divinity. Henceforward he was in residence at Christ Church. Yet he took care that his parish of Childrey should not be neglected, for, "during that Part of his Life, in which his Attendance upon his Professorships and canonical Residence called him to *Oxford* for the greatest Part of the Year, he took a most conscientious Care to supply his Absence by an able Curate, of whom he strictly required the same laborious Course of Duty, and for his Encouragement, allowed him fifty Pounds *per Annum*, besides Surplice Fees, all which amounted to more than a fourth Part of the then Value of that Rectory".[43]

Unlike many of his contemporaries who had suffered under the Commonwealth and Protectorate, Pococke obtained no further preferment after the Restoration. After the death of Selden he lacked influential friends at the court of either the protector or the king. His reputation as an Arabic scholar was not forgotten, however, and on at least one occasion the government had need of his services as a consequence of the passage of Tangier under English rule as a part of the dowry of Catherine of Braganza. "In April, 1668, Dr. *Pocock* had a Letter from Sir *Joseph Williamson*, with an *Arabick* Letter inclosed, from the Emperor of *Morocco* to King *Charles* the Second, desiring from him a Transition of it, they having No-body in Town

Masters enough of that Language, to give the Contents of it."[44] Many years later a Moroccan ambassador came to England, and Anthony Wood describes his arrival in Oxford on 30 May 1682. "About 8 of the clocke at night came into Oxford, Hamet ben Hamet ben Haddu Ottur, embassadour from the emperour of Morocco and put in at the Angell inn within East gate. Where being settled, the vice-chancellor and doctors in their scarlet with the bedells before them congratulated his arrivall; and the orator spoke a little speech, and Dr. [Edward] Pocock something in [A]rabick which made him laugh."[45]

The history of the remaining thirty-one years of Pococke's life after the Restoration is mainly the history of his publications. The first of these, *Carmen Tograi*,[46] his edition and translation of *Lāmiyyat al-'Ajam* of al-Tughrā'ī, is, like *Specimen historia Arabum* and *Porta Mosis*, primarily a text-book. It opens with a preface by Samuel Clarke (1625–1669),[47] who is described under his portrait in the Bodleian Library as "Linguarum Orientalium Post Pocockium Peritissim[us]". Clarke had presumably been given his grounding in Arabic by Pococke, since he became an undergraduate at Oxford in 1640 and remained there until 1649, when he was put in charge of the university press with the title of "architypographus". In 1650, however, he left Oxford and became a schoolmaster in Islington. During the following years he assisted Bryan Walton with the Polyglot, in which he was employed on the Hebrew text, the Aramaic paraphrase and the Latin translation of the Persian gospels. In 1658 he returned to Oxford, and in 1662 he resumed the post of architypographus, which he held until his death. Clarke also wrote, with Pococke's encouragement and assistance, a *Tractatus de prosodia Arabica*, which is bound up with the *Carmen* but has its own title-page.

The Preface is followed by Pococke's introductory lecture to the course, a production which bears a great resemblance to other works of this kind. Pococke begins with an account of the traditional origins of the Arabic language and its links with Hebrew through Ishmael. He then speaks of the traditional origin of the Arabic script, the acquisition of the knowledge of writing by Quraysh, and the difference between the Himyaritic, Kufic and modern Arabic scripts. His information on these subjects is of course entirely derived from Arabic literary sources. Next he gives the reasons why, in his opinion, Arabic is worthy of study. The language, he says, is valuable for four reasons; it is perspicuous, elegant, copious and a language of learning. He then deals more fully with Arabic as a learned language. He runs through the "sciences" of the primitive Arabs—genealogy, astrology, history, the interpretation of dreams, medicine and eloquence. He stresses the importance of poetry among the Arabs. After the Muslim conquests came a great extension of Arabian culture, particularly when the Arabs acquired much of the learning of the Greeks in 'Abbasid times. He recognizes the services rendered to learning by the Arabian writers who preserved in translation the writings of the ancient world throughout the Middle Ages, and he states that their works have continued to be useful, even since the revival of Greek learning in Western Europe: the importance of Arabic works in medicine is admitted, he says, and more use might be made of them. His contemporaries are aware of the existence of Arabian philosophy, but unjustly despise it because it is known to them only through the barbarous translations made in the Middle Ages. A study of these philosophers in the original Arabic would reveal works of high literary merit. There is need to study the Arab historians in order to dispose of common fables and errors (as Pococke himself had already set the example of doing in *Specimen historiae Arabum*), and knowledge of the language would enable Christians to refute genuine Muslim errors instead of the untrue stories fathered upon the followers of the Prophet. Finally a knowledge of Arabic is of assistance to students of Hebrew. Pococke points out the abundance of grammars and lexicons, in which instruments of learning Arabic is second to none, but he warns his students that the study of grammar can be overdone. It is the salt of learning, but too much salt can injure the palate. He concludes with a reference to Laud's donations to the Bodleian.

The text and translation of the poem follow, occupying twenty pages. In the following century Leonard Chappelow, then Sir Thomas Adams's Professor of Arabic at Cambridge, made a metrical translation, or rather an inflated paraphrase, of this poem which was published under the title of *The Traveller* in 1758. This English version is based upon Pococke's Latin and the occasional expansions of meaning in his notes, rather than upon the original Arabic. It is provided with an introduction and notes, the latter being abstracted from Pococke's Latin notes. Chappelow claims that his version, though unrhymed, is in the same metre as the original—a statement which would seem to argue a defect of ear.

The text and translation in Pococke's book are followed by 233 separately numbered pages of Latin notes, which may be taken as the substance of his course of lectures. The method is similar to that followed in his lectures on the Proverbs of 'Alī and the First *Maqāma*. A full commentary is given on almost every word of the text, dealing with the syntax and etymology of the words and frequently comparing them with cognate words in Hebrew and Syriac. The notes show a very accurate and detailed study of the various significances of

Arabic words. Occasionally he deals with matters of other than grammatical interest; for example, he gives an account of the life of al-Ṭughrā'ī, recounts the myth told to account for the phenomenon of the false dawn, and even tells an Arabic joke. His attitude is in general scholarly and objective but he sometimes hits out at what he regards as the religion of the false prophet. A page of Pococke's book after the notes, which would otherwise have been left vacant, contains a short excerpt, all that seems to have survived, from Pococke's inaugural lecture of 1636. In this he speaks of the esteem in which poetry was held amongst the Arabs. The book finishes with an index of Arabic words and another of topics and persons, a list of proverbs quoted in the notes, corrigenda and an index of Hebrew, Aramaic and Syriac words. It is followed by Clarke's *Tractatus de prosodia Arabica.*

Pococke's last scholarly publication in Arabic, the *Historia dynastiarum* of Bar Hebraeus, came out in 1663 and was dedicated to King Charles II. "It may easily be perceived," says Pococke, "how great a boon from God a good King may ever be held; that never has more certain felicity nor more pleasing liberty existed for a people than under a pious King; that never have empires flourished more than when their Majesty is well preserved for Princes; that nothing has ever been more fatal to them than when the Majesty of Princes has become cheap among the people, or than when they who should obey have broken their bounds and have invaded Its function."[48] The preface which follows contains a summary of the life of Bar Hebraeus and mentions the leading part taken by Gerard Langbaine, who had died in 1658,[49] in urging him to carry out this work. Langbaine, provost of Queen's College from 1646 until his death, was both a royalist and an episcopalian and led the opposition to the Parliamentary commissioners when they first came to Oxford. However, he managed to keep his college, perhaps because he was a friend of Selden, and he gave a good deal of help to Pococke when he was deprived by the Parliamentary commissioners, and on other occasions. Pococke mentions him in the *Specimen* as providing some information. The Latin translation of Bar Hebraeus follows this preface and then comes an index with a note on Pococke's system of transliteration from Arabic, which he admits that he has not strictly observed. This section concludes with a table of *Hijrī* and Christian years and a list of errors and various readings. The second part of the book has a fresh title page and a dedicatory letter to Gilbert Sheldon, bishop of London, in which Pococke thanks the bishop for helping him to regain his preferments. The preface which follows states the purpose of this supplement, namely to bring the list of dynasties up to date with a brief account of the rulers after the time of Bar Hebraeus, including the Ottomans. Pococke gives an account of the Īl-Khāns, the Mamluks of Egypt, the nomal 'Abbasid Caliphs of Cairo, the Ottoman Sultans, the Timurids, the Kara-Koyunlu, the Ak-Koyunlu and the Safavids. Finally, so placed to facilitate printing, comes the Arabic text of Bar Hebraeus.

There appears to have been, from the Restoration onwards, something of a decline in the progress of Arabic studies in England. Outwardly this is reflected in Pococke's own life by his failure to obtain from the restored monarchy more than the restitution of those rights of which he had been deprived during the revolutionary years. The academic decline was noted at the time. In 1663 Pococke wrote to Thomas Greaves, "The Genius of the Times, as for these Studies, is much altered since you and I first set about them; and few will be persuaded, they are worthy taking Notice of." To this Greaves replied, "How these studies are esteemed in the Universities, I know not; in these Parts, for ought I observe, they are not much followed or regarded, and receive small Incouragement from those, who, I thought, would have been Fautors and Promoters of them."[50] Greaves was at that time a prebendary of Peterborough so his remarks may be taken to indicate a decline of interest among the higher clergy. A similar loss of interest was noticed at Cambridge in those years. Edmund Castell was appointed the second Sir Thomas Adams's Professor there in 1667, and "His Lectures were heard at first with great Applause, but, in a few Years, were so much neglected, that, being then easy, and disposed to be pleasant, he put up this Affix upon the School-Gates; Arabicae Linguae Praelector cras ibit in Desertum".[51] Pococke mentions the neglect of oriental studies also in the dedication of his *Commentary upon the Prophet Micah* (1676) to Seth Ward, bishop of Salisbury. He there speaks of "the need of patronage and protection that this Work hath, in regard that there is in it much stress laid on such part of Learning (the Oriental I mean), which of late, if not all along, hath had that unhappiness, as to be scarce able to keep itself, not only from neglect, but contempt, as needless; at least of no great use or necessity. In some places abroad where it formerly found great encouragement (if we may believe general complaints,) it hath now little regard, although I doubt not but that it will in good time recover its honour."[52] The reference to the decline of Arabic studies abroad is illuminated by a letter of 1671 from Harder, Golius's successor at Leiden, in which he "writes to Dr. *Pocock*, and gives him a most melancholy Account of the Neglect of *Arabick* Literature in that University, or rather of the Contempt it lay under there; Two Causes he assigns for it; *first*, *Golius*, he thinks, did not exercise the Students, not even those that were maintained at the publick Expence, in these Studies, nor use his Authority to make them take Pains therein; 2dly, He blames the Avarice of the Age, which gave no Attention to any Sciences, that were not greatly lucrative".[53]

Although the negligence of a leading teacher may have been a contributory cause of the decline in one university, it does not explain the phenomenon generally. Moreover, Golius had in his earlier years displayed such energy in promoting Arabic studies that his loss of interest in his later years, if Harder's criticism is correct, may be ascribed to a feeling that circumstances were no longer favouring his work. With regard to Harder's second point, it is hard to believe that Arabic studies had ever been "greatly lucrative".

The cause of the decline become clearer if the motives which had led the men of the seventeenth century to undertake Arabic studies are considered. First among these was the interest in Arabic and other oriental languages in connection with biblical studies. For this reason there had been considerable interest in the Arabic versions in the earlier part of the century. Bryan Walton's Polyglot here represented the culmination of oriental scholarship, according to the means and standards of the time. It must have seemed that little more was to be expected from Arabic in this direction. Moreover there was a distinct alteration in the intellectual atmosphere of post-Restoration Anglicanism. The controversies between Calvinists and Arminians seemed after the Restoration to have become out of date. Fresh emphasis was laid on reason as a means to knowledge of God and as a guide to the good life. In the controversies there was less place for the minute textual arguments which had been the chief weapon of the polemicists of the previous generation. For these reasons the religious interest which had encouraged Laud and Adams to found their chairs of Arabic would no longer move later patrons.

The encouragement of missions had been another motive of the earlier students of Arabic. Here a record of almost unrelieved failure could not but produce ultimate disappointment. Yet the stream of patronage did not dry up. Robert Boyle, whose scientific interests (for which he is now remembered) were no greater than his passion for theology, had, while living at Oxford between 1654 and 1668, made the acquaintance of Pococke and Samuel Clarke. Among his many and generous contributions to missionary activities was his financing of Pococke's translation of Hugo Grotius's defence of Christianity, *De veritate religionis Christianae*, which was published in 1660 and may perhaps have been a delayed result of Pococke's meeting with Grotius in Paris in 1641. The purpose of this translation is described by Twells. "In no Tongue could it be thought more useful, than in the *Arabick*, being a Language understood, not only in the *Ottoman* Empire, but in *Persia*, *Tartary*, and all those part of *India* and *Africa*, where *Mahometism* has prevailed. Among the Professors of that Superstition, doubtless there are some well-meaning People, who would entertain favourable Thoughts of Christianity, were they sufficiently made acquainted with the Reasonableness and Excellency of it. The Conversion of such, Dr. *Pocock* had in view, when he first resolved upon this Work; and not only that, but that the Instruction and better Establishment of the Christians, that are very numerous in some of those Countries, who, by Reason of the Bondage they are under, know but little of the holy Religion they profess, and the Evidence on which it is built; and therefore, to mend their worldly Condition, are too often tempted into Apostasy."[54] Pococke followed this up with a translation of the Anglican Catechism, printed in 1671. In that year Robert Huntington[55] went out as chaplain to the English factory at Aleppo, whence he wrote asking for copies of the translation of Grotius. Pococke sent thirty of these and thirty-six of the new Arabic catechism, together with twelve copies of a Turkish catechism, prepared by William Seaman.[56] In 1673 Huntington wrote again, asking Pococke to make a translation of the Anglican liturgy. This was done; the translation was printed in the following year and in 1675 we find Huntington writing to thank Pococke for the copies he had sent and promising to distribute them. The translation of a catechism into Arabic was not, of course, an original idea. Among the predecessors of Pococke's work was the translation of a catechism of Cardinal Bellarmine, made by Gabriel Sionita and another Maronite, printed by the Savarian Press at Rome in 1613.[57]

Another factor in the decline of Arabic studies in the later seventeenth century was the rise of organized experimental science. This new development is symbolized by the formation of the Royal Society, which received its charter from Charles II in 1662 and developed out of earlier and looser associations of the war-years. The growing emphasis upon experiment and reason as the primary means to knowledge diminished the authority of the classical and Arabian writers. The contributions of Boyle, Newton and others to experimental science, mathematics and astronomy rendered obsolete the medieval oriental texts, which as late as the time of John Greaves had been worth collection, study and printing. The works of the Muslim geographers still retained some value but they were corrected and supplemented by the travels of the Europeans in Asia and Africa.

It is significant therefore that Pococke produced no further works of Arabic scholarship after 1663. His great work on al-Maydānī's collection of proverbs remained unprinted, although various friends, including Castell, encouraged him to publish the book in 1671 and in the following year a specimen was actually put through the press. The fate of another project is thus described by Hearne: "A Book in Arabick written by Abdollatiphi, containing a compendious History of Egypt was begun to be translated by Dr. Pocock and printed at the Theatre in Bp. Fell's time at the expense of Dr. Marshall Rector of Lincoln College, and was a pretty way advanc'd; but on a sudden the Bp. having an occasion for the Latin Letter the Book stop'd wch. so vex'd the good old man Dr. Pocock tht. he could never be prevail'd to go on any farther."[58] This work *al-Ifāda wa'l-i'tibār* of 'Abd al-Laṭīf al-Baghdādī, was at last to be brought to completion, over a century later, by one of Pococke's successors, Joseph White, Laudian Professor of Arabic from 1775 to 1814.

Pococke's only remaining Arabic publications were the missionary literature mentioned, and the later years of his life were occupied with a series of English commentaries on four of the minor prophets. Micah and Malachi were published in 1677, Hosea in 1685 and Joel in 1691. In his exposition of the text, Pococke used his knowledge of Arabic philosophy and oriental customs to throw light upon the meaning. Besides work of this kind, he shared in the business of his college and cathedral and was a delegate of the university press. His most curious productions in these years are sets of Arabic verses for the collections of tributes which the university offered on state occasions. In 1660 he produced Arabic verses with a Latin translation on the Restoration of Charles II and, later in the year, on the death of the Duke of Gloucester. In 1685 he contributed to the collection of verses made on the death of King Charles II. His successor, Thomas Hyde, was a contributor in Persian on such occasions. Pococke died on 10 September 1691 and was buried in the cathedral which he had served so long. Many expected that he would be succeeded as professor of Arabic by his son but the choice of the electors fell on Hyde. The younger Edward Pococke made no more contributions to Arabic studies, and died a country parson at Mildenhall in Wiltshire in the year 1727.

In Pococke's own field of Arabic scholarship he had few worthy successors in England during the century that followed his death. It was unfortunate for his fame that when a revival of Arabic studies did take place, in the nineteenth century, the aims and outlook of the scholars had changed so much from those of Pococke's time that his work was no longer easy to assess and tended to be forgotten. In modern eyes he is an archaic figure, the representative of a dead scholarly tradition. Yet in his time he played a notable part in establishing those links between England and the Muslim countries which have again in our own times become of such singular importance. In an age of religious unrest, political division and civil war, he yet preserved his loyalties, and fulfilled his pastoral and academic duties undismayed.

NOTES

1 There is an account of Pococke in *DNB*, XVI, 7–12 by Stanley Lane-Poole. The principal source of information on his life is the biography by Leonard Twells prefixed to *The theological works of the learned Dr. Pocock* (London, 1740) based on materials now lost. This biography was reprinted in Alexander Chalmers, *The Lives of Dr. Edward Pocock* [*etc.*] (London, 1816). Some of Pococke's manuscripts are in the Bodleian, and a few letters to and from him are extant in various collections. Pococke appears to have spelt his name with the final "e", but the alternative form was used by contemporaries and by his biographer.

2 Twells in *The theological works of . . . Pocock*, I, 1. This source is hereafter referred to as Twells, *Works*.

3 Quoted in J. H. Brown, *A short history of Thame school* (London, 1927), 64.

4 *DNB*, XV, 443.

5 *DNB*, II, 119–20.

6 *D. Iohannis apostoli et evangelistae epistolae catholicae omnes* (Leiden, 1612).

7 Public Record Office, S.P. 105/148, 216.

8 P.R.O., S.P. 105/148, 217.

9 Sāmī al-Kaylānī, "Ṣafḥa min ta'rīkh Ḥalab al-adabī", 8, identifies Fatḥallāh as the poet Fatḥallāh al-Ḥalabī, called Ibn al-Naḥḥās, who died at Medina in 1052/1642: see al-Muḥibbī, *Khulāṣat al-athar* (repr. Beirut, n.d.), iii, 257–66.

10 MS. Poc. 392. *Meidanii Proverbia.* Some of the Arabic script is Pococke's own, the rest appears to have been written by a calligrapher. The first folio bears the following note, written when Pococke was preparing for his second journey to the East:

> "If it please God that I returne not otherwise to dispose of this translation of Proverbes I desire that it may be put in the Archives of [Corpus Christi College] Library. there though very rude and imperfect to be kept for some helpe of those that study the Arabicke language. hopeing that [Mr. Thomas Greaves] or some other may at some time perfect the worke for an edition.
>
> per me Edwardus Pococke April 10th. 1637."

The words in brackets were subsequently scored out. A small portion of the work was published by Henry Albert Schultens, the last member of a dynasty of Dutch orientalists, as *Specimen proverbiorum Meidanii ex versione Pocockiana* (London, 1773). Schultens's book is dedicated to the contemporary Laudian Professor, Thomas Hunt (1696–1774): see *DNB*, X, 279–80.

11 The timing of Laud's decision (if not the decision itself) may be explained by Thomas Adams's undertaking in February 1632 (n.s.) to pay an annual stipend of £40 to Abraham Wheelocke as "publicke professor of the Arabicke tongue" at Cambridge: Cambridge University Library, MS.

Dd. 3.12, f. IV (5). See also A. J. Arberry, *The Cambridge School of Arabic* (Cambridge, 1948), 6–8.

12 Printed in Pococke's *Carmen Tograi* (Oxford, 1661).

13 [Jacobus Golius], *Shadharat al-adab min kalām al-'Arab . . . Proverbia quaedam Alis imperatoris muslemici, et carmen Tograi . . . necnon dissertatio quaedam Aben Sinae* (Leiden, 1629). The work was published anonymously.

14 Twells, *Works*, I, 9–10.

15 MS. Poc. 424, described in the Handlist as *Bibliography of Arabic works.*

16 MS. Poc. 425, described in the Handlist as *Parsing-list of Arabic words.*

17 Thomas Erpenius was professor of Arabic at Leiden from 1613 until his death in 1624. His *Grammatica Arabica* (Leiden, 1613) was the standard grammar in Europe for nearly two centuries, and appeared in numerous reprints and editions, the latest at Palermo in 1746. His *Rudimenta linguae Arabicae* (Leiden, 1620) was a shorter grammar, which also passed through several editions in the seventeenth and eighteenth centures. It formed the basis of the first Arabic grammar to be produced in England, *Elementa Linguae Arabicae* (London, 1730), published by Leonard Chappelow (1683–1786), Sir Thomas Adams's Professor of Arabic at Cambridge.

18 They have been arbitrarily divided between MS. Poc. 427 (*Arabic fragments*) ff. 110, 227–32, and MS. Poc. 428 (*Latin and Greek fragments*) ff. 1–2.

19 They were (i) John Greaves (1602–52): *DNB*, VIII, 481–2; (ii) Sir Edward Greaves (1608–80), physician in ordinary to Charles II: *DNB*, VIII, 480: (iii) Thomas Greaves (1612–76); *DNB*, VIII, 482; (iv) Nicholas. Pococke speaks of John Greaves as "doctissimus mihique amicissimus, *Johannes Gravius*, quo nemo integro magis affectu, se studiaque ac impensas suas publicae rei literariae utilitati dicavit". *Specimen historiae Arabum* (Oxford, 1648/50), 158.

20 *DNB*, XIX, 1278.

21 P.R.O. S.P. 16 381. No. 75. The late Dr. J. Johnson of Oxford kindly made a transcript and photostat of this document available to me.

22 Twells indicates the range of Greaves's orientalist interests, and their links with his mathematical and astronomical studies:

"Very sollicitous, I find, he was for the *Astronomical*, and other *Works* of . . . *Ulug Beg*. . . . He was not less earnest for the *Geography* of *Abulfeda*, *Prince* of Hamah, an *Arabick* writer. . . . The *Alcoran* he desir'd, not only in the original *Arabick*, but also in *Turkish* and *Persian*, with such *Glosses* and *Commentaries* relating to it as could be found. Also *Avicenna de Animâ*, and any other Part of him, that was to be had in *Persian*, *Al Battany*, the *Planisphere and Geography of Ptolemy*, *Gulistan* in *Arabick* and *Mircondus* in *Persian*. . . . He desir'd that Mr. *Pocock* . . . would endeavour to get all the *Manuscripts*, he should think good, in *Persian*, *Turkish*, and *Arabick*, especially, such as relate to *History*, *Philosophy*, *Physick*, *Chemistry*, *Algebra* and *Mathematicks*. And as for *Mathematicians*, that he would carefully remember to enquire after the Ancients, that have been translated out of *Greek*, and either are not yet extant in *Europe*, or else imperfectly published." Twells, *Works*, I, 16.

23 Gabriel Sionita (Jibrā'īl al-Ṣahyūnī: 1577–1648), born at Ihdin (northern Lebanon), studied at the Maronite College in Rome, founded by Pope Gregory XIII in 1584. He taught oriental languages at Rome and Venice, and in 1615 accompanied Savary de Brèves (see below, note 57) to Paris. Among his pupils there was Matthias Pasor. He and his fellow-Maronite, Johannes Hesronita (Yuḥannā al-Ḥasrūnī) published a translation of part of al-Idrīsī's *Kitāb Rujjār* as *Geographia Nubiensis*. He was also a collaborator in the Parisian Polyglot of Le Jay (1645). See Yūsuf Mazhar, *Ta'rīkh*

Lubnān al-'āmm (n.p., n.d.), I, 541–42; Johann Fück, *Die arabischen Studien in Europa bis in den Anfang des 20. Jahrhunderts* (Leipzig, 1955), 141, 157–8.

24 Twells, *Works*, I, 20.

25 County connections had some part in the promotion of Arabic studies in England. Both Pococke and his patron, Laud, were Berkshire men, and subsequently Pococke was protected in his living by the Berkshire branch of the Fettiplace family. The first Arabic professor at Cambridge, Abraham Wheelocke, was a Shropshire man, like his patron, Thomas Adams, and both kept up their ties with their native county: cf. Adams's letter to Wheelocke, written in November 1632:

> "I tould you formerly I was one of the Stewards for our Shropshire feast. The first dish therein is the hearing of the word preached, for where should we begin but with sacrifice to the Authour of our health, peace, plentie, etc. You did formerly proffer your paines if called to do service to your Cuntrimen in this kind. I make reckoning you persist in the same mind, willing to honour your Country wherein you may, and indeed I have engaged my self to my friends to provide them a preacher of our countrymen. Now my request unto you is to prepare your self to preach at this our meeting, which is intended, if God permit, on Tuesday come 3 wickes, which is the 4th of December. The tearme heer [London] endeth the Wednesday before. I hope you shall reckon your paines well bestowed. I entreat you to send your answear by the very first, which I expect to be heer the next wicke without faile, at furthest by the ordinary carrier." (Cambridge University Library: MS. Dd. 3.12; IV (15).)

26 Twells, *Works*, I, 82.

27 Twells, *Works*, I, 22.

28 That Selden was Greaves's patron is indicated by the dedication of Greaves's *Elementa linguae Persicae* (London, 1649), to Selden.

29 Clarendon, *The history of the rebellion and civil wars in England* (Oxford, 1849), IV, 282. Sir Nathaniel Brent was warden of Merton College, William Prynne was the well-known Puritan writer.

30 Letter from Pococke to Selden; Oxford, 11 February 1652/3: Cambridge University Library, Mm.1.47 (Baker MS. 36).

31 Clarendon, *History*, IV, 549.

32 *Specimen historiae Arabum* (Oxford, 1650), 166–7; my translation. For a fuller account of the *Specimen*, see below, pp. 34–6.

33 Anthony Wood, *Athenae Oxonienses* (London, 1692), II, 127.

34 Twells, *Works*, I, 44.

35 George Sale, *The Koran . . . to which is prefixed a preliminary discourse* (London, 1764), I, 100–36.

36 *Contextio gemmarum* (*Annales Eutychii*) *cum versione Latina* (Oxford, 1658).

37 *Contextio gemmarum*: Praefatio Interpretis (unpaginated): my translation.

38 The text is given in S. C. Chew, *The crescent and the rose* (New York, 1937), 185.

39 Twells, *Works*, I, 80.

40 The surviving portion of Pococke's translation consists of four sheets now bound up in MS. Poc. 429, *English fragments*, ff. 1–2, 16–17. For the work in question see *EI*², III, 333–4, ḤAYY B. YAKẒĀN (A.-M. Goichon).

41 Bryan Walton, *Introductio ad lectionem linguarum orientalium* (London, 1655).

42 See B.M. Addit. 4276, 83; Addit. 22905, 7, 9, 13, 15, 18, 20, 22, 27, 29, 33, 35, 37, 42, 48, 50, 57, 62, 79.

43 Twells, *Works*, I, 82.

44 Twells, *Works*, I, 65. Williamson, knighted in 1672, had studied at Westminster under Busby, and at Queen's College, Oxford, under Langbaine. At the Restoration he entered the service of the secretary of state, a post which he himself attained in 1674: see *DNB*, XXI, 473–8.

45 Andrew Clark (ed.), *The life and times of Anthony Wood* (Oxford Historical Society; Oxford), III (1894), 17.

46 *Carmen Tograi cum versione Latina et notis* (Oxford, 1661).

47 *DNB*, IV, 440–1.

48 *Gregorii Abul Pharaji Historia compendiosa dynastiarum cum versione Latina* (Oxford, 1663), Epistola dedicatoria (unpaginated): my translation.

49 *DNB*, XI, 532–4.

50 Twells, *Works*, I, 60.

51 Twells, *Works*, I, 51.

52 E. Pococke, *Commentary upon the Prophet Micah* (Oxford, 1676), reprinted in Twells, *Works*, I, iii.

53 Twells, *Works*, I, 67.

54 Twells, *Works*, I, 56.

55 *DNB*, X, 308–9.

56 William Seaman (1606–80), who had been in the service of Sir Peter Wych at Istanbul, was a Turkish scholar. His Turkish catechism as well as a Turkish translation of the New Testament (1666) and a grammar were published under the patronage of Robert Boyle and Sir Cyril Wych. *DNB*, XVII, 1101–2.

57 The Savarian Press had been set up by Savary de Brèves (1560–1628), who, as French ambassador in Istanbul from 1591 to 1605, had collected over a hundred Turkish and Persian manuscripts, which were placed in the Royal Library in Paris. From 1608 to 1614 he was the French ambassador in Rome, and it was here at his own expense that he set up the press that bore his name. Sionita and another Maronite worked as translators for the press. Savary transferred the press to Paris in 1615. Its fount was used for the Paris Polyglot. It was then lost for over a century (1679–1787) during which period no Arabic text was printed in France.

58 C. E. Doble (ed.), *Remarks and collections of Thomas Hearne* (Oxford Historical Society: Oxford), I (1884), 224. John Fell (1625–86) was dean of Christ Church from 1660 and bishop of Oxford from 1676. Like Pococke, he had been a pupil at Lord Williams's School in Thame. *DNB*, VI, 1157–9.

2

THE STUDY OF ARABIC HISTORIANS IN SEVENTEENTH-CENTURY ENGLAND:

THE BACKGROUND AND THE WORK OF EDWARD POCOCKE

(i) *Arabic Studies in Sixteenth- and Seventeenth-Century Europe*

ARAB historical writing was not a specialized study in the seventeenth century. Organized work in Arabic and Islamic studies was still a recent development in western Europe generally.[1] The first modern English Arabist, William Bedwell (c. 1562–1632), was during most of his life an isolated figure: the principal result of his studies was an Arabic lexicon which was never printed, although he bequeathed the manuscript to Cambridge with a fount of Arabic type for that purpose.[2] In the third decade of the century, however, some younger scholars began to interest themselves in Arabic. Abraham Wheelocke (1593–1654) corresponded with Bedwell from Cambridge, while Edward Pococke (1604–91) studied Arabic under him as a young Oxford graduate. As yet there was no permanent provision for the teaching of Arabic at the English universities. From 1626 to 1629 a refugee German scholar from Heidelberg named Matthias Pasor, had lectured in Arabic, Aramaic, and Syriac at Oxford but no chair of Arabic was established until 1634, when Laud, then chancellor of the university, made an endowment for that purpose. The first Laudian professor was Pococke, who gave his inaugural lecture in 1636. A chair of Arabic had been set up in Cambridge a little earlier. In 1632 Wheelocke had persuaded a somewhat reluctant City draper, Thomas Adams, to make an annual grant of £40 for three years as his stipend to lecture in Arabic.[3] The grant was made permanent in 1636.[4] Wheelocke's successor, who held the Adams professorship from 1667 to 1685, was Edmund Castell. He was a great lexicographer and was followed from 1685 to 1702 by a nonentity, John Luke, whose chief qualification appears to have been a seven years' sojourn in Smyrna. At Oxford Pococke's successor, Thomas Hyde (1636–1703), had been a pupil of Wheelocke's but was primarily interested in Persia.[5] Of these five professors, Pococke alone carried out sustained research into Islamic history. We must therefore consider Arabic studies in general as the background to the study of Arabic historians in seventeenth-century England.

The sixteenth and seventeenth centuries saw an efflorescence of Arabic studies in western Europe. In England the development came late. The first phase of the revival of Arabic learning is chiefly associated with scholars in France and Italy, more specifically Paris and Rome. In those centres development was stimulated by two factors: the political and commercial intercourse between France and the Ottoman Empire resulting from the capitulations of 1535, and the links between the papacy and oriental Christian sects, especially the Maronites after the foundation of the Maronite College at Rome in 1584. The effect of these factors on Arabic studies can be seen, for example, in the journey of the French scholar, Guillaume Postel, to Egypt and Instanbul between 1535 and 1537 to learn oriental languages and collect manuscripts, and also in the career of the Maronite, Gabriel Sionita, who went to the College in Rome and thence to Paris where he was professor of Arabic.

This revival of Arabic studies coincided with the Reformation and the division of western Europe into Protestant and Catholic states. Protestant scholars at first depended mainly on the Catholic centres, especially Paris, for obtaining a knowledge of Arabic. So the great Dutch Arabist, Thomas Erpenius, studied in Paris in 1609. It was also at Paris from Gabriel Sionita that Pasor learnt Arabic in the winter of 1624–5. The development of an important centre of Arabic studies in Protestant Europe began with the appointment of Erpenius as professor of oriental languages (except Hebrew) at Leiden in 1613. He held the post until his death in 1624 and was succeeded by his former pupil, James Golius (1596–1667). Erpenius and Golius made outstanding contributions to the development of Arabic studies by their teaching, their preparation of texts, and their assiduity in collecting manuscripts. The work of the Dutch scholars in its turn served as an inspiration to English scholars and patrons; the foundation of the chairs at Cambridge and Oxford followed, and from this point Protestant orientalism tends to follow its own line of development, apart from Catholic orientalism. But there was an intercourse of ideas between the two groups of orientalists. A very clear example of cross-fertilization is given in Nallino's demonstration that Marracci in his *Prodromus ad refutationem Alcorani* (1691) quoted a considerable number of Arabian authors at second-hand from Pococke;[6] while Denison Ross had earlier shown Sale's indebtedness in his "Preliminary discourse" to Marracci.[7]

(ii) *Motives to the Study of Arabic in Seventeenth-Century England*

The motives which led English scholars to take up the study of Arabic at this time can be deduced from their printed inaugural lectures and similar introductory material. Primarily their interest was religious. The value of Arabic in giving a better understanding of the biblical text and in throwing new light on Hebrew was stressed by Bedwell (1612),[8] Pasor (1626),[9] Pococke (1661),[10] Castell (1667),[11] and Hyde (1692).[12] This theme continues in the following century as Ockley[13] at Cambridge and Hunt[14] at Oxford bear witness. Furthermore a knowledge of Arabic was seen to be essential for polemic with the Muslims which, it was fondly hoped, would bring about their conversion to Christianity. This was, of course, an old mirage, which had been followed in the Middle Ages by Catholic scholars such as Raymund Lull. By the sixteenth century the Roman church had tacitly abandoned hope of converting the Muslim world and had turned its missionary endeavours to more rewarding fields. The less experienced Protestant churches, however, still hoped in the seventeenth century to find common ground with Muslims in opposition to Catholicism. The polemical motive is mentioned by Bedwell and was served by Pococke, who in 1660 translated into Arabic Grotius's propagandist work, *De veritate religionis Christianae*, which had been written by the Dutch scholar for the use of missionaries in the East Indies. Arabic was also a means of establishing an understanding with the oriental Christians of Syria and Egypt. This motive had been anticipated by the Catholics in the fifteenth and sixteenth centuries, when the futility of schemes to convert the Muslims had become obvious. The extent and success of Catholic missionary work during the sixteenth and early seventeenth centuries both alarmed and stimulated the Protestants. Pococke's work reflects in this respect also the concern of his contemporaries. In 1671 and 1674 respectively he translated into Arabic the Anglican catechism and liturgy. This he did on the request of Robert Huntington, at that time the chaplain to the merchants of the Levant Company in Aleppo.

In view of the close connexion between religion and the study of Arabic, it is significant that many of the early Arabists were themselves clerics, such as Bedwell and Pococke. Arabic studies owed much to clerical patronage. The Oxford chair was, as we have seen, founded by Laud, who in 1633 became archbishop of Canterbury. The Cambridge foundation, on the other hand, was by a London merchant; but a deeply pious man, prompted, as his letters show, by religious and not commercial motives. If we go back a generation we find Bishop Lancelot Andrewes, whose disciple in some respects Laud was, offering Erpenius an annual stipend to teach oriental languages in England and preferring Bedwell to the vicarage of Tottenham.[15] Among other clerical amateurs of Arabic and patrons of oriental studies was Archbishop Ussher.

Interest in Arabic was not linked to any significant extent with commercial considerations. The Cambridge authorities, when writing to Adams in 1636 to thank him for undertaking to endow the chair of Arabic in perpetuity, speak of the work as being "also to the good service of the King and State in our commerce with those Easterne nations". Bedwell, following Postel, had spoken briefly of the importance of Arabic in business with the East. But such passages are very exceptional and there is no evidence, on the other hand, that the average English merchant in the Levant had any command of Arabic or any other foreign language.[16]

Although Arabic was not studied for commercial reasons, the motives which led to its study were, in their seventeenth-century context, utilitarian. It could render services to religion, and it could also help to satisfy that desire for general information characteristic of the educated man of the period, which in another direction stimulated the development of experimental science. Arabic was valued as the key to a treasure-house of knowledge, supplementing the inheritance from Greece and Rome. This theme is a commonplace in the seventeenth-century orientalists, who frequently mention the wealth of medical, astronomical, and mathematical works in Arabic. History does not figure so often but Pasor enumerates a number of Arabic historians, saying that they have recorded the deeds not only of the Arabs but also of the Hebrews, Chaldees, Persians, Greeks, and Romans, and claims that the lost books of Livy are extant in Arabic. Arabic historical writings are also mentioned in passing by Thomas Greaves (1637)[17] and Hyde.

(iii) *The Function of Trade*

English trade with the Ottoman Empire nevertheless performed an important function in connexion with the development of Arabic studies. The Levant Company of London was chartered in 1581 and capitulations were finally obtained from Sultan Murad III two years later. Factories of English merchants were established in various ports and towns, notably for our purposes at Aleppo, while an English ambassador took up residence at Istanbul. Thus a permanent means of peaceful contact with the Muslim and Arab lands was established. Merchants acted as intermediaries in obtaining manuscripts, although their ignorance of the languages diminished their utility. So in 1624 Ussher wrote to Thomas Davies in Aleppo, asking him to send books. Davies replied that he had found a Samaritan Old Testament, slightly imperfect, "which notwithstanding I purpose to send by this shipp least I meet not with another". He has sent to Damascus for a perfect Pentateuch "and yf not there to be had to mount Garazin". A messenger has gone to Mount Lebanon and Tripoli for a Syriac Old Testament but without immediate success. With regard to a Hebrew version, for which the large sum of £10 was asked, Davies states that he cannot guarantee it "for neyther my selfe nor any other man here can determine it, only I must be forced to take his word that sells it me who is a minister of the sect of the Marranites, and by birth a Chaldean but not Scholler, neyther is there any to be found in these parts". Davies adds that "to affect business of this nature in these parts requires time, travell being very taedious in these countries".[18] Laud, as a minister of Charles I, was able to improve on this method when in 1634 he obtained a royal letter to the Levant Company "requiring that each of their ships returning from the East should bring one Persian or Arabic manuscript back".[19]

The chaplaincies at the factories were a means by which scholars could obtain a first-hand knowledge of the Near East and its languages. John Luke was, as we have seen, chaplain at Smyrna. Others who turned their time in the Levant to profit were Charles Robson (Aleppo before 1628), Thomas Smith (Istanbul, 1668–70), and Henry Maundrell (Aleppo, 1695–1701), who all wrote travel-books. Smith and John Covel (Istanbul, 1670–6) wrote on the Greek Church. Robert Huntington (Aleppo, 1671–81) was a great collector of manuscripts, which are now in the Bodleian. The most notable of the chaplains at Aleppo was, however, Pococke who went out in 1630 and stayed there for five years. He had already studied Arabic under Pasor and Bedwell and now set to work to improve his knowledge. During this period also Pococke laid the foundation of a great collection of manuscripts concerning which more will be said later.

English diplomatic and commercial representation in the Ottoman Empire facilitated travel in the Levant. The precedent for learned journeys in Muslim lands had been set by Postel but he had few imitators. Erpenius never went east of Venice. Golius in 1622 accompanied a Dutch embassy to Morocco and in 1625 he was sent abroad by the university of Leiden to collect oriental manuscripts. He spent eighteen months in Aleppo, went to Iraq, and returned by way of Istanbul. In 1637 Pococke, after a short spell of teaching at Oxford, set off with his friend, John Greaves, for Istanbul. Greaves is an example of the amateur Arabist of the period. He was primarily interested in astronomy, of which he was professor at Oxford. His object in his journey was not merely to collect antiquities and manuscripts but to make astronomical observations.[20] After spending some months with Pococke, he went to Egypt for this purpose.

Another means which Pococke used to obtain manuscripts was the appointment of a Syrian Muslim as his agent and copyist. This person, a certain al-Darwīsh Aḥmad, wrote five letters to Pococke after his departure from Aleppo and these throw some light on the trade in manuscripts at the time. Al-Darwīsh Aḥmad acted both as a buyer and a copyist.[21] There was a fair amount of competition in the trade: al-Darwīsh Aḥmad mentions particularly as a rival the brother of Golius, who was a Carmelite friar and acted as Golius's agent.

(iv) *The Collections of Manuscripts at Cambridge and Oxford*

As a result of these various activities, several important collections of oriental manuscripts were made by scholars and amateurs of Arabic during the seventeenth century. These collections in turn tended to pass in due course, by gift, bequest, or sale, to the university libraries at Cambridge and Oxford. The Cambridge University Library[22] had at this period resources far inferior to those of the Bodleian. Its oriental collection was founded on the library of Erpenius. The Dutch scholar had intended his manuscripts to go on his death to Leiden. They had, however, been bought by the duke of Buckingham when he was visiting the Hague in 1625–6 for the purpose of pawning the English crown jewels. Buckingham was chancellor of Cambridge university, to which he intended to present the manuscripts. He was assassinated in 1628 with this intention unfulfilled and the university ultimately obtained the collection in 1632, after petitioning Buckingham's widow.[23] There were 85 manuscripts in all but only one of an historical nature, namely that of Eutychius (Sa'īd b. al-Biṭrīq) to which the copyist has appended an Arabic history of Sicily. The next important gift was of 20 manuscripts obtained in Istanbul by Nicholas Hobart. These were presented in 1655 and include three manuscripts of the *Khiṭaṭ* of al-Maqrīzī. In view of this paucity of historical texts, it is not surprising that when Ockley, the Cambridge orientalist, was preparing his *History of the Saracens* in the early eighteenth century, he carried out his research among the more copious stores of the Bodleian Library.

Oxford was fortunate in the seventeenth century in receiving three major collections of oriental manuscripts.[24] Laud himself, as chancellor of the university, presented the great foundation collection of which the Arabic manuscripts alone amount to some hundreds. These reached the Bodleian in instalments between 1639 and 1642. No doubt Pococke had been Laud's agent in the acquisition of some of these. Pococke's own collection was bought by the university in 1693, after his death. The third important source of Arabic manuscripts was Robert Huntington. He presented some to the Bodleian in 1678 and others were purchased in 1693. The bequest of Narcissus Marsh in 1713 should also be mentioned, since Marsh had purchased many of his manuscripts from the library of Golius. Among minor acquisitions we may note the manuscripts acquired in 1659 after the death of Selden, who was chiefly famous as a lawyer and controversialist but was also an accomplished orientalist. Others were acquired in 1670 from the library of Samuel Clarke (1625–69), who had a high reputation as an Arabist in his time but has left little trace to posterity, and in 1678 from the library of Thomas Greaves.

Among these hundreds of manuscripts were many of an historical or biographical nature, although they were not necessarily those that a modern student would regard as of first importance. This was partly due to the circumstances in which many of them were acquired, partly to a difference in outlook. Late authors preponderated since these would most easily be obtainable by purchase and copying.

(v) *The Publication of Historical Texts*

Readers and students of Islamic history in the seventeenth century were not greatly concerned with the critical study of texts or the verification of sources. They wanted information in a compendious form on the historical background of Muslim civilization. Hence early historians were not particularly esteemed; in fact later historians might be preferred since they brought the story down to recent times. This demand was met by the publications of Erpenius, Golius, and Pococke, which were issued for the benefit of the learned world in general, not merely of other orientalists. Four Arabic historical texts were printed during the century, three of which were compendious histories of a derivative nature. The Arabic text was accompanied in each case by a Latin translation so that, in Pococke's words, 'those who seek a knowledge of the history rather than of the language may by omitting the Arabic proceed with unhindered foot'.[25] These historical publications were the following:[26]

1. The second part of al-Makīn's chronicle, dealing with Islamic history. Edited and translated by Erpenius and published posthumously (1625) at Leiden under the title *Historia saracenica.* As a supplement to cover the history of Muslim Spain, the *Historia Arabum* of Rodrigo Jimenez de Rada (1170–1247) was also printed in this book. An English version appeared in 1626 and a French version in 1657.
2. Ibn 'Arabshāh's *'Ajā'ib al-maqdūr* was edited by Golius and published at Leiden in 1636 under the title *Ahmedis Arabsiadae Vitae et rerum gestarum Timuri, qui vulgo Tamerlanes dicitur, historia.*
3. Bar Hebraeus: *Al-Mukhtaṣar fi'l-duwal.*
   (a) A portion of this work was edited with a Latin translation and copious notes by Pococke under the title *Specimen historiae Arabum.* Published at Oxford in 1650.
   (b) The full text was published by Pococke with a translation and supplementary material under the title *Historia compendiosa dynastiarum.* It appeared at Oxford in 1663.

4. Eutychius: *Naẓm al-jawhar.*
   (a) Selden, for polemical purposes, published a translation of a portion of this chronicle under the title *Eutychii Aegyptii . . . Ecclesiae suae origines*: London, 1642.
   (b) The full text with a translation was published by Pococke under the title *Contextio gemmarum* at Oxford in 1658.

Of these chronicles, Erpenius's *Historia saracenica* covered Muslim history to the twelfth Christian century; Pococke's *Contextio gemmarum* began with the Creation and went down to the caliphate of al-Rāḍī in the tenth Christian century, while the *Historia dynastiarum* also opens with the Creation and ends with the reign of the Īl-khān Arghūn in the thirteenth century. Pococke's supplementary material to this work enumerates and gives notes on other Muslim rulers from Arghūn's time to his own. Pococke gives his sources for this supplement; they are Abu'l-Fidā', al-Maqrīzī, Ibn Taghrī Birdī, *al-Jawhar al-thamīn* of Ibrāhīm b. Muḥammad b. Duqmāq, written in 908/1502, al-Jannābī, *Akhbār al-duwal wa-āthār al-uwal* of Aḥmad b. Yūsuf, and *al-Rawḍa al-zāhira fī wulāt Miṣr wa'l-Qāhira* of Muḥammad b. Abi'l-Surūr al-Ṣiddīqī, written in 1036/1626.

Pococke's Specimen Historiae Arabum

Pococke's historical scholarship is most fully apparent in the short work which he entitled *Specimen Historiae Arabum.* The preface of this contains a short account of Bar Hebraeus and ends with a dedication to Selden. The excerpt from Bar Hebraeus's Arabic text occupies 15 pages, which are faced by Pococke's Latin translation. The text begins with an account of the Arab tribes and their groupings, followed by a mention of the pre-Islamic monarchies and a little about religious beliefs in the Jāhiliyya. The proficiency of the early Arabs in the use of language and their knowledge of the stars are noted. The next section recounts the life of the Prophet. A short passage deals with the biblical texts asserted by Muslims to be prophecies of the advent of Muḥammad and with the miracles ascribed to him, particularly the miracle of the Qur'ān. The two remaining groups such as the Mu'tazila, the Khawārij, and the Shī'a, the other describing the four *madhhabs* and concluding with a summary of the main points of religious practice.

This is followed by over 300 pages containing Pococke's notes on the text. The notes were apparently printed in advance of the text since they have a separate title-page with the date 1648, while that to the whole volume is dated 1650, but the pagination continues from the preceding text. They show wide reading, in Hebrew and Greek as well as Arabic, and there are occasional references to other orientalists, especially Erpenius. These notes amplify every point made by Bar Hebraeus. Pococke begins with the etymology of the words "Arab" and "Saracen" and here as elsewhere he rejects some current derivations. He goes on to deal with the Arab tribes and their genealogies and gives an account of the pre-Islamic monarchies drawn from literary sources. In the course of this note he touches on philological questions, such as the ancient royal greeting and the titles *tubba*ʿ and *qayl*, as well as giving an account of Mazdakism.

In the next group of notes he studies the religions of the Jahiliyya. He first discusses the idols mentioned in the Qur'ān, especially the triad al-Lāt, al-ʿUzzā, and Manāt. He is critical of the etymologies advanced by Arab grammarians for Yaʿūq, Yaghūth, and other names. He gives from Arabic sources a euhemeristic theory of the origin of several divinities. Other notes give information about the sects recognized by Muslims as *Ahl al-Kitāb*. In his linguistic notes, Pococke mentions the difference between Himyaritic and North Arabian and connects Himyaritic with Hebrew and Syriac. He tells the traditional stories of the introduction of writing into the Ḥijāz and speaks of the fair of ʿUkāẓ and the Muʿallaqāt. He notes Arab ignorance of philosophical studies until ʿAbbasid times and retells from Bar Hebraeus the legend of the burning of the library of Alexandria.

Next comes a series of notes on the life of the Prophet. Pococke here mentions the doctrine of the Light of Muḥammad. The principal interest of this section, however, lies in the refutation of several inveterate errors still found at that date in learned circles in Europe. He shows the false etymology which would derive the term *Muhājirun* from the name of Hagar. The ancient Christian fable of the entombment of the Prophet in an iron coffin, suspended between earth and heaven is dismissed with ridicule—but in the following century Joseph Pitts, who had made the Pilgrimage as a slave, still thought the tale to be worth refuting.[27] Pococke also deals with the fable of the dove which Christians asserted was trained to eat from Muḥammad's ear and was presented as a miraculous appearance of the Holy Ghost. The story had been perpetuated by Grotius in his *De veritate religionis Christianae* but Pococke obtained from him an admission that it was based on no Muslim authority and it does not appear in Pococke's own Arabic translation of the book.

Pococke's notes on the Islamic sects are enriched by long quotations from al-Ghazālī and other Muslim writers. He gives a particularly full account of the Muʿtazila, as also of the Shīʿa and Nuṣayrīs, whom he may have encountered in Syria. This set of notes concludes with the text and translation of a Muslim statement of beliefs taken from al-Ghazālī. The notes as a whole end with information on the four *madhhabs*, the religious duties incumbent on Muslims, and a long account of various customs and superstitions of the Jāhiliyya.

Pococke shared his contemporaries' interest in Arabic proverbs and cites many in the course of his notes. These are collected together at the end for fuller explanation and Pococke takes the opportunity to make some corrections to a collection published by Erpenius. The book ends with a set of notes on the authors mentioned in the text and notes. Brief biographical details are given, largely derived from Ibn Khallikān. In all, Pococke refers to or quotes from over 70 Arabic writers. Some of these are late but his range is remarkably wide. He makes frequent use of the two great lexicons, *al-ṣiḥāḥ* of al-Jawharī (d.c. 400/1009–10) and *al-Qāmūs* of al-Fīrūzabādī (d. 817/1415). Among historical writers, Abu'l-Fidā', al-Jannābī, and his continuator, Aḥmad b. Yūsuf, are perhaps the most frequently cited and are Pococke's main source for supplementary material on the Jāhiliyya and the life of the Prophet. He draws largely on Ibn Khallikān for information on various matters, for example the origin of the Muʿtazila. His notes on religious beliefs of the Jāhiliyya and on Islamic sects show much use of al-Shahrastānī's *Kitāb al-milal wa'l-niḥal*, written in the twelfth century. Here Pococke had discovered an important authority. Equally important was his realization of the value of al-Ghazālī's writings. Pococke seems to have used an epitome of the *Iḥyā' ʿulūm al-dīn* made by al-Arbalī.

Significance of Seventeenth-Century work on Muslim History

What was the significance of Pococke's work on the Arabic historians? It is difficult to appreciate it to-day, when the study of Muslim history has become so much more critical in its approach and specialized in its nature. Essentially it lies in the fact that he, together with his predecessors Erpenius and Golius and his eighteenth-century successors, Ockley, Sale, and Gibbon, helped to change the image of Islam in Christian and European minds.[28] This he did partly by the refutation of fables such as I have mentioned earlier but more effectively by making available fresh and more authentic material and by demonstrating with all the erudition at his command that Islam and civilization were worthy of serious study by educated men. His publications on Islamic history were not merely learned works but also in a restricted sense works of popularization. In the next century the process was to be carried further. Ockley was to write an English *History of the Saracens* and Sale was to produce an English version of the Qur'ān preceded by a learned and detailed Preliminary Discourse. Finally Gibbon was to integrate Muslim history with that of the Roman and Byzantine empires. These three writers still condition the thinking of the non-specialist on Islam and Muslim history, and the image which they created, as their footnotes and references show, was largely derived from the pioneer work of Pococke. We are now in a third phase, when this image and the Muslim sources from which it derives are being submitted to the techniques of modern historical criticism but this should not obscure the importance of the work of Pococke and the other orientalists of the seventeenth and eighteenth centuries in contributing to a better understanding of the Islamic world and its history.

APPENDIX I

Extracts from Thomas Adams's letters to Abraham Wheelocke concerning the Arabic professorship and related matters

1. (Cambridge University Library, MS. Dd.3.12. IV (2): 3 February 1631/32.

Your letter I have recd. and understand the contents thereof, and as the shortnes of time will permit my thoughts to conceive of it I returne you answeare what my opinion is first I conceive it is no easie nay an impossible thinge to engage the cittie or a particuler company in the busines, neither can I apprehend their is any banke of mony as you call it undisposed, wh may this way be appropriated Yet I conceive the worke is of worthye use and the aimes of the professors to be greatly encouraged and I cannot doubt but what you intend may by Gods' help in due time be effected, and for a beginning to the furtherance of this worke I make no doubt but meanes will be found by particuler freinds to raise a reasonable summe annually for 2 or 3 yeares certeine and if the worke be well accepted in that interim it is most probable that meanes may be found for the establishmt of it: onely in the first place I commend two thinges to be performed by you, first to signifye unto me by your letter what will be the yeerly charge of the lecture intended. 2d. to procure from the Vice-Chancellor and the chiefs of the universitie a certificate or testimoniall that this intended Lecture is of principall use and that the Universitie doth desire the establishmt of it. Heerafter I shall inlarge my writing as occasion shall be offered. at present I thought fit to scribble these few lines for your satisfaction.

2. (3): 16 February 1631/32, sent with the previous letter

I had scribbled the withinwritten 13 daies agoe in answeare of yours then received, but I did forbeare to send it, because I conferred wth one touching the busines intended and he tould me his persuasion was you might read to the bare walls wthout audience, although that conceipt staide me from present sending what I had writt, yet it remooved not the matter from my thoughts, this day your last being brought unto me I could not delay to give you answeare and therfore have sent the former and this together, I againe declare you my opinion that if you can procure a testimoniall from the Vice-Chancellour of Cambridge and the heads of the University that the worke you intend I meane the reading of a lecture in the Syriacke and Arabicke tongues is of necessarie use in the University and wthall desired by them to be established I do not doubt but to procure the summe of 40£ per annum for two or three yeares certeine, and not doubting but if the worke be well accepted that there may be found in the interim meanes for the establishmt of it, to this purpose I writt in my former and second the same.

3. (4): 29 February 1631/32

I have received your letter and for your further satisfaction signifie unto you that when the heads of the university shall be pleased to give the testimoniall required, it is intended that your self shall be preferred in one chaire before any other to enter into the place, and that an espetiall aime is to your owne employment, and improvement of your talent that way received.

4. (5): 3 March 1631/32

I have recd your letter wth the inclosed from the Vice-Chancellor and heads of your famous universitie, my self an unfit obiect in such manner to be saluted by such reverend persons. I am right glad of their good acceptance of the worke intended, although I could have wished the manifestation therof had bine rather to others than to my self, and my name whollie concealed. I pray God make the worke prosperous by his Almightie power that it may be for his owne glorie the increase of learning, the honour of the renowned universitie, the good of the kingdome and his whole Church throughout the world. I am right glad also of their good acceptance of your self wth acknowledgmt of your suffitiencie for the employment intended, your self being the onely person our freinds heer purposed and designed for the honour and burden of that Orientall chaire, and now with the leave and favour of those worthie Cedars or Seraphims rather of your learned Academie I wish you much ioy in your execution of that hopefull employment and that you may be deservedlie honoured in Cambridge and renowned in England.

I cannot doubt but conveniencie of place for the lecture is alreadie settled, and touching the maintenance, wheras I formerlie mentioned I doubted not to procure an exhibition of 40£ per annum for 2 or 3 yeares certeine, wheras it hath pleased the heads of the universitie to understand it for 3 yeares absolutelie, I purpose not to name that contraction, and (God willing) shall provide to be dulie performed unto you 40£ per annum for 3 yeares from the feast of the Annuntiation of the blessed virgin being the 25th of this present march to be paid you quarterlie by x£ a quarter, the first payment to begin at midsummer next and so continuedlie for 3 yeares from the time premised if your self so long live and continue in the employment of publicke professor of the Arabicke tongue in Cambricke, wherto I reckon by the authoritie of the universitie you shall be speedily called and I do further purpose uppon the experience of a good liking of the employment to the furtherance of learning and the honour of the universitie (as it is hoped) to endeavour to perpetuate the same publicke lecture by a setled maintenance for ever. What you mentioned touching thankfulnes from the universitie or your self to mewards, I neither expect it nor conceive my self in any measure worthy therof. . . .

ffinally I give you to understand that I have conferred although very latelie wth our learned and bright shining star mr Holsworth[29] touching the busines intended and desired his opinion of it and in particuler touching the paucitie of Auditers wherat I formerly sticked, as you may remember. His approbation and encouragement to the worke was very great even more than I expected, his satisfaction cleare, his profession of love, of thankfulnes, of readines, to assist in any thing by himself or freinds all wh evince my most grateful acknowledgmt . . . further his good words of your self whom he had formerly knowne, and since heard of, his desire to have his kind love signified unto you wth all possible encouragemt to the prosecution of the worke, so worthy, so commendable, I say, as they evince your gratitude also, so you shall do well to write a few words unto him in manifestation therof and of my kind acceptance of his abundant love.

I hope you still remember that the more wise the Preacher was the more he taught the people and you intend to make all subservient to that great worke the winning of soules, and the Authour of wisdome make us wise to salvation whose glorie I hope you seek above all.

5. (1): 16 March 1631/32

Your letter I received wth the inclosed to Mr Howlesworth, who is gone this afternoone about the busines you mentioned and is minded to let you heare from him the next wicke.

I shall desire you to acquaint the heads of the University at their first conveniencie wth the contents of my last letter touching the promised exhibition for 3 yeares certeine, and the time when it doth begin, and wthall to present my humble request unto them to call you to the worke, and to consummate your election, and to be further pleased to consider of the times for your publicke reading (twise a week as I conceive during the Termes) and at such houres as shall be most opportune in respect of other exercises, all wh I refer solelie as is most meet to their provident consideracions.

Touching your self, since matters have thus proceeded I desire you to alter your purpose to begin with privacie in your chamber for this first quarter and to take resolution to prepare your Oration by the beginning of the next tearme wh is a full moneth from this present day and to give life and beginning to the publicke lecture the next tearme by all possible meanes, and to reckon it greater honour to your famous Universitie at the commencement to have the Arabicke lecture already there established, then to be entred uppon after that long Vacation following, the succeeding tearme being more then vi moneths hence. I cannot doubt but your second thoughts will confirm my purpose herin espetially sithens your oration being to be provided [?] in this convenient time, you are already sufficiently fitted for the publick work.

6. (6): 23 March 1631/32

Yours of the 21st I have recd. and shall present your desired thanks to Mr Howlesworth at the first opportunitie, he tould me the last wicke he was going about the bookes you mentioned but as I remember the vallew of them was not tould me above the one half of the summe you mentioned, however it is very well they are obtained for your Universitie and I conceive the present fruitition of them will be most commodious for yourself and much conducing to the furtherance of the worke intended, and therfore in thankfulnes for the meanes let us say wth the Psalmist, Praysed be the Lord daily even the God that helpeth us and poureth his benefites uppon us etc. and you do well to observe his espetiall providence in every matter. I shall gladly heare that you are called by the heads of the Universitie to the worke that I may warrantablie by their authoritie salute you wth the Title of Professor linguae Arabicae, and most gladly heare of the good successe of the worke under your hand that like that little cloud grewe to the servant of Elias from a hand breadth spreading over heaven, this from a small spark inlightening most remote and darke places, virtus dei de infirmitate, when I am weake then am I strong.

7. (22): 30 March 1632

Yours of this wicke I recd. and whatsoever the feare at Cambridge be least these Orientall bookes will be diverted, yet I hope your Universitie is in better likelihood to have them in regard of some late endeavours then in truth it was formerly, howsoever supposed otherwise. The certeinty is this, Mr Howlsworth uppon the receipt of your letter 3 wickes agoe (as I take it) went immediately to the house of the Dutches[30] and spake to Mr Bowles her Chaplein who promised his furtherance and to moove the Dutches about them wthin a few daies, and Mr Houlesworth replying that my L: of Lincolne[31] had already made way to the Dutches about them, Mr Bowles answered, I wish he had spake unto her, but he did not, onely he acknouledged he spake unto him about them. The second time Mr Holsworth repayring thither recd this answere from Mr Bowles that the dutches replyeth that shee would consider of it. Then did Mr Holsworth understand privately that there was great meanes used to gaine the bookes for Oxford. The 3rd time Mr Holsworth went to Mr Boules for the dutches resolution wh was that shee would speake to the king about them. Heeruppon Mr Holsworth acquainted the Earle of Dover being his parishioner wth the busines and prepared him wth severall arguments to the dutches but not meeting wth her he went to my Lord of Holland[32] by whom meanes was used to his maiestie, and thus it is hoped that the iewells will be reserved for Cambridge and to morrow this nobleman aforenamed will stir againe about it and we hope we shall understand the danger is prevented. Thus you will still say Praised be the Lord daily even the God that helpeth us and poureth his benefites uppon us. Mr Holsworth was willing to write to you but being straitened in time he caused his servant to write to Mr Iohnson to acquaint you wth these circumstances. When I shall understand further I shall advise you. I acknowledge wth respective and most deserved thankfulnes the favours the heads have showed in your election and ordering of the place and time and frequencies of your reading. . . . I recd even yesterday Mrs Bedwells satisfaction that you are as able as any in the kingdome wh report for some reasons no little pleased me.

8. (7): 6 April 1632
I spake this day to Mr Holsworth touching the bookes, and he assured me that he hath bine 3 times this wicke about them and that my Lord of Holland is sollicited and promiseth his best endeavour, and he hopeth they will be shortly obtained, he doth defer to write unto you untill he hath certeine newes about your bookes and promiseth me not to surcease untill he hath brought it unto some period.

9. (8): 14 April 1632
This day I spake to Mr Holsworth and he acquainted me wth the severall passages the last wicke occurring touching the bookes and doth assure me that they will be had for your Universitie and that there is no cause to feare the dispersal of them elsewhere. onely touching the manner to obtain them with expedition he will write the next wicke to the Vice-chancellor if this succeeding wicke do not open the way in a cleare course as it is hoped it will. Mr Howlesworth is no lesse sollicitous then your self for the safe and speedie procuring of them.

10. (9): 18 May 1632
I have read your oration I meane so much of it as my line will fadome, the rest aut Arabicum aut Hebraicum non potest legi, me thinks I heare your Auditors say of the matter, how were we ignorant of these thinges before of the Oration; what pittie were it that this great tallent should be hid in a napkin or rust without use. I have read it I say, and was glad to read the usefulnes of your new language and facilitie to attaine it, and must needs affirme that the matter of your oration was excellent and the composing therof of no small paines. . . . Your letter to Mr Holsworth I have delivered and the next wicke he is purposed to write unto you. The meane time he desireth to be remembered, This day I left him your oration wh he most gladly received and according as I desire he is to show it to Mr Shute[33] and returne it me backe the next wicke. You did well to sever the epistle from the worke otherwise I had scarsely shewne it; you know my mind if the worke be glorious to God, honourable and acceptable to the university, profitable to the kingdome, comfortable to your self, what can I wish more?

11. (10): 8 June 1632
Yours I have recd this wicke certifying that you have begun the Arabicke lecture. I wish and pray it may goe on wth profitable successe. . . . I have not yet your oration from Mr Holswirth. This day I had purposed to speak wth him, but he prevented me by his messenger certifying that the bookes are faithfully promised to be sent to Cambridg this wicke and that he was minded to certifie the same unto you, and his servant tould me, he supposed he saw the trunke at the carriers wherin they were, directed to doctor Mason of St Iohns (as I remember): and touching your booke he had not yet done with it. . . . The next wicke I pray you or the wicke following advise me whether I shall send the promised stipend by Mr Hobson your

carrier[34] in gold or else pay it by the appointmt of some of your Shop-keepers who will faithfully deliver it uppon a note of my paymt of it to any heer as you shall direct. Midsommer draweth on, snd I desire to take your advise, wh way to follow.

12. (11): 6 July 1632

I have spoke to Mr Raymond severall times touching Mr Bedwells lexicon, how it was disposed. He answereth me, that he gave it to Trinitie Colledge by his will, and the words are clear wthout scruple. onely he saith that in conference after his will was made some one saying unto him that if the Colledge would not print the booke what then was his pleasure. He answered let it be then otherwise disposed of.[35] Happily you know already either by Mrs Bedwells letter unto you (if shee have returned answear to yours) or by some other meanes more then I can expresse heerin: at your comming up wth yours wch I desire according to your promise somtime this moneth (your commencemt being now ended) we shall have time further to confer heerof, and to resolve me whether any employmts were for the Arabick professor at the late act.

APPENDIX II

Letter from al-Darwīsh Aḥmad to Pococke

Among Pococke's papers in the Bodleian are some Arabic letters, five of which were written to him by a Muslim friend who signs himself "al-Darwīsh Aḥmad". It is clear from the contents that Aḥmad had known Pococke in Aleppo, and may have taught him Arabic, since in two letters he addresses Pococke as *al-tilmīdh al-ʿazīz*—"the dear pupil". The letters are undated, but internal evidence shows that three of them were written to Pococke in 1636–7, when he was in England after returning from Aleppo, and two while he was residing at Istanbul, between the end of 1637 and August 1640. A great part of each letter consists of formal greetings in rhymed prose: elsewhere the Arabic is semi-colloquial. The principal interest of the letters is the light they throw on the book-trade, since Aḥmad collected and transcribed manuscripts for Pococke, and encountered some competition.

Letter 1. (*Bodleian Library, Oxford, MS. Poc. 432, f.6*)

Addressed to Pococke in "the island of Britain". Aḥmad acknowledges a letter from Pococke, and informs him of his own marriage. He then goes on to write concerning manuscripts as follows:

> "I have got the *Ikhwān al-ṣafā'*[36] which you saw previously, an illustrated one, for sixty piastres. I would not have got it at this price, only Girolamo[37] asked me for it. That one, which you saw on the day you travelled from Aleppo, was unobtainable as you know. As for the book of history of al-Jannābī the judge,[38] some quires of which you saw and said to me that I must take it to the consul when I had finished writing it out, when it is finished I shall take it to him, God willing. The

commentary on the *Gulistān* has been completed and I have sent it to you. God willing, I shall strive on your behalf to send the history of Ibn Khallikān[39] and *Ma'āhid al-tanṣīṣ*[40] and I will send you every book I see which is suitable for you. You must send me a reply to this letter and with it something of the rarities of your homeland and send me the printed geography.[41] Whatever may be of use to you in this respect, send and tell me of it so that I may succeed in executing it."

Letter 2. (*f.7*)

The phraseology of this letter implies that Aḥmad has heard that Pococke has taken his B.D. and been appointed professor of Arabic, since it addresses him as "the teacher of the English sect, the erudite in the Christian sciences, and the researcher into the roots of the Arabic language" (*mu'allim al-ṭā'ifa al-inklīziyya wa'l-mudaqqiq fi'l-'ulūm al-masīḥiyya wa'l-mufaḥḥis 'an uṣūl al-lugha al-'arabiyya*). The portion dealing with Arabic manuscripts runs as follows:

"Previously I had given to Girolamo the *Ḥayāt al-ḥayawān*[42] which I had written for myself, because of my need of goods. I sent you the *Ikhwān al-ṣafā'* which you saw when you were in Aleppo. I only obtained it from its owner for sixty piastres. Then after that I got the book *Ṣubḥ al-a'shā* in two volumes by al-Qalqashandī,[43] each volume for twenty-four piastres, and, God willing, I shall get you the rest of the history of *Ṣubḥ al-a'shā*. Also a man has also [sic] the book *al-Yatīma* by al-Tha-'ālibī[44] which I shall get. I have also got the commentary of al-Bayḍāwī,[45] a copy which has not its like for fifty-five piastres but its price [would be] a hundred piastres, as you will know when it reaches you. I have written out for you a book connected with the Christian religion because Golius (*Kūl*) sent to ask for it from his brother[46] and he had it written out by Thalja,[47] the brother of the Greek Orthodox bishop (*maṭrān al-Rūm*). I have written it out for you and delivered it to Girolamo so it will come to you. I have also happened upon a book about agriculture (*al-filāḥa*) and it will come to you soon. I am working at the writing out of the history of al-Jannābī which I showed you before you went away from Aleppo—some of it, that is. Also I am working at the book *Ma'āhid al-tanṣīṣ 'alā shawāhid al-talkhīṣ* and the history of Ibn Khallikān and the book *al-Mustaṭraf fī kull fann mustaẓraf*.[48] I am staying in the city of Aleppo and I want to go off to Damascus, to visit Jerusalem and return to Aleppo, for I have married and sought for someone to serve me, and have become their servant. I want you to send me a letter in the Arabic tongue, and send also without fail to inform me of your condition. Whatever book you want, write its name in Arabic and send it to Girolamo, and I will send you everything you want. Send and tell Girolamo too, if I bring him a suitable book, to get it, for Golius the Fleming [i.e. Dutchman] has sent to ask his brother for most of the books which I wish to send, especially the book *Ṣubḥ al-a'shā*. He [i.e. Girolamo] did not wish to obtain it, so I went myself to Ibn al-Muwaqqa' and outbid the brother of James Golius and obtained it and brought it to Girolamo, so this was the means of obtaining it. You must send me an Arabic letter specially for I have sent you three letters with this and you have not sent me one."

Letter 3. (*f.8*)

This letter is addressed in affectionate and paternal terms to "my honoured and dear son, Pococke" (*janāb al-walad al-'azīz Pūquq*). Much of it consists of condolences on the death of Pococke's father, which occurred in 1636 or 1637. Aḥmad then passes on to business about manuscripts:

"I have sent you the copy of *Ikhwān al-ṣafā'* which you saw when you were in Aleppo and I got it at a price exceeding its [true] price. The reason for that is that al-Sayyid al-Taqwa took that copy which came from Damascus and gave it to the judge. There arose between him and me conflict and enmity without limit because of *Ikhwān al-ṣafā'*; it became to me a sore trial. When Mawlānā al-Shaykh Najm al-Dīn saw that discord had become great for this reason, he sent and had this copy brought from Ibn al-Ḥuṣrī and handed it over to the owner of the copy brought from Damascus as compensation for it, as the judge had not given him its price. That man said to me, 'I only brought this copy for you and I am suffering loss because of you'. So I went back and got the copy which you saw, and this is the reason for getting the book *Ikhwān al-ṣafā'* at an increased price but yet it is not dear. I want you to have two copies. Also I have given to Girolamo the book *Ḥayāt al-ḥayawān* which I wrote out myself, for twenty-two piastres, for I myself laid out upon it the sum of nineteen piastres, and I would not have sold it to him only that I had married and I needed some money. I have also got a book of the history *Ṣubḥ al-a'shā* which Ibn al-Muwaqqa' had. Great discord arose over them also, and al-Taqwa also wished to get them for he wanted to send them to a man connected with government [*min arbāb al-salṭana*] at a price of twenty-two piastres a book. I outbid him by four piastres and got it somehow, for when I saw them I could not bear to let anyone get them. When they reach you, spend some time reading them, for there is much useful matter in them. I shall, God willing, send you later *Kitāb al-filāḥa* by Ibn Waḥshiyya[49] and the rest of the history *Ṣubḥ al-a'shā* by al-Qalqashandī. I have also written out the preface of al-Kaf'amī[50] and it will come to you, and also the history of Ibn Khallikān will come to you. The history of Ibn al-Shiḥna,[51] which you may know would be of use to you. Send and tell me about it so that I may execute it for you . . . I hope to send you a book connected with the religion of the Christians. The brother of Golius is reading it and I am copying it and it will soon come to you."

Letter 4. (*f.9*)

Addressed to Pococke in Istanbul (*Islāmbūl*).

Aḥmad acknowledges the arrival of a gift from Pococke. He has received a message through a certain al-'Akkārī to join Pococke, and the messenger offered to pay for a mount for the journey. But Aḥmad has not set out, since he awaits information from Pococke as to the length of his stay in Istanbul, lest his own journey should be in vain: "send and inform me of your purpose, for you wrote me a letter from your country and mentioned the occurrence of the plague". The part of the letter dealing with books and manuscripts is as follows:

> "The books which I have got for you are with Girolamo. I have brought them to your recollection before now but he has not mentioned anything about them to you. I think he has sent them to your country and not to you but to someone else. Now however I have a copy of Ibn Khallikān other than that which I sent to you and a copy of the book *al-Milal wa'l-niḥal*[52] and some histories. Also I have *al-Ṣiḥāḥ* of al-Jawharī.[53] a copy of great importance (?) and I have a history about states concluding with the dynasty of 'Uthmān, such as the Tatars, the Mongols, the Kurds, the Turks, the Circassians and the Ottomans.[54] Golius, the brother of the Flemish monk, sent to ask for a copy of the *Dīwān* of al-Ḥāfiẓ in Arabic but it was unobtainable. He also asked for some historical works but did not get anything he asked for. But I saw a fragment of the commentary on the *Dīwān* of al-Ḥāfiẓ in Arabic. I had written a commentary on the *Gulistān* for you but the copy from which the commentary came was defective and now I have completed it and it will soon come to you. I wish to go to Damascus for *Kitāb al-filāḥa* and the book of al-Kafa'mī and I hope to obtain them. But I hope after this letter reaches you, you will send me a letter about the matter which will be in Arabic and detailed in every respect. Do not neglect it. Whatever may be of use to you, send and inform me of it and it shall be done. The *jāwīsh*[55] and Mannā' and the cook all greet you . . . I have got many books and he [i.e. Girolamo] has not mentioned them to you, like *Ṣubḥ al-a'shā* and the history of al-Ṣafadī[56] and *al-Sulwān* and many things which he has not mentioned to you. I think he has got them for someone else as you may know . . . God willing, the books which you have asked for will come soon. I have prepared for you two books all about the religion of the Christians which will also come to you."

Letter 5. (f.5)

The last letter of the series contains further excuses for Aḥmad's failure to join Pococke. Illness alone, he ways, has prevented him from travelling, but after the '*Īd* he hopes, God willing, to set out: "so prepare me a place of residence, if possible, for me to stay in when I come. And farewell."

NOTES

1 A general account of Arabic studies in Europe is given by J. Fück, *Die arabischen Studien in Europa bis in den Anfang des 20. Jahrhunderts* (Leipzig, 1955), supplemented by his article, "Islam as an historical problem in European historiography since 1800", in Bernard Lewis and P. M. Holt (edd.), *Historians of the Middle East* (London, 1926), 303–14.

2 The type had previously belonged to the press set up by Franciscus Raphelengius (1539–97), a learned printer of Leiden (letter of John Greaves to Peter Turner, P.R.O., S.P. 16 381, No. 75). It was modelled on the fount of

the Medicean press, set up in Rome in 1580 by Cardinal Ferdinand de' Medici. See also Appendix I, letter 12.

3 Thirty-two letters from Adams to Wheelocke are in the Cambridge University Library. These throw light on the circumstances in which the chair of Arabic was founded and on the relations between Wheelocke and his patron. See Appendix I.

4 The letter of thanks from the University to Adams is given in A. J. Arberry, *The Cambridge School of Arabic* (Cambridge, 1948), 7–8.

5 Hyde's most celebrated work was *Historia religionis veterum Persarum eorumque Magorum* (Oxford, 1700).

6 C. A. Nallino, 'Le fonti arabe manoscritte di Ludovico Marracci sul Corano' (1932), reprinted in *Raccolta di scritti*, II (Rome, 1940), 90–134. Nallino shows that the Arabic authors quoted by Marracci at second-hand are mainly from Pococke's *Specimen historiae Arabum.*

7 E. Denison Ross, 'Ludovico Marracci', *BSOS*, II, 1, 1921, 117–23. See also his introduction to the edition of Sale's translation of the Koran published by Warne (London, 1921).

8 W. Bedwell, *D. Iohannis apostoli et evangelistae epistolae catholicae omnes* (Leiden, 1612). The 'Praefatio' is the relevant portion.

9 M. Pasor, *Oratio pro linguae Arabicae professione* (Oxford 1627). The lecture was delivered on 25 October 1626.

10 E. Pococke, *Carmen Tograi cum versione Latina et notis* (Oxford 1661).

11 E. Castell, *Oratio . . . cum praelectiones suas in secundum Canonis Avicennae librum auspicaretur* (London, 1667).

12 T. Hyde, *Oratio de linguae Arabicae antiquitate, praestantia et utilitate*, printed in *Syntagma dissertationum*, ed. Gregory Sharpe, II (Oxford, 1767), 449–59.

13 S. Ockley, *Introductio ad linguas orientales* (Cambridge, 1706).

14 T. Hunt (Laudian Professor of Arabic at Oxford, 1738–74), *De usu dialectorum orientalium, ac praecipue Arabicae, in Hebraico codice interpretando* (Oxford, 1748).

15 H. Isaacson, *The Life and death of Lancelot Andrewes*, D.D. . . . *edited and arranged by the Rev. Stephen Isaacson* (London, 1829), 49.

16 How uncommon a knowledge of the local language was amongst the English merchants is indicated by Roger North's account of his brother, Dudley, who resided at Izmir and Istanbul between 1661 and 1680:

"I have heard our merchant say, that he had tried, in the Turkish courts, above five hundred causes; and, for the most part, used no dragomen, or interpreters, as foreigners commonly do, but, in the language of the country, spoke for himself. He observed, that many fair causes were lost by the indiscretion of the dragomen, who neither took nor delivered the matters justly, as he himself, using his own notions and expressions, could do. . . . For these, and other purposes of his negotiation, he had laboured to gain, and had thereby acquired, a ready use of the Turkish language, and could speak it fluently. . . . He not only spoke, but wrote Turkish very well. . . . The Nation maintained a Turkish Effendi, or priest, at a salary, who was to attend every day for the purpose of Turkish writing, especially letters. . . . This was a grave old man, who was a doctor in addresses and forms of concluding; but as to his business, our merchant commonly took the wording of it to himself, not trusting, and often over-ruling the effendi; with whose expressions, in mercantile affairs, he was seldom satisfied." Roger North, *The lives of . . . Francis North, . . . Dudley North, . . . and . . . John North* (London, 1826), II, 373–4.

17 Thomas Greaves acted as Pococke's deputy at Oxford, while the latter was

making his second journey in the East (1637–41). His inaugural lecture was published as *De linguae Arabicae utilitate et praestantia* (Oxford, 1639).

18 Davies to Ussher from Aleppo, 29 August 1624. Cambridge University Library, MS. Dd. 2.13. I, f. 1.

19 A. F. L. Beeston, *The oriental manuscript collections of the Bodleian Library*, 1; reprinted from *Bodleian Library Record*, v, 2, 1954.

20 See above, pp. 7–8.

21 Bodleian Library, MS. Poc. 432, 5–9. See Appendix II.

22 E. G. Browne, *A catalogue of the Persian manuscripts in the Library of the University of Cambridge* (Cambridge, 1896), introduction. Also "Description of an old Persian commentary on the Qur'an", *JRAS*, 1894, 417–22.

23 See Appendix I, pp. 39–41.

24 Beeston, op. cit., 1–2. Further details concerning the various *fonds* of manuscripts may be found in the *Summary catalogue of Western manuscripts in the Bodleian Library*, 7 vols. (Oxford, 1895–1953).

25 E. Pococke, *Specimen historiae Arabum*, Oxford, 1648/50; Praefatio ad Lectorem (unpaginated).

26 C. F. Schnurrer, *Bibliotheca Arabica* (Halle, 1811), 113–17, 113–46.

27 Joseph Pitts, *A faithful account of the religion and manners of the Mahometans*, 3rd edn. (London, 1731), 157.

28 For the formation of the traditional Christian view of Islam, see Norman Daniel, *Islam and the West* (Edinburgh, 1960); R. W. Southern, *Western views of Islam in the Middle Ages* (Cambridge, Mass., 1962).

29 Holsworth (the name is variously spelt in later letters) is Richard Holdsworth (1590–1649), a Cambridge theologian who, at the time of this letter, was rector of a City church in London and professor of divinity at Gresham College. In 1633 he failed to obtain the mastership of St. John's, Cambridge, in a disputed election, but in 1637 he became master of Emmanuel. Although an opponent of Laud, he came to support Charles I against the Parliament, and in 1643 was imprisoned and deprived of his mastership and rectory. See *DNB*, IX, 1018–20.

30 I.e. the duchess of Buckingham; see above, p. 32.

31 John Williams (1582–1650), bishop of Lincoln since 1621, who had played an important part in bringing about Buckingham's marriage in 1620, and became one of Laud's leading opponents. See *DNB*, XXI, 414–20. Laud, as chancellor of Oxford university, was at this time endeavouring to strengthen the Bodleian's oriental collections.

32 Henry Rich (1590–1649), 1st earl of Holland, succeeded the duke of Buckingham as chancellor of Cambridge university. See *DNB*, XVI, 997–1000.

33 Probably Josias (Josiah) Shute (1588–1643), a Cambridge graduate and Hebraist, who was rector of St. Mary Woolnoth in the City from 1611 and from about the time of this letter was chaplain to the East India Company. See *DNB*, XVIII, 170–1.

34 Not the proverbial Hobson, who had died on 1 January 1630/31. See *DNB*, IX, 946.

35 Bedwell had died on 5 May 1632. Two letters from John Clerke (apparently his son-in-law), preserved in Wheelocke's correspondence, relate to this matter:

i. Cambridge University Library, MS. Dd. 3.12. III, 2 (1). Presumably to Wheelocke: 29 June 1632.

I thank you for your kind letter. my mother would have entreated you to acquainte the Head of what hee hath given namelye his Lexicon with the types to print itt and if they will not undertake to print itt that they woulde accept of a booke when it is printed and lett them have itt that will print it.

you know it is pittye it should be tossed and torne in the Librarye and you know it will bee, and there bee manye losed papers in itt wh will be misplaced or lost I praye you do what you can herin and lett mee heare from you as quicklye as maye bee what the Universitye saye to itt.

ii. 2 (2). To M. Cleye, president of Clare Hall, Cambridge: 29 June 1632.

Sir you desire to knowe what my ffather hath given to the Universitye: Why surelye hee hath given a rare and great gift namelye his Arabicke Dictionarye with all the types to print itt withall. it is great pittye itt should lye in the Librarye tost, and torne, as itt will bee if itt bee not printed: my request therfore unto you is that you would bee pleased to move the heades of the Universitye that if they themselves will not bee at the charge to print itt, that they would be pleased to accept of a Copye, I meane a booke when itt is printed and lett them have itt that will print itt. my mother might have made a great benefitt of itt if itt had beene left to her to make the beste of. Sir Killume Digbye [Kenelm Digby] would have given five hundred pounds for the booke and types. I praye you good Sir, acquaint the heades with it, and let me heare from you as speedilye as maye bee. These with my best love to you remembred I rest.

Your loving ffrende

John: Clerke

Tottenham the
29 of June 1632

Some time elapsed before Cambridge received the Lexicon. On 12 October 1632, Adams wrote to tell Wheelocke "that I had bine at Totnam wth Mr Clarke and what promise he had made me that the bookes wthout faile should be sent the last wicke or this present at the furthest, wh I hope is performed." Early in November, he again wrote, "I perceive Mr Clarke hath greatly failed in the discharge of his word wth me as he formerly hath done wth you, and your bookes and types not yet sent. I was better persuaded of his real respect to his promise. Mr Daniell is purposed to call of him and therby to informe you further." (MS. Dd. 3.12. IV, 16, 15.)

36 *Rasā'il ikhwān al-safā'*, "The treatises of the brethren of purity" an encyclopaedic work, written by a number of authors in the fifth/eleventh century, and now recognized as having links with the Ismā'īlī movement. The work was used by Pococke in his notes to *Specimen historiae Arabum*, 207, 385–6.

37 Girolamo (Jaraylmū or Ghirīlmū) seems to have been responsible for the transmission of manuscripts to Pococke, and may have been a dragoman attached to the English factory at Aleppo.

38 Al-Jannābī (d. 999/1590) was for a short time judge in Aleppo. He wrote an Arabic history of the Muslim dynasties, with a Turkish translation and abridgement. His work was cited in Pococke's notes to *Specimen historiae Arabum*, 36, 363.

39 Ibn Khallikān (d. 681/1282) compiler of the biographical dictionary *Wafayāt al-a'yān*, was cited by Pococke as "doctissimus Historicus" in his notes to *Specimen historiae Arabum*, 41, 364–5.

40 *Ma'āhid al-tanṣīṣ* by 'Abd al-Raḥīm b. 'Abd al-Raḥmān al-Qāhirī Zayn al-Dīn (d. 963/1556).

41 "The printed geography" is almost certainly *Geographia Nubiensis* (Paris, 1619), a Latin translation by the Maronites Sionita and Hesronita of a portion of al-Idrīsī's *Kitāb Rujjār*. It is referred to by Pococke in his notes to *Specimen historiae Arabum*, 373.

42 *Ḥayāt al-ḥayawān* of al-Damīrī (d. 808/1405) "is not only a compendium of Arabic zoology but also a store house of Muslim folklore" (L. Kopf,

AL-DAMĪRĪ, *EI*², ii, 107–8. It is cited in Pococke's notes to *Specimen historiae Arabum*, 135, 377.

43 *Ṣubḥ al-a'shā* is an encyclopaedic manual for secretaries compiled by al-Qalqashandī (d. 821/1418).

44 *Yatīmat al-dahr* of Abū Manṣūr al-Tha'ālibī (d. 429/1038), is an anthology of Arabic poetry of his own and earlier times.

45 Al-Bayḍāwī (d. 685/1286 or later) wrote a famous commentary on the Qur'ān entitled *Anwār al-tanzīl wa-asrār al-ta'wīl*, used by Pococke in his notes to *Specimen historiae Arabum*, 64, 369.

46 Peter Golius, the brother of the Dutch Orientalist, James Golius (1596–1667) had become a Carmelite friar, and was known in religion as Celestino di Santa Lidvina. James Golius himself spent some time in Morocco, and subsequently (between 1625 and 1629) travelled in Syria, Mesopotamia and Anatolia.

47 Thalja was another of Pococke's Syrian friends. Pococke, in the preface to his *Contextio Gemmarum*, speaks of him as the copyist of two of the manuscripts of Sa'īd b. al-Biṭrīq used in preparing the work, calling him "Michael Thalgius the Aleppine, an honest man whose friendship I formerly enjoyed, distinguished for his calligraphy rather than for any other part of learning". Three letters from Thalja to Pococke are preserved in the Bodleian (MS. Poc. 432, ff. 14–16) and justify the praise of Thalja's script. It appears from them that Pococke was trying, with rather limited success, to obtain information through Thalja about some Syrian saints.

48 *Al-Mustaṭraf* is an encyclopaedic anthology of Arabic literature, compiled by al-Ibshīhī (d. after 850/1446). The work was used by Pococke in his notes to *Specimen historiae Arabum*, 91, 95, 370, but he was uncertain of the author's name.

49 On the controversies surrounding *Kitāb al-filaḥa al-nabaṭiyya* and its alleged author, Ibn Waḥshiyya, see T. Fahd, IBN WAḤSHIYYA, *EI*², iii, 963–5.

50 Al-Kaf'amī, fl. 895/1489.

51 Ibn al-Shiḥna (d. 890/1485) was the author of an historical work on the history of Aleppo entitled *al-Durr al-muntakhab li-ta'rīkh Ḥalab*.

52 This work, which describes the sects and doctrines of Islam and other faiths, was written by al-Shahrastānī (d. 548/1153). It is cited by Pococke in his notes to *Specimen historiae Arabum*, 52, 368.

53 *Al-Ṣiḥāḥ*, in full *Tāj al-lugha wa-ṣiḥāḥ al-'Arabiyya* is a great Arabic lexicon compiled by al-Jawharī. It is cited in Pococke's notes to *Specimen historiae Arabum*, 43, 365–66.

54 This work is unidentified.

55 *Jāwīsh* (Turkish, *çavuş*), the messenger of the consulate at Aleppo, "who on ceremonial occasions walked before the consul carrying a staff tipped with silver". (A. C. Wood, *A history of the Levant Company* (London, 1935), 228.)

56 The reference is probably to the biographical dictionary, *al-Wāfī bi 'l-wafayāt* of Ṣalāḥ al-Dīn Khalīl b. Aybak al-Ṣafadī (d. 764/1363). Al-Ṣafadī also wrote a commentary on al-Tughrā'ī's *Lāmiyyat al-'Ajam*, which was used by Pococke in his edition of that poem (1661), and also cited in his notes to *Specimen historiae Arabum*, 160–1, 381–2.

3

THE TREATMENT OF ARAB HISTORY BY PRIDEAUX, OCKLEY AND SALE

UNTIL the last years of the seventeenth century, writings upon the history of the Arabs had been, in England as in Europe generally, academic in their purpose and nature. The study of Arab history was not in that period a specialized discipline; oriental studies had developed as ancillaries to Old Testament studies and ecclesiastical history and polemics. Few scholars were primarily interested in Arabic; still fewer made any significant investigations of Arab history. In comparison with his contemporaries, Pococke made an outstanding contribution to historical knowledge, and in his writings he displays the temperament of an historian—a notable achievement as will appear by contrast with some of his successors. Nevertheless Pococke's work was limited both in its scope and its impact. He produced no organized body of history: his publications consisted of the text and translation of two late Christian Arabic chronicles, and the erudite notes, not confined to history but ranging over the whole field of Arab antiquities and Muslim religion, which he appended to his *Specimen historiae Arabum* (Oxford, 1650). Translations and notes were alike in Latin, addressed to an academic audience rather than to the educated public at large. During the last twenty-eight years of Pococke's long life (1604–91), he was preoccupied with Hebrew and the writing of commentaries on the minor prophets. He made no further contributions to the study of Muslim history.[1]

Humphrey Prideaux

Humphrey Prideaux,[2] born in 1648 in Cornwall, was a pupil at Westminster School under Dr. Busby. This was of some importance, since Busby was keenly interested in contemporary orientalism, and added Hebrew, Aramaic, and Arabic to the normal classical curriculum of his school.[3] In 1668 Prideaux went to Christ Church, Oxford, where in 1679 he became a lecturer in Hebrew. He left Oxford in 1686, when James II appointed a Roman Catholic as dean of Christ Church. The remainder of his life was spent in East Anglia. He had already been appointed a canon of Norwich in 1681; from 1688 to 1694 he was archdeacon of Suffolk, and from 1702 until his death in 1724 he was dean of Norwich. When Pococke died in 1691, Prideaux was offered the chair of Hebrew at Oxford, which he declined, and in 1697 he published his most famous work, *The true nature of imposture fully display'd in the life of Mahomet. With a discourse annex'd for the vindication of Christianity from this charge. Offered to the consideration of the Deists of the present age.* The book won an immediate success; there were two editions in 1697 and others subsequently, while a French translation was published in 1698.

The full title of Prideaux's work announces its polemical purpose and its appearance was closely connected with the theological controversies of the late seventeenth century. Prideaux had originally intended to publish a much larger work entitled *The history of the ruin of the Eastern Church*, covering the period 602 to 936, from which he hoped to illustrate by example the dangers of theological disputes. The controversies of the Eastern church, Prideaux believed, "wearied the Patience and Long-Suffering of God", so that "he raised up the *Saracens* to be the Instruments of his Wrath, . . . who taking Advantage of the Weakness of Power, and the Distractions of Counsels, which these Divisions had caused among them, soon overran with a terrible Devastation all the *Eastern* Provinces of the *Roman* Empire".[4] Prideaux saw in this a terrible warning to the sects in England after the Revolution of 1688: "Have we not Reason to fear, that God may in the same Manner raise up some *Mahomet* against us for our utter Confusion . . . And by what the *Socinian*, the *Quaker*, and the *Deist* begin to advance in this Land, we may have Reason to fear, that Wrath hath some Time since gone forth from the Lord for the Punishment of these our Iniquities and Gainsayings, and that the Plague is already begun among us."[5]

Prideaux's composition of this tract for the times was, however, abruptly suspended on the outbreak of the Trinitarian Controversy.[6] He feared that his account of the dissensions in the Eastern Church might unintentionally provide fresh ammunition for those prowling enemies of the Establishment, "the *Atheist*, the *Deist*, and the *Socinian*". He therefore selected the passages of his work which dealt with the life of Muḥammad and published them in the form we have today.[7]

The book forms a curious contrast to an earlier work on the life of Muḥammad and the early history of Islam, which had been circulating for some years in manuscript. Its author, Henry Stubbs (alternatively Stubbes or Stubbe), who died in 1676, had also studied at Westminster under Busby, and had graduated at Oxford. He had served in the Parliamentary army during the Civil War. In later life he practised medicine and involved himself in controversy about the Royal Society, towards which he was hostile. His book, which was not printed until 1911,[8] existed in several different recensions[9] and is notable for its sympathetic attitude towards Islam. In essence it is an anti-Trinitarian tract.[10] For his materials concerning Islam, Stubbs depended upon the translations and writings of Hottinger, Erpenius, Pococke, and others, and upon the accounts of travellers.

Prideaux's book is therefore a two-handed engine of controversy: not only is it intended to expose the errors of Islam (a traditional exercise of Christian apologists), but more immediately to point the contrast between the origins of Islam and Christianity, and thereby to constitute a defence of Christianity against contemporary Deism. For the Deists were Prideaux's particular obsession. As a controversialist, he does them less than justice, seeing in them merely followers of a fashionable belief that Christianity is an imposture.[11] Their one merit is that they, 'seeming to retain the common Principles of Natural Religion and Reason, allow a sufficient Foundation whereon to be discoursed with". The atheist and the epicurean deist (who denies God's providence), by contrast "do leave no room for any Argument but that of the Whip and the Lash, to convince them of those impious Absurdities, and therefore deserve not by any other Method to be dealt with".[12]

Prideaux's book consists of two parts; the first, entitled "The Life of Mahomet" occupies 125 pages. The pagination continues for the second part, shortly entitled "A Letter to the Deists, etc.", which has however a separate title-page. The final section (pp. 235–60) contains "An Account of the Authors quoted in this Book". I am not here concerned with the "Letter to the Deists" which is, as it were, the sermon for which the preceding "Life of Mahomet" is the text.

Prideaux's sources, and his use of them, are of some interest. He is anxious to present his biography as a well-documented work, so that he "may not be thought to draw this Life of *Mahomet*, with Design to set forth his Imposture in the foulest Colours the better to make it serve (his) present purpose". In his "Account", Prideaux lists thirty-six Arabic authors of works, and makes a great display of their names in his footnotes. Upon examination, however, it becomes clear that his knowledge of them was derived at secondhand, from translations or quotations in the works of orientalists.

Three major works which he used were the printed editions (with Latin translations) of al-Makīn by Erpenius, Bar Hebraeus by Pococke, and Eutychius, also by Pococke.[13] For the Qur'ān, he appears to have relied chiefly on the twelfth-century Latin translation of Robert of Ketton, which had been printed by Bibliander in 1543.[14] He strongly criticizes this version as "an absurd Epitome of it, . . . whereby the Sense of the Original is so ill represented, that no one can scarce anywhere understand what is truly meant by the other". Although a printed Arabic Qur'ān had recently become available[15] and is mentioned by Prideaux, he seems to have been unable to use it, since he says, 'Had he [the editor] added a *Latin Version*, he would have made it much more useful." Prideaux also speaks of du Ryer's French translation[16] (of which he remarks "it must be said that it is done as well as can be expected from one who was only a Merchant") and the faulty English version made from this by Alexander Ross.[17] Another important translation used by Prideaux was that erroneously called *Geographia Nubiensis*.[18]

Prideaux appears to have known the great majority of his Arabic authorities only through citations and references in Christian writers. Pococke above all provided a mine of information in his *Specimen historiae Arabum*. A comparison of Prideaux's bibliographical notes with those appended by Pococke to his *Specimen* (359–89) indicates the extent of his dependence. In few of his notices does he add anything to Pococke's account of the authors; he is mostly content to translate, perhaps to curtail, Pococke's paragraphs, and to convert the *hijrī* to Christian years. An impressive array of Arabic authorities in a footnote usually implies the incorporation of material from Pococke's notes in the *Specimen*. In a few cases he draws upon other seventeenth-century Orientalists, particularly the *Historia orientalis* of the Swiss scholar, Hottinger;[19] and the *Historia Arabum* of the Maronite, Abraham Echellensis.[20]

Side by side with this information, drawn, albeit at secondhand, from Arabic authors, Prideaux uses the writings of anti-Muslim controversialists. Two of these, "Disputatio Christiani contra Saracenum de Lege Mahometis", reputedly translated from Arabic into Latin early in the twelfth century, and "Confutatio Legis Saracenicae" composed by Richard, a Dominican, in the thirteenth century, were printed with Bibliander's Qur'ān. Another, which Prideaux particularly esteemed, was *De confusione sectae Mahometanae*, written by Joannes Andreas, a Muslim converted at Valencia in 1487. The edition used by Prideaux was a reprint, published at Utrecht in 1656, of a Latin translation made from an Italian rendering of the Spanish original.[21] Prideaux states that the works of Richard and Joannes Andreas "are the best of any that have been formerly published by the Western Writers on this Argument, and best accord with what the *Mahometans* themselves teach of their Religion".[22]

Prideaux uses his sources with little discrimination. Materials from Muslim writers and Christian controversialists are treated as equally valid, and with the aid of his footnotes it would be a possible, if unprofitable, exercise to disentangle information derived from each of the two groups of sources. The resultant biography is an unskilful combination of Muslim tradition and Christian legend, inspired by a sour animosity towards its subject. Yet it marks a real if limited advance, when compared with accounts of Muḥammad's life current earlier. In Prideaux's work there is at least a historical framework although much overlaid by legendary material (both Christian and Muslim) and distorted by polemical bias.

Simon Ockley

A much more solid contribution to historical knowledge was the work produced by the Cambridge scholar, Simon Ockley, which is generally known as *The history of the Saracens*. Ockley was born at Exeter in 1678.[23] In 1693 he entered Queens' College, Cambridge, and in 1705, having taken holy orders, he became vicar of Swavesey in Cambridgeshire, where he died in 1720. In 1711 he was appointed to the Sir Thomas Adams chair of Arabic at Cambridge. His *History* was prepared and written in circumstances of great hardship. The first volume, entitled *The conquest of Syria, Persia, and Aegypt, by the Saracens*, was published in London in 1708. The second volume, to which the title *The history of the Saracens* was first given, appeared ten years later. The whole was reissued with this title in 1757 at the suggestion of Dr. Long, then master of Pembroke College, Cambridge, and Long is believed to be the author of a life of the Prophet prefixed to this edition. There was a reprint of the 1757 edition by Bohn in 1847.

Ockley's *History* is a landmark in two respects. It is the first attempt to write a continuous history of the Arabs in English, and it is based very largely on then unpublished manuscript sources. Chronologically the scope of the work is curious. The first volume begins with the election of Abū Bakr to the caliphate, and deals very fully with his reign and that of 'Umar. The volume ends with a short account of the reign of 'Uthmān. As the original title indicates, Ockley concerns himself principally with the wars of conquest and deals at great length with the Syrian campaigns. The second volume covers the period from the caliphate of 'Alī to the death of 'Abd al-Malik (35–86/656–705).

The omission of any account of the life of the Prophet is explained by the current popularity of Prideaux's book. In the introduction to his second volume, Ockley sounds a faint note of criticism:

> "I mention the *Life of* MAHOMET because it is the foundation of all our History; and though what hath been written of it by the Reverend and Learned Dr. *Prideaux* is sufficient to give a general *Idea* of the Man and his Pretensions, and admirably accommodated to his principal Design of showing the nature of an Imposture; yet there are a great many very useful Memoirs of him left behind, which would tend very

much to the Illustration of the succeeding History, as well as the Customs of those Times wherein he flourished."[24]

The abrupt termination of the *History* with the death of 'Abd al-Malik is sufficiently explained by the troubles and distractions which beset Ockley in his daily life. The penury of his later years is mentioned in his introduction to the second volume. "I was forced," he says, "to take the Advantage of the Slumbers of my Cares, that never slept when I was awake; and if they did not incessantly interrupt my Studies, were sure to succeed them with no less constancy than Night doth the Day."[25] As is well known, the second volume of the *History* was introduced to the world from Cambridge Castle, where Ockley was imprisoned for a debt of £200.

Ockley's difficulties were increased by the necessity of seeking his manuscript materials in the Bodleian Library. The oriental resources of the Cambridge University Library were at that time inferior to those of Oxford, which by the end of the seventeenth century had acquired the great manuscript collections of Laud, Pococke, and Huntington.[26] Ockley began by making a draft from the printed histories available to him, al-Makīn, Bar Hebraeus, and Eutychius. On his first visit to the Bodleian, he came upon what he believed to be an authentic history of the conquest of Syria, the *Futūḥ al-Shām* of the pseudo-Wāqidī. It was from this manuscript[27] that he drew the bulk of his material for the first volume of his history: in the original work of 891 pages, 21 to 115, 131 to 237, and 265 to 342 are closely based on the *Futūḥ*. No other author was used extensively by Ockley for this first volume, but his marginal references show an acquaintance with manuscripts of Abu'l-Fidā''s *al-Mukhtaṣar fī akhbār al-bashar*, Ibn Duqmāq's *al-Jawhar al-thamīn fī sīrat al-khulafā' wa'l-salāṭīn*, Ibn 'Abd Rabbih's *al-'Iqd*, and two works on Jerusalem, one by Muḥammad b. Ibrāhīm al-Suyūṭī, the other entitled *al-Uns al-jalīl bi-ta'rīkh al-Quds wa'l-Khalīl*.[28]

Ockley's second volume deals with the political history of the caliphate after the death of 'Uthmān, and in writing this part he was not dependent mainly on a single source, as in his first volume. Once again he had recourse to the Bodleian. He spent on this occasion five months in Oxford (his first volume had entailed two visits, each of less than six weeks), and was permitted by Bodley's Librarian to take the books he needed out of the library—a favour which was in breach of the statutes and had not been accorded to King Charles I! Ockley's marginal references and a table prefixed to Volume II show that he made use of manuscripts of Abu'l-Fidā' Ibn al-Athīr, and al-Ṭabarī, as well as of an anonymous historian which he greatly valued.[29] In addition he obtained a good deal of information, especially about 'Alī, from d'Herbelot's *Bibliothèque orientale*,[30] a pioneer encyclopaedic dictionary of orientalism, first published in 1697. Ockley's acquaintance with the Persian writers was acquired through d'Herbelot. With this exception, Ockley makes little use of secondary sources.

It will be clear from the foregoing that Ockley, unlike Prideaux, was a scholarly historian who based his work upon an investigation of original sources. His discrimination was not faultless, although it must be borne in mind that his most serious error, the acceptance of the *Futūḥ al-Shām* as a genuine work of al-Wāqidī, was not revealed until the nineteenth century. On the whole his instinct was sounder than that of Pococke, in his preference for early over later sources, and Muslim rather than Christian writers. Lacking the criteria which historical scholarship has assembled in the last two centuries, he is content to paint a full picture rather than to investigate the accuracy of details. His limitations in this respect appear in the remarks he makes on the author of *Futūḥ al-Shām*, whom he believes, from internal evidence, to have lived "above two hundred years after the Matter of Fact which he relates". He continues:

> "And if so, 'tis the same thing as if he had lived six hundred years after. For that Author that lives 1000 years after any Matter of Fact, is as much a Witness of it, as he that lives but at 200 years Distance. They are both of them oblig'd to take upon Trust, and if there be no Loss of good Authors during that Interval; he that writes latest is as credible an Historian as the first."[31]

One technical virtue of the historian he displays to the full; in the second volume especially he is meticulous in his dating. Each volume has a chronological table prefaced, while the second has marginal date-headings to each page. Where the chronology of his sources is obscure or confused, he draws attention to the discrepancies.[32]

The scholarly character of Ockley's work appears in his attitude towards the people with whom he deals. He does not fail to follow common form by stigmatizing Muḥammad, in his first line, as "the great Impostor"; he describes the Arab conquests as "that grievous Calamity", but the body of his work is totally lacking in the virulence which Prideaux displays. There is an echo of Prideaux in the preface to Ockley's first volume, where he speaks of the desirability of a knowledge of Arab history,

> "Not only because they have had as great Men, and perform'd as considerable Actions, as any other Nation under Heaven; but, what is of more concern to us Christians, because they were the first Ruin of the Eastern Church."[33]

The impression which one gains from reading Ockley is, however, that he is much more interested in the great men and considerable actions of the Arabs than in the ruin of the Eastern Church. Indeed, he tells us that his original purpose was "to take in the whole Series of the Affairs of the Christians during the Period; but upon second Thoughts it appeared to me to be foreign to my Purpose".[34] This transfer of interest, from the study of Arab history as ancillary to that of ecclesiastical history, to Arab history as in itself a subject of valid enquiry, is perhaps the most important aspect of Ockley's work.

George Sale

George Sale (?1697–1736)[35] was the first notable English Arabist who was not in holy orders. His father was a London merchant. He himself was a student of the Inner Temple in 1720, and subsequently practised as a solicitor. His interest in Arabic having been aroused, he received tuition from a Syrian Christian, Dadichi, who was in London in 1723. He may also have been taught by another Syrian, Negri,[36] who was also in London about this time and was commissioned by the Society for the Promotion of Christian Knowledge to produce an Arabic version of the Psalter and the New Testament. Sale was a corrector of the Arabic New Testament, and from 1726 to 1734 he was closely associated with the S.P.C.K., which he served in his legal capacity. Meanwhile he was working on a translation of the Qur'ān, the publication of which, in 1734, is a landmark in the history of Qur'anic studies. Not only was his translation far more accurate than its only English predecessor, the seventeenth-century version by Ross, but it was annotated from the Muslim commentators (particularly al-Bayḍāwī and al-Suyūṭī) and other sources, and preceded by a long Preliminary Discourse which forms a compendium of the information then available on the origins, doctrines, practices, and sects of Islam. The enlightened and objective attitude displayed by Sale may have been responsible for his gradual dissociation from the activities of the S.P.C.K. after 1734. Sale died in 1736, leaving his wife and family in financial difficulties. His collection of manuscripts ultimately passed to the Bodleian.

The purpose of the present account is not to give an appreciation of Sale's translation, which has been done by Professor Fück,[37] nor to analyse in general his sources of information. Over thirty years ago, Denison Ross indicated the dependence of Sale upon Marracci,[38] while in 1931 C. A. Nallino showed that Marracci himself quoted a considerable number of Arabic authors at secondhand, mainly from Pococke's *Specimen historiae Arabum*.[39] I shall confine myself to the first two sections of the Preliminary Discourse, the subject-matter of which is specifically historical, and examine briefly their sources and outlook.

The first of these sections deals with the Jāhiliyya, the second with the career of the Prophet. Taken together they supersede Prideaux. The insufficiency of Prideaux's work, in spite of its popularity, had appeared almost at once. Its publication nearly coincided with that of d'Herbelot's *Bibliothèque orientale* (1697) and Marracci's *Alcorani textus universus*, with its Latin translation (1698).[40] Then in 1723, Gagnier published at Oxford the text of Abu'l-Fidā' dealing with the life of the Prophet. This was the first Muslim Arabic account of Muḥammad to be printed *in extenso* and it was accompanied by a Latin translation.[41] The change of intellectual climate in western Europe in the later seventeenth and early eighteenth centuries was however producing a new attitude towards Islam and its Prophet, which rendered the tone of Prideaux as outdated as his sources were inadequate. Indicative of this is a French *Vie de Mahomet* by Count Henri de Boulainvilliers (1658–1722),[42] published posthumously in London in 1730.[43] Like Prideaux, Boulainvilliers uses the origins of Islam as the vehicle of his own theological prejudices, which are markedly anticlerical but these lead him to look with sympathy on his subject. He rejects the traditional axioms of Christian polemic with Muslims,

> "that there is not any rational inducement in all that they believe or practise; insomuch that common sense must be discarded in order to embrace their system",

and

> "that *Mahomet* was so coarse and barbarous an impostor, that he is not a man, who does not or cannot perceive plainly his cheat and corruption."

Boulainvilliers still assumes the superiority of Christianity but there is no acerbity in his tone; "with respect to the essential doctrines of religion, all that [Muḥammad] has laid down is true; but he has not laid down all that is true; and that is the whole difference between our religion and his."

La vie de Mahomet, again like Prideaux's book, is not a work of scholarship. The author admits that he does not understand Arabic and is indebted to d'Herbelot's *Bibliothèque* and to translations. Factually his book is sounder than Prideaux's which he criticizes, but there are some errors and a good deal of embroidery. Boulainvilliers left his work incomplete, at A.H. 5, and the English publisher invited Gagnier to write the closing section. According to Gagnier, the negotiations broke down and the sequel as we have it is anonymous.[44] In 1732, Gagnier in fact came out with his own *Vie de Mahomet*,[45] a work of serious scholarship. He makes his attitude perfectly clear in a lengthy "Préface: où l'on réfute les Paradoxes avancés par Mr. le Comte de Boulainvilliers, dans sa Vie de Mahomet". He criticizes particularly the favourable picture which Boulainvilliers gives of the Prophet, and the style of the work, which, he says, is romance rather than history.

Sale's account should be seen in connexion with these two recent biographies. In the first section of his Preliminary Discourse he deals with five main topics: the geography of Arabia; the Arab tribes; the history of the Jāhiliyya; the pre-Islamic religions of Arabia; and the culture of the Arabs. His account of the geography is based partly on Greek and partly on Arabic sources, notably al-Idrīsī (known through Pococke and the *Geographia Nubiensis*), Bar Hebraeus and Abu'l-Fidā', a fragment of whose *Taqwīm al-buldān* had been printed by Gagnier at Oxford in 1726–7. Pococke's notes in the *Specimen* and those of Golius to his edition of al-Farghānī[46] also contributed information. It is interesting to note that Sale also used the *Account* of Joseph Pitts, the first Englishman known to have visited Mecca.[47]

In the remainder of this section a very great deal of information is derived from or through Pococke's *Specimen*. This is clear from Sale's footnotes, but these conceal the full extent of his borrowing since sometimes they cite only the author used by Pococke. A comparison of Sale's text with that of Pococke makes it clear, however, that the English account is often little more than a translation or summary of passages of the *Specimen*. This is particularly obvious in Sale's account of the pre-Islamic religions of Arabia, where Sale's footnote references to *al-Mustaṭraf*, al-Shahrastānī, al-Jannābī, al-Bayḍāwī, and *Naẓm al-durr* can, with two dubious exceptions, be traced back to the *Specimen*. Sale's other sources show an acquaintance with the printed, rather than the manuscript, material available at the time; d'Herbelot's *Bibliothèque orientale*, Gagnier's texts of Abu'l-Fidā', al-Makīn, and Bar Hebraeus. He mentions Prideaux's *Life of Mahomet* five times, once to correct an error, and has one reference to the first volume of Ockley's *History*.

The second section of Sale's Preliminary Discourse falls into two parts. First he describes the condition of Christianity, Judaism and the Persian empire on the eve of the Muslim conquests. Here he naturally draws little information from Arabic sources: apart from a reference to the Qur'ān and one to Pococke's account of Mazdakism, which is derived from Abu'l-Fidā' and al-Shahrastānī, he cites only the two Christian Arabic writers, al-Makīn and Bar Hebraeus. They are mentioned on a single point; for the rest he depends largely on

Byzantine and modern sources. He refers to Prideaux, Ockley, and Boulainvilliers when describing the errors and schisms of Christendom, and follows his predecessors by saying that the Arabs "seem to have been raised up on purpose by GOD, to be a scourge to the *Christian* Church, for not living answerably to that most holy religion which they had received".[48] But his pages, unlike those of Prideaux, are not imbued with a sense of warning and retribution; the theory of a divine judgement is unemotionally stated and probably not very seriously entertained.

Sale's principal source for the career of the Prophet was Gagnier's edition of Abu'l-Fidā', to which there are numerous references in his footnotes. On two points he corrects Boulainvilliers's narrative, and in the course of ten references to Prideaux he makes seven critical comments of greater or less importance. Characteristic of the difference in outlook between the two writers is Sale's remark, "I cannot possibly subscribe to the assertion of a late learned writer [i.e. Prideaux, op. cit., 76], that he made that nation exchange their idolatry for another religion altogether as bad."[49] Sale's dependence upon late sources and lack of historical criteria for assessing his material caused him some difficulties. Like his predecessors, he accepted the story of the *Mi'rāj* as an authentic part of the Prophet's teaching. To Prideaux this had been an outstanding piece of evidence in support of his view of Islam. Sale finds it awkward since, as he says, "I do not find that *Mohammed* himself ever expected so great a regard should be paid to his sayings, as his followers have since done; and . . . he all along disclaimed any power of performing miracles."[50] He does not, however, reach the correct conclusion that the story may be a later accretion but says, rather lamely, that it seems "to have been a fetch of policy to raise his reputation".

The picture of early Arabia and the origins of Islam which is drawn by Sale is therefore still seriously at fault. Sale's range of sources was more limited and his Arabic scholarship perhaps less profound than appeared to his contemporaries. Nevertheless his work was of great importance. His freedom from religious prejudice (in which respect he compares favourably with many of his nineteenth- and twentieth-century successors), his obvious conviction that Arabic writers were the best source of Arab history, and Muslim commentators the fittest to expound the Qur'ān, marks an enormous advance on the hodgepodge of "authorities" advanced by Prideaux. His work complements that of Ockley, and for over a century the two played a leading part in creating the notion of the Prophet and the Arabs held by educated Englishmen.

NOTES

1 See above, pp. 3–26, 34–6.
2 *DNB*, XVI, 352–41.
3 *The Diary of John Evelyn*, Everyman Edition (London, 1945), i, 357, entry of 13 May 1661: "I heard and saw such exercises at the election of scholars at Westminster School to be sent to the University in Latin, Greek, Hebrew and Arabic, in themes and extemporary verses, as wonderfully astonished me in such youths, with such readiness and wit, some of them not above twelve, or thirteen years of age." Letter from Edmund Castell to Samuel Clarke in 1667, Baker MSS., Cambridge University Library, Mm. 1. 47, 347: "I also send you some papers from Dr. Busby, who . . . desires the cast of your eye, and your most exact censure, alteration, and emendation of the Hebrew, Chaldee, Arabique . . . Papers, which he sends to you, as also that you would, with his service, present them to Dr. Pococke . . . Our request is, that he would also be pleased to do the like with you, to read, censure, etc. with as much severity as may be." Busby wrote his own Arabic grammar for use in the School. His inclusion of Arabic in the curriculum was one reason for his acrimonious disagreement with Edward Bagshaw, the Second Master: John Sergeaunt, *Annals of Westminster School* (London, 1898), 86, 1156–16; *DNB*, I, 874–5; III, 481–3.
4 Prideaux, *Life of Mahomet*, 8th edition (London, 1723), "To the Reader", vii, viii.
5 Ibid., xi–xii.
6 For the Trinitarian Controversy, see E. M. Wilbur, *A history of Unitarianism in Transylvania, England, and America* (Cambridge, Mass., 1952), 226–31.
7 Prideaux, xiii–xiv.
8 Henry Stubbe, *An account of the rise and progress of Mahometanism with the life of Mahomet and a vindication of him and his religion from the calumnies of the Christians* (London, 1911). For Stubbs, see *DNB*, XIX, 116–17 and P. M. Holt, *A seventeenth-century defender of Islam: Henry Stubbe (1632–76) and his book* (London, Dr. Williams's Trust, 1972).
9 The manuscripts include the following in the British Museum: (i) Sloane 1709, 1786: two fragments of a single manuscript; (ii) Harley 1876, 6189: two complete manuscripts.
10 Stubbe is not mentioned in either H. J. McLachlan, *Socinianism in seventeenth century England* (London, 1951) or E. M. Wilbur, op. cit.
11 For the Deists, see G. R. Cragg, *From Puritanism to the Age of Reason* (Cambridge, 1950), 136–55.
12 Prideaux, xv.
13 See above, pp. 13, 18–19, 33.
14 See J. Fück, *Die arabischen Studien in Europa bis in den Anfang des 20. Jahrhunderts* (Leipzig, 1955), 3–9. On Robert of Ketton and his associates, see James Kritzeck, *Peter the Venerable and Islam* (Princeton, N.J., 1964).
15 Abraham Hinckelmann, *Al-Coranus s. lex Islamica Muhammedis* . . . (Hamburg, 1694). See Fück, *Die arabischen Studien*, 94–5.
16 André du Ryer, *L'Alcoran de Mahomet* (1647).
17 Alexander Ross, *The Alcoran of Mahomet* (London, 1649).
18 See above, p. 24, n. 23.
19 J. H. Hottinger, *Historia orientalis* (Zürich, 1651 and 1660).
20 Abraham Echellensis, *Historia Arabum*; supplement to *Chronicon orientale* (Paris, 1651).

21 Prideaux, 257.

22 Ibid., p. 259.

23 See *DNB*, XIV, 807–10; also the "Memoir of Ockley" prefixed to the edition of *The History of the Saracens* published by Bohn (London, 1847); and A. J. Arberry, *The Cambridge School of Arabic* (Cambridge, 1948), pp. 13–16. A detailed study of Ockley as an Orientalist has been made by Dr. A. M. A. H. Kararah in "Simon Ockley: his contributions to Arabic studies and influence on western thought" (Cambridge, Ph.D. thesis, 1955).

24 Ockley, *History of the Saracens* (Cambridge, 1757), II, xxxv.

25 Ibid., p. xxxix.

26 See above, pp. 32–3.

27 J. Uri, *Bibliothecae Bodleianae codicum manuscriptorum orientalium catalogus* (Oxford, 1787), 150, No. DCLV, MS. Laud. A. 118. Ockley also mentions another manuscript of the pseudo-Wāqidi, MS. Pocock. 326; Uri, 154, DCLXXXIV.

28 The manuscripts are described in Uri's *Catalogus*: (1) Abu'l-Fidā', *al-Mukhtaṣar*; MS. Pocock. 303; Uri, 155, No. DCLXXXVI. The manuscript contains the first part of the work, going to A.H. 454. Ockley's marginal reference (p. 9) numbers the MS. Pocock. 330. (2) Ibrāhīm b. Muḥammad b. Duqmāq, *al-Jawhar*; MS. Laud. B. 129; Uri, 148, DCXLVIII. Ockley's marginal reference (p. 8) numbers the MS. Laud. 806.11. (3) Aḥmad b. Muḥammad b. 'Abd Rabbih, *al-'Iqd*; MS. Huntington. 554; Uri, 172, DCCLXXXII. (4) Muḥammad b. Ibrāhīm b. Muḥammad al-Suyūṭī, *Itḥāf al-akhiṣṣā' bi-faḍā'il al-masjid al-aqṣā*; MS. Huntington. 510; Uri, 179, DCCCXXI. (5) Muḥyi'l-Dīn b. 'Abd al-Raḥmān, *al-Uns*; MS. Pocock, 362; Uri, 154, DCLXXX. Anonymous in Ockley, who calls the work *The history of the Holy Land*, or *The history of Jerusalem*.

29 (1) For Abu'l-Fidā', *vid. supra* n. 28 (1). (2) Ibn al-Athīr, *al-Kāmil*; MSS. Pocock. 137 and 103; Uri, 156, DCXCIV and DCXCVI. These two manuscripts cover the years A.H. 7–61 and 76–130. (3) Ockley's use of al-Ṭabarī is a matter of some complexity. (*a*) After giving up the Arabic version for lost, he states (*History*, II, xxxix–xl) that he "luckily found a Piece of it in *Folio* amongst Archbishop *Laud's* Manuscripts". He cites this in his table of "Mss. Authors" (p. xli) as "The Second Volume of *Altabari*'s Great History", *Laud's* MSS. *Num.N.* 55, 124. There is no Laudian historical folio manuscript with such a number in Uri's *Catalogus* (which gives the older numbers) and the only Laudian manuscript bearing the name of al-Ṭabarī is Laud. A. 124, al-Makīn, *Mukhtaṣar ta'rīkh al-imām Abū* (sic) *Ja'far Muḥammad b. Jarīr al-Ṭabarī*; Uri, 160, DCCXV. Ockley may have had the second part of al-Makīn's compendium in mind. It is perhaps relevant to note that another manuscript, with a similar number, Marsh. 124; Uri, 161, DCCXXII, is in fact described as the second part of al-Ṭabarī. The Marsh manuscripts were a bequest to the Bodleian in 1713 and so would be available to Ockley for his second volume. (*b*) Ockley also lists as Laud. 161. A. (for Laud. A. 161; Uri, 149, DCL) "An Imperfect Historian (and therefore Anonymous) . . . of singular Use in this History." This, which is also marked on the manuscript itself as Laud. 265, was identified by de Goeje as a portion of al-Ṭabarī covering the years A.H. 61–82. It is described in his communication in *ZDMG* (1862), 16, 759–62, and in Guidi's note printed in the Introductio, pp. lv–lvi, to de Goeje's edition of *Annales quos scripsit . . . At-Tabari* (Leiden, 1901). (*c*) A fragment of al-Ṭabarī, so identified in Uri, covering the years A.H. 77–79, forms part of MS. Huntington, 198; Uri, 159, DCCXI, which seems to have been missed by Ockley. It may be noted in passing that the Uri references of MSS. Huntington, 198 and Marsh, 124,

are transposed in de Goeje's communication cited above. (4) The other fragment listed as anonymous by Ockley is MS. Huntington, 495; Uri, 185, DCCCLVII, covering the early Umayyad period.

30 Fück, *Die arabischen Studien*, 98–100.

31 Ockley, *History*, I, xx.

32 E.g., *History*, I, 159, 371; II, 77–8, 296.

33 *History*, I, ix.

34 *History*, II, v.

35 *DNB*, XVII, 668–70.

36 See Fück, *Die arabischen Studien*, 95–7, for Negri and Dadichi.

37 Fück, *Die arabischen Studien*, 104–5.

38 E. Denison Ross, "Ludovico Marracci" in *BSOS* (1921), II, 118–23; cf. also his introduction to the Warne edition of Sale (1921) in which he says, "I have therefore been forced to the conclusion that with the exception of al-Baidhawi, Sale's sources were all consulted at second hand; . . . so much had been achieved by Marracci that Sale's work might also have been performed with a knowledge of Latin alone, as far as regards the quotations from Arabic authors."

39 C. A. Nallino, "Le fonti arabe manoscritte di Ludovico Marracci sul Corano" (1932), reprinted in *Raccolta di Scritti* (1950), II, 90–134.

40 Marracci's polemical *Prodromus ad refutationem Alcorani* had been separately published in 1691.

41 J. Gagnier, *Ismael Abul-Feda, de vita et rebus gestis Mohammedis* . . . (Oxford, 1723). For Gagnier, a French cleric who became an Anglican clergyman, settled at Oxford and became Lord Almoner's Professor of Arabic, see *DNB*, VII, 708–9.

42 Boulainvilliers's primary interest was in his own illustrious ancestry, which impressed other French genealogists less than himself. This led him to write on the history and antiquities of France.

43 Fück, *Die arabischen Studien*, 103 and n. 269[a]. An English translation (the translator is anonymous) was published in the following year: *The Life of Mahomet, Translated from the French Original by The Count of Boulainvilliers* . . . (London, 1731). The quotations that follow are taken from this translation, at p. 243.

44 The article on Gagnier in *DNB* states that he was in fact responsible for the anonymous continuation. This would seem to be disproved by Gagnier's own words in his Préface and his stringent denunciations of Boulainvilliers's work.

45 J. Gagnier, *Vie de Mahomet*, 2 vols. (Amsterdam, 1732).

46 Fück, *Die arabischen Studien*, 82 and n. 224. This source, which was used by others besides Sale, is commonly referred to as "Golius ad Alfraganum".

47 Joseph Pitts, *A faithful account of the religion and manners of the Mahometans* . . . (London, third edition, 1731). Partially reprinted and edited by Sir William Foster in *The Red Sea and adjacent countries* (Hakluyt Society, Series II, C, London, 1949).

48 G. Sale, *The Koran, commonly called the Alcoran of Mohammed* (London, 1764), I, 47.

49 Ibid., p. 51.

50 Ibid., p. 61.

II

STUDIES IN SUDANESE HISTORY

4

THE COMING OF THE FUNJ

(A) HYPOTHESES OF FUNJ ORIGINS

THE Funj Sultanate was the most easterly of the chain of Muslim dynastic states which at one time stretched south of the Sahara through *Bilād al-Sūdān*. Founded early in the sixteenth century by a king traditionally called ʻAmāra Dūnqas, its centre was on the Blue Nile, around the town of Sinnār. At the height of their power, the Funj sultans exercised a hegemony over the rulers and tribes of the Nile at least as far north as the Third Cataract. In a much debilitated form, the Sultanate lingered on until the early nineteenth century, when in 1821, Bādī VI, the last titular Funj ruler, submitted to the Turco-Egyptian forces sent by Muḥammad ʻAlī.

The problem of Funj origins is one of the most controversial in Sudanese history. It was discussed in a series of contributions to *Sudan Notes and Records* between 1930 and 1935, and, more recently, in another article by Dr. A. J. Arkell in the same periodical,[1] and in two books by Crawford[2] and al-Shāṭir Buṣaylī.[3] Early contributions to this discussion are vitiated by the uncritical attitude of their writers to the tradition of an Umayyad pedigree of the Funj, and by their equally uncritical acceptance of data derived from the final recension of the Funj Chronicle. The value of these sources was queried by Arkell in his first article "Fung Origins",[4] and further research has supported his very damaging criticisms.

Three hypotheses have crystallized out of the controversy. The first would bring the Funj from Abyssinia. This hypothesis was propounded by Crawford, and also by al-Shāṭir Buṣaylī, in a form which deserves serious consideration. The second hypothesis represents the Funj as a war-band of Shilluk, coming from a tribal homeland on the White Nile. Originally propounded by Bruce in the eighteenth century, this hypothesis was defended by Arkell in "Fung Origins" (1932). The third hypothesis was mooted by Arkell in his later article, "More about Fung Origins" (1946), and was more briefly stated in his book, *A history of the Sudan to 1821* (2nd ed., London, 1961), pp. 208–9. This would derive the ruling dynasty of the Funj from a refugee prince from Bornu, who settled among the Shilluk. Arkell thus regards this hypothesis as supplementary to the previous one.

The actual sources which provide data on the problem of Funj origins are few in number, mostly late (at least in the form in which we have them), and difficult to evaluate. Chronologically they may be listed as follows:

(1) The account of the Jewish traveller, David Reubeni, who passed through territory ruled by a king called 'Amāra, identified with the first Funj ruler of Sinnār, in 1523.[5]

(2) The Umayyad genealogy of the Funj. Al-Shāṭir Buṣaylī prints a Funj document giving a variant of this which seems to date from the later seventeenth century.[6] Other variants are given by H. A. MacMichael in his *History of the Arabs in the Sudan*, from manuscripts dating only from the nineteenth and twentieth centuries, although claiming in some cases to derive from originals of the eighteenth, seventeenth, or even sixteenth century.[7]

(3) The account given by the Scottish traveller, James Bruce, who passed through the Funj kingdom in 1772, and derived his information from various persons, notably Aḥmad Sīd al-Qōm, a high officer at the court of Sinnār.[8]

(4) The Funj Chronicle. Several recensions of this are extant, one of which, represented by manuscripts now in the Nationalbibliothek, Vienna, and the University of Nottingham Library, is particularly important in this connexion. A critical edition of the Chronicle was published by al-Shāṭir Buṣaylī 'Abd al-Jalīl as *Makhṭuṭat Kātib al Shūna* (n.p., n.d. [? Cairo, c. 1961]). The author of the original nucleus of the Chronicle was Aḥmad b. al-Ḥājj Abī 'Alī, who was born in 1199/1784–5.

(5) Traditions current in the nineteenth and twentieth centuries have been collected by various persons, and are to be found especially in the articles, referred to above, in *Sudan Notes and Records*. They were recorded uncritically, and their independent evidential value is slight.

(6) Linguistic data have been adduced by supporters of all three hypotheses. Both the presentation and the interpretation of much of this alleged evidence are amateurish and highly unscientific. Pending a systematic and expert investigation of the very complex problems involved, these hazardous analogies and intuitive derivations are best disregarded.

The Bornu Hypothesis

Of the three hypotheses, that of the Bornu origin lacks any supporting evidence in the sources originating in the Nilotic Sudan. Arkell's arguments in its favour rest on material from the central and western *Bilād al-Sūdān*, as translated and annotated by H. R. Palmer.[9]

Essentially, Arkell's hypothesis asserts that a sultan of Bornu,

'Uthmān b. Kaday, who was defeated by a rival and expelled from his homeland, made his way to the Nile valley, where he or one of his descendants first "acquired dominion over the Shilluk, and then over the old Nubian kingdom of Soba".

What is the evidence for this? Arkell's basic reference is an Arabic chronicle (little more than a king-list) of the rulers of Bornu, 'Dīwān Salāṭīn Burnū', of which two copies were obtained by the explorer, Barth, in 1853. One of these was translated by Palmer,[10] who subsequently published the Arabic text.[11] This version does not mention the expulsion of 'Uthmān b. Kaday, but a footnote by Palmer mentions that in the other version (the Blau MS.) 'Uthmān "is said to have died at Makada or Mâkida, i.e. northern Kordofan, to which most of the princes of the Daud branch [i.e. 'Uthmān's clan] seem ultimately to have fled".[12]

Palmer's note is cited to this point by Arkell, who, however, omits the concluding sentence. This states that the "Girgam", another king-list, also translated by Palmer, "has 'Malakata' a corruption of Mâkita, i.e. country of the Amakitan (Tuwareg)". Essentially, then, the assumption that 'Uthmān b. Kaday and his clan emigrated to the east depends on a doubtful place-name in a single copy of a nineteenth-century chronicle.

Arkell seeks to buttress his assumption by citing other accounts of the migration, also translated and annotated by Palmer. One of these, the chronicle "Ngizam and Bulala", speaks of the rule of Sultan Dā'ūd b. Ibrāhīm for two hundred years in the land of Malkda. Palmer annotates this as meaning that the Da'udid princes fled to Malkda, which, he says, "here means the region generally called Mâkida, the country of the Amakitan, i.e. northern Kordofan".[13] This interpretation is inconsistent with his other assertion, that the Amakitan are Tuwareg, who are not found in northern Kordofan. With this citation, Arkell groups a passage from another chronicle, "Mai Daud", which states that 'Uthmān b. Kaday "went to the land of Malakâda (Makâda)". It is not clear whether Palmer found the bracketed form in his text, or inserted it as a gloss. In any case he provides a footnote which gives a third interpretation of the term Makâda, inconsistent with both his other identifications, but more favourable to Arkell's hypothesis. Makâda, he says, is "the Kingdom of Sen'ar [*sic*] on the Blue Nile". He gives no reason in support of this identification.[14]

Thus there are two uncertainties: the name of the place to which 'Uthmān b. Kaday fled, and its location. Arkell has arbitrarily selected the name and interpretation most favourable to his hypothesis. He is also aware that Makāda means Abyssinia (more strictly, parts of western Abyssinia), but resolves this further complication by declaring that "The Bornu MSS. just quoted must mean Sennar when they say Makāda". He supports this from the statements in the chronicles "Ngizam and Bulala" and "Mai Daud" that the refugee Da'udids were ultimately overthrown by the Turks,[15] and equates this event with the Turco-Egyptian conquest of Sinnār in 1821. But both these chronicles speak of the Turkish leader as Yūsuf Pasha, a name not associated with the Turco-Egyptian conquest, although, I suggest, it may signify Yūsuf Pasha Qaramānlī, governor of Tripoli, who sent expeditions into the territory north of Bornu in the early nineteenth century.

Arkell further assembles other material from Palmer, some of which may serve as evidence that there has been on occasions in the past a connexion between the Nilotic Sudan and the Bornu region, but which is irrelevant to his specific assumption of the eastwards migration of 'Uthmān b. Kaday. Thus, he cites a statement by Palmer that "At least one tradition survives of a time when the Meks [*Makks*, i.e. kings] of Senaar . . . were in some sense either theoretically subject to or at least connected with the early Bornu Mais of Wadai." But the context in which this occurs shows that Palmer, although muddled, is thinking of a period before the Funj Sultanate, and Arkell ignores his further remark that "All that had, however, by 1470 passed away." Arkell links with this another assertion by Palmer, that "the Bornu Keyi . . . claim a connection with Senaar".[16] This is so vague and tenuous as to be devoid of evidential value: it is an *obiter dictum* in a passage of wild amateur philology. Another tradition to which Arkell makes allusion implies a migration, or rather an extension of power, in precisely the reverse direction to that which he seeks to establish. This tradition, given by Palmer in "A Native Chronicle of Wadai", represents the founder of the Tunjur dynasty as having become "king in the island of Sennar". "Their [i.e. the Tunjur] kingdom afterwards extended to Darfur and Wadai."[17] Finally, a tradition obtained by Arkell from Palmer's "Middle Ifrikia" "classes the Tunjur with the Bulala".[18] The document concerned is a twentieth-century text. A cursory examination of its contents indicates its unhistorical quality. Moreover, to demonstrate a connexion of the Bulala with the Tunjur does not corroborate Arkell's main assumption.

In addition, Arkell shows, irrelevantly in this context, the existence of a connexion between medieval Bornu and Darfur. He indulges in some philological speculation, and indicates some possibilities of archaeological investigation. But his hypothesis must stand or fall by the alleged documentary evidence cited from Palmer, and in the opinion of the present writer he has completely failed to make out his case.

The Shilluk Hypothesis

The Shilluk hypothesis of Funj origins was first propounded by Bruce. In the notes printed at the end of his *Travels* we are given the data (but not necessarily *all* the data) on which he based it. These data are clearly taken from several informants: they exhibit inconsistencies of nomenclature and topography, but they bear witness to a strong tradition, held at Sinnār in 1772, that the ruling *élite* of the Funj were a branch of the Shilluk, a tribe domiciled on the White Nile.

Bruce's narrative, which should be regarded as his considered synthesis of the material derived from various informants, rather than as a report of a single current tradition, consists of the following passages:

> "In the year 1504, a black nation, hitherto unknown, inhabiting the western banks of the Bahar el Abiad [*al-Baḥr al-abyaḍ*, the White Nile], in about latitude 13°, made a descent, in a multitude of canoes, or boats, upon the Arab provinces, and in a battle near Herbagi [Arbajī], they defeated Wed Ageeb [Wad 'Ajīb], and forced him to a capitulation, . . . and he thus became as it were their lieutenant.
>
> This race of negroes is, in their own country, called Shillook. . . . It was the year 1504 of the Christian aera, that Amru, son of Adelan, the first of their sovereigns on the eastern side of the Nile, founded this monarchy, and built Sennaar, which hath ever since been the capital. . . .
>
> At the establishing of this monarchy, the king, and the whole nation of Shillook, were Pagans. They were soon after converted to Mahometism, for the sake of trading with Cairo, and took the name of Funge, which they interpret sometimes lords, or conquerors, and, at other times, free citizens. All that can be said with certainty of this term, as there is no access to the study of their language, is, that it is applicable to those only that have been born east of the Bahar el Abiad."[19]

In his article, "Fung Origins",[20] Arkell supports the Shilluk hypothesis. Writing in reply to two earlier contributors, Chataway and Nalder,[21] who had advanced the hypothesis of an Abyssinian or upper Blue Nile origin for the Funj, he is first concerned to show the unreliability of their principal sources: the Umayyad genealogy of the Funj, and the early portion of the Funj Chronicle in its final recension. He is further concerned to defend the accuracy of Bruce, which Nalder and Chataway had impugned. Thirdly, he seeks to support Bruce's hypothesis by other evidence, but this part of his article is less convincing than the previous parts.[22]

Arkell has added little of substance to Bruce's statements, and it is by Bruce's account that the Shilluk hypothesis must in the last resort be judged. Its inherent weakness is that it lacks support in the other early sources. Reubeni is silent on Funj origins, but the earliest version of the Funj Chronicle agrees with him in showing the Funj as a land-based, cattle-owning, nomadic group. There is no suggestion of the invasion of canoe-men from the White Nile, to which Bruce alludes. It is indeed difficult to see how the Shilluk, by raids down the White Nile, reached Arbajī and made their headquarters in Sinnār on the Blue Nile. A possible explanation is that the story of the canoe-raid of 1504 is an interpolation by Bruce himself, since we know from his notes that he had heard of the Shilluk raids, which continued as late as the nineteenth century.

Another difficulty is that the Shilluk traditions themselves lend no support to the idea that the Funj were derived from them. Such memories as remain of relations with the Funj Sultanate are of warfare. These are confirmed from the Funj Chronicle. The various versions of this work speak of a campaign of the Funj against the Shilluk about the middle of the seventeenth century, presumably undertaken to secure the White Nile river-crossing, since it was followed by an expedition against Taqalī. By 1772, as Bruce showed, the region of Alays, in the north of Shilluk-inhabited territory, was under the rule of Sinnār. Hostilities in the seventeenth century are not, however, conclusive evidence that the Funj did not derive their origin from the Shilluk at an earlier period, and the argument from the silence of the oral Shilluk tradition should not be pressed too far. When all objections are made, the nucleus of the Shilluk hypothesis is difficult to reject.

The Abyssinian Hypothesis

The Abyssinian hypothesis of Funj origins need imply no more than that the Funj, before the foundation of Sinnār, had their homeland in the marches of Abyssinia. The principal testimony in support of this opinion is that of David Reubeni, who speaks of "the king's city" of Lam'ul or La'ul on the sources of the Nile, eight days' journey from Sinnār.[23] An inscription on a Funj royal drum, dating from the mid-eighteenth century, states that the ancestral home of the dynasty was Lūl'[24] which may perhaps be identified with La'ul/Lam'ul, especially since a passage in the Funj Chronicle implies that Lūl was a district on the upper Blue Nile (*fi'l-Ṣa'īd*).[25] The use of a single name for both a district and its principal town is not, of course, unusual.

It has been usual to cite in support of the Abyssinian hypothesis the references, in several variants of the Umayyad genealogy of the Funj, to the coming of their ancestor from Abyssinia. This is legitimate enough so far as it goes, since the obviously spurious Umayyad element in the genealogy does not necessarily invalidate its geographical content. The lack of precision in the term "Abyssinia" is a more serious objection. Generally speaking, this indication is more valuable as evidence against the Bornu and Shilluk hypotheses than as a positive contribution to the identification of the Funj homeland.

An expanded form of the Abyssinian hypothesis has been propounded by Crawford,[26] followed by al-Shāṭir Buṣaylī,[27] both of whom would bring the Funj from the region of modern Eritrea. Crawford rests his hypothesis largely on an identification, "on purely geographical grounds", of Lam'ul with Gallabat, again in the Abyssinian marches but to the north of the upper Blue Nile. This, it seems to me, is quite arbitrary, and disregards the geographical indications provided by Reubeni. Seeking to bring 'Amāra and his people from a region still farther north, Crawford cites traditions about the Funj current in the twentieth century in Eritrea. Buṣaylī also has recourse to these traditions, and adds others of conflicts between the Funj and tribes in the Sawākin region.

While these traditions, late and sparse as they are, provide evidence of contact *at some date* between the Funj and the tribes of the Red Sea region, it is quite unwarrantable to associate them specifically with the original migration of the Funj to Sinnār. Paul, from whom Buṣaylī derives one of his traditions, prudently rejects an early sixteenth-century date for the clash between the Funj and the Red Sea tribes, and links it with a late sixteenth-century expansion of 'Abdallāb power to the east.[28] At best these traditions preserve tribal reminiscences of warfare and other contacts between tribes of the Eritrea-Sawākin region and the Funj, or their vassals, at uncertain dates. One may note also in passing that Crawford, followed by Buṣaylī, indulges in philological speculation.

Against the hypothesis of a homeland on the upper Blue Nile one must set some traditions reported by J. W. Robertson in 1934.[29] The Funj chiefs of Fāzūghlī and Keili in his time asserted that their ancestors came thither from Sinnār at an uncertain period. Robertson believes that "They undoubtedly have been in this part of the world for two or three hundred years". Robertson would favour a still later date for the establishment of Funj control over most of the territory now known as Dār al-Funj, i.e. the country to the west of the upper Blue Nile above al-Ruṣayriṣ. Here the paramount chief (the shaykh of Gule) was a descendant, not of the Funj, but of the Hamaj regents, who controlled the Sultanate of Sinnār in the last sixty years of its existence. The ancestor of Robertson's chief fled to the area after the Turco-Egyptian conquest of Sinnār in 1821.

These traditions do not, it seems to me, invalidate the contention that the original homeland of the Funj lay in this region. They are traditions of dynastic origins, and say nothing about the mass of the people, or about the situation before the dynasties were established. Robertson, indeed, quotes from the shaykh of Gule another tradition, that Dār al-Funj was tributary to Sinnār before the establishment of his dynasty. These traditions are in no way inconsistent with the hypothesis that the original homeland of the Funj was in this region.

Conclusions

The conclusions I have reached from an examination of the evidence, real or supposed, on Funj origins are largely negative. The more ambitious hypotheses, which would bring the Funj to Sinnār from a remote homeland, Bornu or Eritrea, must fail, since the data adduced are quite insufficient to support the conclusions of their authors. There remain two hypotheses which have a firmer basis of local tradition, which would place the homeland of the Funj respectively among the Shilluk, and in the Abyssinian marches of the upper Blue Nile.

Of these two, I believe that the upper Blue Nile theory has rather stronger claims to consideration. In a sense, however, it only pushes the problem back one stage further: were the Funj indigenous to Lūl (as the Funj Chronicle and the drum-inscription would imply), or had they come thither from some still earlier home? This is likely to remain an unanswerable question.

One further consideration remains. In 1932, Professor Evans-Pritchard reported on an ethnological survey he had undertaken in the modern Dār al-Funj. Among the conclusions he reached was that linguistic evidence "lends great probability to the contention that the Shilluk have exercised wide cultural influence in this area and, in consequence, that they have at one time or other invaded it".[30] While he is rightly cautious about building any hypothesis on his findings, one is perhaps justified in suspecting that Bruce's awkward tradition of a Shilluk origin for the Funj may embody a memory of a Shilluk contribution to the population of the territory on the upper Blue Nile whence the Funj were later to emerge.

(B) THE EVIDENCE OF THE FUNJ CHRONICLE

Some light on the early history and customs of the Funj, when they were still a migratory group in the region of the Blue Nile, is afforded by the recension of the Funj Chronicle represented by MSS. Vienna and Nottingham, which contain material not found elsewhere. In the following translation of the relevant passage, I have followed Buṣaylī's printed edition of the text, checked against my own reading of the two manuscripts.[31]

(1) And let us return, God willing, to the mention of the kings, and the disclosure of the years of each one of them, and the end of his rule, and what occurrences and events happened in his time, so far as is possible.

(2) Now the origin of their kingdom, according to what passes on the tongues of men, is that, at the beginning of the matter of the Funj, they were at a place called Lūl[32] (with two emphatic *lāms* and *jazma*), and they were there as long as God willed them to remain there.

(3) [MSS. Vienna and Nottingham: *A section concerning the genealogy of the Funj*

It is said that they were from Banū Umayya. When the kingdom was snatched from them, and Banu'l-'Abbās caused them to flee, two of their men came to that place, and had children by the women,[33] and the Funj were from their descendants. And it is said that they were Banū Hilāl.

(4) The common story is that their great men would assemble at the place of their chief, and they would bring food, and the first to arrive would eat the food.[34] They were living at Jaylī[35] until a man arrived from downstream. He settled among them, and looked into their affairs. So he advised them, and whenever food came, he would keep it until they were assembled. Then he would arise and distribute it among them, and they would eat, and the remainder would be left over. So they said, "A man of *baraka*—why should he leave us?" So they married him to the daughter of their king, and she bore him a son. When he grew to maturity, his grandfather died. So they agreed to put him in the place of his grandfather and all follow him. They did so, and therefore they were called the Unsāb. They abode in their known place, and when they wished to move from it, they made an *'anqarīb* of *sh.r.ṭān*,[36] and likewise for his wife, and they carried him until they settled with them at Jabal Mūya. They were tall, strong and tough: one of them would carry his provisions and water upon his shoulder, and go about, and journey. When they obtained the kingdom, the *'anqarīb* of *sh.r.ṭān* became a sacred object [*'āda*]. When they appointed a new king, they married him to one of the descendants of that woman, and called her "the daughter of the sun's eye" [*bint 'ayn al-shams*]. They would carry her [*or* them both][37] in the way aforesaid to the compound of the *jundī*, and would shut him [MS. Nottingham, them both] up there for seven days. Then they would go with him to a place known to them, where there were sacred objects [*'awā'id*] coming out to them from the earth. They

would take omens from their coming out, and bode ill from their absence. These [customs] remained among them until the end of their kingdom. God knows best, and I seek pardon of God, and repent before him.]

(5) Then they moved to Jabal Mūya, which is a well-known hill, and abode there. When God wished to disclose His command, and to make them sultans over His people, they had cattle, among them a bull. It would come, arising by night, and go towards the forest of Sinnār, where at that time there was no settlement [*'imāra*], save that they mention that a slave-girl called Sinnār was there, sitting on the river-bank, and the town, when it was settled, was called after her. Then that bull would go and graze in the forest, and return on the same night, and one day they followed it, and saw her abode and her river. So they came down from Mūya, and King 'Amāra Dūnqas exalted her.[38] He was the first of them, and became their king [*or* their kingdom was established there], after he had fought the 'Anaj with 'Abdallāh al-Quraynātī al-Qāsimī, the father of 'Ajīb al-Kāfūta, and had returned there. His kingdom remained there, and he appointed the said 'Abdallāh as shaykh in Qarrī.[39] The kingdom remained to him and his descendants after him until Nūl.

Some Observations on this Passage

The account of the history of the Funj before the foundation of Sinnār contained in the above passage is of considerable importance, since it is the most detailed and coherent group of Funj traditions which has come down to us. This narrative is written in barbarous Arabic and seems to be mainly the record of an oral account. Paragraph (3), which mentions the legends of Umayyad and Hilālī descent, contains themes which are much amplified in Sudanese genealogies. It appears to be an interpolation in the narrative which would otherwise proceed smoothly from paragraph (2) to paragraph (4). The account of Funj traditions given in paragraphs (4) and (5) contains obvious legendary elements, in the story of the Wise Stranger, and the tale of the bull which led the Funj to the site of Sinnār. The ceremonies (not otherwise recorded) connected with the installation of the Funj sultans are given an historical explanation.

The legend of the coming of the Wise Stranger, who teaches a barbarous people civilized habits, is found in various parts of the modern Republic of the Sudan: I note the following occurrences:

(*a*) The Funj. The Wise Stranger comes from down the Nile, reforms eating habits, marries the king's daughter, and founds a dynasty.

(*b*) Darfur. The Wise Stranger comes from Tunis, brings security and order (the reform of eating habits is specifically mentioned), marries the king's daughter, and founds a dynasty.[40]

(*c*) Taqalī (a Muslim state in the pagan Nuba Mountains). The Wise Stranger (Muḥammad al-Ja'alī) comes "from the north", converts the people to Islam, marries the king's daughter, and founds a dynasty.[41]

(*d*) Nabtāb (the ruling clan of Banū 'Āmir, a Bija tribe on the Sudanese-Eritrean border). The Wise Stranger is a Ja'alī from al-Matamma on the Nile, a holy man. He marries the king's daughter, and founds a dynasty.[42]

Some provisional conclusions may be drawn from these stories.

(1) They are all legends of cultural contact between an ancient centre of civilization and barbarous peripheral regions. In (*a*), (*c*), and (*d*) the centre is on the Nile; more specifically in (*c*) and (*d*), the Ja'alī region, i.e. Upper Nubia. The Fūr alone claim a cultural link with the Maghrib.

(2) The emphasis on the Nile, or the Ja'alī region, as a centre of civilization, may be a folk-memory of cultural influence *anterior to* the islamization of Upper Nubia. The Wise Stranger in (*a*) is not represented as a Muslim, although his counterparts in (*c*) and (*d*) are. The Wise Stranger in (*b*), although brought from a Muslim locality and given an Arabic name, is not represented as bringing Islam to Darfur. It is possible that (*c*) and (*d*) are Islamized forms of older legends.

(3) The assertion that a dynasty is derived from the marriage of a king's daughter to a stranger should, in the absence of supporting evidence, be viewed as a folk-lore theme rather than an historical fact. Where it occurs it is probably evidence of cultural contact. It may also be an aetiological legend, explaining the anomalous persistence of *Mutterrecht* (or related customs) in an Islamized society.

The Funj are represented in the narrative as a whole as being, by origin, a group of migratory herdsmen (cf. the bull legend); an impression which is confirmed by Reubeni's description of 'Amāra. He says that "The king has many horses and captains who ride on them, and fine camels, and innumerable herds of cattle and sheep." Rather earlier, he has stated that "the king used to travel about his domains, month by month, from station to station". The tradition shows the Funj gradually extending the range of their wanderings northwards over the territories to the west of the upper Blue Nile. The conclusive identification of Jaylī is impossible: the Chronicle perhaps indicates that it was synonymous with Lūl. I would suggest, very tentatively indeed, that it may be the hill conventionally called, on modern maps of the Sudan, Jebel Keili, lying south-west of Fāzūghlī. Whether this be so or not, the tradition then brings the Funj to a clearly identifiable site at Jabal Mūya [Jebel Moya], part of a conspicuous isolated massif in the Gezira plain, about twenty miles west of Sinnār. Thence, as the bull legend indicates, they followed the grazing until they reached the Blue Nile at Sinnār, the most northerly of their settlements. Reubeni's account clearly shows that the more southerly territories were not abandoned as the Funj extended their grazing-grounds to the north: in his time 'Amāra's headquarters were at Lam'ul/La'ul, while Sinnār itself was under one of his subordinates.

(C) RELATIONS BETWEEN THE FUNJ AND THE ARABS

The thrust of the Funj northwards synchronized with the latest phase of a southward migration by nomad Arabs which had been going on for centuries.[43] At the time of the Arab conquest of Egypt in the seventh century, the Nilotic territories from the First Cataract south to an indeterminate distance beyond the confluence of the Blue and White Niles had formed two Nubian Christian kingdoms. The northern kingdom, al-Muqurra, penetrated by Arab immigrants, foundered under pressure from the Mamluk Sultanate of Egypt: in 717/1317 the church of Old Dongola, its capital, was converted into a mosque. The southern kingdom, 'Alwa, which had its capital at Sūba on the right bank of the Blue Nile, survived longer, but the time and circumstances of its collapse are obscure. Ibn Khaldūn, describing the situation late in the eighth/fourteenth century, speaks of the Arabs as having reached the borders of Abyssinia, but this is a vague and general statement.[44]

Sudanese traditions, first committed to writing in the late eighteenth or early nineteenth century, tell (as we have seen) of an alliance between the Funj ruler, 'Amāra Dūnqas, and an Arab chief, 'Abdallāh al-Quraynātī al-Qāsimī (otherwise called 'Abdallāh Jammā'), to fight the 'Anaj, meaning the indigenous inhabitants of the lands into which both Arabs and Funj were moving. The *Ṭabaqāt* of Wad Ḍayfallāh, in a passage which was copied into the Funj Chronicle, gives another tradition:

> "Know that the Funj took possession of the land of the Nubians and gained the mastery over it in the first of the tenth century; the year ten after nine hundred, and the town of Sinnār was laid out; King 'Amāra Dūnqas laid it out. And the town of Arbajī was laid out thirty years before; Ḥijāzī b. Ma'īn laid it out."[45]

The mention of Arbajī is significant, since it implies Arab penetration up the Blue Nile a generation before the Funj settlement at

Sinnār, and throws light on the tradition narrated by Bruce of a clash between Funj and Arabs at Arbajī in 1504.[46]

These traditions thus preserve memories of both co-operation and hostility between the Arabs and the Funj: co-operation against the 'Anaj, and hostility over their respective spheres of control on the Blue Nile. The tradition in the Funj Chronicle that 'Amāra appointed 'Abdallāh as shaykh in Qarrī, implying the superior status of the Funj ruler, suggests that Bruce's tradition of a Funj victory over the Arabs at this period is veracious. In later recensions of the Funj Chronicle these sparse traditions are padded out with extraneous material.

The traditions of the 'Abdallāb (i.e. the clan claiming descent from 'Abdallāh Jammā') were not put into writing until the present century, and indeed the extensive collection of material from oral sources is very recent.[47] When all allowance is made for the lateness of their recording, and for possible sophistication from the well-known literary sources of the *Ṭabaqāt* and the Funj Chronicle, these traditions yet contribute some new and important items of information.

(1) *The Antecedents of 'Abdallāh Jammā'*

'Abdallābī tradition represents 'Abdallāh Jammā' as being a *sharīf* by descent.[48] While this is a claim as common as it is specious, its significance lies in its formal legitimation of *religious* leadership, i.e. it implies that 'Abdallāh and his kin were a holy family, not primarily tribal chiefs. Rather, they became tribal chiefs by virtue of their religious prestige. 'Abdallāh, named significantly *Jammā'*, "Gatherer", creates a warrior-horde from Juhayna, the principal Arab immigrant tribe.[49] In this connexion, it should be noted that to the Arabs the war against the 'Anaj, the last representatives of Christian 'Alwa, was presumably a holy war, although this is not stated explicitly in the traditions.

(2) *Relations with the Funj*

Not surprisingly, the 'Abdallābī traditions tend to reverse the impression of Funj military and political superiority given by Bruce and implied by the Funj Chronicle. What is interesting, however, is the emphasis on the religious element in hostilities between the Arabs and the Funj: in this connexion, the obvious confusion of one tradition itself has evidential value:

> " 'Amāra Dūnqas was the leader of the Christian Nubians. 'Abdallāh fought 'Amāra, and defeated him. Thereupon 'Amāra asked 'Abdallāh Jammā' about the reason for the war, and 'Abdallāh answered that he

would fight him until he accepted Islam. 'Amāra showed himself ready to pay *jizya*, if he were left with his religion. But 'Abdallāh refused, saying, 'Two religions, the Christian religion and the Muhammadan religion, cannot exist in the Sudan.' Faced with the insistence of 'Abdallāh, 'Amāra announced his acceptance of Islam, and they made a confederation. There they fought the 'Anaj and the Fūnj and the Christian Nubians."[50]

When we pass on from the time of 'Abdallāh Jammā' to that of his son, 'Ajīb al-Kāfūtā,[51] the evidence for hostility between the Arabs and the Funj becomes more detailed and precise. The account in the Funj Chronicle is as follows:

"Then after him [i.e. the Funj king, 'Abd al-Qādir II] ruled *Makk* 'Adlān walad Āyā,[52] the lord of the battle of Karkūj. It was he who killed Shaykh 'Ajīb al-Kāfūtā when he disobeyed him and went out from submission to him. He advanced against him from Sinnār, and it is said that he stopped at Altī. He sent the army against him. So the said Shaykh 'Ajīb and those who were with him met them at a place called Walad Abī 'Amāra, known in the vicinity of Karkūj. They fought there, and the said Shaykh 'Ajīb was killed. The army of the *makk* was victorious, and the sons of Shaykh 'Ajīb fled to Dongola. Then the *makk* sent to them Shaykh Idrīs walad al-Arbāb,[53] . . . and he gave them the *amān*; so they came to him, and he [i.e. 'Adlān] appointed one of them, al-'Ujayl, as shaykh."[54]

'Abdallābī tradition depicts the battle of Karkūj as the last episode in a struggle between Shaykh 'Ajīb and the Funj. 'Ajīb is represented as the paragon of a Muslim ruler, who "extended the boundaries of his dominions and combined with martial exploits the virtues of a holy man".[55] Even more than his father, 'Ajīb was "holy" by descent, since his mother was a daughter of Ḥamad Abū Dunāna, one of the pioneer Ṣūfī teachers in the Nilotic Sudan.[56] He is said to have fought for religious reasons against 'Abd al-Qādir II, and to have driven him into Abyssinia, after which he built mosques in the Abyssinian marches, and appointed judges (i.e. of the *Sharī'a*) in the territories under his control. After making the pilgrimage to Mecca, he found the Funj ready to make war on him, and his defeat and death at Karkūj ensued.[57]

The 'Abdallābī and Funj accounts are thus complementary, and it is clear that not until the battle of Karkūj in 1016/1607–8 was the supremacy of the Funj over the 'Abdallāb assured. The alliance between 'Amāra and 'Abdallāh Jammā' did not regulate in perpetuity the relations between the two ruling houses: it was an early phase in their competition to dominate the central Nilotic Sudan.

(D) SULTAN SELIM I AND THE FUNJ

Several writers during the present century have given credence to a belief that Sultan Selim I, after overthrowing the Mamluk sultanate in Egypt, intervened in Lower Nubia and the region between Suakin and Massawa, to bring these territories under Ottoman domination. Budge, MacMichael, Crawford and Arkell all associate the establishment of Ottoman control over these two regions with Selim I.[58] The data on which this belief is based are derived from the Arabic *Ta'rīkh al-Sūdān*,[59] written in the opening years of this century by the Lebanese Na'ūm Bey Shuqayr (Naum Shoucair), or from the résumé of Shuqayr's material given in English in Wallis Budge's *The Egyptian Sudan*, published in 1907. Shuqayr must therefore be the point of departure for investigating the historicity of this belief.

Shuqayr's *Ta'rīkh al-Sūdān* is a very good work indeed. Its author possessed great advantages. As an Arabic-speaking member of the Egyptian Military Intelligence organization,[60] controlled by Major (later Sir) F. R. Wingate, he took an important part in the gathering of information from Sudanese sources in the later years of the Mahdia and during and after the Anglo-Egyptian reconquest of the Sudan. After the fall of Omdurman in September 1898, he was responsible for assembling and investigating the Mahdist archives, and he incorporated numerous documents in his *Ta'rīkh*. Other material was derived from Sudanese manuscript chronicles and oral sources. Shuqayr was careful in reproducing his sources, and discriminating in his use of them, but Budge (and those who have used Budge) blurred the distinctions which Shuqayr maintained.

The relevant passages of the *Ta'rīkh* are four in number. Two of these[61] are mere summaries of information which is given more fully later. These may be ignored, but the two longer passages require to be translated almost *in extenso*.

The long passage dealing with Nubia is as follows:[62]

> "And they said concerning the entry of the Turkish troops into Nubia, that the Jawābira had gained power over the Gharbiyya, and these sent messengers to Sultan Selim. In the year 1520, he sent with them an expedition of Bosniak troops under the command of Ḥasan Qūsī [*sic*], and they expelled the Jawābira to Dongola, so that only a few of them remained in Ḥalfā and al-Dirr. They repaired the ancient fortresses in Aswān, Ibrīm and Sāy, and dwelt in them . . .
>
> And Qūsī Ḥasan was commandant of the troops and independent governor of Nubia . . . And Ḥasan Qūsī died, and his offspring were appointed to the government of Nubia after him. They made their capital at al-Dirr, and were known as the Ghuzz *kāshifs*.
>
> Then [they said] that the Fūnj, after subduing Upper Nubia in 1505 A.D.,

coveted Lower Nubia, and conquered it up to the Third Cataract, and wanted to advance northwards. It was said, 'And the governor from the Ghuzz at that time was Ibn Janbalān. When he heard of the advance of the Fūnj army to his country, he prepared a numerous army, and awaited them on the frontier, near to Ḥannak. The two armies met, and a great battle took place, in which the Ghuzz army won a great victory. They repulsed the Fūnj army with losses, after filling the earth with their slain.' It was said, 'And the blood collected in a pool there, and the place was called the Basin of Blood (*Ḥawḍ al-Dam*). They built a dome over it, and made it a boundary between themselves and the Fūnj.' This story is well-known generally among the people of Dongola and al-Maḥas."

This passage collates two traditional anecdotes, and sophisticates both by attempts at dating. The first, centring around Ḥasan 'Qūsī', is (although Shuqayr does not say so) derived immediately from the narrative of the Swiss traveller, John Lewis Burckhardt,[63] who passed through Lower Nubia in 1813. Burckhardt was a careful and accurate narrator, and was obviously reproducing Nubian oral tradition. His account is rendered into Arabic with substantial accuracy by Shuqayr, but there are some slight, yet significant, differences. Burckhardt gives no precise date for the episode, which is merely referred to "the reign of the great Sultan Selym". He does not connect the incident in any way with Selim's conquest of Egypt, but says that the Gharbiyya "sent an embassy to Constantinople". Furthermore, he calls the commander of the Bosniaks "Hassan Coosy". "Coosy", transliterated by Shuqayr *Qūsī*, may better be taken to represent *Ghuzzī*, a term which, in the usage then current in Egypt and Nubia, was equivalent to "Mamluk". It should be noted, finally, that Burckhardt does not speak of the *kāshifs* of Nubia as Ghuzz: indeed, the one instance of his use of the term almost seems to exclude them from this category.[64]

The second anecdote seems to have been first recorded by Shuqayr himself. It centres around another personage called Ibn Janbalān, and it makes no mention of Ḥasan. Although Shuqayr implies that the Ghuzz in this anecdote are to be equated with the Ghuzz *kāshifs*, whose origin he has described just previously, this may not be so. His insertion of the date 1505 is something of a red herring: his intention is to establish a *terminus a quo*, not to imply that the battle of Ḥannak took place during, or shortly after, that year. The anecdote is essentially an actiological legend, to explain a place-name, but it preserves a tradition of a frontier-fight. It is probable that the "Ibn Janbalān" mentioned is the Sulaymān Jānbulād (Soliman-Gianballat), whom Vansleb describes as the first bey to govern Upper Egypt, and who appears to be identical with Sulaymān Bey b.

Qubād.[65] This identification would mean that the battle of Ḥannak took place after Ḥijja 983/March 1576, when Sulaymān Bey was appointed to office.

Another passage deals with the alleged connexion between Selim and the Red Sea littoral. It occurs in Shuqayr's account of the Funj kingdom, and is entered under his notice of 'Amāra Dūnqas, the first Funj ruler, who flourished in the first half of the tenth/sixteenth century. It runs as follows:[66]

> "It was said, 'And in his days, Sultan Selim advanced to Suakin and Massawa, and took possession of them both, and entered Abyssinia, aiming to march towards Sinnār. He wrote to its king, summoning him to obedience, and he answered him thus, "I do not know what has incited you to fight me and take my land. If it is to aid the religion of Islam, then I and the people of my kingdom are Arab Muslims, following the religion of the Apostle of God. If it is for some material aim, then know that most of the people of my kingdom are desert Arabs, who have migrated to this country to seek a livelihood, and have nothing from which you may collect an annual tribute." With the letter, he sent him the book of genealogies of the Arab tribes in his kingdom, which had been collected for him by the Imām al-Samarqandī, one of the '*ulamā*' of Sinnār. When the two writings reached Sultan Selim, their contents amazed him, and he turned aside from the war of Sinnār.' It was said, 'And he took the book of genealogies with him to Istanbul, and it remains to this day in the library there.' "

The anecdote of the personal conquest of Suakin and Massawa by Selim, followed by an invasion of Abyssinia, and an intended invasion of the territories of Sinnār, is wholly legendary. It is interesting to note that a variant of the same anecdote substitutes for the king of Sinnār the chief of the 'Abdallāb.[67]

The connexion of Selim I with these exploits is entirely fictitious. The detailed account of his acts in Egypt, recorded by Ibn Iyās,[68] completely excludes any personal invasion of the Suakin-Massawa region, or of Lower Nubia. Even the setting of these events within the reign of Selim is untenable. The Ottoman conquest of Lower Nubia and the Red Sea littoral was accomplished, certainly in the reign of Sultan Süleyman, and probably about the middle of the tenth/sixteenth century, by Özdemir Pasha, a Circassian Mamluk from Egypt.[69] The ascription of events of Süleyman's reign to that of his predecessors is in line with an Egyptian mythopoeic tendency, during the Ottoman period, to enhance the deeds and person of Selim.[70] As the overthrower of the old-established Mamluk sultanate, and the only Ottoman ruler to visit Egypt before the nineteenth century, Selim occupied a prominent place in popular imagination.

The anecdote of the correspondence between the Funj king (or the

'Abdallābī chief) and Selim may well preserve a memory of contact between a ruler on the Nile and an expansionist Ottoman governor in Suakin, perhaps even Özdemir himself, but the date cannot now be established. The Imām al-Samarqandī, mentioned in the story, is a ghostly figure to whom, down to the time of Shuqayr and MacMichael, genealogical information was ascribed. The scattered references in the pedigrees collected and summarized by MacMichael suggest the existence of a quasi-hereditary school of genealogists, resembling those of jurists and Ṣūfī adepts which are described in the *Ṭabaqāt* of Wad Ḍayfallāh. Four otherwise unknown persons who are cited as genealogists are Abū Sulaymān al-Baḥrānī, who was the shaykh of Maḥmūd (or Abū Maḥmūd) al-Samarqandī, and 'Abd al-Raḥmān al-'Irāqī, while 'Abdallāh b. Sa'īd al-Samarqandī may have been a descendant or collateral of the previous al-Samarqandī.[71] The date of their activities cannot be ascertained. The sophisticated pedigrees of certain arabized groups are probably ultimately due to this school.

NOTES

1 A. J. Arkell, "More about Fung origins", *Sudan Notes and Records* [*SNR*], XXVII (1946), 87–98.
2 O. G. S. Crawford, *The Fung kingdom of Sennar* (Gloucester, 1951).
3 Al-Shāṭir Buṣaylī 'Abd al-Jalīl (Chater Bosayley A. Galil), *Ma'ālim ta'rīkh Sūdān Wādī al-Nīl* (Cairo, 1955).
4 *SNR*, XV (1932), 201–50.
5 See S. Hillelson, "David Reubeni, an early visitor to Sennar", *SNR*, XVI (1933), 55–66.
6 Buṣaylī, op. cit. 270–1.
7 H. A. MacMichael, *A history of the Arabs in the Sudan* (Cambridge, 1922), II, 36–7 (BA), 104–5 (A2), 132 (A11), 196 (D1), 213 (D2), 346 (D6), also tree illustrating B1, before p. 145. Cf. also J. D. P. Chataway, "Notes on the history of the Fung", *SNR*, XIII (1930), 257; L. F. Nalder, "Fung origins", *SNR*, XIV (1931), 63–4.
8 James Bruce, *Travels to discover the source of the Nile* (2nd ed., Edinburgh, 1805), VI, 370–2; VII, 85, 87, 89–94, 96, 98.
9 A. J. Arkell, "More about Fung origins", *SNR*, XXVII (1946).
10 H. R. Palmer (tr.), *History of the first twelve years of the reign of Mai Idris Alooma of Bornu (1571–1585) by his Imam, Ahmed ibn Fartua* (Lagos, 1926), 84–91.
11 Aḥmad al-Burnūwī, *Hādha'l-'kitāb huwa min sha'n Sulṭan Idrīs Alūma* (Kano [1930]), 130–7.
12 Palmer, *History of . . . Mai Idris*, 90 footnote.
13 H. R. Palmer, *Sudanese memoirs*, II (Lagos, 1928), 32 and footnote.
14 Ibid., 47 and footnote.
15 Ibid., 32, 47.
16 Palmer, *History of . . . Mai Idris*, 5, 114.
17 Palmer, *Sudanese memoirs*, II, 25.
18 Ibid., 54.

19 Bruce, *Travels*, VI, 370–2.
20 *SNR*, XV (1932).
21 See above, footnote 7.
22 Arkell's attempt to corroborate Bruce rests on three types of alleged evidence: (1) a supposed Shilluk origin of certain Funj names and terms; (2) tribal genealogies, derived from MacMichael; (3) reports of traditions current in the nineteenth and twentieth centuries.
23 *SNR*, XVI (1933), 57, 60.
24 *SNR*, IV (1921), 211–12.
25 MS. Vienna, f. 8b. Later recensions of the Funj Chronicle give the variants Lūlū and even Lu'lu'—an attempt at arabicization.
26 Crawford, *Fung kingdom*, 147–55.
27 Buṣaylī, op. cit., 28–34.
28 A. Paul, *A history of the Beja tribes of the Sudan* (Cambridge, 1954), 76–7.
29 J. W. Robertson, "Fung origins", *SNR*, XVII (1934), 260–6, especially pp. 261–3.
30 E. E. Evans-Pritchard, "Ethnological observations in Dar Fung", *SNR*, XV (1932), 58–9.
31 Al-Shāṭir Buṣaylī 'Abd al-Jalīl, *Makhṭūṭat Kātib al-Shūna* (n.p., n.d. [?Cairo, c. 1961]), 6–7; MS. Vienna, ff. 3a–4b. MS. Nottingham, pp. 5–6. Buṣaylī's edition of the Funj Chronicle is hereafter designated *FC*.
32 Buṣaylī, *FC*, reads "Lūlū", omitting "and *jazma*". Here the reading of MS. Vienna must be preferred, supported as it is by the drum-inscription (see above, p. 72). The explicit mention of the *jazma* (not found in MS. Nottingham) shows that originally the name had no final vowel.
33 MS. Nottingham adds "and they became very numerous".
34 Thus Buṣaylī, *FC*, *al-akl*; but both MSS. Vienna and Nottingham read *al-kulwa*, "the kidney".
35 "Jaylī" is my reading of MS. Vienna. There is a lacuna in Buṣaylī's text, while MS. Nottingham (which is very corrupt here) appears to read *ṣayla 'aẓīma*.
36 Buṣaylī, *FC*, reads *s. r. ṭān*, which he glosses *khashab al-s. rtī*, i.e. *s. rtī* wood. The reading *sh. r. ṭān* may stand for *shurṭān*, an unusual plural of *sharīṭ*, a rope of palm-fibres.
37 Here (as elsewhere) the pronouns are indistinct in MS. Vienna, the calligraphy of which is very poor.
38 So MS. Vienna. MS. Nottingham reads "and the greatest of them was the King 'Amāra Dūnqas". Buṣaylī, *FC*, reads "the *Makk* 'Amāra Dūnqas cut her trees", following a later recension.
39 In MSS. Vienna and Nottingham the passage translated "al-Quraynātī . . . as shaykh" is missing, owing to a copyist's error.
40 R. C. [von] Slatin, *Fire and sword in the Sudan* (2nd ed., London, 1896), 38–41. There are numerous variants of the legend, including forms which make the Wise Stranger a Hilālī or an 'Abbasid (i.e. a Ja'alī). See my article DĀR FŪR, in *EI*², II, 122.
41 R. J. Elles, "The Kingdom of Tegali", *SNR*, XVIII (1955), 7–8.
42 Crawford, *Fung kingdom*, 112; Paul, op. cit., 82–3.
43 A detailed study of the Arab penetration of the Nilotic Sudan is provided by Yūsuf Faḍl Ḥasan, *The Arabs and the Sudan* (Edinburgh, 1967).
44 Ibn Khaldūn, *Kitāb al-'ibar* (ed. Y. A. Daghir, Beirut, 1956–61), VI, 10; tr. de Slane, *Histoire des Berbères* (Paris, 1925), I, 10.
45 Thus following the text of the critical edition by Yūsuf Faḍl Ḥasan, p. 39; for which edition see below, p. 101, n. 1: page-references to this edition are prefixed by *T*. It is significant, however, that where this passage is cited in

the early recension of the Funj Chronicle (MSS. Vienna and Nottingham) and in Buṣaylī's printed text (*FC*, 4), the reading is "in the first of the tenth century after the nine hundred", i.e. 901/1495–6, not 910/1504–5.

46 See above, p. 71.

47 A. E. D. Penn, "Traditional stories of the 'Abdullab tribe", *SNR*, xvii/1, 1934, 59–82; the translation of a chronicle completed in 1916 or later. I have not seen the Arabic original. Current oral traditions of the 'Abdallāb are studied in Sīd Ḥasan Muḥammad Khalīl, *Jawānib min ta'rīkh al-'Abdallāb min khilāl riwāyātihim al-samā'iyya* (unpublished essay, University of Khartoum, 1969). The same writer has also published recordings of these traditions as *Ta'rīkh al-'Abdallāb min khilāl riwāyātihim al-samā'iyya* (Sudan Research Unit, University of Khartoum, 1969).

48 Sīd Ḥasan, *Jawānib*, 23.

49 Sīd Ḥasan, *Jawānib*, 5.

50 Sīd Ḥasan, *Jawānib*, 5.

51 Otherwise known as 'Ajīb al-Mānjilak. *Mānjil* or *mānjilak* was the title bestowed on 'Ajīb and his successors by the Funj rulers; it does not seem to have been held by 'Abdallāh Jammā'.

52 'Adlān's regnal dates are given in *FC* as 1013–16/1604–7, and in Bruce's king-list (Bodleian, MS. Bruce 18 (2), ff. 54b–57a) as Rajab 1015/November 1606 to 1020/1611–12.

53 Idrīs walad al-Arbāb was a very influential holy man, related traditionally to the 'Abdallāb, since his mother and the mother of Shaykh 'Ajīb were both daughters of Ḥamad Abū Dunāna. His biography is given in *T*, 49–65. See also MacMichael, *Arabs*, II, 246–7; Hill, *Biographical dictionary*, 179.

54 *FC*, 8–9.

55 Penn, "Traditional stories", 61.

56 Sīd Ḥasan, *Jawānib*, 24–5. Cf. Crawford, *Fung kingdom*, 174–5.

57 Penn, "Traditional stories", 61–4. Bruce mentions the flight of 'Abd al-Qādir to Abyssinia, but does not ascribe it to a defeat by 'Ajīb. He represents 'Abd al-Qādir as living in exile "under the mutual protection" of the Abyssinian and 'Abdallābī rulers, and names the latter "Nile Wed Ageeb", i.e. Nā'il walad 'Ajīb: Bruce, *Travels*, III, 300, 312–13.

58 E. A. Wallis Budge, *The Egyptian Sudan* (London, 1907), II, 200–1, 207–8. MacMichael, *Arabs*, I, 189; II, 6. O. G. S. Crawford, *Fung kingdom*, 123, 170. A. J. Arkell, *A history of the Sudan to A.D. 1821* (London 1955, 1961), 204.

59 Na'ūm Shuqayr, *Ta'rīkh al-Sūdān al-qadīm wa'l-ḥadīth wa-jughrafiyyatuh* (Cairo [1903], 3 vols. in 1).

60 See his biography in Richard Hill, *A biographical dictionary of the Sudan* (2nd ed., London, 1967), 293, 405.

61 *Ta'rīkh*, I, 66; II, p. 55.

62 *Ta'rīkh*, II, 108–9.

63 J. L. Burckhardt, *Travels in Nubia* (London, 1819), 133–5.

64 *Travels*, 138. Burckhardt, discussing the blood-wite payable in Nubia, speaks of 'one of the governor's tribe, or an El Ghoz (الغُزّ a name given in Egypt and Nubia to the Mamelouks) or any of the people of Ibrim' as if these were three distinct categories. Nevertheless, *kāshifs* in Ottoman Egypt were almost invariably Mamluks, and the probability that "Coosy" = *Ghuzzī* supports the belief that Shuqayr is right in speaking of "the Ghuzz *kāshifs*".

65 See below, p. 183.

66 *Ta'rīkh*, II, 73–4.

67 Penn, "Traditional stories", 66–7. The incident is there related of the 'Abdallābī chief 'Ajīb III, who flourished in the early eighteenth century.

68 Mohamed Mostafa (ed.), *Die Chronik des Ibn Ijās*, V (2nd ed., Cairo, 1961), 148 ff. Hereafter indicated by Ibn Iyās.

69 See below, p. 179. An earlier date (935/1528) for the conquest of Lower Nubia, and its accomplishment by Sulaymān Pasha al-Khādim, is proposed in Stanford J. Shaw, *The financial and administrative organization and development of Ottoman Egypt 1517–1798*, Princeton, 1962, 12–13.

70 See below, pp. 171–2.

71 MacMichael, *Arabs*, II, 127. For other references, see under these names in the index. MacMichael's own discussion of the problem of al-Samarqandī is in II, 6–8. His reference to al-Samarqandī "the Great" (p. 7) should be "the Elder", a common signification of *al-kabīr*.

5

THE SONS OF JĀBIR AND THEIR KIN: A CLAN OF SUDANESE RELIGIOUS NOTABLES

AWLĀD JĀBIR, the Sons of Jābir, were eminent religious teachers in the Nilotic Sudan during the later part of the sixteenth century. Apart from their individual importance, they and their kinsmen by blood and marriage formed a complex group of holy families. Information concerning numerous members of this clan is provided by the biographical dictionary of Sudanese holy men known as the *Ṭabaqāt* of Wad Ḍayfallāh (Muḥammad al-Nūr b. Ḍayfallāh), which is the main source used in this article.[1]

The Ancestry of the Sons of Jābir

Concerning the ancestry of the Sons of Jābir, there is a significant ambiguity. The *Ṭabaqāt* gives the text of an *ijāza* granted by ʻAbd al-Raḥmān b. Jābir to one of his disciples, Ibrāhīm b. Umm Rābiʻa, dated 982/1574–5, which concludes with the words:

> "Written by *al-faqīr* Ibn Jābir, the Juhanī among the Arabs as to lineage; and it has reached me [sc. apparently Wad Ḍayfallāh] that he is established as to lineage from the offspring of the wandering ascetic Aḥmad b. ʻUmar, and he was from the offspring of ʻAqīl b. Alī b. Abī Ṭālib, but the first is the continuous tradition from our fathers."[2]

By the testimony of ʻAbd al-Raḥmān b. Jābir himself, therefore, his family were Arabs of Juhayna, members of which tribe had been moving southwards from Egypt since the third/ninth century, and by the late eighth/fourteenth century were dispersed throughout Nubia, which they controlled.[3]

The ascription of a Talibid pedigree to the Sons of Jabir, which would of course make them kinsmen of the Prophet, is an example of a process whereby a family eminent for religious learning and piety established its standing in a Muslim community. The genealogical claim, that is to say, is essentially an origin myth, legitimating the current status of the family: it is not necessarily or even probably a statement containing a kernel of historical fact. The persistence of the older and more authentic pedigree, as in this instance, is unusual.

A more elaborate form of the genealogy can be seen in the pedigree supplied in the *Ṭabaqāt* for Ibrāhīm al-Būlād b. Jābir, the brother of ʻAbd al-Raḥmān, where he is described as "Ibrāhīm, the son of Jābir, the son of ʻAwn, the son of Salīm, the son of Rubāṭ, the son of Ghulāmallāh, [who was] the father of the Rikābiyya *sayyids*".[4] A variant in one manuscript reads as follows:

> ". . . the son of *al-sayyid* Muḥammad ʻAwn, the son of *al-sayyid* Aḥmad Salīm al-Majdhūb, the son of *al-sayyid* Muḥammad al-Murābiṭ, the son of al-Ghulām Aḥmad al-Muḥammad, the son [sic, *ibn*; read *abī*, "father"] of the Rikābiyya *sayyids*."[5]

Who was Ghulāmallāh or al-Ghulām Aḥmad? There is no information about him in the *Ṭabaqāt*. He is, however, a considerable figure in a genealogical work, widespread in manuscript form in the Sudan, and entitled (on the manuscript known to me) as *Kitāb maʻārif furūʻ uṣūl al-ʻArab wal-ḥasab waʼl-nasab*, hereafter referred to as *Fūrūʻ*.[6] His lineage is there given as "Ghulāmallāh, the son of ʻĀyid [ʻĀʼid], the son of al-Maqbūl, the son of *al-shaykh* Aḥmad, the son of ʻUmar al-Zaylaʻī, the inhabitant of al-Luḥayya, a village in the Yemen, the son of Maḥmūd, the son of Hāshim, the son of Mukhtār, the son of ʻAlī, the son of Sirāj, the son of Muḥammad, the son of Abuʼl-Qāsim, the son of *al-imām* Zāmil etc., to Abū Ṭālib, the son of ʻAbd al-Muṭṭalib [etc. to Luwayy]."[7]

A later passage gives an account of Ghulamallāh and his immediate family:

> "His mother went out one day and left him in the cradle. When she returned, she found the house burning on every side, and sought to rush in and enter it to him, being bewildered at what had happened to her. His father, *al-sayyid* ʻĀʼid b. al-Maqbūl, took her and prevented her, and said to her, 'If he be my son, the fire will not burn him, God Most High willing.' When the house had collapsed and fallen to pieces, and the fire had died down, his father went in to him and found him in excellent condition with no trace of burning and no pain, except that his clothes were blackened from the smoke of the fire.
>
> God (praised and exalted be He) destroyed the people of Ismāʻīl by his *baraka*. They were an uncountable number, yet they were quickly destroyed in a very little time. Through this miracle the most abundant prestige accrued to his offspring, pupils and disciples from the kings of the Funj at Sinnār and their soldiers, the dignitaries and the great men.
>
> As regards his origin, he was born in an island called Nawāwa [?Nawāra] after his father had come from al-Luḥayya in the land of the Yemen. His two sons, Rubāṭ and Rikāb, were born in an island called Sākiya, one of the islands of the Red Sea [*al-Māliḥ*]. Thence he went out with his sons to the land of Dongola, because it was in extreme perplexity and error [*al-ḍalāl*] for lack of scholars [ʻ*ulamā*ʼ]. When he settled

there, he built the mosques and taught the Qur'ān and the [religious] sciences. All the holy men [*al-marātib*] there were from his pupils, either directly or through his offspring, the four Sons of Jābir."[8]

The data provided by the *Furū'* have some interesting implications. In the first place, Ghulāmallāh came of a family of wanderers, who had made their homes at different times in Zayla', the Yemen and the islands of the Red Sea; in this connexion, it is significant in the *Ṭabaqāt* passage cited earlier, Aḥmad b. 'Umar (al-Zayla'ī) is called "the wandering ascetic" (*al-sā'iḥ*). Secondly, since Ghulāmallāh is represented as living five generations before the Sons of Jābir, who flourished in the late sixteenth century, his settlement in the land of Dongola may be dated approximately to the early fifteenth century, i.e. the period immediately following the decline of Christianity in that region.[9] This situation obviously offered scope to a Muslim missionary. The phraseology of the *Furū'* indeed suggests a Christian population: *al-ḍalāl* echoes *al-ḍāllīn* in *Sūrat al-Fātiḥa*, "those who go astray", traditionally interpreted as meaning the Christians. Thirdly, the tracing of Ghulāmallāh's lineage to Abū Ṭālib is a further example of the device already mentioned for legitimating the status of a holy family in an Islamic community.

The dubious nature of the genealogical connexion between the Sons of Jābir and Ghulāmallāh is heightened by a consideration of the intervening generations. If the pedigree were authentic, one would expect most information to be transmitted about the later generations. In fact one finds the reverse. Ghulāmallāh, as we have seen, is the subject of a fair amount of tradition, and there is some semi-legendary material in the *Ṭabaqāt* concerning the next two generations, Rubāṭ and Salīm, but nothing about their successors, 'Awn and Jābir himself.[10] Thus, by the efforts of the genealogists, a family belonging to the tribe of Juhayna became kinsmen of the Prophet by being linked to an earlier family, whose claim to such a pedigree was no less specious.

The sons of Jābir

Table 1

Jābir

Ibrāhīm | 'Abd al-Raḥīm | Ismā'īl | 'Abd al-Raḥmān | Fāṭima

'Abd al-Raḥmān → Idris

Fāṭima → *Table 2*

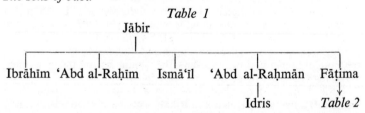

With the sons of Jābir we emerge from the mists of genealogical legend into the light of history. Their careers can be dated with some precision, and the abundance of detail which is provided about them in the *Ṭabaqāt* contrasts with the sparse traditions available concerning their ancestry. Their respective qualities were summed up in a saying: "The four sons of Jābir were like the four elements; each one had his own virtue. The most learned of them was Ibrāhīm, the holiest of them 'Abd al-Raḥmān, the most pious of them Ismā'īl, and the most devout of them 'Abd al-Raḥīm; and their sister, Fāṭima, . . . was their equal in learning and faith."[11]

It was Ibrāhīm al-Būlād b. Jābir[12] who established the family's reputation for learning. He was born on the island of Turunj[13] in the territory of the Shāyqiyya. He went to Cairo, where he studied law and grammar under Shaykh Muḥammad al-Banūfarī, a distinguished Mālikī teacher who died between 967/1559 and 1000/1592.[14] He returned to his homeland at the beginning of the reign of the 'Abdallābī shaykh, 'Ajīb al-Mānjilak. This must have been about the year 1570, since the date of Shaykh 'Ajīb's death, after a reign of 41 years, is placed by the *Ṭabaqāt* in 1019/1610–11,[15] while in Bruce's king-list, the battle of Karkūj, in which he met his end, is dated 1016/1607–8.[16] He set up a school in Turunj, at which he taught two standard textbooks of Mālikī law, the *Mukhtaṣar* of Khalīl and the *Risāla* of Ibn Abī Zayd al-Qayrawānī. He was, according to the *Ṭabaqāt*, the first to teach Khalīl in Funj territory. His period of teaching lasted for only seven years, but during that time he had numerous pupils.

Ibrāhīm's brother, 'Abd al-Raḥmān,[17] studied under him and under al-Banūfarī, and continued the school after his brother's death. He founded two other mosque-schools in Shāyqiyya territory, at Kūrtī and al-Dufār, and divided the year among the three of them. 'Abd al-Raḥmān clearly attained wealth and importance: he had a body-guard of 40 slaves carrying swords. He wrote a law-book as well as a book on Sufism entitled *Murshid al-murīdīn fī 'ilm al-taṣawwuf.*

After 'Abd al-Raḥmān's death, his school passed to the third brother, Ismā'īl,[18] who had studied under him and al-Banūfarī. We are told little about Ismā'īl except that he made the Pilgrimage to Mecca with his sister, Fāṭima, and her son. The fact that this is noticed indicates that it was at that time an unusual observance for a Sudanese Muslim: it further suggests that Ismā'īl and his kin were rich. One anecdote recounted of him is significant:

> "His piety reached such a point that he would not use water which came in the irrigation channels of the Shāyqiyya, and he said, 'Their oxen are taken by force'."

The oxen (*jarāriq*) referred to were those used to turn the waterwheels (sing. *sāqiya*) which fed the irrigation-channels. This is perhaps the earliest reference to the predatory character of the Shāyqiyya, which made them the terror of their neighbours until the Turco-Egyptian conquest. Ismā'īl's protest against injustice has several parallels in the acts of religious teachers both during the Funj period and afterwards: a late example is the refusal of Muḥammad Aḥmad, later the Mahdi, to eat food provided by the Turco-Egyptian administration in the Sudan.

Ismā'īl's position as teacher passed on his death to his nephew, Idrīs b. 'Abd al-Raḥmān.[19] The fourth son of Jābir, the very devout 'Abd al-Raḥīm, seems to have taken no part in his brothers' public activities, and has no notice in the *Ṭabaqāt*. The career of Idrīs marked the zenith of his family's fortunes, since he married the queen of Kajba,[20] one of the petty kingdoms of the Shāyqiyya. This, however, led to the decline of the school, since she resented the absence of Idrīs except during vacations, and urged him to transfer his teaching to her house. His pupils refused this, saying, "She has beautiful serving-women, who will go in and out amongst us. We fear that they will corrupt our religion." So his disciples dispersed, and attached themselves to other teachers.

With Idrīs, the importance of the male line of Jābir comes to an end. Later generations of teachers were descended from Jābir through his daughter, Fāṭima. It may be noted also that Zahrā', the daughter of Idrīs, married al-Zayn b. Ṣughayirūn b. Fāṭima (see below, p. 94), and their daughter, Ḥawsha, was the mother of the jurist, Abu 'l-Ḥasan.

Fāṭima b. Jābir and her descendants

Table 2

Sirḥān al-'Ūdī = Fāṭima

Muḥammad Ṣughayirūn → *Tables 3, 3a*

'Umar → *Table 4*

Abu 'l-Qāsim

Āmina → *Table 5*

As we have seen above Fāṭima, the sister of the sons of Jābir, herself had a reputation for learning and piety, and made the Pilgrimage to Mecca. She was also the ancestress of two families of religious teachers, through her son, Muḥammad Ṣughayirūn, and her daughter, Āmina.

Fāṭima married a certain Sirḥān b. Muḥammad b. Sirḥān[21] (called

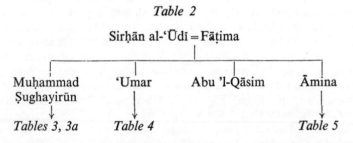

Sirḥān al-'Ūdī), who was by origin a cultivator from Arqū Island, south of the Third Cataract. He had studied the Qur'ān, and made the Pilgrimage to Mecca. After a quarrel with his kinsmen, he loaded the timbers of his *sāqiya* into a boat, and made his way up-stream into Shāyqiyya territory. He settled on the east of the island of the sons of Jābir, and sent his son, Idrīs, to study at their school. He obtained Fāṭima b. Jābir in marriage from her brother 'Abd al-Raḥmān, and she bore him three sons and a daughter.

(*a*) *The family of Ṣughayirūn*

Table 3

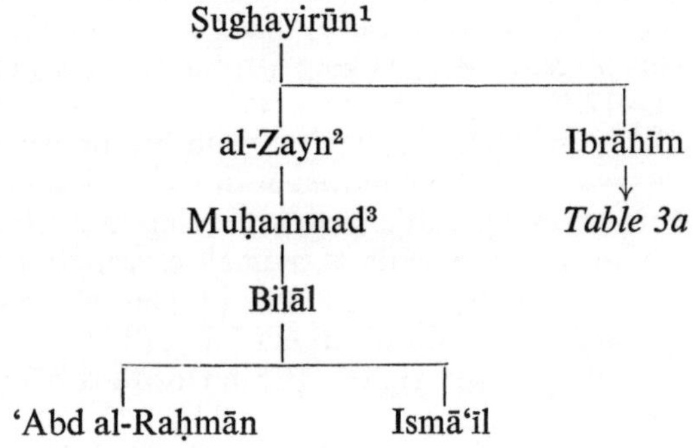

Notes

1 Ṣughayirūn's other children were Abukr and (daughters) Rābi'a, Ḥājja, and Zaynab. Rābi'a married her cousin, Madanī b. 'Umar (see Table 4); Ḥājja married Muḥammad b. al-Tinqār (see Table 5); and Zaynab married her cousin, Muḥammad b. Abi 'l-Qāsim.

2 Al-Zayn had also two daughters: Barra, who married her cousin, Nūrayn b. Madanī (see Table 4) and Ḥawsha, who married her cousin, Ṣāliḥ b. Ibrāhīm (see Table 3a).

3 Muḥammad b. al-Zayn married his cousin, Ḥājja, the daughter of Zaynab and Muḥammad b. Abi 'l-Qāsim.

The eldest son of Fāṭima b. Jābir, Muḥammad, commonly known by his nickname of Ṣughayirūn,[22] was the most prominent religious teacher in the generation which followed the sons of Jābir. He studied under his uncle, Ismā'īl b. Jābir, from whom he obtained his *ijāza*, and then went on to Cairo, where he too was a pupil of Shaykh Muḥammad al-Banūfarī. Subsequently he taught in the school of the sons of Jābir, but this aroused the jealousy of his maternal cousins.

The episode which followed throws some light on an obscure period of Funj history. Incited by Ṣughayirūn's jealous cousins, Zumrāwī, the king of the Shāyqiyya, came to the mosque to kill him.

His purpose was divined by Fāṭima, and Zumrāwī fell fainting from his horse, and was cured by the incantation of Ṣughayirūn. Zumrāwī then offered him gifts: four *sāqiyas*, four mares in foal, and four slaves. But Ṣughayirūn rejected these, saying, "Your wealth is unlawful to me, and dwelling in your country is unlawful to me!" Ṣughayirūn, meanwhile, had found an adherent in the prince, Bādī Abū Rubāṭ, the *sīd al-qōm*[23] of the Funj King ʻAdlān w. Āya. After defeating and killing the ʻAbdallābī viceroy, Shaykh ʻAjīb al-Mānjilak, at the battle of Karkūj (c. 1016/1607–8 *ut supra*), ʻAdlān led his army northwards to the territory of Dongola. He reached Mushū, just south of the Third Cataract, which was the frontier-post of the Funj kingdom. There, for reasons which are not disclosed in the *Ṭabaqāt*, he was deposed by the Funj, who appointed Bādī as king in his place. In Bruce's king-list, the accession of Bādī is dated 1020/1611–12.[24]

On Bādī's invitation, Ṣughayirūn with his mother and family left the Shāyqiyya country and moved up-stream. His disciples quarrelled over where he should settle, and, according to the tradition, he was guided by al-Khiḍr to settle at a small clearing (*al-Fujayja*) in the bush on the river-bank. This was in Dār al-Abwāb, the Jaʻalī territory lying between the junction of the Atbara with the main Nile and the Sabalūqa gorge. He sent to Sinnār to ask Bādī to grant him a parcel of land to live on, and a landing-place on the river-bank. The king would have granted him whatever he wished, but he refused to take more. There he established his school, which succeeded that of the sons of Jābir as a principal centre of religious and legal education in the northern Funj territories. His tomb and shrine were a few miles up-stream at al-Qōz.

Ṣughayirūn was succeeded by his son, al-Zayn,[25] under whom the school flourished. Al-Zayn taught for about 50 years, dying in 1086/1675–6, and is said to have had a thousand pupils in his school, which provided *faqīhs* and judges for a wide area of *Bilād al-Sūdān*, as far west as Dār Ṣulayḥ (Waddāy).[26] He left two daughters, Barra and Ḥawsha.

He was succeeded as teacher by his favourite son, Muḥammad al-Azraq,[27] who was taught by his father and his uncle, Ibrāhīm b. Ṣughayirūn. He died in 1108/1696–7, and was succeeded as teacher by his son, Bilāl,[28] who acquired a reputation for magical powers: "he never uttered an imprecation at the tomb of his father against anyone who had done him harm, but that person was rapidly destroyed". An anecdote told of him is as follows:

> "Baqawī w, ʻAjīb took by force a cow belonging to the *faqīh* Abu 'l-Ḥasan. They [i.e. Abu 'l-Ḥasan and Bilāl] overtook him at Walad

Bān al-Naqā. He refused to return it, and said, 'O Bilāl Zayn, [wait] until I come back.' So he [i.e. Bilāl] entered the *qubba* of Shaykh al-Zayn and said to them [i.e. the spirits of his father and grandfather], 'If I'm no use, maintain the posterity for yourselves. Baqawī says to me, "O Bilāl Zayn, [wait] until I come back". and says to Walad Bān al-Naqā, "My lord!" '. The *faqīh* Muḥammad al-Miriq said, 'I heard the tomb of al-Azraq say, "Ka'! Ka'!".' Baqawī went forth, and did not return: it is said that he was killed in the war of Ja'al with al-'Ujayl."

The anecdote preserves a memory of the cattle-raiding and border warfare which went on between the 'Abdallāb (the Awlād 'Ajīb), and their northern neighbours, the Ja'aliyyūn. Baqawī and 'Ujayl cannot at present be identified. The *faqīh* Abu 'l-Ḥasan is probably Bilāl's cousin, Abu 'l-Ḥasan b. Ṣāliḥ al-'Ūdī (see below), but is identified by Dr. Yūsuf Faḍl Ḥasan as being perhaps Abu'l-Ḥasan Dafa'allāh b. Ḍayfallāh (*T*, 65). The point of the story is a competition for prestige between the guardians of rival shrines, the descendants of Ṣughayirūn at al-Qōz and the descendants of Bān al-Naqā, a Ṣūfī family, whose centre was a few miles up-stream.

Bilāl died about the year 1138/1725–6, and was succeeded as teacher by his son, 'Abd al-Raḥmān,[29] who had studied under his father and under Abu 'l-Ḥasan b. Ṣāliḥ. He had a high reputation as a jurist, and was still young received permission to give *fatwās* and to teach. The school flourished in his time, and he died in 1155/1742–3, after maintaining it for 17 years. A certain Ismā'īl b. Bilāl, who was an informant of the compiler of the *Ṭabaqāt*, was probably a brother of his.

Table 3a

Ibrāhīm al-Ḥajar
|
Ṣāliḥ al-'Ūdī
|
Abu 'l-Ḥasan

Al-Zayn's brother, Ibrāhīm b. Ṣughayirūn,[30] studied under his cousin, Madanī b. 'Ūmar[31] (see below), and also taught in the family school. Like Madanī, he was nicknamed *al-Ḥajar*. His interests, however, seem to have lain elsewhere. He is represented as a rich man, the owner of 80 mares. Ibrāhīm died at Sinnār in 1099/1687–8, while on a mission to the Funj sultan, Ūnsa w. Nāṣir. He had gone to complain of the 'Abdallābī viceroy, or the king of the Sa'dāb. The Sa'dāb were the ruling clan of the Ja'aliyyūn in Dār al-Abwāb, where the family of Ṣughayirūn were settled, and the 'Abdallābī shaykh was, at least in theory, the overlord of the region. There is a suggestion that the complaint was connected with a movement of population. There had been a severe drought in 1095/1683–4, which was known ironically as *Umm Laḥm*, "the Mother of Flesh", leading to a dispersal in search of pasture. A good Nile flood in 1098/1687 caused the people to return to their old resorts, and some kind of conflict or tension in the 'Abdallābī territories seems to have ensued.

Ibrāhīm al-Ḥajar was the father of Ṣāliḥ al-'Ūdī, who, through marriage with his cousin, Ḥawsha b. al-Zayn, was the father of Abu 'l-Ḥasan.[32] Abu 'l-Ḥasan was taught by his grandfather, Ibrāhīm, and acquired a very high reputation as a jurist. We are informed that he maintained a brotherly union with 'Abd al-Raḥmān w. Usayd and Sa'd, two teachers of Nūrī. The account goes on to say:

> "They[33] used to come round to him every year with gifts of fruits from the north [lit., down-stream], such as dates and *dōm* nuts. The *faqīh* Abu 'l-Ḥasan would give them bulls for cultivation, and clothes for themselves and their women."

The anecdote may indicate the development of a system of regular and organized barter, safeguarded by the religious prestige of the *faqīhs*. Abu 'l-Ḥasan died in 1133/1720.

(b) The descendants of 'Umar

Table 4

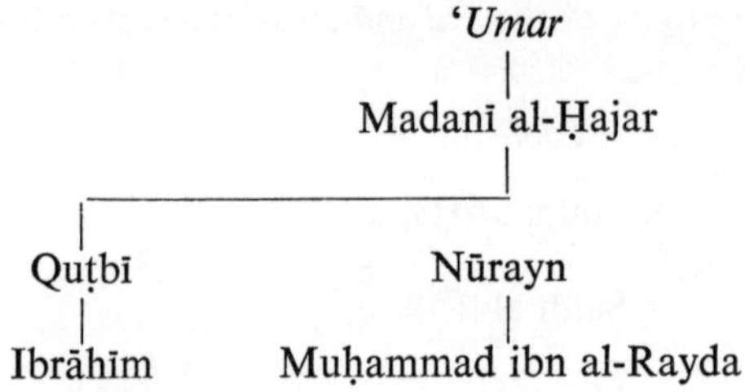

Madanī,[34] the son of 'Umar b. Fāṭima, studied law under his paternal uncle, Ṣughayirūn, whose daughter, Rābi'a, he married. On Ṣughayirūn's death, he shared the teaching in the family school with his cousin, al-Zayn, until Ibrāhīm b. Ṣughayirūn grew up. He had two sons, Quṭbī and Nūrayn, the latter of whom married Burra b. al-Zayn, and had a son, Muḥammad, called Ibn al-Rayda.

Ibn al-Rayda, who studied under Bilāl b. Muḥammad al-Azraq and Abu 'l-Ḥasan b. Ṣāliḥ, as well as at a school at Nūrī, became a celebrated jurist. His cousin Ibrāhīm b. Quṭbī is also described as a very learned man.

(*c*) *The descendants of Āmina*

Table 5

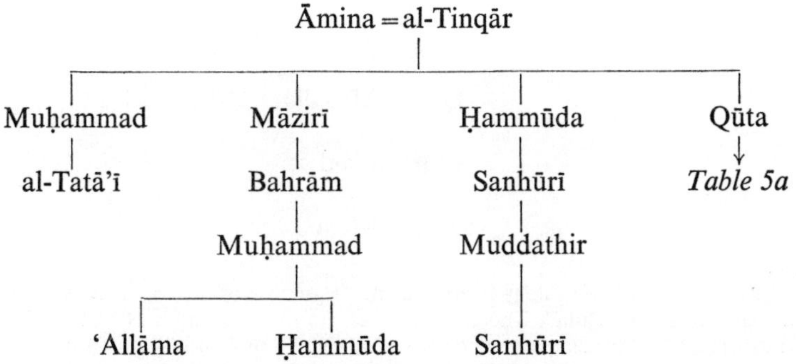

Āmina, the daughter of Fāṭima b. Jābir and sister of Ṣughayirūn, was a good and learned woman. She married a certain Ja'alī named al-Tinqār. All three of their sons receive notices in the *Ṭabaqāt*. They were closely associated with Ṣughayirūn. Two of them, Muḥammad[35] and Māzirī,[36] are explicitly said to have studied under him, while the third, Ḥammūda,[37] was nicknamed *Jayyāb al-'ajwa min al-Rīf* "the bringer of dates from Upper Egypt", because he brought dates to cure Ṣughayirūn when he was sick.

The descendants of Āmina moved away from the family school, and set up new establishments. Muḥammad b. al-Tinqār set up a teaching-mosque at al-Muways, between al-Fujayja and Shandī, the capital of the Sa'dāb. Subsequently he moved to al-Bursī in the south (*fī arḍ al-Ṣa'īd*)—presumably the village of that name east of the Blue Nile, near Abū Ḥarāz. The Shandī district seems, however, to have been the real centre of the family's activities. Al-Tatā'ī, the son of Muḥammad b. al-Tinqār, maintained a mosque on the edge of the town and ran a great law-school. This was perhaps the mosque in Shandī at which Muḥammad b. Bahrām and his son, 'Allāma (the grandson and great-grandson respectively of Māzirī b. al-Tinqār) were teachers. Ḥammūda b. al-Tinqār's great-grandson, Sanhūrī, studied law under 'Abd al-Raḥmān b. Bilāl (see above).

Qūta, the daughter of Āmina, married Musallam al-Ḥalanqī. The Ḥalanga are an arabized group, originally of Tigre origin but settled since the eighth Christian century in the Bija territory of the Tāka, around the present site of Kasala. Qūta's son, Muḥammad,[38] studied law under his maternal uncle, Muḥammad b. al-Tinqār. He became the outstanding jurist of the region, and wrote books of *fatwās* and legal decisions. He maintained a school at al-Qōz (almost certainly not al-Qōz of the Ṣughayirūn family, but Qōz wad Ḍiyāb, south of Khartoum), but subsequently removed to al-Hilāliyya, on the east bank of the Blue Nile. His son, Sharaf al-Dīn[39] also a jurist, died at Qōz wad Ḍiyāb.

Table 5a

Qūta = Musallam al-Ḥalanqī
|
Muḥammad
|
Sharaf al-Dīn[1]

Note

1 Sharaf al-Dīn's genealogy is given at the beginning of his notice as "the son of 'Alī, the son of Qūta". There is, however, no other mention of 'Alī; and in Muḥammad b. Musallam's notice, Sharaf al-Dīn is spoken of as his son.

Conclusion

The information provided by the *Ṭabaqāt* about the kin of Awlād Jābir fades out about the middle of the eighteenth century. The clan seems to have produced no outstanding figures subsequently. It is indeed remarkable how long it subsisted on the cultural capital acquired under al-Banūfarī in Cairo in the later sixteenth century. After Ṣughayirūn, there is no indication that any of its members studied outside Sudanese territories. Their contribution to the Islam of the Sudan was by the transmission of a modicum of law and theology to newly or superficially islamized regions—Dār al-Shāyqiyya, Dār al-Abwāb, the Blue Nile—rather than the development of schools enjoying a wide reputation in the older Islamic lands, or the production of scholarly works.

This frustrated development is not easy to explain. The geographical remoteness and isolation of the Nilotic Sudan from the ancient centres of Islamic learning should not be exaggerated. There was regular commercial contact with Egypt, as the accounts of European travellers, of Evliya Çelebi, and Muḥammad b. 'Umar al-Tūnusī indicate. It was not overwhelmingly difficult either to travel to Cairo, or to obtain books thence. The notice of 'Ammār b. 'Abd al-Ḥafīẓ al-Khaṭīb[40] in the *Ṭabaqāt* (largely based on an autobiography), depicts its subject as spending over four years (from 1077/1677) as a student and pilgrim in Egypt and the Ḥijāz, and as bringing back to Sinnār two or three loads of books. A century and a half later, Burckhardt visited the flourishing school of the Majādhīb clan at El Damer, and described how books were brought there by the young *faqīhs* after studying in al-Azhar and Mecca.[41]

The *Ṭabaqāt* of Wad Ḍayfallāh was compiled just before new forces made an impact on the indigenous Islam of the Nilotic Sudan.

The revival of Islam, which was manifested in the eighteenth and early nineteenth centuries by such phenomena as the spread of the Naqshbandī *ṭarīqa*, the challenge of Wahhābism, and the emergence of new orders such as the Tijāniyya and the Sanūsiyya, was communicated to the Sudanese Muslims by al-Sayyid Muḥammad 'Uthmān al-Mīrghanī during his visit in 1232/1816–17.[42] Four years later, in 1236/1820–1, the Nilotic Sudan was conquered by Turco-Egyptian forces, and annexed to Muḥammad 'Ali's Egypt. Far-reaching consequences flowed from these events: the organization of the influential Khatmiyya order under the direction of the Mīrghanī family, the establishment of a hierarchy of salaried '*ulamā*' on the late Ottoman model, the strengthening of cultural links between Egypt and the Sudan, the transmission of Western influences on concepts and institutions. The tension between these new forces and the traditional Sudanese Islam, which the sons of Jābir had done so much to foster, was to result in the Mahdia.

APPENDIX

The Traditions concerning Rubāṭ and Salīm

The name of Ghulāmallāh's son is given in the *Ṭabaqāt* as Ribāṭ (usually vocalized Rubāṭ), and in the *Furū*' also as Irbāṭ. We have also noted a variant reading, Muḥammad al-Murābiṭ,[43] i.e. "Muḥammad the man of the frontier-settlement", which suggests that Rubāṭ/Irbāṭ may represent an original *Sāḥib al-Fibāṭ*, "the master of the frontier-settlement". Since a *ribāṭ* was a pious community of warriors, established on the frontier between Muslim and non-Muslim territory, it is possible that Rubāṭ may have played a part in the islamization of Nubia.

The *Ṭabaqāt* gives the following anecdote concerning Rubāṭ:

"The Ṣawārda married him to a bondwoman (*amma*) of theirs, by whom they deceived him. She bore him Salīm. Then they confessed the deception to him, and said to him, 'She is a bondwoman'. He complained of them to the judge, who gave him a decision that his son was free, and required of him the price of the bondwoman [or: of his mother]. This occurrence was in the time of the Fūnj."[44]

The last sentence is certainly corrupt, as Rubāṭ must have lived well before the establishment of the Funj dynasty. Almost certainly there has been confusion in the Arabic manuscripts between Fūnj/Funj and 'Anaj, the latter being a term applied to the autochthons of the Nilotic Sudan.

Rubāṭ's marriage to a bondwoman is probably an instance of a custom which survived into the nineteenth century, and was observed in 1833 by the English traveller, Hoskins. He describes it as follows:

> "They [*sc.* the *makks* of Shandī, Berber, Dār al-Shāyqiyya, and Dongola] purchased, or made captive in their wars, female slaves; of which some possessed thirty, others as many as a hundred, and some five hundred. These unfortunate creatures . . . were placed by the meleks [*makks*] in the different villages, and obliged to gratify the avarice of their masters, and earn their own scanty livelihood by the abandonment of their virtue. The only privilege these most wretched of slaves possess is, that when they have paid to the melek a sum equal to their purchase money or present value, the custom of the country precludes him from selling them. It is at his option to sell or not the child to the father. . . . The sons of these slaves . . . are sometimes sold, particularly when the melek is in want of money; but generally they are brought up to cultivate the ground of their chief, and, when necessity requires, rally around his standard, and accompany him to battle. From their earliest infancy, they are entirely devoted to the despotic will of their melek, evincing great attachment to his person, and zeal in the execution of his commands, as the only means by which they can hope for emancipation."[45]

The anecdote quoted from the *Ṭabaqāt* reflects the conflict between this custom and the *Sharī'a*. Among Nubians, Salīm would inherit his mother's servile condition, while Rubāṭ, as a Muslim, would regard his son as free-born, irrespective of the mother's status. The judge's decision shows an interesting compromise, accepting the provision of the *Sharī'a* in respect of the son, while compensating the clan by requiring the redemption of the bond-woman. The evidence of Hoskins, however, shows that in this matter the *Sharī'a* failed to overcome local custom.

The variant reading calls Rubāṭ's son Aḥmad Salīm al-Majdhūb, i.e. "the ecstatic", implying that he was a Ṣūfī adept. The traditions recorded, however, are only concerned with his marriages, and give further evidence of the fluid society of fifteenth-century Nubia. They are as follows:

> "Then Salīm sought in marriage the daughter of his paternal uncle, Rikāb, and her name was Junayba. She refused him because of [his] servile status [*al-'abūdiyya*]. Qindīl al-'Awnī had a sick daughter. Salīm made an incantation for her, and she was cured. He married him to her, and she bore 'Awn. . . . Also *Malik al-Kanīsa* had a sick daughter, and she was cured. So he married him to her, and she bore him Hadhlūl. Then Junayba the daughter of his paternal uncle regretted her refusal, since he was a holy man, and the people desired him. So he married her, and she bore him four children. . . ."[46]

These traditions present several points of interest. The name of *Malik al-Kanīsa* suggests a Nubian Christian, rather than an Arab Muslim background: *Malik al-Kanīsa*, "the King of the Church", indicates a chief living at a Christian site, even if the church was no longer in use.[47] The name of 'Awn, and the epithet al-'Awni attached to Qindīl,[48] suggest a link with the 'Awniyya, a sub-tribe of the Shāyqiyya living on the left bank of the Nile around Kūrti.[49] *Al-Kanīsa* may be a locality of that name on the left bank of the Nile, five miles upstream of Nūri, which is also in Shāyqiyya territory.[50] For what they are worth, these indications suggest that Ghulāmallāh's immediate descendants lived as Muslim frontiersmen among the Shāyqiyya, beyond the territory of Dongola properly speaking. The reputation of Salīm rested upon his magical powers, rather than upon his Islamic scholarship: the practice of incantation (of the Qur'ān and other religious texts) is one which is still found in the Sudan.[51] Both 'Awn (Muḥammad 'Awn in the variant reading) and his son, Jābir, are shadowy figures, of whom no anecdotes are recorded in the *Ṭabaqāt*.

The genealogies provide Rubāṭ with a brother, Rikāb. His notice in the *Ṭabaqāt* merely gives him as the ancestor of five clans, which were widely dispersed and included the Dawālīb of Kordofan, as well as groups in Taqalī (in the Nuba Mountains, on the southern fringe of Arab penetration) and others with the Shukriyya nomads of the Buṭāna, east of the main and Blue Niles. The generic term Rikābiyya seems, however, to have been extended in common usage to all who claimed descent from Ghulāmallāh—who himself is sometimes called (by anticipation) al-Rikābī. Jabrallāh, the brother of Jābir, seems also to have been a genealogists' fiction, since he is shown only as the progenitor of a clan (Awlād Umm Shaykh) who were the proprietors of a mosque at al-Hilāliyya, on the Blue Nile. Since we have no information concerning the migration of Jabrallāh's descendants to this remote region, this is probably merely an attempt by Awlād Umm Shaykh to ennoble their ancestry.

NOTES

1 See the critical edition by Yūsuf Faḍl Ḥasan, *Kitāb al-ṭabaqāt fī khuṣūṣ al-awliyā' wa'l-ṣāliḥīn wa'l-'ulamā' wa'l-shu'arā' fi'l-Sūdān* (Khartoum, 1971). The completion of the *Ṭabaqāt* is dated in the colophon 16 Rabī' I 1166/21 January 1753, but internal evidence shows that work on it continued until at least 1219/1804–5. References, where relevant, are also given to the summary-translation in MacMichael, *Arabs*.

2 *T*, 104.

3 See Yūsuf Faḍl Ḥasan, *The Arabs and the Sudan* (Edinburgh, 1967).

4 *T*, 45.

5 *T*, 45, n. 4. An almost identical variant is given in the uncritical edition of Ibrāhīm Ṣidayq (Cairo, 1348/1930), p. 6, n. 2, but reading "al-Ghulām Aḥmad al-Mujammir".

6 School of Oriental Studies, University of Durham: Sudan Archive, *Provisional hand-list of Arabic manuscripts and lithographs: Africa, Arabia* (Second draft, 1961), No. 256/19; [?] al-Ṭāhir b. 'Abd Allāh, *Kitāb ma'ārif furū' uṣūl al-'Arab wa'l-ḥasab wa'l-nasab*: 97/5/11. A summary-translation, from a different manuscript, is given in MacMichael, *Arabs*, II, 16–59.

7 *Furū'*, f. 4a.

8 *Furū'*, f. 5a.

9 The church at Old Dongola was converted to a mosque by the first Nubian Muslim king in 717/1317. A bishop of Ibrīm and Faras was, however, consecrated in Cairo as late as 1372; P. L. and M. Shinnie, "New light on medieval Nubia", *JAH*, VI (1965), 265.

10 See, pp. 99–101.
11 *T*, 46, 251.
12 His notice is at *T*, 45–6. It is not found in MacMichael's summary-translation, which was made from a defective manuscript.
13 Turunj is on the right bank of the Nile, near to Karīma and opposite Nūrī. There are numerous fertile islands in the vicinity.
14 Cf. Najm al-Dīn al-Ghazzī, *al-Kawākib al-sā'ira bi-a'yān al-mi'a al-'āshira*, III (Harissa/Beirut, 1958), 82.
15 *T*, 42.
16 Bodleian Library, Oxford: MS. Bruce 18 (2), f. 55b.
17 *T*, 251; MacMichael, *Arabs*, II, 224 (17).
18 *T*, 46–7. Not found in MacMichael's summary-translation.
19 *T*, 47–8. Not found in MacMichael's summary-translation.
20 Cf. Crawford, *Fung kingdom*, 47–8.
21 *T*, 225; MacMichael, *Arabs*, II, 266 (233).
22 *T*, 234–7; MacMichael, *Arabs*, II, 268–70 (241).
23 The *sīd al-qōm* (*sayyid al-qawm*) was a high officer of royal blood at the Funj court.
24 MS. Bruce 18 (2), f. 55b.
25 *T*, 73–5; MacMichael, *Arabs*, II, 272 (258).
26 That Dār Ṣulayḥ or Waddāy was a watershed between the eastern *Bilād al-Sūdān*, which was culturally dependent on Egypt and the east, and the western *Bilād al-Sūdān*, which was similarly dependent on the Maghrib, is confirmed by Burckhardt, who observed in 1813–14 that "the Fakys, as well as Saley as of the countries to the east of it, all write the eastern Arabic Nuskh characters though very much corrupted; while those to the west and north have uniformly adopted the Moggrebyn character" (J. L. Burckhardt, *Travels in Nubia* (London, 1819), 481.
27 *T*, 356–7; MacMichael, *Arabs*, II, 260 (204).
28 *T*, 124; MacMichael, *Arabs*, II, 236 (79).
29 *T*, 285–6; MacMichael, *Arabs*, II, 224 (16).
30 *T*, 76–7; MacMichael, *Arabs*, II, 246 (139).
31 *T*, 360; MacMichael, *Arabs*, II, 246 (139).
32 *T*, 77–8; MacMichael, *Arabs*, II, 228 (47).
33 In some manuscripts the pronouns in this passage are in the singular: cf. *T*, 78 and notes 4 and 5.
34 *T*, 360; MacMichael, *Arabs*, II, 253 (161). This notice covers both Madanī al-Ḥajar and Muḥammad ibn al-Rayda.
35 *T*, 360–1; MacMichael, *Arabs*, II, 260 (202).
36 *T*, 361–2; MacMichael, *Arabs*, II, 253 (160).
37 *T*, 186; MacMichael, *Arabs*, II, 244 (130).
38 *T*, 362; MacMichael, *Arabs*, II, 259 (196).
39 *T*, 232; MacMichael, *Arabs*, II, 267 (239).
40 *T*, 117–19; MacMichael, *Arabs*, II, 263 (219).
41 Burckhardt, *Travels in Nubia*, 267.
42 *FC*, 73–4.
43 See above, p. 89.
44 *T*, 215. An interesting variant is given in n. 5.
45 G. A. Hoskins, *Travels in Ethiopia*, London, 1835, 89–90; cf. 59.
46 *T*, 215.
47 In Sudanese colloquial usage, the plural form, *kanā'is*, signifies "ruins", cf. S. Hillelson, *Sudan Arabic: English–Arabic vocabulary* (London, 1925); 245.

48 MacMichael, *Arabs*, II, 304, suggests that Qindīl al-ʻAwnī may be identical with Qindīl al-Ṣāridī, referred to in another notice (*T*, 293). This would establish a link with the Ṣawārda, who appear in the anecdote of Rubāṭ's marriage. See also Dr. Yūsuf Faḍl Ḥasan's comments (*T*, 293, n. 13).

49 MacMichael, *Arabs*, I, 220; II, 336–7.

50 Cf. Count Gleichen, *The Anglo-Egyptian Sudan*, London, 1905, I, 38.

51 Cf. J. S. Trimingham, *Islam in the Sudan* (London, 1949), 167.

6

FOUR FUNJ LAND-CHARTERS

Introductory Remarks

In 1967, the Rev. Dr. A. J. Arkell presented to the School of Oriental and African Studies in London a collection of papers relating to his Sudanese researches. These included transcriptions of four charters, the brief particulars of which are as follows:

Arkell I (Arkell Papers: Box 1, File 5, Piece 82): grant by Shaykh Raḥma b. Yūnus to Shaykh Ya'qūb b. Muḥammad Zayn, 23 Dhu'l-Ḥijja 1146/27 May 1734.

Arkell II (AP: 1, 5, 81): confirmation by Sultan Bādī IV of the preceding grant, 1 Muḥarram 1147/3 June 1734.

Arkell III (AP: 1, 5, 72): grant by Shaykh Muḥammad b. 'Adlān to the *Faqīh* Muhammad 'Alī w. al-'Abbās, 10 Muḥarram 1228/13 January 1813 [*sic*].

Arkell IV (AP: 1, 5, 73): confirmation by Shaykh Ḥusayn b. Muḥammad Abī Likaylik of the preceding grant, 12 Muḥarram 1228/15 January 1813 [*sic*].

The Arabic texts of these charters (plates i–iv respectively) have never previously been published, although English translations of the first two were published by Dr. Arkell as an appendix to his article, "Funj Origins", *SNR* XV/2, 1932, at pp. 248–50. I have here given new translations of these, in order to secure uniformity of presentation with the translations of the third and fourth charters.

In the commentary, I have not attempted an exhaustive analysis of the charters, but rather have sought to relate them to the documents earlier published by Dr. Abu Selim,[1] to elucidate some problems of their diplomatic and terminology, and to relate them to their immediate historical contexts. Further information on aspects not here examined in detail, e.g. the technical terms in the lists of immunities and the identification of the great officers of state who attest the charters, may be found in Dr. Abu Selim's introduction to his book. With regard to the sites of the estates granted in the charters: that referred to in Arkell I and II lay in the region of Hujjaj, west of the Blue Nile and about 25 miles north-west of Sinnār. The estate mentioned in Arkell III and IV may have lain to the east of the Blue Nile, in the hinterland of the present village of Wad al-'Abbās, about 16 miles down-stream from Sinnār.

Arkell I (PLATE I)

This is a title-deed and customary charter [given] in Sinnār, the divinely guarded and protected (may God Most High exalt her), in the presence of her warden, the governor at the present time of what is within her, the chief of the knights, the bravest of the brave, the treasure of security, he who is known for goodness and benefaction, he who trusts in the Bountiful King, Shaykh Raḥma, the son of the late Shaykh Yūnus, the *Amīn al-Sulṭān*—may God be with him wherever he is and guard him with the chapters and verses of the Qur'ān. Amen.

And thereafter: Shaykh Raḥma, the son of the late Shaykh Yūnus, has granted as alms to Shaykh Ya'qūb an estate in the land of Umm Marāḥīk; alms for the sake of God and for the reward of the world to come, for the Day wherein neither wealth nor children will avail save unto him who comes to God with a secure heart.

The boundaries are known on the four sides: on the east side, al-Ṭunḍuba and Naqr Hantūla; on the south side, 'Azzāz Jarrūra and the reservoir of Walad Bilāl; on the west side, Umm Marāḥīk, the boundary going in a northward direction to the track of Umm Ṭalḥa, and going eastwards in the direction of al-Ṭunḍuba, terminating beyond the purchased cultivable land of Shaykh Ya'qūb.

Let none approach the messenger of Shaykh Raḥma, the son of Shaykh Yūnus, or draw near to him, or stop at his door.

Ḥamad walad Khayyār, the herdsman of the estate, was present to delimit the estate.

There were present as witnesses thereto: Shaykh Bishr, his brother; Kitfā, his brother; Wārit, his brother; Hārūn, his brother; Naṣr, his brother; the *Arbāb* Mas'ūd; 'Alī walad Nuwayr; the *Arbāb* Muḥammad walad walad [*sic*] Ḍuwayw; 'Alī, his son; Muḍḍawī, *muqaddam al-qawāwīd*; al-Ṭāhir al-Ghadawī; 'Umar al-Ghadawī; Ḥasan, *qawwād al-shaykh*; Zāyid al-Ḥarrās; Muṣṭafā of the Blacks [*al-Sūdān*]; Sa'īd of the *Marājina*; Ismā'īl, brother of Shaykh Raḥma; Anqala, his brother; Shawwāl, his brother; Ramaḍān; 'Alī, his son; Ṣābūn; Kūrāb; 'Abd al-'Āṭī; the *Arbāb* Ibrāhīm walad Badawī; and the writer of the letters, Muḥammad, the son of the *faqīh* Aḥmad, clerk and witness.

On the forenoon of Thursday, 23 Dhu'l-Ḥijja, in the year 1146 from the Emigration of the Prophet—on whom be the most excellent blessings and the purest peace.

Arkell II (PLATE II)

A sultanic title-deed and customary charter from the presence of the sultan of Islam, who brings unanimity among the believers, who destroys the people of iniquity and tyranny, the ruler of the kings of the land and the sea, who orders the affairs of the peoples of the nations, who establishes places of hospitality and kindness, who demolishes foundations, who has power to compel; he whom conquest and victory encounter when he sets forth, who clothes the Muslims with the clouds of his excellence; he whom God has chosen as his commissioner over men—may God be his Guardian and Security; our lord the sultan, the son of the sultan, the victorious and divinely aided king, Sultan Bādī, the son of the late Sultan Nūl—may the days of his justice be increased, and the nights of his felicity renewed, by the influence of Muḥammad and his kin. Amen.

To all to whom this charter shall come, and to him who looks into its veracious contents.

And thereafter: The pious, divinely assisted and victorious sultan has confirmed and ratified the act of Shaykh Raḥma, the son of Shaykh Yūnus, in the grant as alms to Shaykh Ya'qūb, the son of Shaykh Muḥammad Zayn, of an estate in the land of Umm Marāḥik; alms for the sake of God Most High, and for the reward in the Day of Resurrection.

The boundaries are known in the charter of the said Shaykh Raḥma as to the four sides: on the east, al-Ṭunḍuba and Naqr Hantūla; on the south, 'Azzāz Jarrūra and the reservoir of Walad Bilāl; on the west, Umm Marāḥik, the boundary going in a northward direction to the track of Umm Ṭalḥa, and going eastwards in the direction of al-Ṭunḍuba, terminating beyond the purchased cultivable land of Shaykh Ya'qūb.

Let none approach him, or draw near to him, or impede him in the way; the rope which he has cast aside, let no fellow carry away; let none drink his dark water [?] therein. [The estate is] free from all evils and damages.

Beware, then, beware of disobedience, and let the disobedient blame none but himself.

There were present as witnesses thereto: Shaykh Raḥma, the son of Shaykh Yūnus; the *Jundī* Yūnus; Shaykh Ismā'īl, maternal uncle of the king; the *Arbāb* Idū, grandfather of the king; Shaykh Shā' al-Dīn Darwīsh, shaykh of the River; Shaykh Ḥamad, shaykh of al-Qarrabīn; Shaykh Muḥammad, *muqaddam al-sajjāda*; the *Qāḍī* Ibrāhīm; the *Khaṭīb* 'Abd al-Laṭīf; 'Ammār Abu'l-Naqā; and the writer of the charter, Muḥammad 'Abd al-Ghanī.

And God is a sufficient witness.

On the first day of Muḥarram in [the year] 1147 from the Emigration of the Prophet—on whom be the most excellent blessings and peace.

Arkell III (PLATE III)

This is a copy of a sultanic charter.

In Thy Name, O Generous One.

In the Name of God, the Compassionate, the Merciful.

Praise be to God, and blessings and peace on the Seal of the noble Apostles of God.

A sultanic title-deed, written and approved in the Funj territories, in the divinely guarded and protected city of Sinnār (may God Most High exalt her), in the presence of her warden and the son of her warden, the master of her bridles, her remote and near places, her cultivators and nomads, the governor at the present time of those over her and within her; he whom men dread, whose strength heroes fear in the day of war and conflict; he who is protected from error by God the Judge; Shaykh Muḥammad, the son of the late *wazīr*, Shaykh ʻAdlān—may God grant him victory. Amen.

To all to whom this charter shall come, and to him who looks into its veracious contents.

And thereafter: the divinely preserved, pious, divinely assisted and victorious Shaykh Muḥammad has granted as alms to the *faqīh* Muḥammad ʻAlī walad al-ʻAbbās an estate from the cultivable land of [Dār] ʻAjīb, being waste rainland; alms for the sake of God and his Apostle, and for the Day wherein neither wealth nor children will avail, save unto him who comes to God with a secure heart.

The estate is known as to its site and boundaries: its boundary on the east the estate of Shaykh al-Ṭurayfī, the son of Shaykh Yūsuf; on the north, beyond al-Ṭanāḍib and Walad Maḥmūd; on the west, ʻIdd Mulayḥa, and beyond Jannīn, and beyond Sharaf al-Dīn walad Dūra and Ḥusayn walad Dūra, and beyond the reservoir of Shammīn; and on the south, beyond the estate of the Fūr and the estate of Khamīs walad Janqal: the boundaries end there.

And the said estate with its known boundaries has become the property and possession in full freehold of the *faqīh* Muḥammad ʻAlī walad al-ʻAbbās, for himself, his offspring, and the offspring of his offspring; they shall inherit it from heir to heir until God shall inherit the earth and those upon it, and He is the best of heirs. Let him not be exposed therein to the litigation of any, or the trespass of any. [It shall be] free and delivered from all evils, rights of way, and damages. It shall not be liable to *jasāra*, or *khasāra*, or ʻ*aẓm*, or ʻ*āna*, or *raghm*, or *zarība*, or *ḍiyāfa*, or *ḥasab*, or *dam*, or *nār*, or *qawār*, or *nuzūl*, or *makhlā*, or *matūrat*, or *kalīgha*, or anything small or great.

And we command you peremptorily, all shaykhs and *maqdūms*, especially Ḥassān and his followers and all his successors, you and your tax-collectors and your successors to the Last Day, that none of you shall trespass upon the *faqīh* Muḥammad 'Alī in this [estate], and none of you shall trespass upon his offspring, or the offspring of his offspring. Whoever trespasses upon him after my declaration and this my charter exposes himself to destruction, Beware, then, beware of disobedience, and let the disobedient blame none but himself.

And farewell.

There were present as witnesses thereto: Shaykh Aḥmad walad al-Nūr, *shaykh al-qawwāriyya*; Shaykh 'Adlān walad Shanbūl, shaykh of Arbajī; the *Arbāb* Qāsim walad al-Shaykh Muḥammad; the *Arbāb* Naṣr, his brother; the *Arbāb* Idrīs walad Bādī; the *Arbāb* Mūsā, his brother; the *Arbāb* Muḥammad walad Ḥusayn; the *Arbāb* Ḥasan, his brother; the *Arbāb* Muḥammad walad Idrīs; the *Arbāb* 'Alī, his brother; the *Arbāb* Ḥasan walad Rajab; the *Arbāb* Ibrāhīm, his brother; the *Arbāb* Nāṣir walad *al-Arbāb* Rajab; the *Arbāb* Idrīs, the *Arbāb* Ibrāhīm, the *Arbāb* Ḥasan, the *Arbāb* 'Īsāwī, the *Arbāb* 'Alī, sons of the late *wazīr*, Shaykh 'Adlān; the *Arbāb* Dafa'allāh Aḥmad; the *Arbāb* Dafa'allāh Ḥamad; the *Arbāb* Ibrāhīm 'Uwayḍa; the *Arbāb* 'Alī Ilyās; the *Arbāb* 'Alī walad Muḥammad; the *Arbāb* Aḥmad b. al-Ḥājj Sulaymān; the *Arbāb* Khūjalī walad Khālid; Ḥasan walad 'Iwaḍallāh; Ḥusayn, his brother; Shaykh Farajallāh; Shaykh Tayfara; the *Arbāb* 'Abdallāh walad Sukkūt; the *Arbāb* Muḥammad walad Jamīlallāh; the *Arbāb* Muḥammad walad Kāb; the *Mankarūkan*[2] Bakhīt; the *Mankarūkan* Karrūma; 'Alī Abū Zuwayr; 'Adlān walad Maḥjūb; Faḍl Karan Dūs; 'Abd al-Raḍī walad al-Bayt; 'Īd walad al-Bayt; Ḥāmid walad al-Bayt; Aḥmad walad al-Baqara; and the clerk, Aḥmad al-Makkī.

And God is a sufficient witness.

Executed on Thursday, in the daytime of 10 Muḥarram, in the year 1228 from the Emigration of the Lord of the Apostles—the blessing of God be upon him and peace, and may God be pleased with all his Companions.

And farewell.

Arkell IV (PLATE IV)

This is a copy of a sultanic charter.

In Thy Name, O Generous One.

In the Name of God, the Compassionate, the Merciful.

Praise be to God, and blessings and peace on the Seal of the noble Apostles of God.

A sultanic title-deed, written and approved in the Funj territories, in the divinely guarded and protected city of Sinnār (may God Most High exalt her), in the presence of her warden and the son of her warden, the master of her bridles, her remote and near places, her cultivators and nomads, the governor at the present time of those over her and within her, the candlestick of the age and the lamp of the countries, the destroyer of the people of abomination, iniquity and injustice; the *amīn* of the army of the sultan, who trusts in God the Eternal, the *wazīr*, Shaykh Ḥusayn, son of the late *wazīr*, Shaykh Muḥammad Abū Likaylik—may God grant him victory. Amen.

To all to whom this charter shall come, and to him who looks into its veracious contents.

And thereafter: The divinely preserved, pious, divinely assisted and victorious *wazīr*, Sultan [*sic*] Ḥusayn, has confirmed and ratified the act of Shaykh Muḥammad ʻAdlān to the *faqīh* Muḥammad ʻAlī al-ʻAbbāsī concerning the cultivable land of Dār ʻAjīb, being waste rainland. And I, the *Wazīr* Ḥusayn, have confirmed and ratified [this] to the *faqīh* Muḥammad ʻAlī al-ʻAbbāsī, for the sake of pleasing God and for the reward in the life to come, and for the Day wherein neither wealth nor children will avail, save unto him who comes to God with a pure heart.

The estate is known as to its site and boundaries: its boundary on the east, the estate of Shaykh al-Ṭurayfī, the son of Shaykh Yūsuf; on the north, beyond al-Ṭanāḍib and Walad Maḥmūd; on the west, ʻIdd Mulayḥa, and beyond Jannīn, and beyond Sharaf al-Dīn walad Dūra and Ḥusayn walad Dūra, and beyond the reservoir of Shammīn; and on the south, beyond the estate of the Fūr and the estate of Khamīs walad Janqal: the boundaries end there.

And the said estate with its known boundaries has become the property of the *faqīh* Muḥammad ʻAlī al-ʻAbbāsī, for himself, his offspring, and the offspring of his offspring; they shall inherit it from heir to heir until God shall inherit the earth and those upon it, and He is the best of heirs. Let him not be exposed therein to the litigation of any, or the trespass of any. [It shall be] free and delivered from all evils, rights of way, and damages. It shall not be liable to *jasāra*, or *khasāra*, or *ʻaẓm*, or *ʻāna*, or *ḥasab*, or *dam*, or *nār*, or *qawār*, or *nuzūl*, or *raghm*, or *zarība*, or *ḍiyāfa*, or *ʻulūq*, or *makhlā*, or *matūra*, or anything small or great.

And we command you peremptorily, shaykhs, *maqdūms*, and tax-collectors, that none of you shall trespass upon the *faqīh* Muḥammad ʻAlī al-ʻAbbāsī, especially Ḥassān, thou and thy company, to the Last Day let none of you trespass upon him. Whoever trespasses upon him after my declaration and this my charter exposes himself to destruction. Beware, then, beware of disobedience, and let the disobedient blame none but himself.

There were present as witnesses thereto: Shaykh Wāwrit walad Hārūn, *amīn al-sulṭān*; the *Jundī* Kitfāwā, *jund*[*ī*] *al-sūq*; Shaykh Nāṣir walad al-Amīn, shaykh of Qarrī; Shaykh Muḥammad walad Badr, shaykh of Alays; Shaykh ——ān walad al-Faḍīl, shaykh of Atbara;

Shaykh Kamtūr walad Aḥmad, shaykh of the River; Shaykh Muḥammad al-'Arakī, shaykh of Bayla; Shaykh al-Nūr walad Muḥammad, shaykh of al-Qarrabīn; Shaykh Muḥammad walad Idrīs, shaykh of the Household of the king's son; Shaykh 'Adlān walad Shanbūl, shaykh of Arbajī; the *Arbāb* Ḥamad, son of the late *wazīr*, Shaykh 'Adlān; Qāsim walad Muḥammad; Naṣr walad Muḥammad; the *Arbāb* Dafa'allāh Muḥammad [*sic*]; the *Arbāb* Ibrāhīm 'Uwayḍa; Aḥmad walad Muḥammad Abu'l-Qāsim; the *Mankarūkan* Farajallāh; the *Mankarūkan* Tayfara; the *Mankarūkan* 'Abdallāh walad Sukkūt; the *Mankarūkan* Faḍlallāh walad Salāma; the *Mankarūkan* 'Abd al-Bayyin; the *Mankarūkan* Ḥamad al-Sayyid; Faḍl walad Qāsim, *muqaddam al-mahr*; and the clerk, Aḥmad al-Makkī.

And God is a sufficient witness.

Executed on Saturday, in the daytime of 12 Muḥarram, in the year 1228 from the Emigration of the Lord of the Apostles—the blessing of God be upon him and peace, and may God be pleased with all his Companions.

COMMENTARY

1. *Types of Land-Charter*

The land-charters of the late Funj period (i.e. the reigns of Bādī IV and his successors) fall into two categories: those which originate, and those which confirm, a grant of land and examptions. In his valuable collection of documents, Dr. Abu Selim has published five originating, and thirteen confirmatory charters. Of the originating charters, two (AS 1, 3) were granted by Sultan Bādī IV (1136–75/1724–62); the remaining three emanated respectively from Shaykh Muḥammad al-Amīn b. Musmārr, the 'Abdallābī viceroy of Qarrī (AS 7), Shaykh Ḥammād b. 'Arabī of the Dāniyāb (AS 5), and a certain Shaykh Ḥamad b. 'Alī (AS 13). Of the confirmatory charters, four confirming existing rights were granted by Sultan Bādī IV (AS 2, 18, 29, 30), one (AS 16) by Sultan Nāṣir (1175–83/1762–9), and one (AS 28) by Sultan Bādī V (1204/1789–90); three confirmed grants made by subordinates, one of these emanated from Sultan Nāṣir (AS 12), one (AS 11) from Sultan Rānfī (1213–19/1798–1804), and one (AS 6, confirming AS 5 above) from the 'Abdallābī viceroy, Shaykh 'Ajīb b. 'Abdallāh of Qarrī; four confirmed grants made by previous rulers, one (AS 19) emanating from Sultan Nāṣir, one (AS 21) from Sultan Ismā'īl (1183–90/1769–76), one (AS 22) from Sultan 'Adlān II (1190–1203/1776–88), and one (AS 8) from the 'Abdallābī viceroy, Shaykh Nāṣir b. Muḥammad al-Amīn.

The four documents of which transcriptions are preserved in the

فهذه حجة

وو ثيقة ملوكية بسنار المحروسة المحمية اجلها الله تعالى لدامتولبها والحاكم
يومئذ بما فيها رئيس الفرسان واشجع الشجعان صندوق الامان المعروف بالخير
والاحسان الواثق بالملك المنان الشيخ رحمه ابن المرحوم الشيخ يونس امين رر
السلطان كان الله حين كان وحرسه بالسور وءايات القران امين اما
بعد فالشيخ رحمه ابن المرحوم الشيخ يونس تصدق على الشيخ يعقوب بدار في ارض ام
مراحيك صدقة لابتغاء وجه الله تعالى وطلبا للثواب الدار الاخرة ليوم لا ينفع
فيه مال ولا بنون الا من اتا الله بقلب سليم ومعلومة الحدود من الجهات
الاربعة من جهة الصبح الطنضب وتقرهنتوله ومن جهة الصعيد عزاز جروره
وحفير ولد بلال ومن جهة الغرب ام مراحيك يمشي الحد مسغل بنظر مسغل
الى عن درب امطلحه يمشي مصبح ابناظر الدطنضب ويركز فوق بطين الشيخ
يعقوب المشتري ومرسال الشيخ رحمه ابن الشيخ يونس لا احد يعترله ولا يدنيه
ولا يقف على بابه ومحمد ولد خيار راعي الدار حضر على قطع الدار حضر وشهد بذلك رر
الشيخ بشر اخيه وكتفا اخيه ووارث اخيه وهارون اخيه ونصر اخيه ومنصور
والارباب مسعود وعلي ولد نوير والارباب محمد ولد دولد ضو بو وعلي ولده
ومضوي مقدم القواويد والطاهر الغدوي وعمر الغدوي وحسن قواد الشيخ وزايد
الحراس ومصطفي السودان وسعيد المراجنة واسماعيل اخو الشيخ رحمة وتقله
اخيه وشوال اخيه ورمضان وعلي ولده وصابون وكوباب وعبد العاطي
والارباب ابراهيم ولد بدوي ومصطفى الاحرف محمد ابن الفقيه احمد
كاتب وشاهد ضحا الخميس ثلاثة وعشرين في ذي الحجة
سنة مائة وستة واربعين من بعد الالف من الهجرة النبوية
على ساكنها افضل الصلاة وازكى التسليم

PLATE I

حجة سلطانية ووثيقة ملوكية من حضرة سلطان الاسلام وجامع كلمة
الايمان ومدمر اهل البغا والطغا مالك ملوك البر والبحر ناظم مصالح جماهير الامم ماسس
بناء الكرم والالطاف هادم اساس ورد الاعتساف الذي اذا توجه استقبله
الغنم والظفر من ارتع المسلمين سحايب فضله الذي اختاره الله على العباد امينا وكان
الله حافظا وامينا مولانا السلطان ابن السلطان الملك المظفر المجاهد السلطان
بادي ابن المرحوم السلطان نول زيدت ايام عدله وجددت ليالي سعده بجاه محمد واله
امين الى الكل من تقف عليه هذه الوثيقة والناظر لها فيها من الحقيقة وبعد
فان السلطان المبرور المؤيد المنصور تمم وامضا ما فعله الشيخ رحمه ابن الشيخ يونس
من الصدقة على الشيخ يعقوب ابن الشيخ محمد زين بدار فجارض ام رحيك صدقة
ابتغاء لوجه الله تعالى وطلبا للثواب في يوم الماب وهي معلومة الحد وربع وثيقة
الشيخ رحمه المذكور من الجهات الاربعة من الصبح الطنضبة وتقرهتو له ومن الصعيد
عزاز جروره وجعفر ولد بلال ومن الغرب ام راحيك يمشي الحد بنظره مسغل
الى عند درب ام طلحة يمشي الحد مصبح بناظر الطنضبة ويركز فوق طين الشيخ يعقوب
المشتري لاحد لغرب ولا يدنيه ولا يقف له على طريق وحبله المرمي لايشيله زول
وماءه الازرق لا يشرك به في ذالك سالمة من جميع الشرور والمضار والحذر ثم الحذر
من المخالفة والمخالف لا يلوم الا نفسه حضر ذالك وشهد به الشيخ رحمه ابن
الشيخ يونس ومحمد يونس الجعفري والشيخ اسماعيل خال الملك والارباب ابدو جد الملك
والشيخ شاء الدين درويش شيخ البحر والشيخ محمد شيخ العربين والشيخ محمد
مقدم السجادة والقاضي ابراهيم والخطيب عبد اللطيف وعمار ابو النقا ومسطر
الوثيقة محمد عبد الغني وكفا بالله شهيدا اول يوم من محرم لسبعة
واربعين ومايه بعد الالف من الهجرة النبوية على صاحبها افضل الصلاة
والسلام

PLATE II

هاذه صورة وثيقة سلطانية

الحمد لله والصلاة والسلام على خاتم رسل الله الكرام

باسمك يا كريم — بسم الله الرحمن الرحيم

حجة سلطانية محررة مرضية بالديار الفنجية بمدينة سنار المحروسة المحببة جعلها الله تعالى لدى منوبها وابن منوبها
ملكا اعنتها وقاصيها ودانيها وحاضرها وباديها والحاكم يومئذ بمن عليها ومن فيها من نهاب الرجال وتخشى من صولته الابطال
يوم الحرب والنزال المعتصم بالله الديان الشيخ محمد ابن المرحوم الوزير الشيخ عدلان نصره الله آمين الى حضرت كل من تقع عليه
هذه الوثيقة والناظر لما فيها من الحقيقة وبعد ان المحفوظ المبرور والمؤيد المنصور الشيخ محمد تصدق على الفقيه محمد علي ولد
العباس بدار من طين عجيب رمز مسطر موان صدقة لله ولرسوله وليوم لا ينفع فيه مال ولا بنون الا من اتى الله بقلب سليم والدار معلومة
البقعة والحدود وحدها من جهة الصبح دار الشيخ الطريفي ولد الشيخ يوسف ومن جهة السافل فوق الطنا ضب وولد
محمود ومن جهة الغرب عد مليحه وفوق جنيد وفوق شرف الدين ولد دوره وحسين ولد دوره وفوق فولة تمبين
ومن جهة الصعيد فوق دارفور ودار خميس ولد جنقل هناك انتهت الحدود وصارت الدار المذكورة بحدودها
المعلومة للفقيه محمد علي ولد العباس ملكا وحوزا وتصرفا وله ولذريته وذريت ذريته يتوارثونها من وارث الى وارث
حتى يرث الله الارض ومن عليها وهو خير الوارثين لا ينازعه فيها منازع ولا يتعرض له فيها متعرض سالمة مسلمة
من جميع الشروط [illegible] والمضار لا عليها جبايه و[illegible] ولا [illegible] ولا [illegible] ولا [illegible] [illegible] ولد [illegible]
ولا قوار ولا نزول ولا محلاة ولا منورت ولا كلفة ولا حل ولا حل ونؤكد عليكم يا جميع الشيوخ والمقاديم وحصوص [illegible] وكل
من يات بعده انتم وجرايكم ومن يات من وراءكم الى قيام الساعة لا احد منكم يتعرض للفقيه محمد علي في هاذه ولا احد منكم يتعرض
لذريته ولا ذريت ذريته ومن يتعرض له بعد كلامي هذه فقد عرض نفسه للهلاك والحذر ثم الحذر من الخلاف
والمخالف لا يلوم الا نفسه والسلام وقد حضر ذلك وشهد به الشيخ احمد ولد النور شيخ الغوارية والشيخ عدلان ولد شنبول
شيخ ابركي والارباب قاسم ولد الشيخ محمد والارباب نفر اخيه والارباب ادريس ولد باد والارباب موسى اخيه والارباب محمد ولد حسين
والارباب حسن اخيه والارباب محمد ولد ادريس والارباب علي اخيه والارباب حسن ولد رجب والارباب ابراهيم اخيه والارباب ناصر ولد الارباب
رجب والارباب ادريس والارباب ابراهيم والارباب حسن والارباب عيساوي والارباب علي ابناء المرحوم الوزير الشيخ عدلان والارباب
دفع الله احمد والارباب دفع الله محمد والارباب ابراهيم عويسة والارباب علي الياس والارباب علي ولد محمد والارباب احمد ابن الحاج سليمان
والارباب خوجلي ولد خالد وحسن ولد عوض الله وحسين اخيه والشيخ فرج الله والشيخ تبغره والارباب عبد الله ولد سكوت والارباب
محمد ولد جميل الله والارباب محمد ولد كاب والمنكروك تخيته والمنكروك كروسه وعلي ابو زيد وعدلان ولد محجوب وفضل كرن دوس وعبد الرحيم
ولد البيت وعيد ولد البيت وحامد ولد البيت واحمد ولد البيغره والكاتب احمد الحلبي وكفى بالله شهيدا وقع ذلك يوم الخميس نهار عشرة
ايام من شهر الله المحرم سنة ١٢٣٨ الف وماتين وثمانية وعشرين من هجرة سيد المرسلين صلى الله عليه وسلم وارضى اللهم صحابه اجمعين والسلام

PLATE III

هاذه صورة وثيقة سلطانية ١

باسمك يا كريم بسم الله الرحمن الرحيم الحمد لله والصلاة والسلام على خاتم رسل الله الكرام

حجة سلطانية محررة مرضية بالديار الفنجية بمدينة سنار المحروسة المحمية اجلها الله تعالى لدى متوليها وابن متوليها مالك عقنها
وقاصيها ودانيها وحاضرها وباديها والحاكم يومئذ بمن عليها ومن فيها قنديل الزمان وسراج البلدان ومدمر اهل المنكر والبغي
والطغيان وامين جيش السلطان الواثق بالله الصمد الوزير الشيخ حسين بن المرحوم الوزير الشيخ محمد ابو لكيلك نصره الله
وامين الحضرة كل من تقف عليها هاذه الوثيقة والناظر فيها من الخليفة وبعدان المحفوظ المبرور المؤيد المنصور الوزير
الشيخ حسين شمم واعطى ما فعله السلطان محمد عدلان الى الفقيه محمد علي العباسي من طين دار عجيب ارض مطر موان
وانا الوزير حسين شمم واعطيت للفقيه محمد علي العباسي ابتغاء مرضات الله تعالى وطلبا للثواب في دار المئاب واليوم
لا ينفع فيه مال ولا بنون الا من اتى الله بقلب سليم والدار معلومة البقعة والحدود وتحدها من جهة الصبح
دار الشيخ الطريفي ولد الشيخ يوسف ومن جهة السافل فوق اسطا صنب وولد محمود ومن الغرب عد مليحه
وفوق جنين وفوق شرف الدين ولد دوره وحسين ولد دوره وفوق فولت شمين ومن جهة الصعيد فوق دار فور
ودار خميس ولد جنقل هناك انتهت الحدود وصارت الدار المذكورة بحدودها المعلومة ملكا للفقيه محمد علي العباسي له
ولذريته وذرية ذريته يتوارثونها من وارث الى وارث حتى يرث الله الارض ومن عليها وهو خير الوارثين لا ينازعه
فيها منازع ولا يتعرض له فيها متعرض سالمة مسلمة من جميع الشرور والسبل والمضار لا عليها جارة ولا خسارة
[illegible] ولا عانة ولا حسب ولا دم [illegible] ولا ازريبة ولا ضيافة ولا علوق [illegible]
ونؤكد عليكم ايها الشيوخ والمعاديد والجاري لا احد منكم يتعرض للفقيه محمد علي العباسي خصوصا حسان [illegible] وجماعتك
الى قيام الساعة لا احد منكم يتعرض له ومن تعرض له بعد كلامي وو[illegible] هذه فقد عرض نفسه للهلاك والحذر ثم الحذر من الخلاف
والمخالفة لليوم الا نفسه حضر ذلك وشهد به الشيخ وارث ولد [illegible] امين السلطان والجندي كتفاوا جند السوق والشيخ
ناصر ولد الامين شيخ قري والشيخ محمد ولد بدر شيخ اليس والشيخ [illegible] ولد الفضيل شيخ النهر والشيخ منو ولد احمد
شيخ البحر والشيخ محمد العركي شيخ بيله والشيخ النور ولد محمد شيخ القريبين والشيخ محمد ولد ادريس شيخ حوش ولد مكر
والشيخ عدلان ولد شنبول شيخ اربجي والارباب حمد ابن المرحوم الوزير الشيخ عدلان وقاسم ولد محمد ونصر ولد محمد والارباب
دفع الله محمد والارباب ابراهيم عويضه واحمد ولد محمد ابو القاسم والمكروكي فرج الله والمكروكي نبطره والمكروكي
عبد الله ولد سكوت والمكروكي فضل الله ولد سلامة والمكروكي عبد البين والمكروكي حمد السيد وفضل ولد قاسم
مقدم المهر والكاتب احمد المكي وكفى بالله شهيدا وقع ذلك يوم السبت نهار اثنا عشر من شهر الله المحرم سنة ١٢٢٨
الف ومايتين وثمانية وعشرين من هجرة سيد المرسلين صلى الله عليه وسلم وارضى اللهم عن اصحابه اجمعين

PLATE IV

Arkell Papers form two pairs, each consisting of one originating and one confirmatory charter. The first pair (Arkell I and II) is early in date, and is of interest since none of the sultanic confirmations published by Dr. Abu Selim is accompanied by its originating charter. The second pair (Arkell III and IV) was issued in the reign of Bādī VI, the last Funj sultan, during the period of the Hamaj regency.

2. *The Structure of the Charters*

The four documents under consideration conform to the pattern of the charters published by Dr. Abu Selim. Each charter falls into three main sections; namely, the introductory formulae, the body of the text, and the concluding formulae.

(a) *Introductory Formulae*

In the original charter, the introductory formulae would begin with an *invocatio* consisting probably of the *basmala* and *ḥamdala*. These are missing in Arkell I and II; of the six charters of Bādī IV published by Dr. Abu Selim, not all have these elements, and where they are present, they display some variation. The closest in time to Arkell II is AS 30 (Sha'bān 1145/January–February 1733), which has no *basmala*, but opens with a *ḥamdala*.[3] In the second pair of documents (Arkell III and IV) the *invocatio* is of an elaborate type, consisting of a double and rhyming *basmala*; and a rhyming *ḥamdala*. The double *basmala* had, however, appeared in an earlier charter of Bādī IV (AS 29; Rajab 1141/January–February 1729), and a very elaborate *ḥamdala* appears in one of his later charters (AS 18; Rajab 1166/May–June 1753). The *invocatio* would, in an original document, be followed by the seal. This is lacking in these transcriptions, but Dr. Arkell has indicated the place of the royal seal in Arkell II, while in Arkell I he has copied a validating mark, used in lieu of a seal. The seal of Bādī IV is known from Dr. Abu Selim's collection; it bears a rhyming inscription and the date 1137/1724–5. The use of validating marks instead of seals is also known from two documents (AS 31, 32).[4]

The character of the document is then described in a dual formula. In Arkell I, the first portion of this is reduced, but Arkell II gives a full rhyming formula: *ḥujja sulṭāniyya wa-wathīqa mulūkiyya*. Both parts of the formula present problems. The phrase *ḥujja sulṭaniyya*, "a sultanic title-deed", appears to have been used not only (as would be expected) in documents emanating from the Funj sultan, but also in those of the Hamaj who usurped his position. It occurs in Arkell III and IV, and also in a fragmentary document published by Dr. Abu Selim (AS 32): all these are Hamaj charters. By contrast, the phrase does not occur in the charters of the 'Abdallābī viceroys of Qarrī, who were traditionally second in status to the Funj sultan. In their documents, the terms used are *ḥujja far'iyya* (AS 6, 25, 26), *qaṭ'iyya* (AS 7, 8, 10, 17) and *'ādiyya* (AS 24).[5] The second portion of the formula, *wathīqa mulūkiyya,* is curious, both because of the unusual form of the adjective, and because it would seem to be an example of parallelism. But this phrase also appears in charters that do not emanate from sultans or the Hamaj. In Dr. Abu Selim's collection, it is used by two 'Abdallābī viceroys (AS 6, 8) and a tribal chief (AS 27), while in Arkell I it is used by the grantor of the estate, an official of Bādī IV. Its meaning should therefore perhaps be elicited from a corresponding phrase in other documents. Three published by Dr. Abu Selim (AS 5, 7, 10—the last two emanating from 'Abdallābī viceroys) use the term *wathīqa 'urfiyya,* i.e. a charter based on *'urf,* custom or usage not resting upon the *Sharī'a.* The adjective *mulūkiyya* may therefore imply that the validity of the document derives from the customary power of the issuing authority, whether sultan, viceroy, official or chief, and not signify "royal" in the strict sense.

The next element in the introductory formulae is the *intitulatio,* the listing of the titles and honorifics of the issuing authority. Here the best starting-point is Arkell II, which is the latest of three extant charters of Bādī IV (the others are AS 29, 30) written by the royal clerk Muḥammad b. 'Abd al-Ghanī. In all these charters, the titulary opens with the phrase *min ḥaḍrat . . . ,* "from the presence of . . .", followed by a string of honorifics which vary in each instance. This is a different opening from that in all the later sultanic charters, written by other clerks. The earliest of these (AS 1), written in 1156/1743–44, during the reign of Bādī IV, may be taken as an example. After the formula characterizing the document, its place of issue, Sinnār, is specified. The epithets describing Sinnār, viz. *al-maḥrūsa al-maḥmiyya,* "the [divinely] guarded and protected", were applied in Ottoman usage to Cairo and Istanbul, but were elsewhere used in connexion with other great Muslim cities.[6] The titulary is then introduced with the words *ladā mutawallīhā,* "in the presence of her warden", and honorifics. In both the earlier and the later charters, the titulary then proceeds with the formula *mawlānā al-sulṭān ibn al-sulṭān,* "our lord the sultan, the son of the sultan", whose name and patronymic are given.

The other three Arkell documents belong broadly to the second pattern described above, in that they begin by specifying the place of issue, Sinnār, and introduce the *intitulatio* proper with the phrase *ladā mutawallīhā.* The term *mutawallī,* here perhaps best translated "warden", is thus used of the sultan and his officials indiscriminately.

A series of honorifics follows, concluding with the name of the grantor of the charter. In Arkell I, this is Shaykh Raḥma b. Yūnus, entitled *amīn al-sulṭān*; in Arkell III, Shaykh Muḥammad b. ʿAdlān, and in Arkell IV, Shaykh Ḥusayn b. Muḥammad Abī Likaylik, entitled *amīn jaysh al-sulṭān* and *wazīr*. The *intitulatio* concludes, in all four charters, with a prayer (*du*ʿ*a*) for the grantor of the charter.

(b) *The Body of the Text*

This portion of the charter gives the essential information about the grant, beginning with the names of the donor of the estate and its recipient, as well as (in Arkell II and IV) the name of the confirming authority. The precise nature of the grant is defined; as alms (*ṣadaqa*) in all four documents, but with additional terms emphasizing the recipient's absolute possession in freehold in Arkell III (*milk wa-ḥawz wa-taṣrīf*) and less fully in Arkell IV (*milk*). The delimitation of the estate granted, with reference to the four cardinal points, is characteristic of both originating and confirming charters. The usages *al-sāfil* (or a derivative), "downstream", and *al-ṣa*ʿ*īd*, "up-stream", for north and south respectively, may be noted.

The grant of land is accompanied by the concession of certain immunities. In Arkell I these amount to no more than a general interdict on interference with the emissary (*mirsāl*) of Shaykh Raḥma b. Yūnus, the donor. This term would appear to mean the recipient, Shaykh Yaʿqūb, regarded as the bearer of a message (i.e. the charter) from the donor. In the confirmatory charter (Arkell II) the immunities are more detailed, albeit the phraseology is obscure: their import would appear to be that the recipient is secured against interference, his goods, however trifling, are sacrosanct, and that his water-rights on his estate are absolute. The exemption of the estate from *shurūr* and *maḍārr*, here translated "evils" and "damages", may refer to specific extortions.

In Arkell III and IV, charters granted at a time when political conditions in the Funj territories were anarchic, the immunities are specified in detail and at length. As we have already seen, the legal status of the estate as *milk* is emphasized, and the recipient is declared not to be subject to litigation or trespass. In the list of exemptions, the terms *shurūr* and *maḍārr*, already met with, are associated with *s.b.l.*, perhaps to be read *subul* and possibly signifying (as translated) "rights of way". A list of levies from which exemption is granted then follows. The terms (but not the order) are the same in both charters, with the exception that *kalīgha* in Arkell III is replaced by ʿ*ulūq* in Arkell IV. These and other terms relating to exemptions are defined by Dr. Abu Selim: he does not give the sources of his information, and different interpretations of some of them have been given by other writers.[7] It is perhaps also significant of the decline of the Hamaj regency that whereas in Arkell II the body of the text ends with a general warning against disobedience, this in Arkell III and IV is preceded by a peremptory command, addressed in precise terms to various types of officials, and even specifically to a certain Ḥassān, restraining them from trespass upon the estate granted.

(c) *Concluding Formulae*

A characteristic feature of these four charters, as of those published by Dr. Abu Selim, is the list of witnesses attesting the document. A comparison may usefully be made between Arkell II and the two other known charters of Bādī IV written by the royal clerk, Muḥammad b. ʻAbd al-Ghanī. Of the eleven witnesses to Arkell II (1147/1734) ten also attest AS 30 (1145/1733), and five of these also witness the earliest of the three charters, AS 29 (1141/1729). Almost a decade intervenes between Arkell II and the next known charter of Bādī IV, AS 1 (1156/1743–4), which was written by a different royal clerk, Yaʻqūb Ḥumayrā, and appears (the document is damaged) to have no names of witnesses in common with it.

3. *Historical and Biographical Notes*[8]

(a) *Arkell I and II*

Arkell II, the confirmatory charter of Arkell I, is dated 1 Muḥarram 1147/3 June 1734, and is the third oldest of the known charters of Sultan Bādī IV, being preceded only by AS 29 (Rajab 1141/Jan.–Feb. 1729), and AS 30 (Shaʻbān 1145/Jan.–Feb. 1733).[9] Bādī IV b. Nūl reigned from 16 Shawwāl 1136/8 July 1724 to 2 Ramaḍān 1175/27 March 1762, and is the earliest Funj sultan whose charters are extant. His father and predecessor, Nūl, had been appointed sultan on 1 Shaʻbān 1132/8 June 1720, after a revolt of the Funj against the previous monarch, Ūnsa III. The facts that Nūl was connected only on his mother's side with the old royal clan, the Ūnsāb; that he died after a short reign; and that Bādī IV succeeded as a minor, all contributed to a weakening of the royal authority, of which the concessions of estates and exemptions may be a symptom, if not a consequence. Bādī IV's efforts, on assuming personal rule, to re-establish the royal power, produced in the end another revolt of the Funj in which he too was deposed. The beneficiary of this *coup* was its manager, Shaykh Muḥammad Abū Likaylik, a man who was of Hamaj (i.e. neither Funj nor Arab) origin. Effective power was henceforward in the hands of Abū Likaylik and his kinsmen who succeeded him, nominally as *wazīrs*, in fact as regents of the Funj sultans.

Shaykh Raḥma b. Yūnus, the grantor of the originating charter, Arkell I, is there described as *amīn al-sulṭān.* The title of *amīn* appears to have been held by the chief of the sultan's officials before the establishment of the Hamaj regency. A revolt against Sultan Bādī III (1103–28/1692–1716) was headed by the *amīn* Irdāb, who is also described as *amīn al-Funj.* In a war between the Funj sultan and the Abyssinians in 1157/1744, Bādī IV put the *amīn*, whose name is not given, in command over his army. A later sultan, 'Adlān II, who tried to regain power from the Hamaj regent, similarly put an *amīn* named Raḥma w. Kitfā[10] in command of his army. The position of *amīn jaysh al-sulṭān*, the *amīn* of the sultan's army, was, as Arkell IV shows, distinct from that of *amīn al-sulṭān.*

There is fairly clear evidence from the charters that the office of *amīn al-sulṭān* was hereditary in the reigns of Bādī IV and his successors. Raḥma b. Yūnus, whom we know from Arkell I to have been *amīn al-sulṭān*, heads the list of witnesses to the confirmatory charter, Arkell II. The implication that the first witness to a royal charter is the *amīn al-sulṭān* is supported by Arkell IV, where alone this title is appended to the name of the first witness, Wāwrit (?Wārit) b. Hārūn.[11] From this evidence, eight members of the family in three generations held the office of *amīn al-sulṭān.* Four members of the family held the title of *jundī* or *jundī al-sūq*, a post which seems to have had some of the police functions associated with the officers of the *shurṭa* in other Islamic societies. For details of the family see Table 1.

The recipient of the estate granted in Arkell I and II, Shaykh Ya'qūb b. Muḥammad [al-] Zayn, was a member of an old-established holy clan, the Ya'qūbāb, which went back to the early Funj sultanate.[12] His ancestor in the fourth generation, Bān al-Naqā Muḥammad al-Ḍarīr, was related through his mother to the Funj, and was at one time the *jundī* of Sultan Nāyil (940–57/1533–51). Bān al-Naqā was one of the first Nilotic Sudanese initiates into the Qādiriyya *ṭarīqa*, of which his family became hereditary local heads. Several members of the clan receive notices in the *Ṭabaqāt* of Wad Ḍayfallāh: see Table 2.

Among the witnesses to Arkell II, the *Khaṭīb* 'Abd al-Laṭīf was the son and successor as *khaṭīb* at Sinnār of a scholar named 'Ammār b. 'Abd al-Ḥafīẓ. He was a Shafi'ite jurist, and after a clash with a Funj sultan (? Bādī IV) made the Pilgrimage to Mecca. After an accusation by members of his family, he was put to death by Bādī IV—an act for which his biographer sees retribution in the death of the sultan and the downfall of the Funj. The Funj Chronicle places his death in the year 1170/1756–7.[13]

(b) *Arkell III and IV*

The date of Muḥarram 1228/January 1813 borne by these two charters presents serious difficulties, and must be rejected as, presumably, a copyist's error. The reasons for its unacceptability are: first, that three of the persons mentioned (Ḥassān and Farajallāh in Arkell III and IV, Ḥusayn w. 'Iwaḍallāh in Arkell III only) are identifiable as having died before 1228/1813; secondly, that the political situation in which Shaykh Ḥusayn b. Muḥammad Abī Likaylik was regent obtained only for a few months in 1223/1808.

The Hamaj regency, established by Muḥammad Abū Likaylik in 1175/1762, passed on his death to his paternal nephew, and then successively to four of his sons (see Table 3). The fourth of these, the sixth regent, 'Adlān, was killed (16 Ramaḍān 1218/30 December 1803) in a conspiracy led by Muḥammad w. Rajab and Muḥammad w. Nāṣir (referred to subsequently by their patronymics, Walad Rajab and Walad Nāṣir), the sons of the third and fourth regents. Walad Rajab thereupon became regent, but the political situation was most complex and unstable and he was soon at open enmity with Walad Nāṣir. The intermittent struggles of Walad Rajab and Walad Nāṣir (who made his headquarters at Kasala) occupied the next few years. In 1221/1806 Walad Nāṣir set up his uncle, Ḥusayn b. Muḥammad Abī Likaylik, as anti-regent. Then in Rajab 1222/Oct.–Nov. 1807, Walad Nāṣir was poisoned. The Nasirid faction did not, however, disappear: it was held together by Muḥammad w. Ibrāhīm (referred to subsequently as Walad Ibrāhīm), another grandson of Abū Likaylik, and by the solidarity of Walad Nāṣir's slave-household. The slaves were indeed the real holders of power, and appointed one of themselves, Tayfara, or al-Tayfara (mentioned in Arkell III and IV) in the place of a regent. Shortly afterwards, however, they conferred a nominal regency on Muḥammad w. 'Adlān (referred to subsequently as Walad 'Adlān), the son of the sixth regent, who was in their power. There were thus, in 1223/1808, three claimants to the regency: Walad Rajab, Ḥusayn b. Muḥammad Abī Likaylik, and Walad 'Adlān.

In the middle of the year (summer 1808), Walad Ibrāhīm (in agreement with Tayfara) succeeded in breaking the independent power of the Nasirid slave-household (and by implication invalidating the regency of Walad 'Adlān), confirmed the regency of Ḥusayn, and captured Walad Rajab, who was put to death by Walad 'Adlān to avenge the killing of his father. The Rajabid faction was thus overthrown, but hostility immediately developed between Walad Ibrāhīm and Walad 'Adlān. This is the situation reflected in Arkell III and IV. Arkell IV represents Ḥusayn as bearing the title of *wazīr* and functioning as regent by confirming Arkell III. Bādī VI, who as sultan might have been expected to confirm the charter, was a figure-head. It may be noted, however, that several of the honorifics bestowed on Ḥusayn in Arkell IV are also bestowed on Walad 'Adlān in the originating charter, an indication perhaps of his former status or continuing ambitions. On 23 Jumādā II 1223/16 August 1808, Walad 'Adlān's slaves inflicted a heavy defeat on Walad Ibrāhīm, and Walad 'Adlān was recognized as regent. He retained this position until he was murdered in Rabī' II 1236/Jan.–Feb. 1821, on the eve of the Turco-Egyptian conquest.

The purpose of the grant in Arkell III and IV was clearly to build up support for Walad 'Adlān against his rival, Walad Ibrāhīm. The beneficiary, Muḥammad 'Alī w. al-'Abbās, may almost certainly be identified with a former minister (*wazīr*) of Walad Nāṣir, who conspired with Walad 'Adlān against Walad Ibrāhīm but was put to death when the plot failed. It was, in fact, a sudden and unexpected reversal of fortune after the failure of this plot which brought Walad 'Adlān to the regency in Jumādā II 1223/August 1808. After he had achieved power, a brother of the beneficiary, the *faqīh* Madyan w. al-'Abbās, was one of Walad 'Adlān's chief assistants. Another of Walad 'Adlān's partisans mentioned in the charters was Farajallāh, who had been closely associated with him since the death of the Regent 'Adlān in 1218/1803. The non-Arabic title *mankarūkan*, which he and Tayfara bear in Arkell III, presumably indicates a rank in the slave-household. Others who are mentioned in the Funj Chronicle as leading associates of Walad 'Adlān were the *arbābs*, 'Alī Ilyās and Dafa'allāh Aḥmad, and Ḥusayn w. 'Iwaḍallāh, as well as Tayfara himself. It is relevant to notice that Ḥassān, against whom special immunity is granted in the charters, is described in the Funj Chronicle as a famous horseman of the retinue of Walad Ibrāhīm, and was killed in the fight that brought Walad 'Adlān to power.

[Tables 1–3 follow

Table 1: The Hereditary Amīns *and* Jundīs

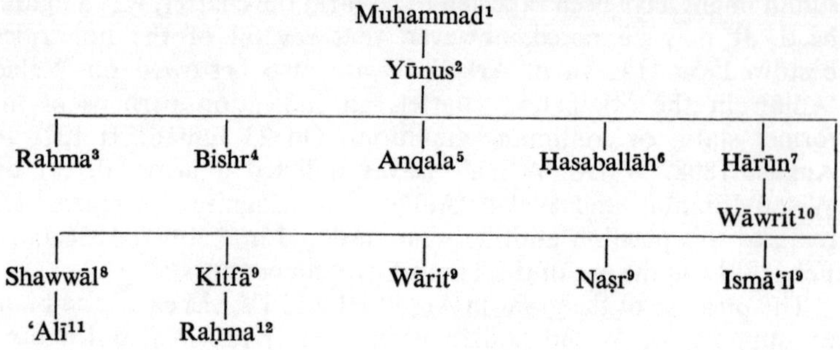

Notes

[1] Muḥammad, *jundī* (AS 29).
[2] Yūnus, *amīn* (AS 29); *fl.* 1141/1729.
[3] Raḥma, *amīn* (AS 30, Arkell I, II), *fl.* 1145–7/1733–4.
[4] Bishr, *amīn* (AS 1, 2, 3), *fl.* 1156–7/1743–5.
[5] Anqala, *amīn* (AS 18), *fl.* 1166/1753.
[6] Ḥasaballāh, *amīn* (AS 12, 16), *fl.* 1177–9/1763–5.
[7] Hārūn, *jundī* (AS 12, 16), 1177–9/1763–5; *amīn* (AS 21, 22, 28), 1184–1206/1770–91. In *FC* 25 he is entitled *amīn* by anticipation.
[8] Shawwāl, *jundī* (AS 21, 22), *fl.* 1184–95/1770–81.
[9] Mentioned in Arkell I.
[10] Wāwrit, *amīn* (Arkell IV), *fl.* 1228/1813.
[11] 'Alī, *jundī* (AS 28), *fl.* 1206/1791.
[12] Raḥma, *amīn* (*FC* 35), *fl.* 1203/1788–9.

Table 2: The Ya'qūbāb

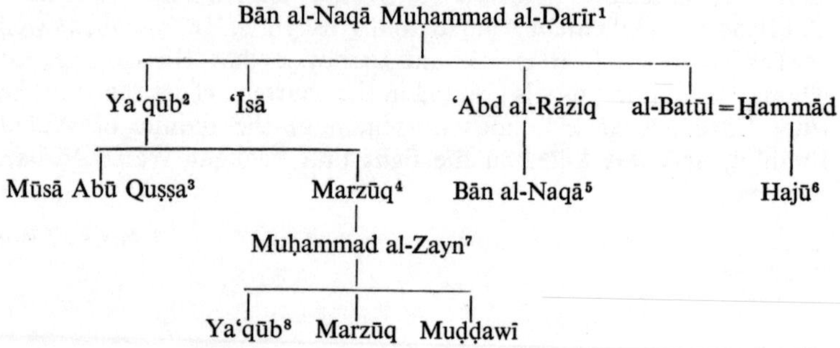

Notes

[1] Biography, *T*, 108–9.
[2] Biography, *T*, 372–3.
[3] Biography, *T*, 324–8. Contemporary of Sultan Bādī II (1054–91/1644–80).
[4] Biography, *T*, 328.
[5] Biograph, *T*, 114–15.
[6] Biography, *T*, 368.
[7] Biography, *T*, 328.
[8] Arkell I, II.

Table 3: The Hamaj Regents

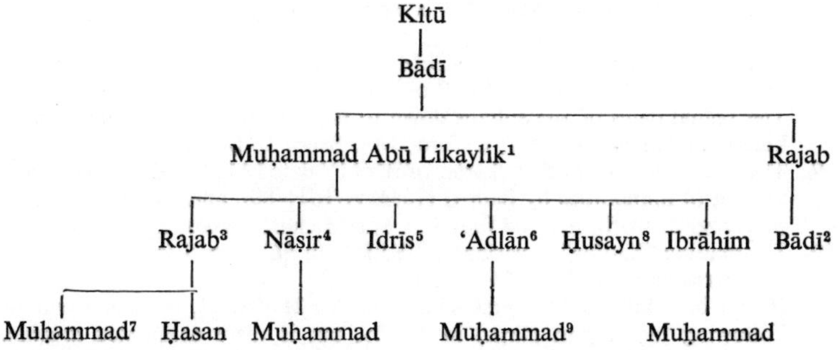

Notes

The table is based on data provided in the Funj Chronicle. The regents are numbered in order of succession:

[1] Muḥammad Abū Likaylik (1175–90/1762–1776 or 1777).
[2] Bādī w. Rajab (1190–4/1776 or 1777 to 1780).
[3] Rajab b. Muḥammad Abī Likaylik (1194—Muḥarram 1200/1780—Nov. 1785).
[4] Nāṣir b. Muḥammad Abī Likaylik (held effective power 1203–13/1788 or 1789 to summer 1798).
[5] Idrīs b. Muḥammad Abi Likaylik (early 1213—16 Jumādā II 1218/summer 1798—3 Oct. 1803).
[6] Adlān b. Muḥammad Abī Likaylik (Jumādā II—16 Ramaḍān 1218/Oct.—30 Dec. 1803).
[7] Muḥammad w. Rajab (1218–23/1803–8).
[8] Ḥusayn b. Muḥammad Abī Likaylik: rival to (7) (1221–3/1806–8).
[9] Muḥammad w. 'Adlān puppet regent (1222/1807); with full powers (23 Jumādā II 1223—Rab' II 1236/16 Aug. 1808–Jan.–Feb. 1821).

NOTES

1 M. I. Abu Selim (ed.), *Some land certificates from the Fung*, Sudan Research Unit; Occasional Papers, no. 2, Khartoum 1967 (in Arabic). Documents published in this book are indicated by AS, followed by the number of the document.

2 In the form *mancrocna*, this non-Arabic term is given as an alternative to *shauis* (*shāwīsh*, from Turkish *çavuş*) and glossed *ṣarrāf* in G. B. Brocchi, *Giornale delle osservazioni fatti nei viaggi . . . nella Nubia* (Bassano, 1841–3), v, 331 f. I am obliged to Mr. R. L. Hill for this information.

3 A photograph of this charter appears as Plate V to Sadik Nur, "Land tenure during the time of the Fung", *Kush*, IV, 1956, 48–53, on which no *basmala* appears, but it is not clear whether the document has been photographed in full. The *ḥamdala* begins *al-ḥamdu li-walīhi*, not *al-ḥamdu lillāhi*, as in AS 30.

4 For photographs of Bādī IV's seal, see Plates IV and V, and for validating marks, see Plate VI to Nur, "Land tenure", *ut sup*.

5 For Dr. Abu Selim's interpretation of these terms, see *Some land certificates from the Fung*, 19.

6 See John Wansbrough, "A Mamlūk commercial treaty concluded with the republic of Florence" in S. M. Stern (ed.), *Documents from Islamic chanceries*, Oxford 1965, where *al-maḥrūsa* is applied to Alexandria (p. 52), Cairo (p. 54) and Damascus (p. 56).

7 Abu Selim, op. cit., 31–33; cf. MacMichael, II, 79; J. A. Reid, "Some notes on the tribes of the White Nile Province", *SNR* XIII/2, 1930, 170.

8 The regnal dates of the sultans down to Ismā'īl are derived from Bruce's king-list (Bodleian Library, Oxford; MS. Bruce 18 (2), ff. 54b–57a).

9 The translation of another charter of Bādī IV dated 1145/1732–3, confirming a grant of immunities by Bādī II (1054–91/1644–80), and incorporated in a genealogical work, may be found in MacMichael, *Arabs*, II, 70–1.

10 The reading "Kitfāw" (a variant of "Kitfā") in *FC* 35, n. 5, is to be preferred to the reading "Kadnāwī" in the text.

11 Hārūn b. Yūnus, who is first witness in AS 21 and 22, is second witness (following the Regent Nāṣir) in AS 28, but is there designated *al-amīn*. Ḥasaballāh b. Yūnus is second witness (following the Regent Muḥammad Abū Likaylik) in AS 12, but first witness in AS 16.

12 Some information on the clan is to be found in Arkell, "Fung Origins" *ut sup.*

13 *T*, 299–300, 140–1; *FC*, 23.

7

HOLY FAMILIES AND ISLAM IN THE SUDAN

THE islamization of the Nilotic Sudan has been (and indeed still is) a continuing process. Since the Arab conquest of Egypt in the early seventh century, Nubia and the Upper Nile regions have been in contact with Islam, and the frontier of islamization has, during the last thirteen hundred years, moved southwards up the Nile in fairly well-defined stages. One such stage was inaugurated during the fourteenth century, when the northern Nubian kingdom of al-Muqurra with its capital at Old Dongola, gradually ceased to be Christian, and broke up into arabized principalities. A dark age ensued. When a clear historical tradition is resumed, in the opening years of the sixteenth century, the southern Nubian kingdom of ʻAlwa (which had its capital at Sūba, near modern Khartoum) had also foundered. Arab tribes had pushed southwards into the Gezira, between the Blue and White Nile, but the Arabs themselves were subject to alien overlords. These were the Funj: a dark-skinned people, whose immediate provenance (their remoter origins are highly controversial) was the upper Blue Nile.[1] They were quickly islamized, and so under their domination (which lasted nominally until the Turco-Egyptian conquest in 1821) the southern frontier of Islam was stabilized roughly along the line of 13° N. It was in this period of approximately three centuries, that the effective islamization of the northern Sudan was carried out, and this was the time in which the older holy families established themselves.

Wherein does the "holiness" of these families, and of their individual members, lie? In the first place, they act as agents for the transmission and propagation of the Islamic faith, its associated Holy Law, and Muslim culture. Secondly, they are traditionally regarded as possessors of *baraka*, which has been defined as "beneficent force, of divine origin, which causes superabundance in the physical sphere and prosperity and happiness in the psychic order".[2] *Baraka* is heritable, and the claim to possess it is closely linked with the further claim to be Sharīfs (*Ashrāf*), descended from the Prophet, and hence to derive *baraka* from this exalted source. The claims to Sharīfī descent and to the possession of *baraka* are thus not, as they may appear, arbitrary and gratuitous pretensions, but are closely linked with function, and are indeed a species of mechanism for validating the assumption of a certain role in traditional Islamic society. The point is brought out clearly in a discussion of the genealogy of a Sudanese holy man, Muḥammad b. Surūr, who lived in the seventeenth century. He was of Ja'alī origin, and his family tree followed the usual pattern, tracing the legendary ancestry of the Ja'aliyyīn to al-'Abbās, the uncle of the Prophet and the eponym of the 'Abbasid dynasty. When, however, Muḥammad b. Surūr assumed the role of a holy man (being initiated into the Qādiriyya order of Ṣūfīs, living a life of notable piety, and founding a mosque, where his tomb became a place of pilgrimage), an attempt was made to superimpose on his established pedigree a Sharīfī ancestry going back to the Prophet. This caused difficulty, and alternative solutions of the incongruity were proposed: one explaining that the descent from the Prophet was through the female line, the other that Muḥammad b. Surūr had been spiritually adopted by the Prophet in a vision.[3]

Ghulāmallāh b. 'Ā'id and his reputed descendants offer perhaps the best example of a family which owed its reputation chiefly to the teaching of religion and law. Other holy families were primarily important as providing a succession of Ṣūfī leaders. One such was the Ya'qūbāb. The founder of the family, Bān al-Naqā Muḥammad al-Ḍarīr, who was related to the Funj on his mother's side, was initiated into the Qādiriyya order about the middle of the sixteenth century by a wandering Ṣūfī from Baghdād. His descendants can be traced through as many as six generations to the early nineteenth century. One branch of the family established themselves in Ja'alī territory, where they were rivals of the descendants of Ṣughayirūn.

Some holy families, fulfilled the functions of both religious teachers and Ṣūfī leaders. Indeed, the distinction between the two roles is not always easy to draw in Sudanese Islam. This may be illustrated from linguistic usage. The colloquial term for a teacher, whether of religion or Sufism, is *fakī*, a dialect-form of *faqīh*, meaning in standard Arabic, a jurist. For its plural, however, *fakī* takes *fugarā*, i.e. *fuqarā'*, which has the standard meaning of dervishes, members of Ṣūfī orders. Again, the colloquial term for a Qur'anic school is *khalwa*, meaning in standard Arabic a Ṣūfī retreat.

A very interesting example of a Sudanese family who claimed *Sharīfī* descent, and acted as both religious teachers and Ṣūfī leaders, is provided by the Majādhīb of al-Dāmir, just south of the junction of the 'Aṭbarā with the Nile.[4] The founder of the family, a Ja'alī known as Muḥammad al-Majdhūb al-Kabīr (i.e. the Elder), flourished in the early eighteenth century. His son, Ḥamad, made the Pilgrimage to Mecca and was initiated into the Shādhiliyya order. He was a teacher and a practising jurist who gave *fatwās* and judgements, as well as being a famous Ṣūfī. He died in 1190/1776–77, and was buried at al-Dāmir.[5] His son, Aḥmad Qamar al-Dīn, born in 1159/1746–7, had an equally high reputation for scholarship and piety.[6] In effect, an indigenous sub-order, the Majdhubiyya, was formed locally by adherents of the family.

John Lewis Burckhardt, who visited al-Dāmir in 1814, has left a striking description of the town under Ḥamad's grandson Muḥammad al-Majdhūb al-Ṣaghīr, born in 1210/1795–6. His account throws light on several aspects of the role of a holy family.

> "Damer is a large village or town, containing about five hundred houses. It is clean, and much neater than Berber, having many new buildings, and no ruins. The houses are built with some uniformity, in regular streets, and shady trees are met with in several places. It is inhabited by the Arab tribe of Medja-ydin [*sic pro* Majādhīb], who trace their origin from Arabia; the greater part of them are Fokara or religious men. They have no Shikh, but a high pontiff, called El Faky el Kebir (the great Faky), who is their real chief, and decides all matters in dispute. The family of Medjdoule [*sic pro* Majdhūb], in whom this office is established, has the reputation of producing necromancers, or persons endowed with supernatural powers, from whom nothing remains hidden, and whose spells nothing can withstand. . . . Here are several schools, to which young men repair from Darfour, Sennaar, Kordofan, and other parts of Soudan, in order to acquire a proficiency in the law, sufficient to enable them to figure as great Fakys in their own countries. The learned men of Damer have many books, but they treat exclusively of religious and judicial subjects. . . . These books are brought from Cairo by the young Fakys of Damer themselves, many of whom go to study there in the mosque El Azher, or in the great mosque at Mekka, where they remain for three or four years, living during that time principally upon alms and stipends. . . .
>
> The affairs of this little hierarchical state appear to be conducted with great prudence. All its neighbours testify much respect for the Fakys; the treacherous Bisharein[7] even, are so completely kept in awe by them, that they have never been known to hurt any of the people of Damer when travelling from thence across the mountains to Souakin. They particularly fear the power of the Fakys to deprive them of rain, and thus to cause the death of their flocks. Caravans pass occasionally from Damer to Souakin, for many of the Fakys are traders. . . . There are several public wells in the town, as well as at some distance along the roads leading to it."[8]

Although the principal function of the holy families was to transmit and propagate the religion and culture of Islam, they had also (as this passage from Burckhardt shows) political and economic roles in Sudanese society. The Funj Sultanate, under which they developed and flourished, was a fragile domination. Outside its heartland on the upper Blue Nile, it exercised a lax and precarious hegemony, and the ruling dynasty was repeatedly weakened by inner tensions, the nature of which remains obscure. In 1762 the last effective sultan was deposed by a powerful minister, who established a permanent regency in his own family. But after his death, this regime, the Hamaj Regency, became the prey of warring factions, and when Muḥammad 'Alī Pasha's forces invaded the Sudan in 1820, the Funj Sultanate had disintegrated into a congeries of tribal monarchies.

By contrast with the frail and unstable dynasties of the rulers, the holy families acquired power and prestige, so that they became the true scaffolding of Sudanese society. The *fakīs*, like the men of religion in other Muslim lands, had a recognized place as mediators and intercessors. A notable example of this function was the intercession, about the year 1016/1607–8, of the great Ṣūfī shaykh, Idrīs al-Arbāb, when the Funj sultan, 'Adlān I, had defeated and killed his rebellious 'Abdallābī viceroy of the north, Shaykh 'Ajīb. The sons of Shaykh 'Ajīb fled to Dongola, but through the mediation of Idrīs they were pardoned and re-established in office. In places where, and at times when, the political rulers were weak, a *fakī* might himself acquire power. So, for example, Ḥasan b. Ḥassūna, the grandson of a Maghribī immigrant, established himself as a nomadic chief on the eastern fringes of the Funj Sultanate. He had a retinue of armed slaves and household officers imitated from those of the Funj court. His death in 1075/1664–5 was caused by the back-firing of a handgun—one of the very few recorded instances of firearms in the Sudan at this period.[9]

Ḥasan's political power was personal, and died with him. In the riverain lands, however, there is some evidence that the holy families strengthened their position, perhaps at the expense of the Funj dynasty itself, through land conceded to them by the sultans. These estates were granted by regular and formal charters.[10] They were not endowed as *waqf*, but conceded as free gifts (*ṣadaqa*). The family which had the greatest success in the acquisition of political power was the Majādhīb, who, as we saw in Burckhardt's description, established in the late eighteenth century a theocratic enclave in al-Dāmir. In theory, al-Dāmir was a portion of the tribal kingdom of the Ja'aliyyūn, which was subject to the 'Abdallābī viceroy descended from Shaykh 'Ajīb, who in turn was a dependant of the Funj sultan. In practice, as Burckhardt makes clear, *al-Fakī al-Kabīr* was its undisputed master.

Burckhardt also alludes to the economic role of the Majādhīb, who kept open the trade-routes, especially to Suakin on the Red Sea coast, through the fear that their *baraka* inspired. His reference to the activities of the *fakīs* themselves in trade throws light on one or two obscure passages in the *Ṭabaqāt*. A nephew of Ṣughayirūn, Ḥammūda, was nicknamed *Jayyāb al-ʿajwa min al-Rīf*, "the bringer of dates from Upper Egypt", because, according to the biographer, when dates were needed to cure Ṣughayirūn, Ḥammūda brought them from Egypt. A great-grandson of Ṣughayirūn named Abu'l-Ḥasan, who died in 1720 or 1721, maintained "companionship, brotherhood and union" with two *fakīs* of Nūrī in Shāyqiyya territory. Every year they would bring him gifts of northern produce, such as dates and *dom*-nuts, and he would give them bulls for cultivation and woven cloths. In both these anecdotes we surely catch a glimpse of organized trade passing up and down the Nile valley under the auspices of men of great religious prestige.

The decline of the Funj Sultanate and the establishment of the Hamaj Regency in the later eighteenth century were the harbingers of a period of profound changes and unsettlement in the Nilotic Sudan. The conquest of the former Funj dominions and of Kordofan by the troops of Muḥammad ʿAlī Pasha in 1820–1 inaugurated a more centralized and vigorous administration than the Sudanese had previously known. Europe began, at first indirectly, to make an impact on these remote peoples. The penetration of the upper White Nile and the Baḥr al-Ghazāl resulted in a southwards movement of the frontier of islamization after three centuries of stability, the consequences of which movement are still being felt. Apart from these basically political changes, there were also changes in the religious life of the Sudan, reflecting Islamic movements in the outside world. The eighteenth century witnessed a Ṣūfī revival, especially in the Arab provinces of the Ottoman Empire. The Naqshbandiyya order made considerable advances through the efforts of ʿAbd al-Ghanī al-Nābulusī of Damascus. A similar efflorescence of the Khalwatiyya resulted from the efforts of another Damascus shaykh, Muṣṭafā al-Bakrī al-Ṣiddīqī. In the Ḥijāz a new order came into existence, known as the Sammāniyya from its founder, Shaykh Muḥammad b. ʿAbd al-Karīm al-Sammān.

The Sammāniyya order was brought into the Nilotic Sudan by a certain Shaykh Aḥmad al-Ṭayyib b. al-Bashīr, who was born in 1155/1742–3, and was initiated into the order in Medina by its founder, about the year 1171/1757–8.[11] Shaykh al-Ṭayyib was the great-grandson of the holy man, Muḥammad b. Surūr, the problem of whose genealogy was mentioned earlier. He thus came from an established holy family, although a minor one: Muḥammad b. Surūr is the only member of it to find mention in the *Ṭabaqāt*. Under Shaykh al-Ṭayyib, however, the family achieved the kind of renewed surge forward that may be observed in the descendants of some other holy men. On his return to the Sudan, probably shortly before 1190/1776–7, after many years spent in the Ḥijāz and Egypt, Shaykh al-Ṭayyib acquired an immense reputation as a Ṣūfī teacher and worker of miracles. His principal residence was at Umm Marriḥi, north of Omdurman, where were the mosque and the tomb of Muḥammad b. Surūr, but he made a prolonged and initially successful visit to Sinnār and its vicinity, at the invitation of the Hamaj Regent Nāṣir b. Muḥammad Abī Likaylik between 1785 and 1798. He effected a miraculous cure of one of the regent's brothers, and was given an estate near Sinnār. There he remained for seven years, but finally, apparently after a clash with an old-established holy family of the district, he completely abandoned this holding and returned to Umm Marriḥi, where he died in 1239/1824. During his lifetime, he had built up a very large following for the Sammāniyya in the Sudan, and after his death the local headship of the order remained with his descendants.

Through Aḥmad al-Ṭayyib, a minor holy family had advanced to the first rank, and a new Ṣūfī order had been successfully established in the Sudan. This twofold achievement was repeated by his younger contemporary, Muḥammad 'Uthmān al-Mīrghanī, in the early and middle decades of the nineteenth century.[12] The Mīrghanī family seems at one time to have been domiciled in Central Asia (a remote ancestor was named Mīrkhōnd al-Bukhārī), but in the middle of the eighteenth century was resident in the Ḥijāz at Mecca and al-Ṭā'if. 'Abdallāh b. Ibrāhīm al-Mīrghanī, who died in 1207/1792–3, was an eminent Ṣūfī, and claimed Sharīfī descent. His obituary appears in al-Jabartī's chronicle.[13] Muḥammad 'Uthmān, 'Abdallāh's grandson, was a disciple of Aḥmad b. Idrīs al-Fāsī, in whose teaching both the mystical revival and the rigorist reforming spirit characteristic of the Wahhābīs, were combined.

On behalf of his master, Muḥammad 'Uthmān, then twenty-six years of age, made a propagandist tour of the Sudanese territories in 1232/1816–17—on the very eve, that is, of the Turco-Egyptian invasion. He spent some time in Dongola, in Kordofan (then administered by a governor from the sultan of Darfur), and at the Funj capital. In both Kordofan and Sinnār he met with opposition, but obtained some adherents. After the death of Aḥmad b. Idrīs al-Fāsī, Muḥammad 'Uthmān developed his own Ṣūfī order, sometimes called the Mīrghaniyya, but more usually the Khatmiyya. In the Sudan, he was followed as its head (after his death in 1853) by al-Ḥasan, his son by a woman of the Jallāba Hawwāra, a trading tribe belonging to the diaspora of riverain peoples.

Both the Sammāniyya and the Khatmiyya gained adherents in the Sudan at the expense of the older orders. This at times led to tension, such as that which caused Shaykh al-Ṭayyib to leave the vicinity of

Sinnār, and return to his ancestral home. It was, however, the Khatmiyya which aroused the greater odium. The coming of Muḥammad 'Uthmān coincided very nearly with the coming of the Turco-Egyptian invaders, and in Sudanese eyes the two events were connected. Aḥmad b. Idrīs al-Fāsī is reported by a Sudanese chronicler to have said that what befell the Sudan was because its people insulted Muḥammad 'Uthmān.[14] But, after the Turco-Egyptian regime had been established, the Khatmiyya flourished. Na'ūm Shuqayr, the Lebanese historian of the Sudan, quotes a Sudanese informant as follows:

> "The people, especially the heads of the orders, were also wronged by the preference shown to the Mīrghanīs above the other orders in the Sudan, so that their followers increased and their prestige became great. Although this did not explicitly originate from the government in Egypt, it was occasioned by it. For the administrators and holders of power among the departmental heads were not Sudanese, from whom they differed in their ways of eating, drinking, dress and dealings. So they tended to have to do with the Mīrghanīs, first because they resembled them, and secondly because the Mīrghanīs were connected with Mecca. For this reason, the Shāyqiyya troopers generally, because of their closeness to the governing people, inclined to them, and entered their order. . . . Thereby the authority of the Mīrghanī *khalīfas* increased, and they started to behave arrogantly towards the heads of the other orders, insulting and belittling them, so that they in turn bore rancour towards them and the government, which was the cause of their elevated status."[15]

Under the Turco-Egyptian regime, the status of the *fakīs* as a whole declined. Although the authorities were generally conciliatory towards them and subsidized their *khalwas*, the establishment of an official hierarchy of '*ulamā*' diminished both their prestige and their political functions. Access to Egypt, and hence to al-Azhar, was facilitated, so that the products of the traditional Sudanese schools were confronted with more authoritative expositors of the religious sciences. There thus developed the possibility of a schism between the official religious establishment, with which the Khatmiyya had close links, and the older indigenous Muslim leadership, less orthodox in its theology than the recognized '*ulamā*', but still with infinitely more appeal to the mass of the Sudanese.

For sixty years, however, the schism remained potential rather than actual. Sometimes the line of division between the two groups was obscured. A case in point is that of a holy family which had great influence in Kordofan. The founder of the family was a certain *fakī* of Dongola, named Bishāra al-Gharbāwī, who had studied under Ibrahīm al-Būlād, and flourished in the seventeenth century.

He received a grant of land from the Funj Sultan Bādī II (1054–91/1644–80) which was confirmed by Sultan Bādī IV in 1145/1732–3. Bishāra's descendant in the fourth generation, a merchant named 'Abdallāh, settled in Kordofan. There his son, Ismā'īl, became a teacher of religion, and acquired a great reputation for piety. At one time, Ismā'īl was closely attached to Shaykh Aḥmad al-Ṭayyib, but when Muḥammad 'Uthmān al-Mīrghanī visited Kordofan, he became his leading adherent. In 1842, he formed an autonomous order, the Ismā'īliyya of Kordofan, with a highly localized following. Ismā'īl's prestige is demonstrated by the fact that he is known as *al-walī*, "the saint", i.e. "the possessor of *baraka*". Unusually, the family did not claim to be *Ashrāf*, but were content with an 'Abbasid (i.e. Ja'alī) pedigree.[16]

Ismā'īl al-Walī left two sons. One of them, Muḥammad al-Makkī, succeeded him in the headship of the order in 1863, and died only in 1906, having in the meantime been one of the Mahdi's foremost supporters in Kordofan. The younger son, Aḥmad, had a very different career and fate. He spent twelve years as a student and teacher at al-Azhar (whence he was known as al-Azharī), and then returned to teach law in Kordofan. Unlike his brother, he strenuously opposed the claims of the Mahdi, which he denounced in a manifesto, written in 1882.[17] Shortly afterwards he was appointed *qāḍī* and *muftī* of the western Egyptian Sudan, and was killed in battle by the Mahdi's followers. His son, Ismā'īl al-Azharī (1868–1947) had a distinguished career as an Islamic jurist under the Condominium, finally holding the appointment of *muftī* of the Sudan.[18] The grandson of this man, another Ismā'īl al-Azharī, the founder of the nationalist *Ashiqqā'* party, became the first prime minister of the Sudan in January 1954, and saw the country through the final stages leading to independence two years later.

This survey has carried us rather ahead of our period. In passing, however, one may note that the role of Ismā'īl al-Walī in the islamization of Kordofan is a particular example of a widespread phenomenon. Not only Kordofan, but also Darfur and Waddāy, were probably to a very large extent converted by a diaspora of arabized Nubians (Ja'aliyyūn and Danāqla, that is to say) from the main Nile. Numerous western families and groups preserve traditions linking their ancestry with the River, and some of these traditions seem to go back to remote periods. There are, for example, foundation-legends in which a wise stranger from the River spreads enlightenment among an aboriginal people, into whose ruling family he marries. Such are found in connexion with the family ruling the Muslim enclave of Taqalī in the Nūba Mountains, and the Kayra dynasty, from which came the sultans of Darfur. Again, there are clans such as the Dawālīb in northern Kordofan who claim to be desdendants of Ghulāmallāh through a son (Rikāb) other than the ancestor of the Sons of Jābir.[19]

Sixty years after the Turco-Egyptian invasion, khedivial rule in the Sudan was threatened and ultimately overthrown by the Mahdia. The origins of this movement are complex, but in one aspect it was the vehicle of a protest by the indigenous and traditional Islamic leadership against the regime which had diminished their status. From this point of view, it was a revolt of the *fakīs*, and very appropriately its leader was a holy man who had undergone the traditional education of the Sudan. In the person of Muḥammad Aḥmad al-Mahdī, the last of the great holy families of the Sudan was to emerge.

A certain pattern is observable in the history of three families already discussed—those of Aḥmad al-Ṭayyib, the Mīrghanīs and Ismā'īl al-Walī—namely that their emergence was in two stages. In the first, the founder of the family—and by this I mean its first notable member, not its legendary ancestor—establishes a reputation for holiness, and perhaps a claim to *Sharīfī* descent. In the second, some generations later, the prestige of the family is revived and augmented by an individual who carries it forward into the front rank. This pattern can also be traced in the Mahdi's family. Traditions survive of a pious and holy man, six generations before Muḥammad Aḥmad, who may be regarded as the founder.[20] The family was then living in the vicinity of Dongola, and claimed to be *Ashrāf*. Virtually nothing is known of its members, however, before 'Abdallāh, the father of the Mahdi. He was a boat-builder, and moved up the Nile to the neighbourhood of Khartoum in search of timber. His sons continued the family craft after his death, except for Muḥammad Aḥmad, who studied in various *khalwas*, and was initiated into Sufism as a member of the Sammāniyya order. Subsequently, however, dissension arose between Muḥammad Aḥmad and the head of the order, Muḥammad Sharīf Nūr al-Dā'im, and from this point he began to act with increasing independence, until, on 1 Sha'bān 1298/29 June 1881, he publicly manifested himself as the Expected Mahdi.

In the four years that ensued, victories in the field and the collapse of khedivial power (consequent on 'Urābī's revolt in Egypt and the ensuing British occupation) transformed the Mahdi from the leader of a weak holy community, seeking refuge in the remoter parts of the Egyptian Sudan, into the territorial sovereign of an Islamic state. This had important results for the holy families of the Sudan. It brought to the fore a number of individuals and groups who had previously been only of minor importance, and it produced varied reactions among the older-established holy families.

The most obvious beneficiaries from the success of the revolt were the Mahdi's own kinsmen, to whom specifically the term *Ashrāf* was applied in the new regime. Their emergence at this stage was, however, curiously frustrated. During the Mahdi's lifetime, they had by no means a monopoly of power. Of the three *khalīfas*, who occupied the second position in the Mahdist state, only one (and he the most junior in both age and standing) was a relative of the Mahdi: this was *Khalīfat al-Karrār* Muḥammad Sharīf. Three or four other *Ashrāf* only seem to have had real authority or influence. As a group, however, they acquired a good deal of unpopularity because of the privileged position they had arrogated to themselves, and they were publicly denounced by the Mahdi himself only ten days before his death. They were thus in an unfavourable position for obtaining the succession when the Mahdi died after a short illness on 9 Ramaḍān 1302/22 June 1885, and the headship of the state passed to the Mahdi's closest assistant, the most senior of the three *khalīfas*, 'Abdallāhi b. Muḥammad. In spite of two attempts to seize power, in 1886 and 1891, the *Ashrāf* failed to obtain the position to which they felt themselves entitled.

This shift of sovereignty from the Mahdi's family bears a curious but fortuitous resemblance to what happened in the Almohad state, seven and a half centuries previously, when the Mahdi Muḥammad b. Tūmart was succeeded by 'Abd al-Mu'min. With the competition of the *Ashrāf* virtually eliminated, the Khalīfa 'Abdallāhi seemed well placed to found a Sudanese dynasty. His own family originated outside the boundaries of the Egyptian Sudan, between Waddāy and Bornu. His grandfather had travelled eastwards, intending to make the Pilgrimage to Mecca, but had settled among the Ta'āisha Baqqāra of Darfur, and married a woman of the tribe.[21] 'Abdallāhi's father had a reputation for piety and acted as a diviner, advising the tribe on the success or failure of their intended raids. 'Abdallāhi himself led his family further east in the troubled times which followed the khedivial annexation of Darfur (1874), and became a disciple of Muḥammad Aḥmad shortly before the Mahdia, which he may himself have instigated his master to proclaim.

After having established himself as head of the Mahdist state, 'Abdallāhi proceeded to entrench his own tribe, the Ta'āisha in general, and his own kinsmen in particular, in the chief positions. Throughout his reign, his half-brother, Ya'qūb, acted as his *wazīr*, with very great powers of control over the administration. In his later years, 'Abdallāhi was grooming his son, 'Uthmān, for the succession. 'Uthmān, who was given the honorific of *Shaykh al-Dīn*, "the Master of the Faith", appears to have been a young man of intelligence and insight, and, together with his uncle Ya'qūb, he served as one of the Khalīfa's chief advisers. In the event, of course, the Khalīfa's dynastic schemes collapsed: not so much because of inner weaknesses in the Mahdist state, as because of the superior military and technical resources of the Anglo-Egyptian forces under Kitchener's command. Ya'qūb died in battle in 1898, the Khalīfa similarly in the following year, while 'Uthmān *Shaykh al-Dīn* survived only a few months as a prisoner in Rosetta.

At the beginning of the Mahdi's revolt, much of his appeal was, as we have seen, to the *fakīs* and the old holy families. Some of these brought important bodies of adherents to his side. Muḥammad al-Makkī welcomed Muḥammad Aḥmad to his house at El Obeid, the provincial capital of Kordofan, even before he manifested himself as the Mahdi. Another religious leader with a large local following was the *fakī* al-Manna Ismā'īl, a member of the Sammāniyya order, whose ancestor in the fifth generation had emigrated from Ja'alī territory and attached himself to a group of Baqqāra, who moved from Darfur to Kordofan. The family had provided hereditary *fakīs* to these nomads (the Jawāma'a and the Jim'a) and so al-Manna was able to summon tribal warriors in support of the Mahdi. In the early days of the revolutionary war, he had enormous power, but his ambitions clashed with those of the Khalīfa 'Abdallāhi, and he was put to death in 1883.[22] Among the Bija nomads of the Red Sea Hills, the support of the Majādhīb was of critical importance to the Mahdi, and the circumstances in which it was given were significant. Since the eighteenth century (as Burckhardt's account suggests) the Majādhīb had been extending their influence over the Bija in the region between al-Dāmir and Suakin. The establishment by al-Ḥasan al-Mīrghanī of his headquarters near Kasala, about the middle of the century, created competition between the Majdhūbiyya and the Khatmiyya for the support of the tribes in the eastern Egyptian Sudan. At the Mahdia the two groups polarized, the Mīrghanīs and the Khatmiyya remaining loyal to the khedivial government, the Majādhīb and their adherents supporting the Mahdi. This was strikingly demonstrated when 'Uthmān Diqna, a former merchant from Suakin, was sent in 1883 as the Mahdi's emissary to the region. He was greeted by the influential head of the Majādhīb, Muḥammad al-Majdhūb al-Ṣaghīr's nephew and successor, Shaykh al-Ṭāhir al-Ṭayyib al-Majdhūb, who was able to swing on to the side of the Mahdi thousands of Bija tribesmen.[23] The long guerrilla warfare which 'Uthmān Diqna waged around Suakin and in the Red Sea Hills is a familiar episode of the Mahdia, but 'Uthmān owed his initial success largely to the decision of Shaykh al-Ṭāhir to support the Mahdi.

With the Mahdia began a new phase in the history of the Sudanese holy families. Although the Mahdia cannot be described (except in a very loose sense) as a national leader, he differed from earlier great *fakīs* in the overtly political aspect and the extensive scope of his aims. By assuming the title of *mahdī*, Muḥammad Aḥmad claimed a direct and divine authority for his acts, which rendered him superior to the governments of the khedive and the sultan, tainted as they were with infidelity. Through his proclamations and his decisions on points of law, he legislated for an Islamic theocracy, for which he created an administrative framework through his appointments to office. Ideally, the theocracy was to be universal: in practice, the Mahdi did not seriously look beyond the territories of the former Egyptian Sudan—and indeed the Mahdist state at its greatest extent never included all these. Nevertheless, the Mahdi and his successor were political sovereigns on a scale that dwarfed the achievement of the former Majādhīb rulers of al-Dāmir.

A second consequence of the Mahdia was the polarization of Sudanese Islam between the *Anṣār*, that is the followers of the Mahdi, and the adherents of the Mīrghanī family. The other holy families, however ancient, however numerous their following, fell into the background. At the beginning of the Condominium, this was not, indeed, apparent. The families of both the Khalīfa and the Mahdi had for all practical purposes been eliminated. Sayyid 'Alī al-Mīrghanī and his kin reaped the reward of their loyalty to the khedive, and were recompensed for their sufferings under the Mahdia.

The revival of the religious and political power of the Mahdi's family after a protracted eclipse of nearly forty years was the achievement of his posthumous son, 'Abd al-Raḥmān, whose mother was a princess of Darfur. 'Abd al-Raḥmān's youth was spent in disagreeable penury. Like all the surviving members of his family, he was suspect to the Condominium government, which long feared a recrudescence of Mahdism. The inner history of the resurgence of the family fortunes under his management has yet to be written, but some of the landmarks are clear.[24] During the twenties and thirties he gradually built up his wealth, mainly from cotton grown on the estates conceded to him by the Sudan Government. The ban which had been placed on the religious practices of the *Anṣār* was withdrawn, and 'Abd al-Raḥmān was able to build up a loyal body of adherents. While the mass of these were unsophisticated tribesmen, there was also a nucleus of educated and westernized townspeople, chiefly members of families who had supported the Mahdi in the previous generation. By the beginning of the Second World War, Sayyid 'Abd al-Raḥmān al-Mahdī was a leader of equal prestige and standing with his older rival, Sayyid 'Alī al-Mīrghanī.

It was against this background of two great holy families, each with a devout religious following, and standing in mutual opposition, that the politics of Sudanese nationalism emerged. The politically-conscious entourage of the leaders found in them the vehicle for mediating the new ideas to the masses, and in return obtained mass-support for their claims to national leadership. Nor was 'Abd al-Raḥmān al-Mahdī, at any rate, a passive instrument in the hands of his political associates. He has himself described the transformation of his religious following into a nationalist party:

> "I proclaimed [in 1924] the slogan which I have held until today, 'The Sudan for the Sudanese': that slogan which subsequently became the slogan of the independence movement in the Sudan; then the slogan of all after independence. I started to make propaganda for this principle, and to gather around myself a number of educated men, while, of course, the *Anṣār* were the popular support on which I depended in this propaganda."[25]

Although the identity and the roles of the holy families have changed during the past five centuries, it will be clear from what has gone before that they have constituted an element of great and durable importance in Sudanese society. In two departments of the national life, they may well still have an important part to play; in the formation of political groupings, and in the islamization of the southern Sudan. The early holy families developed in consequence of the southwards shift of the frontier of islamization between the fourteenth and sixteenth centuries. The shift which began in the early nineteenth century is now far advanced. It would not be surprising if the phenomena so characteristic of the islamization of the Nilotic Sudan, as well as of Kordofan and Darfur, were to recur in the south.[26]

NOTES

1 See above, "The coming of the Funj", pp. 67–87.
2 *EI*², I, 1032, *sub voce.*
3 'Abd al-Maḥmūd Nūr al-Dā'im, *Azāhīr al-riyāḍ* (Cairo, 1954), 18–19. Compare the acquisition of kinship to the Prophet by the Sons of Jābir; above, p. 88.
4 A valuable memorandum on the Majādhīb, written by Na'ūm Shuqayr on 31 May 1915, is now in the Sudan Archive at the School of Oriental Studies, Durham (195/2, pp. 9–14).
5 *T*, 187–8. J. S. Trimingham, *Islam in the Sudan* (London, 1949), 224–6.
6 The birth-date appears in the summary-translation in MacMichael, *Arabs*, II, 242.
7 For the Bisharein (Bishārīn), see *EI*², I, 1239–40, *sub voce.*
8 J. L. Burckhardt, *Travels in Nubia* (London, 1819), 266–8.
9 *T*, 133–48; summary-translation in MacMichael, *Arabs*, II, 244–5.

10 See above, "Four Funj land-charters", pp. 104–20.
11 Trimingham, op. cit., 226–8. *Azāhīr al-riyāḍ* (see note 3 above) is a most important, though hagiographical, biography of Aḥmad al-Ṭayyib, and also gives much information about his disciples. It was written by a grandson of Aḥmad al-Ṭayyib.
12 Trimingham, op. cit., 231–5.
13 'Abd al-Raḥmān al-Jabartī, *'Ajā'ib al-āthār* [Būlāq, 1880], II, 240–1.
14 *FC* 74.
15 Shuqayr, *Ta'rīkh*, III, 112.
16 MacMichael, *Arabs*, II, 61 ff. (a genealogical work compiled by Aḥmad b. Ismā'īl al-Azharī); Trimingham, op. cit., 235–6; Shuqayr, op. cit., I, 139.
17 Text of this manifesto in Shuqayr, *Ta'rīkh*, III, 383–91.
18 See Hill, *Biographical dictionary*, 402. Biographical notices of some other persons mentioned in this study may also be found in this work.
19 See above, p. 101.
20 Shuqayr, *Ta'rīkh*, III, 114; *Azāhīr al-riyāḍ*, 304.
21 Shuqayr, *Ta'rīkh*, III, 71.
22 A. R. C. Bolton, "El Menna Ismail; fiki and emir in Kordofan", *SNR*, XVII/2 (1934), 229–41.
23 'Uthmān Diqna's MS. report to the Mahdi has been reproduced by the Central Records Office of the Sudan, Khartoum, as *Daftar waqā'i' 'Uthmān Diqna* (Archives/P/002), undated. Translation in F. R. Wingate, *Mahdiism and the Egyptian Sudan* (London, 1891; 2nd edn., London, 1968), 509–21.
24 A record of events, in the form of memoirs of Sayyid 'Abd al-Raḥmān al-Mahdī has been published by al-Ṣādiq al-Mahdī (ed.), *Jihād fī sabīl al-istiqlāl* (Khartoum, n.d. [1965]).
25 Al-Ṣādiq al-Mahdī (ed.), op. cit., 24.
26 The role of the holy families and their adherents in the Condominium and subsequently is surveyed by Dr. Gabriel Warburg in "Religious Policy in the northern Sudan: 'Ulamā' and Ṣūfism 1899–1918" in Gabriel Baer (ed.), *The 'ulamā' in modern history: African and Asian Studies*, 7 (Jerusalem, 1971); and "Popular Islam and tribal leadership in the socio-political structure of the north Sudan" (in the press).

8

MODERNIZATION AND REACTION IN THE NINETEENTH-CENTURY SUDAN

By "modernization" I mean the introduction of methods of political and economic organization, and techniques of production, transport and communications, derived from those employed in European states, all of which substantially modified the structure of the antecedent traditional society. The term "reaction" is used quite literally, to signify the response of elements in the traditional society to modernization: it does not signify a value-judgment. "The Sudan" is used in the sense it acquired during the nineteenth century, to mean the territories of the eastern *bilād al-Sūdān* which were brought under Egyptian rule—substantially the area of the present-day Republic of the Sudan.

Within these territories, which have as their axis the river-system of the middle and upper Nile, the process of modernization differed in two important respects from that which took place elsewhere in the African interior. First, it was inaugurated at a very early date, since it was a direct consequence of the Turco-Egyptian conquests in the years 1820–2. Secondly, it was modernization at one remove; the extension to a dependent region of a process which was at the same time going forward in Egypt under Muḥammad ʿAlī and his successors. Hence during the first phase of modernization, the agents of change were Ottoman subjects, Turkish and Arabic speaking, from Muḥammad ʿAlī's domains. In the second phase, between the accession of Ismāʿīl and the outbreak of the Mahdia (1863–81), Europeans and Americans assisted in the process, with consequences that will appear.

Sudanese Traditional Society before the Turco-Egyptian Conquests

To speak of "Sudanese traditional society" is a gross over-simplification: there were many traditional societies, differing among themselves in ways of life, languages, customs and religions. An important distinction can however be drawn between those lying north and south respectively of the frontier of islamization. This has moved southwards up the Nile since the Muslim conquest of Egypt in the early seventh Christian century. From the early sixteenth to the early nineteenth century, it was practically stable at approximately 13° N. While it is important not to exaggerate differences in the level of culture between northern and southern societies at this period, the fact remains that north of the frontier of islamization there was a literate society with a greater potential of homogeneity, and a greater openness to influence from the Arab Muslim civilization of the Middle East, than the society of the southern territories. It is with this developing northern society that this paper is concerned.

What were its characteristics? It was, first, a society undergoing arabization. There had been for centuries inter-marriage between infiltrating Arab nomads and indigenous peoples: the Nubians of the main Nile, and the Bija of the Red Sea Hills. Furthermore, except among the Bija, Arabic won an almost complete victory over the indigenous languages north of the frontier of islamization. Arab prestige was demonstrated in another way when genealogies were elaborated to demonstrate the descent of the arabized Nubians, the "Black Sultanate" of the Funj, and even the Bija, from the early Islamic dynasties and the Companions of the Prophet.

The powerful yet impalpable bonds of Islam and Arabness linked the peoples of the northern Sudan more effectively than any political organization. Local and tribal loyalties were strong, although the genealogies which provided their rationale perhaps suggested a fictional antiquity, and imposed an artificial rigidity on fairly fluid groupings. Political fragmentation was the norm, with hereditary chiefs ruling the settled territories or the nomad tribes. From the early sixteenth to the mid-eighteenth century, the Funj dynasty had exercised a precarious hegemony as far north as the Third Cataract, but by the early nineteenth century no vestige of central authority survived.

The islamization of this region was a gradual process. The northern riverain territories were the site of an ancient Nubian Christian culture, which may have lingered on after the establishment of Arab political control.[1] The Arab tribal immigrants, mostly nomads from Upper Egypt, are unlikely to have been devout and instructed Muslims. In the southern parts of the region were pagans, including originally the Funj themselves, and their numbers were increased by the importation of slaves from beyond the frontier of islamization. The effective islamization of the northern society was the work of religious teachers (*fakīs*)[2] who established the Mālikī *madhhab* and the Qādiriyya *ṭarīqa*. Several of these men were the founders of religious clans which had both spiritual power and political influence, and thereby provided an element of stability and continuity which contrasted with the fragility of the governmental structure. Their followers were devout and credulous, profoundly affected by the Ṣūfī elements in their teaching, and attached to the cults of the local saints. Although new, reformed orders, the Sammāniyya and the

Khatmiyya were introduced in the late eighteenth and early nineteenth century respectively, these were rapidly assimilated in structure and social functions to the traditional Sufism of the Sudan.[3]

Although the northern society, in both its sedentary and its nomadic sectors, was dominated economically by a harsh subsistence economy, important trade-routes ran across the territory, linking the African interior with the coast-lands of the Mediterranean and the Red Sea. By the end of the period at least, there were fairly regular trading-caravans passing between Sinnār or Darfur and Egypt. Other routes ran from west to east, serving not only trade but also the stream of pilgrims who made their way from the states of the western *Bilād al-Sūdān* to the Ḥijāz, often taking years on the journey, and even forming permanent settlements. In the generation before the Turco-Egyptian conquest, Shandī was the great emporium of the riverain Sudan: its commercial activity has been vividly described by Burckhardt, who visited it in 1814.[4] In this trade, slaves, obtained by raiding beyond the frontier of islamization, were a staple export, while other slaves, retained within the region, worked in the fields, served in the houses, and fought as armed retainers of the chiefs and notables.

Modernization in the Turco-Egyptian Period: 1820–85

The Turco-Egyptian campaigns of 1820–2 conquered only the nucleus of what was to be the Egyptian Sudan. Of the region inhabited by the northern society, the river-lands and the plain of Kordofan passed under the rule of Muḥammad ʻAlī. The Bija lands were not acquired until late in his reign; Darfur, not until the time of Khedive Ismāʻīl. Of greater importance, however, was the beginning of expansion southwards. The frontier of islamization, fixed for three centuries, became fluid, with results for both the northern and southern societies which are still continuing. The southwards expansion, up the White Nile, opened with voyages of exploration between 1839 and 1842. These were followed by commercial activity, and not until the reign of Khedive Ismāʻīl was any really effective administrative control established.

The three aspects of modernization in the Turco-Egyptian period with which this study is concerned are, first, the introduction of technical devices; secondly, the development of a modern administrative system; and, thirdly, the direct impact of the West, the original source of "modernization", on Sudanese society.

Two western inventions played an important part in the nineteenth-century Sudan: firearms and steamers. Although handguns had been known in the Sudan by the second half of the seventeenth century at latest,[5] they were not used on any large scale. The superiority of the Turco-Egyptian forces in this respect enabled them to overcome the resistance of the Shāyqiyya and of the Fūr in Kordofan with great slaughter. Steamships, first used on the Egyptian Nile about 1828, were not introduced into Sudanese waters for another generation, but in the sixties and seventies a substantial fleet was built up, maintained by a dockyard at Khartoum.[6] A third invention, of rather less significance, was the electric telegraph.

Firearms and the steamer played a great part in the southward movement of the frontier of islamization in the Turco-Egyptian period. At first the expansion into the south was tentative and hesitant, but these new devices enabled the northern society and its Turco-Egyptian rulers to overcome the two principal obstacles to advance up the White Nile: namely, the cohesive and bellicose Shilluk, whose canoe raids had on occasion struck far to the north,[7] and the immense barrier of the *sadd*, blocking the approach both to the Equatorial Nile and the Baḥr al-Ghazāl.

The opening of the south offered new opportunities to a particular sector of the northern society, the sedentaries of the main Nile, notably the Ja'aliyyūn, the Shāyqiyya and the Danāqla. Already before the Turco-Egyptian conquest, there was a diaspora of Danāqla and Ja'aliyyūn in other Sudanese territories, and origin-legends of several royal clans suggest that this may have been very ancient. As the Upper Nile and Baḥr al-Ghazāl became more accessible to traders from the north, a new diaspora was formed in these regions. Its members were at first the servants and armed retainers of alien merchants, European and others, but as time went on, many of them acquired increasing responsibility and power. A few, of whom the most notable was the Ja'alī, al-Zubayr Raḥma Manṣūr, became real merchant-princes, combining the commercial and political control of great tracts of country.[8] Others commanded private armies of slave-troops (*bazingers*).[9] Other again came as officials or soldiers of the administration, when the khedivial authority was at last extended to the southern Sudan.

The kind of government which was established in the Egyptian Sudan was something wholly new. European writers have concentrated on its faults, and have painted a dark picture of oppression, incompetence and corruption, relieved only during the few years when General Gordon held office. Faults must be admitted, as must the low quality of many of the Turco-Egyptian administrators: it must be remembered that with the vigorous modernization going on in Egypt itself, the supply of trained, competent and honest administrators was never equal to the demand. Quite apart from all this, however, was the contrast between the types of government to which the northern society was accustomed, and the new model established by the Turco-Egyptians.

In the first place, the Turco-Egyptian administration was highly centralized. Even the phases of so-called "decentralization", when the governorate-general was abolished, simply meant that the Sudanese provinces were brought directly under a department in Cairo. Although representatives of the old chiefly families continued to hold office, and might (especially in the nomad tribes) have very real and extensive power, they were quite clearly no longer autonomous but agents of a central authority, which could appoint, remove and circumvent them, exploiting their family rivalries in doing so. The strength of the government lay in its new powers of control, especially in its armed forces. The bulk of these consisted of regular infantry (*jihādiyya*), recruited (usually as slaves) from the south, and irregular cavalry, most of whom were recruited from an early date amongst the Shāyqiyya tribesmen. Control was also helped by improvements in communications, although too much must not be made of these. No roads were constructed. At the end of the Turco-Egyptian period, the only railway consisted of a few miles of track in the far north.[10] Hence troop movements by land (and *a fortiori* the sending of reinforcements from Egypt) were slow and cumbersome—a fact which placed the administration at a disadvantage when faced with scattered tribal risings at the beginning of the Mahdia. On the other hand, the introduction of steamers greatly increased control over the central riverain areas (here again the military history of the Mahdia is instructive), while the development of a telegraph network in the time of Ismā'īl was an important, although vulnerable, contribution to centralization.[11] Armed with these instruments, the Turco-Egyptian administration largely succeeded in maintaining public security in the settled areas and along the main routes, in repressing the turbulence of the nomads, and, above all, in enforcing the payment of taxes.

The religious life of northern Sudanese society was also greatly affected by changes resulting from Turco-Egyptian rule. Previously, as we have seen, the religious leadership consisted of the hereditary teachers (*fakīs*) of the religious sciences and Sufism—two groups which overlapped but were not quite identical. Although there are traces of an official organization of *Sharī'a* courts when Funj power was at its height, the evidence is sparse, and the *fakīs* seem to have fulfilled at need the functions of *muftīs* and arbitrators.[12]

In the Turco-Egyptian period, the traditional Islam of the Sudan suffered two severe blows. Although the new régime on the whole maintained friendly relations with the *fakīs*, and subsidized them (as previous rulers had done), it diminished their prestige, created and maintained a formal hierarchy of *qāḍīs*, *muftīs* and other cult officials, and facilitated the education of Sudanese *'ulamā'* at al-Azhar. Thus the traditional and indigenous Muslim leadership was confronted with a rival group, more orthodox and alien in its outlook, and more directly dependent on the government. But there was another development. In the Sudan, as in Egypt itself and the Ottoman Empire generally, it was the policy of the rulers to weaken the independence of the whole Muslim Institution as a partner in the state. Although at the outset, the newly established *Sharī'a* courts had possessed jurisdiction over the whole range of civil and criminal causes, their powers were rapidly diminished. By the end of the period they dealt only with matters of personal status and inheritance, while through a system of local councils (*majālis maḥalliyya*) set up in 1850, general civil and criminal jurisdiction was devolved on amateur benches of notables and merchants applying customary law.[13] Thus the prestige, not only of the traditional religious leaders, but also of the Islamic hierarchy established under the Turco-Egyptian regime, had undergone considerable diminution.

The process of modernization was accompanied and fostered by an increasing number of Western expatriates, both European and Americans. During the Funj period probably not more than a dozen Europeans visited the northern Sudan, and none penetrated south of the frontier of islamization. The Turco-Egyptian conquest opened the Sudanese territories to the West.[14] A line of later visitors combined adventurous tourism with more serious interests. During the middle decades of the nineteenth century there grew up a fair body of travel literature. Although it was still remote, the Sudan was not inaccessible to men of some means and resolution.

Apart from the travellers, the expatriates appeared in the Sudan in three principal roles: as traders, as missionaries, and as employees of the administration. European trade in the Sudan was hampered in the early years of the Turco-Egyptian regime by Muḥammad 'Alī's system of state monopolies: a restriction which became more galling after the break-through into the Upper Nile seemed to offer untold opportunities to the pioneers of organized commerce. Although the monopolies were formally abolished in 1842, freedom of trade was not really established until the end of Muḥammad 'Alī's reign. After 1850, the barriers were swept away.[15] The exploitation of the ivory of the south began, and an ancillary slave-trade rapidly grew up, and began to overshadow legitimate commerce. In this opening phase, the European traders led the way, but their domination of the commerce of the Upper Nile was transient, and after little more than a decade they were superseded by merchants who were mostly of Sudanese or Egyptian origin.

The expansion of missionary activity into the Upper Nile accompanied the European commercial initiative, and receded with it. A Catholic mission set up its headquarters in Khartoum in 1848, and mission-stations were established on the Upper Nile in the following decade. Their success in proselytizing was almost negligible, and by 1860 the southern stations had been abandoned. A later attempt to reopen them failed, and, at the outbreak of the Mahdia, the farthest south of the missionaries was the Nuba Mountains.[16] Yet, in spite of the almost total failure of missionary activity, the presence of Christians in Khartoum and other towns of the Sudan, the building of churches, and the appearance of priests and members of religious orders, represented an innovation in the traditional and exclusively Islamic society of the northern Sudan. It was also a visible sign that the old relationship between Muslims and *dhimmīs* no longer existed.

During the reign of Khedive Ismā'īl, Western employees of the government began to make an impact on Sudanese society, both in the arabized north and in the south. They were men of varied background, recruited from several countries. Some were Americans, veterans of the Civil War, who had accepted appointments in the khedivial army, such as Colston and Prout, who carried out a reconnaissance of Kordofan and Darfur, and Chaillé-Long who served in the south. Others were British, such as Baker, who after journeys through the Sudan as an explorer and big-game hunter, was employed by the khedive to pacify and govern the southern provinces; or Gordon, a courageous and eccentric soldier, whose exploits in China and the Sudan have almost invariably been viewed by the British through a rosy haze. Among other expatriate officials were Gessi, who had fought under Garibaldi, and was to administer the Baḥr al-Ghazāl under Gordon; Emin, of Silesian Jewish origin, a naturalist by choice and an administrator by necessity; and Slatin, whose best-seller, *Fire and sword in the Sudan*, created for European readers a durable, if not wholly accurate, picture of the Mahdia.

The decade preceding the outbreak of the Mahdia was the heyday of the expatriate officials. They were appointed by Ismā'īl to promote the efficiency of the administration. Above all, they were employed to establish the hold of the khedivial government over the newly acquired territories in the south and west—the Upper Nile to the Equatorial lakes, the great basin of the Baḥr al-Ghazāl, and Darfur. Apart from friction between individual Europeans or Americans and their Egyptian or Sudanese colleagues, tension was bound to be created by the rapid introduction into the service of this group of officials, who in language, customs and religion were alien both to the old Turco-Egyptian administrators and to the mass of the Sudanese. Since, moreover, the extension of khedivial rule over the south and west was concurrent with, and partly justified by, attempts to suppress the slave-trade—a policy to which Ismā'īl publicly committed himself by a convention with Britain in 1877—the expatriates acquired additional odium, especially among the diaspora of northerners whose fortunes were closely bound up with the trade.

The Mahdist Reaction

It will be clear from the foregoing that, during the sixty years of Turco-Egyptian domination of the Sudan, the traditional society of the north had been considerably affected. These changes had not worked wholly to the detriment of sections of that society: nevertheless, by 1881 a revolutionary situation was in being, which was to turn into active revolution with the manifestation of Muḥammad Aḥmad as Mahdi.

The supporters of the revolutionary movement may be divided, apparently paradoxically into two categories: those who had suffered in consequence of the changes induced by the Turco-Egyptian regime, and those who had gained as a result of those changes. The former category included the religious leaders and the tribal communities. Both of these groups experienced internal as well as external tensions. As we have seen, the modernizing policy of the government was inimical to the existence of an autonomous Muslim Institution, and the hierarchy of '*ulamā*', which it had itself established after the conquest, was partially deprived of judicial functions and depressed in status. The indigenous, and non-hierarchic *fakīs* had earlier undergone a similar depression as a consequence of the conquest. Hence there was a general tension between the men of religion and the administration, but at the same time an internal tension between the *fakīs* and the '*ulamā*'. This was to show itself in the fact that the '*ulamā*' were divided in their reactions to the claims of the Mahdi—a leader standing in the indigenous Sufist *fakī* tradition. The *fakīs* were much more sympathetic in their attitude, although one important order, the Khatmiyya, under the leadership of the Mīrghanī family, remained unwaveringly hostile to the Mahdia. In this connexion, it is worth noticing that the Khatmiyya was an order of recent introduction, which had very close links with the Turco-Egyptian administration. Thus, although from the outset the Mahdi found many adherents among the men of religion, and especially the *fakīs*, they were not monolithic in their support for him and their opposition to the existing regime.

The tribes and their chiefly families had suffered, like the men of religion, from the encroachments of the government. In the Sudan, as in Egypt, during the nineteenth century the trend of policy and action was to curtail the autonomy of the tribal chiefs, and generally to extend a uniform administration over the desert and the sown. By 1881 this process had not gone as far in the Sudan as in Egypt, but it had attained some success, especially among the sedentaries of the riverain lands. There the great historic tribes had early been brought into submission, while the new diaspora had drained their homelands of the men with the greatest initiative and resolution. The nomad tribes still remained a problem, but as khedivial rule was extended to the Baḥr al-Ghazāl and Darfur, the Baqqāra were put under increasing administrative pressure. Hence it is not surprising that the Mahdi was able, in the first few months after his manifestation, to build up a revolutionary army of tribesmen. But again their adherence was not monolithic. The most committed were the Baqqāra, whose freedom had most recently been curtailed with the annexation of Darfur.

The Mahdi also found supporters among the northerners of the diaspora in Kordofan, Darfur, the Baḥr al-Ghazāl and the Upper Nile. These were, on the whole, people who had profited from the opportunities resulting from the Turco-Egyptian regime, but had been frustrated by the events of the preceding decade. The extension of khedivial rule to the south and south-west had been partial, and the administration set up was frequently inefficient. Nevertheless, it had destroyed the power of the great merchant-princes, and placed in jeopardy the careers and prosperity of their assistants and subordinates. The merchants (*jallāba*) who worked across the frontier of islamization suffered from measures taken against slave-trading, and (with Gordon's authorization) were atrociously harried by the Baqqāra in 1879. Other members of the diaspora had, to all appearance, secured their future in alliance with the regime; such were Ilyās Pasha Umm Birayr, a rich merchant of El Obeid who was for a time governor of Kordofan, and Muḥammad Bey Khālid, also a merchant by origin, who was a sub-governor in Darfur. Nevertheless, the readiness with which men like these conspired to subvert the Turco-Egyptian regime is a measure of the frustration which they felt.[17]

The form taken by the Mahdist reaction is itself an indication of the extent of the changes that had occurred under Turco-Egyptian rule. There was no attempt—indeed there could be no attempt—to restore the old political structures of the Nilotic Sudan. The Funj sultanate, the ʻAbdallābī shaykhdom, the Hamaj regency, even the once-powerful tribal kingdom of the Jaʻaliyyūn and the Shāyqiyya confederacy had gone beyond recall. Some of the nomadic tribal chiefs sought to regain their autonomy, and in Darfur the former royal clan struggled to regain the independence lost only in the previous decade. These, however, were peripheral and ultimately abortive attempts.

The Mahdist reaction drew much of its emotional strength and its religious and political concepts from the indigenous Islam of the Sudan. At its core lay the revolt of the *fakīs*, and the *fakīs*, as we have seen, had been, even in the Funj period, more effective than the political leaders as a focus of stability and continuity. Yet even here the sixty years of Turco-Egyptian rule had diminished the authority of the old religious clans. The men of religion who inaugurated and headed the revolt were parvenus. While the Mahdi and his relative, the Khalifa Muḥammad Sharīf, claimed to be *Ashrāf*, they did not belong to one of the greater old-established religious clans. The other two khalifas came from tribal groups on the frontiers of the northern Sudanese society; ʻAbdallāhi was conscious of bearing, among the sedentaries, the stigma of an uncouth barbarian. Of the old religious clans, only one, the Majādhīb, played a part of any distinction in support of the Mahdia, and its field of activity was not in its original homeland on the main Nile, but among the fringe-nomads, the Bija of the Red Sea Hills.

It would, however, be wrong to see in the Mahdist reaction and the state, which was its outcome, merely a resurgence of the Sufist, unintellectual and unorthodox Islam of the Funj period. Ever since the middle of the eighteenth century, currents of reform had been working in the Muslim society of the Near East, and the Mahdia was a response to these developments also. The reform-movements, of which Wahhabism is the prototype, looked back to an image of primitive Islam, and were rigorist in their interpretation and application of the *Sharīʻa*. The Sudanese Mahdi and his followers went one step further: they were not merely guided by the precedents of primitive Islam; they were re-enacting it in the end-time, and re-establishing the *Umma* against a schismatic Muslim society.

Thus the Mahdist state embodied a theological rather than a political concept. It developed from the holy community of those who had left all in answer to the Mahdi's summons:

> "The alteration of the age and abandonment of the *Sunna* are not hidden, nor will the man of faith and understanding be satisfied therewith; but he will rather leave his desires and his home to raise up the religion and the *Sunnas*."[18]

Phrases such as "the alteration of the age", which have, of course, eschatological overtones, are related in the Mahdi's letters to the activities of three principal groups: the "Turks", "the evil ʻ*ulamā*ʼ " (ʻ*ulamā*ʼ *al-sū*ʼ),[19] and the unbelievers. The letters are directed to specific individuals or groups, but, taking them as a whole, it is clear that what the Mahdi reprehends is the change in Islam (i.e. the modification of the traditional Muslim and Sudanese way of life) for which they are responsible. The three groups are associated in this innovating process. By the "Turks" he means the alien officials of the Turco-Egyptian administration; by "the evil *'ulamā'* " the members of the official Islamic hierarchy who have connived at the innovations of the "Turks" and have denounced Muḥammad Aḥmad's claim to be the Mahdi. Behind these two groups, at the very source of authority, the khedive's court, are the unbelievers, i.e. specifically, the British.[20]

The Mahdia thus presented itself as a primitivist and rigorist movement, fundamentally opposed to change and to the modernization which had been induced, both in Egypt and the Sudan, by the impact of the West. This ideology, developed by the Mahdi, was never formally abandoned by his successor, the Khalifa 'Abdallāhi, under whom the revolution was brought to a successful political conclusion. In practice, however, things were rather different.

I do not here allude principally to the failure of the Mahdist community to maintain the rigorist ideals of its founder. From what has been said above, it will be clear that the men of religion and the devout formed only a section of the mass-movement against the Turco-Egyptian regime. What I have rather in mind is that even within the fields of technical modernization and administration, so much was taken over from the Turco-Egyptian regime by the Mahdist state, that in many respects it was its successor. The three chief technical innovations of the Turkiyya were, as we have seen, firearms, steamers, and the electric telegraph. All these were used by the new regime. Firearms were sanctioned by the Mahdi with some reluctance: their use infringed the precedents of the Prophet's wars, and caused problems of internal security. The telegraph network was almost wholly destroyed during the revolutionary war, but a link between Omdurman and the Dockyard at Khartoum was kept in service throughout the Mahdia. The fleet of steamers, inherited from the previous administration, played an important part in the communications-system of the Mahdist state, and kept open the way to the south where a tenuous hold was maintained over some riverain areas.[21]

In these respects the Mahdist state was living on acquired capital, and problems of maintenance and supply increased with every passing year. In the sphere of administration, on the other hand, the new regime maintained and even extended the centralized control which the Turco-Egyptians had inaugurated. The Mahdist revolution contributed to this. For the first time, almost all the communities of the northern Sudan became involved in a combined action against a common opponent. It was not a consciously nationalist movement; it found little support in the south, and there were unwilling participants and internal tensions even among its northern adherents. Yet it created a revolutionary spirit, which gave an emotional and ideological unity to the diverse inhabitants of territories more or less fortuitously assembled under Turco-Egyptian administration.

The Mahdist period contributed in another way to the unification of the northern Sudan. It was a time of rapid and widespread population movements. The *hijra* of adherents to the Mahdi in Abā or at Qadīr in the first stage, was followed by the *jihād* against the Turco-Egyptians, in which the western tribes played so large a part.[22] The Mahdist capital at Omdurman was a congeries of uprooted populations. The Khalifa's own tribal policy involved the forced migration of the nomadic Baqqāra from Darfur to Omdurman, and their conversion into a tribal garrison, maintained by the corn of the Gezira. This was an ambitious experiment in sedentarization. It was always precarious, and it broke down with the dispersal of the tribes after the battle of Kararī in 1898. But for nearly two decades, the tribal system and population-pattern of the northern Sudan had undergone a series of violent shocks, and in spite of the later efforts of administrators under the Condominium, Humpty-Dumpty could not be put together again.

The Mahdist state, being ideologically the nucleus of a revived and universal Islamic *Umma*, was of necessity unitary and centralized in structure. Its practical establishment was the work of the Khalifa 'Abdallāhi, since the Mahdi himself died in the closing stages of the revolutionary war. Within restricted limits (since most of the recent khedivial acquisitions of territory in the south and south-west could not be held), the Khalifa combated particularist and separatist movements, and repressed challenges to his own authority within the Mahdist *élite*. He established a personal autocracy, sustained by a bureaucracy inherited from the previous régime, and operating through provincial governors (mostly his kinsmen and clients) with whom he was in almost daily communication. In this way, the Sudanese became further habituated to centralized and authoritarian government, which had been an innovation of the Turco-Egyptians. This in its turn was to prepare the way for the British administration of the Condominium period.

Thus the Mahdist reaction, for all its ideological hostility to the modernization which had preceded it, made large compromises. The Mahdia can be seen from many angles: from one it may be described as an early attempt to assimilate the consequences of modernization to an inheritance of indigenous Islam.

NOTES

1 See P. L. and M. Shinnie, "New light on medieval Nubia", *JAH*, VI/3 (1965), 263–73, especially p. 265.

2 The term *fakī* has a wider range of meanings than the classical Arabic *faqīh*, from which it is derived; cf. J. S. Trimingham, *Islam in the Sudan* (London, 1949), 140–1.

3 See Trimingham, op. cit., 226–8, 231–5.

4 J. L. Burckhardt, *Travels in Nubia* (London, 1819), 277–361.

5 I have noted two references to firearms in the *Ṭabaqāt*. Shaykh Ḥasan w. Ḥassūna was killed (1075/1664–5) when his musket misfired (*T*, 148). 'Uthmān w. Ḥamad, a Shāyqī chief who defeated the Funj in the seventeenth century, also possessed a musket (*T*, 227). But Bruce, speaking of the Funj in 1772, says, "The Mek has not one musket in his whole army" (Bruce, *Travels*), VI, 392. At the time of the Turco-Egyptian invasion, the Shāyqiyya had apparently no firearms (cf. An American in the service of the Viceroy [G. B. English]), *A narrative of the expedition to Dongola and Senaar* (London, 1822), 83–5).

6 See Richard Hill, *Sudan transport* (London, 1965), 2–5.

7 Bruce (*Travels*, VI, 370–1) identifies the emergence of the Funj with a Shilluk raid "in a multitude of canoes, or boats, upon the Arab provinces" in 1504. The identity of Shilluk and Funj is open to question (cf. above, pp. 71–2), but there is other evidence of devastating canoe-raids. A passage in the *Ṭabaqāt* (*T*, 344) records a tradition that "from al-Khurṭūm [the confluence of the Blue and White Niles] to Alays [the Funj frontier-post on the White Nile near the modern al-Kawwa] there were seventeen schools, and the Shilluk and Umm Laḥm [the famine of 1095/1683–4] destroyed them all". Petherick, describing conditions as late as 1853, writes: "During the inundation of the Nile, marauding bands of Shillooks in their canoes frequently drop down the stream, and surprise Eleis [Alays] and the Arab population on either side of the river as low down as the vicinity of Wallad Shallai [82 miles upstream from Omdurman]." He also speaks of raids across the Gezira to the vicinity of Sinnār (J. Petherick, *Egypt, the Soudan and Central Africa* (Edinburgh and London, 1861), 342.)

8 His autobiography, from an oral account, is given by Shuqayr, *Ta'rīkh*, III, 60–87.

9 *EI*², I, 1156–7, BĀZINḲIR.

10 Hill, *Sudan transport*, 8–17.

11 Richard Hill, *Egypt in the Sudan, 1820–1881* (London, 1959), 130–1, 157–8.

12 An elaborate account of the Funj judicial system is given by Ḥusayn Sīd Aḥmad al-Muftī, *Taṭawwur niẓām al-ḥukm fi'l-Sūdān*, I (n.p. [? Khartoum], 1378/1959), 15–43. The details of organization appear to be derived from the ms. memoirs of a modern Sudanese historian, Muḥammad 'Abd al-Raḥīm. Incidental information on the judicial functions of the *fakīs* may be found in the *Ṭabaqāt*.

13 Al-Muftī, op. cit., 76, 112–13. See also *Report on the Soudan by Lieutenant-Colonel Stewart*; Parliamentary Papers, Egypt No. 11 (1883); C. 3670, 11–13.

14 The invasion itself was witnessed and described by an American, serving Muḥammad 'Alī as an artillery officer ([G. B. English], op. cit.) and by two Cambridge dons with antiquarian interests, to whom the expedition "seemed to present a fortunate opportunity of carrying into effect those designs, of

which the success must otherwise have been very uncertain" (George Waddington and Barnard Hanbury, *Journal of a visit to some parts of Ethiopia* (London, 1822), iii–iv).

15 Ahmed Abdel-Rahim Mustafa, "The breakdown of the monopoly system in Egypt after 1840", in P. M. Holt (ed.), *Political and social change in modern Egypt* (London, 1968), 291–307.

16 On the penetration of the south, see J. R. Gray, *A history of the southern Sudan, 1839–1889* (London, 1961).

17 The links between local politics in Kordofan and the Mahdia appear clearly in the memoirs of Yūsuf Mikhā'īl; see Salih Mohammad Nur, *A critical edition of the memoirs of Yūsuf Mikhā'īl* (Ph.D., London, 1962). The attitude of Muḥammad Khālid (Zuqal) is described by R. C. Slatin, *Fire and sword in the Sudan* (London, 1896), 149–51, 219–222.

18 Muḥammad al-Mahdī, *Manshūrāt* (photographic reproduction by the Central Records Office of the Sudan, Khartoum, 1963–4), II, 47.

19 The term '*ulamā' al-sū*' was earlier used by Shaykh 'Uthmān dan Fodio, and has been traced back in western Sudanese usage to the jurist al-Maghīlī in the time of Muḥammad Askia (1493–1528): see M. Hiskett, "An Islamic tradition of reform in the Western Sudan from the sixteenth to the nineteenth century", *BSOAS*, XXV/3 (1962), 580–1.

20 Cf. the following passage from the Mahdi's letter to the Khedive Muḥammad Tawfīq (*Manshūrāt*, II, 277–84; Shuqayr, *Ta'rīkh*, III, 347–51) dated 3 Ramaḍān 1302/16 June 1885, six days before the Mahdi's death:

> "You delivered the command of the *Umma* of Muḥammad to the enemies of God, the English, and you have made lawful to them their [i.e. the Muslims'] blood and property and honour. . . . It was not right of you to take the unbelievers as friends rather than God, and to seek their help in shedding the blood of the *Umma* of Muḥammad."

21 The armaments and steamers of the Mahdist state were listed in a letter from the Khalifa to Rābiḥ Faḍlallāh, dated 22 Qa'da 1303/22 August 1886 (Shuqayr, *Ta'rīkh*, III, 447). For the steamers, see also Hill, *Sudan transport*, 27–31.

22 The pattern of *hijra* and *jihād* has an obvious precedent in the career of the Prophet, but the possibility of influences from the western *bilād al-Sūdān* cannot be excluded: cf. the teaching and actions of 'Uthman dan Fodio and others in I. M. Lewis (ed.), *Islam in tropical Africa* (London, 1966), 324–6, 408–24; Murray Last, *The Sokoto Caliphate* (London, 1967); J. R. Willis, "*Jihād fī sabīl Allāh*—its doctrinal basis in Islam and some aspects of its evolution in nineteenth-century West Africa", *JAH* VIII/3 (1967), 395–415.

III

STUDIES IN EGYPTIAN HISTORY

9

OTTOMAN EGYPT (1517–1798): AN ACCOUNT OF ARABIC HISTORICAL SOURCES

HISTORICAL writing in Arabic on Ottoman Egypt during the period from the conquest to the French occupation is reasonably copious and varied in kind. It has not yet been adequately evaluated, and its full exploitation is still far in the future. Very little of the material has been published, nor has much work been done on the manuscript sources. The consequence of this is that writers on the period have depended excessively on the few published works, especially on the chronicle of al-Jabartī, and on the writings of French scholars, especially those who were associated with Bonaparte's expedition to Egypt. This in turn has led to a certain distortion of the history of the first two centuries of Ottoman rule, owing to the retrojection of conditions and institutions of the later eighteenth century.

The historical writing which will be surveyed in this paper was produced in Egypt by persons who were domiciled in, or native to, that country. A certain amount of information may also be obtained from external Arabic sources.[1] The Egyptian material is mostly in the form of chronicles, the framework of which, however, is not necessarily strictly annalistic. There are two grave limitations on the scope of this material. First, there is an almost complete absence of contemporary writing for about seventy years from the termination of Ibn Iyās's chronicle in 928/1522, and this period is only thinly covered by later writers. This lack of contemporary chronicles, and the sparseness of the data provided by sources of the eleventh/seventeenth century, suggest that this "dark age" was, in fact, a time in which there were few dramatic political occurrences. Nevertheless it was an important period of institutional transition, and our ignorance of developments in the middle and later tenth/sixteenth century seriously affects our understanding of events in the following period.

The second limitation of scope of the Egyptian material persists throughout the whole of the period here surveyed. The data provided refer almost exclusively to Cairo, and particularly to the governing and military *élite* of the city. While it is no doubt true that the capital dominated the political life of Egypt, and the military grandees dominated the capital, there were, even in the political sphere, developments outside Cairo of which we obtain only infrequent and inadequate glimpses from the chroniclers. It is, for example, clear that for nearly three centuries after the Ottoman conquest, Upper Egypt played a political role of immense importance: over long stretches of time it was a virtually autonomous region, under tribal or beylical rulers; alternatively, it was a territory of refuge for members of factions defeated in the capital. This we can trace from the chroniclers, but only in episodic fashion. Another grave deficiency is the lack of data on the tribes. Here again it is clear that the nomads and semi-nomads of the desert fringe had an important and complex influence on Egyptian political history, but it is impossible to study their significance in detail, by regions and periods. Since our information even on political events is so limited and one-sided, it goes without saying that the chroniclers alone are inadequate sources for reconstructing the social and economic history of Ottoman Egypt.

The following survey gives a brief account of various sources in chronological order. It is not exhaustive, but includes all the works with which I am personally acquainted.[2]

(A) WRITING OF THE EARLY OTTOMAN PERIOD IN EGYPT

1. Al-Ishbīlī, *al-Durr al-muṣān*

This short work, which was completed on 10 Ṣafar 923/4 March 1517 (i.e. while Selim I was still in Egypt) is an Arabic literary *fethname*.[3] Written in a mixture of *saj*ʿ and verse, it is full of encomia of Selim, who is presented as the successor of the Patriarchal Caliphs, and as a quasi-messianic figure engaged in holy war against the Safavids and Mamluks. The historical events reviewed are the Chāldirān campaign and its sequel, the overthrow of ʿAlāʾ al-Dawla, and in much greater detail the operations against the Circassian Mamluk sultanate. As a record of events, the work should be regarded with caution, but it throws an interesting light on the propaganda used to justify Selim's warfare against other Muslim sovereigns.

2. Ibn Iyās, *Badāʾiʿ al-zuhūr*

The author's eyewitness account of the collapse of the Circassian Mamluk sultanate, and the establishment of Ottoman rule in Egypt, forms the last portion only of a long and detailed chronicle. It is the sole reliable first-hand account in Arabic of developments from the appearance of the Ottoman threat to the events immediately following the death of the viceroy, Khāʾir Bey (Muḥarram 922—Dhu'l-Ḥijja 928/February 1516—November 1522.)

3. Ibn Zunbul, *Ta'rīkh ghazwat al-sulṭān Salīm khān ma' al-sulṭān al-Ghawrī*

Although this work appears to supplement that of Ibn Iyās in providing a history of the Ottoman conquest and early Ottoman period, it must be used with very great caution. Dating from the middle years of the tenth/sixteenth century, it is a collection of heroic prose sagas rather than a sober narrative. The campaign of Selim against al-Ghawrī forms only the first part of the work, and is contained in pages 2 to 24 of the published edition. The core of this romance of chivalry (for such it is), is constituted by an account of the valiant life and death of Ṭūmān Bāy, who is depicted as a kind of Circassian Roland, a doomed hero encountering overwhelming odds. This saga of Ṭūmān Bāy occupies pages 24 to 113. It is characterized by literary devices and legendary features. Ṭūmān Bāy and his faithful followers stand in contrast to the traitors to their race, Khā'ir Bey, Jānbirdī al-Ghazālī, the *kāshif* Jānim al-Sayfī, and to the treacherous Arab chief, Ḥasan b. Mar'ī. Sultan Selim is a somewhat colourless figure, the tool of Khā'ir Bey. Numerous speeches by the leading figures give an impression that the narrator is possessed of inside knowledge, not to say omniscience, but these should be regarded as purely literary devices, incidental to the unfolding of the plot. The narrator then goes on to describe the dispositions made in Egypt by Selim, his return to Istanbul and his death (pages 113 to 120). A final section (pages 120 to 129) deals with the revolt of Jānbirdī al-Ghazālī in Damascus against Sultan Süleyman, and brings the story down to the death of Khā'ir Bey (Dhu'l-Qa'da 928/October 1522) and the participation of the contingent which he had sent from Egypt in the conquest of Rhodes (Ṣafar 929/December 1522). This appears to be the original end of the work, although additional material is tacked on in some of the manuscript versions.

The central theme of Ibn Zunbul's romance is the decline and fall of the Circassians in Egypt. He does not seek to elucidate historical causation: it is sufficient that God willed the end of the Circassian sultanate and the Ottoman triumph. Nevertheless he harks back repeatedly, and resentfully, to the Ottoman use of artillery and fire-arms. It was these unfair weapons which, under God, brought about the destruction of the Circassian chivalry.

(B) WRITINGS OF THE ELEVENTH/SEVENTEENTH AND TWELFTH/EIGHTEENTH CENTURIES

4. Al-Isḥāqī, *Akhbār al-unwal*

This work has acquired an unmerited importance through publication: it is by no means in the same category as the other published chronicles, those of Ibn Iyās and al-Jabartī. It is a jejune compendium of Islamic and Egyptian history in ten chapters. Of these, only the tenth, amounting to under an eighth of the whole work, deals with events in Ottoman Egypt, but an account of the actual conquest appears in the previous chapter under the notice of Sultan Selim I. The tenth chapter deals in succession with the viceroys from Khā'ir Bey to Ibrāhīm Pasha, who was recalled in Ramaḍān 1032/July 1623. The practice of using the periods of office of viceroys as units of chronology, in preference to writing annals in the strict sense, was widely followed by later historians of Ottoman Egypt.

5. The Continuation of al-Isḥāqī

A manuscript in the Bibliothèque Nationale (MS. arabe 1854), which lacks both a title and the name of the author, is a recension and continuation of the ninth and tenth chapters of al-Isḥāqī's *Akhbār al-uwal.* Within the period covered by the original, there is some additional material, notably accounts of the revolts of Jānim and Īnāl (fols. 52a–57a), and of Khā'in Aḥmad Pasha (fols. 58a–63a). The material taken from *Akhbār al-uwal* has been reorganized, so that the notice of each Ottoman sultan (from Chapter 9 of *Akhbār*) is followed directly by the notices of the viceroys who governed Egypt in his reign (from Chapter 10). The chronicle is continued down to 1084/1673. On f. 110b, the author speaks of himself as Muḥammad b. Isḥāq, but since al-Isḥāqī died in 1060/1650, his authorship of at least the final portion of the Continuation is excluded.

6. Mar'ī b. Yūsuf, *Nuzhat al-nāẓirīn*

A minor chronicle of little worth, which goes down to the viceroyalty of Bayram Pasha (appointed 1035/1626).

7. Al-Ghamrī, *Dhakhīrat al-i'lām*

Another minor chronicle, written in atrocious verse and therefore presumably intended for entertainment rather than for edification. It goes down to 1040/1630.

8. Ibn Abi'l-Surūr

Two versions of Ibn Abi'l-Surūr's chronicle of Ottoman Egypt, form part of two distinct works:[4]

(*a*) *al-Rawḍa al-zahiyya.* The second part of this work (50 out of 76 folios in the Bodleian MS. Pocock. 80) gives an account of the rulers of Egypt from antediluvian times. Of this, the final portion (fols. 57–76) covers the Ottoman period to the viceroyalty of Khalīl Pasha, which began in Rabī' I 1041/October 1631.[5]

(*b*) *al-Kawākib al-sā'ira.* This is a general work on Egypt in twenty chapters. The British Museum manuscript consists of 132 folios. The third chapter deals with the rulers of Egypt from antediluvian times, the last portion (fols. 13b–69a) covering the Ottoman period down to Muḥammad Pasha (1062/1651–2). The text appears to be identical with that of *al-Rawḍa al-zahiyya* as far as 1041/1631.

In both versions Ibn Abi'l-Surūr's chronicle, which follows the usual pattern of division into viceroyalties, is a source of primary importance for the events of the first half of the seventeenth century. The longer version is particularly valuable for the information it gives about the career of Riḍwān Bey al-Faqārī.

9. Anon., *Qahr al-wujūh*

This pseudo-historical genealogical work purports to trace the descent of Riḍwān Bay al-Faqārī (d. 1066/1656) from the Circassian Mamluk sultan, Barsbāy, and, further, to demonstrate the origin of the Circassians from a clan of Quraysh. The work is chiefly valuable for the insight it affords into Mamluk aims in the mid eleventh/eighteenth century.[6]

10. Al-Ṣāliḥī, *Waq'at al-ṣanājiq*

Two chapters of historical narrative are inserted in a framework of religious texts and pious reflections: in the Paris manuscript the historical portion occupies 42 out of 96 folios. The second chapter of the work (fols. 12a–45a) deals with the great revolt of the Faqārī beys in 1071/1660, which led to the almost complete annihilation of this faction. The third chapter (fols. 45a–53b) deals with the earlier revolt of Muḥammad Bey al-Faqārī in Upper Egypt (1069/1658). Both accounts are minutely detailed, forming a diary of the events they describe.

11. Anon., *Zubdat ikhtiṣār*

This is a chronicle of Ottoman Egypt, constructed on the usual pattern of viceroyalties. The unique manuscript, in the British Museum, consists of forty-one folios. The detailed account of events begins (fol. 6a) with the middle decades of the eleventh/seventeenth century, and goes down to 1111/1699, with an additional entry for 1113/1701–2. The author has clearly used *Waq'at al-ṣanājiq* for his account of the troubles of 1069/1658 and 1071/1660, since his narrative follows this closely, although his phraseology is more colloquial than that of al-Ṣāliḥī. The later part of the work is so full as to be almost a diary. It is a most valuable source for the last decades of the seventeenth century.

12. Anon., Paris Fragment

This work, of which neither the title nor the author's name has survived, consists of seventy-eight folios containing parts of two chapters. The first, of which the beginning is lacking, is a history of the Ottoman sultans, starting (in the present state of the manuscript) about the middle of the fifteenth century. As its close (fol. 25b) Ahmed III is spoken of as the reigning sultan, and the last event to be mentioned is the war with Russia in Dhu'l-Qa'da 1123/July 1711. The second chapter (denoted Chapter 4 in the manuscript) deals with the viceroys of Egypt in the Ottoman period, the extant portion ending with the events of Dhu'l-Qa'da 1120/February 1709: thus about three *hijrī* years are lacking. The later part of this chapter is very full. It both supplements and continues *Zubdat ikhtiṣār*, but the details of the narrative and the phraseology show it to be an independent source.

13. Aḥmad Çelebi, *Awdaḥ al-ishārāt*

This work, extant in a unique manuscript in Yale, deals with the viceroys of Egypt from Khā'ir Bey to the departure of Bakīr Pasha in Jumādā II 1150/ September 1737. For the period covered also by the Paris Fragment, there is a fairly close resemblance in subject-matter (but not in phraseology) between the two chronicles.[7]

14. The Damurdāshī Group of Chronicles

This group of chronicles may be distinguished from those surveyed above by the following characteristics:

(i) The language in which they are written is very colloquial, while the earlier chronicles at least attempt to present a literary style.

(ii) The framework of viceroyalties is no longer carefully preserved: these chronicles are constructed episodically around the exploits of the military grandees of the Faqāriyya and Qāsimiyya.

(iii) After an introduction describing the Faqārī and Qāsimī factions, all these chronicles begin with the opening of the twelfth *hijrī* century.

Although the chronicles of this group exhibit a marked family resemblance, they also show considerable variations of phraseology, suggesting that they are different narrators' versions of a common theme, rather than recensions of a written original. Like the work of Ibn Zunbul, these chronicles contain many reported speeches, conveying an impression of inside knowledge, but again this is, probably, a literary device. There is probably a saga element in these chronicles, and the data they appear to provide should be used with caution.

Three versions are distinguishable in the manuscripts known to me:

(*a*) Al-Qīnalī, *Majmū' laṭīf*. This is a large fragment, which in its present form goes down to 1152/1739.

(*b*) Anon., *Kitāb* (*Majmū'*) *al-durra al-munṣāna*. In its complete form (in the Bodleian manuscript), this version goes down to 1168/1754–5. There is a large fragment in the Cambridge manuscript.

(*c*) Al-Damurdāshī, *al-Durra al-muṣāna*. This version goes down to 1169/1756, and shows marked differences from the anonymous version.

15. Anon., *History of the Year 1191*

This is a work of the same type as the Damurdāshī Group. Written in colloquial Arabic, it deals with the exploits of the grandees.

WRITINGS OF THE EARLY THIRTEENTH/NINETEENTH CENTURY

16. Al-Sharqāwī, *Tuḥfat al-nāẓirīn*[8]

This work was composed at the request of the retinue of the Grand *Vezir* Yusuf Pasha, whom the author met at Bilbays in Ramaḍān 1214/January–February 1800. It is a very thin compendium of Egyptian history, and is practically worthless.

17. Al-Khashshāb[9]

Two short historical works may be attributed to this writer:

(*a*) *Tadhkira*. This is a brief chronicle of Ottoman Egypt in the eighteenth century, down to the beginning of the French occupation, contained in twenty-six folios.

(*b*) *Khulāṣat mā yurād*. Although the author is not named, a note in French (fol. 1a) states that the manuscript is an autograph of the archivist of the Divan of Cairo in 1216 (i.e. 1801–2). Al-Khashshāb held under Menou a post which might be so described. The work, in thirty folios, is a biography of Murād Bey, and appears to be the only work of this type in the period here surveyed.

18. Al-Jabartī, *'Ajā'ib al-āthār*

Of al-Jabartī's monumental work, the first two volumes, dealing with events from 1100/1688–9 to the eve of the French invasion in 1213/1798, fall within the period surveyed in this paper. The principal problems relating to the composition of the work have been discussed in detail by Professor Ayalon, and the remarks which follow should be read in connexion with his studies.[10]

The first volume, which ends with 1189/1775–6, presents particular difficulties. It should be regarded as an historical introduction to the main body of the work. Al-Jabartī himself draws attention to the year 1190 as that from which he kept a regular record of events. His own account of his sources for the first volume is neither full nor explicit. He speaks of the neglect and dispersal of Egyptian historical manuscripts, culminating in the action of the French, who 'took what they found to their country'[11] thereby giving us a *terminus a quo* for the composition of this volume. He refers, rather contemptuously, to writings by common soldiers, and, with rather more respect, to the chronicle of Aḥmad Çelebi, which, he says, like the other works, ended in 1150. Owing to the absence of chronicles after that date, he had recourse to informants, official registers, and funerary inscriptions. From 1170 to 1190, he was himself a witness of events—he was born in 1167/1753.

Al-Jabartī's use of four identifiable sources can be established for this first volume. These are:

(i) The chronicle of al-Isḥāqī, and probably its Continuation;
(ii) The chronicle represented by the Paris Fragment;
(iii) A chronicle or chronicles of the Damurdāshī Group;
(iv) The chronicle of Aḥmad Çelebi.

He also includes some folk-tales of a legendary nature. From this it follows that the first volume is of uneven value. Down to the middle of the eighteenth century, he combines (although he does not fully synthesize) sources of varying quality. Only from 1170/1756–7 onwards, after the end of the Damurdāshī Group, does his chronicle acquire independent evidential value: before that date, recourse should be had to the older sources.

BIBLIOGRAPHICAL APPENDIX

(1) 'Alī b. Muḥammad al-Lakhmī al-Ishbīlī al-Maghribī al-Dimashqī, *al-Durr al-muṣān fī sīrat al-muẓaffar Salīm khān*, ed. Hans Ernst (Cairo, 1962). *GAL, S*, III, 1303.

(2) Muḥammad b. Aḥmad b. Iyās, *Badā'i' al-zuhūr fī waqā'i' al-duhūr*, ed. Mohamad Mostafa, vol. V (2nd edn., Cairo, 1380/1961). *GAL*, II, 295; *S*, II, 405.

Partial translation by W. H. Salmon, *An account of the Ottoman conquest of Egypt in the year* A.H. *922* (A.D. *1516*) (London, 1921). Full translation by Gaston Wiet, *Journal d'un bourgeois du Caire*, Tome ii (Paris, 1960). The latter translation is made from a better text, and is preferable in itself.

(3) Aḥmad b. Zunbul al-Rammāl al-Maḥallī. The lithographed edition gives the title of the work in the corrupt form: *Kitāb ta'rīkh al-sulṭān Salīm khān b. al-sulṭān Bāyazīd khān ma' Qānṣawh al-Ghawrī sulṭān Miṣr wa-a'mālihā*. It is dated in the colophon Rabī' II 1278 [October 1861]. No place of publication is given. In MS. Bruce 21 (Bodleian Library, Oxford) the title is given as: *Ta'rīkh*

ghazwat al-sulṭān Salīm khān ma' al-sulṭān al-Ghawrī. *GAL*, II, 43, 298; *S*, II, 409.

(4) Muḥammad b. 'Abd al-Mu'ṭī al-Isḥāqī al-Manūfī, *Kitāb akhbār al-uwal fī man taṣarrafa fī Miṣr min arbāb al-duwal* (Cairo, 1311). *GAL*, II, 296; *S*, II, 407.

(5) [The Continuation of al-Isḥāqī.] Author's name and title lacking. Bibliothèque Nationale, Paris; MS. arabe 1854. At fol. 110b (within the portion derived from al-Isḥāqī), the author's name is given as Muḥammad b. Isḥāq: this, of course, gives no clue as to the continuator.

This was perhaps the first Arabic chronicle of Ottoman Egypt to be translated into a European language: it was almost certainly the source of the 'Abrégé chronologique de l'histoire de la Maison Ottomane et du gouvernement de l'Égypte', in M. Digeon, *Nouveaux contes turcs et arabes* (Paris, 1781).

(6) Mar'ī b. Yūsuf al-Ḥanbalī al-Maqdisī, *Nuzhat al-nāẓirīn fī ta'rīkh man waliya Miṣr min al-khulafā' wa'l-salāṭīn*. Bodleian, MS. D'Orville 544. The portion dealing with the viceroys of Ottoman Egypt also appears as the continuation of Ibn Zunbul in the British Museum, London; MS. Or. 3031. *GAL*, II, 369; *S*, II, 496.

(7) Ahmad b. Sa'd al-Din al-Ghamrī, *Dhakhīrat al-i'lām: Ta'rīkh umarā' Miṣr fi'l-Islām*. British Museum, MS. Or 6377. *GAL*, II, 297; *S*, II, 408.

(8) Shams al-Dīn Muḥammad b. Abi'l-Surūr al-Bakrī al-Ṣiddīqī:

(*a*) *al-Rawḍa al-zahiyya fī / wulāt Miṣr wa'l-Qāhira*. Bodleian, MS. Pocock 80. / *akhbār Miṣr wa'l-Qāhira al-mu'izziyya*. Bodleian, MS. Bruce 35.

(*b*) *al-Kawākib al-sā'ira fī akhbār Miṣr wa'l-Qāhira*. British Museum, MS. Add. 9973. *GAL*, II, 297; *S*, II, 408.

Al-Kawākib was described in detail by Silvestre de Sacy in *Notices et extraits des manuscrits de la Bibliothèque du Roi*, I (1788), 165–280. The portion of the third chapter dealing with the Ottoman period is translated in full.

(9) Anon., *Kitāb qahr al-wujūh al-'ābisa bi-dhikr nasab al-Jarākisa min Quraysh* (Cairo, 1316 [1898–99]); also MS. Or. 3030 (British Museum). In MS. Arabic 791, fols. 236–66 (Rylands Library, Manchester) the title is given as: *Qahr al-wujūh al-'ābisa bi-dhikr nasab umarā' al-Jarākisa wa'ttiṣālihi bi-Quraysh*. *GAL*, *S*, II, 406.

(10) Ibrāhīm b. Abī Bakr al-Ṣāliḥī al-Ḥanbalī, *Tarājim al-ṣawā'iq fī waq'at al-ṣanājiq*. Bibliothèque Nationale, MS. arabe 1853. *GAL*, II, 299; *S*, II, 410.

(11) Anon., *Zubdat ikhtiṣār ta'rīkh mulūk Miṣr al-maḥrūsa*. British Museum, MS. Add. 9972.

(12) [Paris Fragment.] Author's name and title lacking. Bibliothèque Nationale, MS. arabe, 1855.

(13) Aḥmad Çelebi b. 'Abd al-Ghanī al-Ḥanafī al-Miṣrī, *Awdaḥ al-ishārāt fī man tawallā Miṣr al-Qāhira min al-wuzarā wa'l-bāshāt*. Yale University Library; Landberg MS. no. 3.

(14) (*a*) Muṣṭafā b. Ibrāhīm al-Maddāḥ al-Qīnalī, *Majmū' laṭif*. Nationalbibliothek, Vienna; MS. Hist. Osm. 38. *GAL*, II, 299; *S*, II, 410.

(*b*) Anon., *Kitāb* (*Majmū'*) *al-durra al-munṣāna fī waqāī'* (*sic*) *al-kināna*. Bodleian, MS. Bruce 43; University Library Cambridge; MS. Add. 278[7]. *GAL*, *S*, II, 411 (the Cambridge manuscript only).

(*c*) Aḥmad al-Damurdāshī, *kâhya* of '*Azeban*, *al-Durra al-muṣāna fī akhbār al-kināna*, British Museum, MS. Or. 1073–4. *GAL*, II, 300.

(15) [*History of the year 1191*.] Anon., no title. Bibliothèque Nationale, MS. arabe 1856. The first line after the *basmala* is a species of title, and reads: *Fī ta'rīkh 'ām 1191 mā waqa'a fi'l-kināna min dawlat Muḥammad Bayk*. *GAL*, *S*, II, 411.

(16) 'Abdallāh b. Ḥijāzī al-Sharqāwī, *Tuḥfat al-nāẓirīn fī man waliya Miṣr min al-wulāt wa'l-salāṭīn*. Printed in the margin of 4. Al-Isḥāqī, *Akhbār al-uwal* (Cairo, 1311). *GAL*, II, 479; *S*, II, 729.

(17) Ismā'īl b. Sa'd al-Khashshāb:

(*a*) *Tadhkira li-ahl al-baṣā'ir wa'l-abṣār ma' wajh al-ikhtiṣār*. Bibliothèque Nationale, MS. arabe 1958. This brief chronicle of Ottoman Egypt in the twelfth *hijrī* century forms the basis of Delaporte, "Abrégé chronologique de l'histoire des Mamlouks d'Égypte", *Description de l'Égypte, État moderne*, II, i, 165 ff. *GAL*, *S*, II, 720.

(*b*) *Khulāṣat mā yurād min akhbār al-amīr Murād*, Bibliothèque Nationale, MS. arabe 1859. The completion of the manuscript is dated in the colophon 18 Muḥarram 1216/31 May 1801.

(18) 'Abd al-Raḥmān b. Ḥasan al-Jabartī, *'Ajā'ib al-āthār fi'l-tarājim wa'l-akhbār* (Būlāq, 1297). *GAL*, II, 480; *S*, II, 730.

NOTES

1 Among the external Arabic sources may be noted (i) the biographical dictionaries of al-Ghazzī, al-Muḥibbī, and al-Murādī; (ii) Quṭb al-Dīn Muḥammad b. Aḥmad al-Nahrawālī, *al-Barq al-yamānī* (see below, p. 217, n. 13), for information on the Mamluk and Ottoman exploits in the Yemen, and sidelights on Egypt in the early Ottoman period; (iii) Aḥmad b. Zaynī Daḥlān, *Khulāṣat al-kalām fi umarā' al-balad al-Ḥarām*, for relations between Ottoman Egypt and the *amīrs* of Mecca. The Syrian and Lebanese sources for the intervention in Syrian affairs of *Bulut Kapan* 'Ali Bey and Muḥammad Bey Abu'l-Dhahab are fully indicated by Dr. Abdul-Karim Rafeq in *The Province of Damascus 1723–1783* (2nd edn., Beirut, 1970).

2 Shortened forms of the authors' names and the titles of the works are given in the text. For further particulars, see the Bibliographical Appendix.

3 See *EI*², II, 839–40, FATḤNĀME (G. L. Lewis).

4 A detailed study of Ibn Abi'l-Surūr's historical writings has been prepared by Dr. Abdul-Karim Rafeq.

5 Thus the Bodleian MS. Pocock 80. The Bodleian MS. Bruce 35 resumes the list of governors down to Ṣafar 1061/January 1651, but this appendix is a mere list of names and dates, probably added by another hand.

6 See below, pp. 220–30.

7 For a comparison of some passages in the two chronicles, see below, pp. 232–33.

8 See Gamal El-Din El-Shayyal, *A history of Egyptian historiography in the nineteenth century* (Alexandria, 1962), 12–14.

9 See El-Shayyal, op. cit., 14–15; David Ayalon, "The historian al-Jabartī and his background", *BSOAS*, vol. xxiii, 2 (1960), 241–3.

10 Ayalon, "The historian al-Jabartī and his background", *BSOAS*, xxiii, 2 (1960), 217–49; *EI*², V, 355–7, AL-DJABARTĪ.

11 Al-Jabartī, *'Ajā'ib*, I, 6.

10

AL-JABARTĪ'S INTRODUCTION TO THE HISTORY OF OTTOMAN EGYPT

1. *Analysis of al-Jabartī's Account*

Al-Jabartī's chronicle, *'Ajā'ib al-āthār fi'l-tarājim wa'l-akhbār* formally begins with the year 1100/1688–9 (p. 24 of the first volume of the Būlāq edition). He precedes his annals, however, with an introduction, of which the last part (p. 20, line 23–p. 24, line 4) is concerned with Ottoman Egypt from the time of the conquest by Selim I to the beginning of the twelfth *hijrī* century.

This concluding portion of the introduction is by no means a systematic synopsis of events; it is indeed remarkable for the almost total absence of historical data. Its composite nature is indicated both by the heterogeneity of its contents, and by its varied styles of composition, which alternate between *saj'* and ordinary prose. Its component parts are as follows:

(A) p. 20, lines 23–33	This is written in prose and comprises:
p. 20, lines 23–27	(*a*) A brief note on the conquest of Egypt by Selim I, citing Ibn Iyās, al-Qaramānī, Ibn Zunbul, and others not named as detailed authorities for the period.
p. 20, lines 27–33	(*b*) A short account of the dispositions made by Selim in Egypt, including his pardon to the Circassians and his confirmation of existing *waqfs*, stipends, and other financial arrangements.
(B) p. 20, line 33–p. 21, line 11	A eulogy of Sultan Süleyman I, followed by a eulogy of the rule of the Ottoman sultans in the heyday of the Empire. This is in *saj'*.
(C) p. 21, lines 11–23	An anecdote concerning the appearance of corruption in the Ottoman Empire, in which the characters are Sultan Selim II and Shemsi Pasha al-'Ajamī. The anecdote is taken from al-Isḥāqī, and is in prose.
(D) p. 21, line 23–p. 23, line 19	A long passage in *saj'* comprising:
p. 21, lines 23–27	(*a*) Reflections on the above anecdote, concluding with a line of verse.

p., 21, lines 28–31	(*b*) The appearance of the Faqāriyya and Qāsimiyya factions in Ottoman Egypt; and their connexion with the factions of Sa'd and Ḥarām.
p. 21, line 31–p. 23, line 19	(*c*) An anecdote of the origin of the Faqāriyya and Qāsimiyya in the time of Selim I concluding with a line of verse.
(E) p. 23 line 20–p.24, line 4	A passage in prose comprising:
p. 23, lines 20–29	(*a*) An alternative anecdote of the origin of the Faqāriyya and Qāsimiyya in A.H. 1050.
p. 23, lines 29–33	(*b*) An account of their distinctive insignia.
p. 23, line 22–p. 24, line 4	(*c*) A list of the Faqārī and Qāsimī beys at the beginning of the twelfth *hijrī* century.

Al-Jabartī is extremely reticent about his sources for this period. His allusion to Ibn Iyās, al-Qaramānī, and Ibn Zunbul as authorities for the Ottoman conquest lacks weight, since his account of this event is so brief that it precludes the identification of sources. His use of al-Isḥāqī will be considered below. Speaking of his sources, he says (p. 6, lines 20–24):

> "After search and investigation, I found only some quires written by some common soldiers, which were incorrectly composed, ill arranged and planned, and rendered thin by the lack of correct expressions in some of the occurrences. I obtained a history of these kinds, but on the whole in good order, by a person called Aḥmad Çelebi b. 'Abd al-Ghanī, beginning with the time when the House of 'Uthmān gained possession of Egypt, and ending like the others we have mentioned in A.H. 1150."

This chronicle, he states, was subsequently lost.

2. *The Literary Chronicles*

Two types of chronicle were produced in Egypt during the seventeenth and eighteenth centuries, which we may denote respectively the literary and popular chronicles. The literary chronicles are written in an Arabic which, although pedestrian and sometimes ungrammatical, implies a background of some literary education. These are chronicles of the "sultan-pasha" type: their main framework, that is to say, is provided by the reigns of the Ottoman sultans and the viceroyalties of their pashas in Egypt. Within this framework the treatment of events is annalistic. Although these chronicles are sometimes copious, especially in their later parts, where the writers are dealing with the events of their own lifetimes, they make little attempt to explain the causes behind developments. The reader feels that they are descriptions from the outside, and he often lacks a key to the motives of the actors in the narrative.

One such literary chronicle, which was known to al-Jabartī, is the *Kitāb akhbār al-uwal fī man taṣarrafa fī Miṣr min arbāb al-duwal* of Muḥammad b. ʻAbd al-Muʻṭī al-Isḥāqī.[1] Professor Ayalon has commented that "as al-Isḥāqī's chronicle ends in the year 1033/1623–4, it could hardly be of much use to al-Jabartī".[2] While this is true of the main body of al-Jabartī's chronicle, it does not apply to the introductory material. Furthermore it is very probable that al-Jabartī had access to a recension of al-Isḥāqī which continued the narrative of events down to a later date than that of the versions that have been printed.

One recension of this kind is extant today in the Bibliothèque Nationale (MS. arabe 1854).[3] In this Paris recension the chronicle is continued down to 1084/1673, but the later portion cannot be by al-Isḥāqī, who died in 1060/1650. There is a slight indication that al-Jabartī used the text represented by this Paris recension. In his first volume, p. 91, line 12, he states that (89) Riḍwān Bey[4] died in A.H. 1065. This is the date given by the Paris recension, whereas other chronicles place the death in Jumādā II 1066. The event, of course, falls outside the standard versions of al-Isḥāqī.

Al-Jabartī's use of al-Isḥāqī's chronicle is established by his own statement that the anecdote of Selim II and Shemsi Pasha (Passage C) is derived from that source. The story is not found in the Paris recension, but appears in the standard versions as printed. It may be noted, in passing, that al-Jabartī's phraseology is closer to the text of the Cairo edition of 1286/1869 than to that of 1296/1879.[5] It is possible that al-Jabartī's account of Selim I's pardon of the Circassians and confirmation of their financial privileges (Passage A (*b*)) may be derived from another anecdote, the legend of Selim, Khā'ir Bey, and Yūnus Pasha (see below, p. 171), which is recounted by al-Isḥāqī as historical evidence for the rights of the neo-Mamluks.

Since al-Jabartī was acquainted with the chronicle of al-Isḥāqī, both in its original form and, probably, in a continuation, a further question arises. Why did al-Jabartī fail to draw on al-Isḥāqī's abundant data on early Ottoman Egypt for his introduction? To this problem we shall return in the concluding section of this article.

3. *The Popular Chronicles*

These are chronicles composed by persons of little or no literary education for the primary purpose of entertainment. They form a single family, in which the same basic material is presented in several recensions. They are all eighteenth-century in date, and have no known predecessors in the historical writing of the seventeenth century. All begin, after a short introduction, with the opening of the twelfth *hijrī* century. Although their construction shows traces of the "sultan-pasha" framework, this is not stressed (e.g. by short accounts of the acts of the sultans) as in the literary chronicles. In style, they are characterized by abrupt, colloquial, often highly ungrammatical sentences, stages in the narrative being marked by recurrent clichés, such as *wa-idhā bi . . .* , *wa'l-narja' ilā. . . .*

The impression produced on the reader is that the chronicles are fundamentally the records of colloquial, oral narrations. This impression is heightened by other characteristics. In contrast with the literary chronicles, their dating is sparse and imprecise. The variants of phraseology among the chronicles are so great as to suggest different narrations of a common theme, of which the principal incidents and framework were fixed by a traditional model, rather than recensions of a written original. The narrative abounds in the alleged speeches of the actors: these should probably be regarded rather as a narrator's device than as authentic records. There is also some evidence of the transposition of events in order to heighten the dramatic effect.

Thus these popular chronicles are probably less reliable than the literary chronicles as sources for reconstructing the order of events. In one respect, however, they are of great value. They were composed, as far as can be discovered, by soldiers for the entertainment of their comrades. While the interest of their narrators is limited to the doings of the military grandees and the Seven Corps of the Ottoman garrison, a narrower field than that of the literary chroniclers, they afford us a greater depth of insight into the motives of the actors, and the significance of events. In sum, the popular chronicles may supply the missing key to the more sober factual accounts of the literary chronicles.

This family of eighteenth-century chronicles may be designated as the Damurdāshī Group (short reference, D Group),[6] since Brockelmann ascribes them to a certain Aḥmad al-Damurdāshī, who held the post of *kâhya* of the *'Azeban* Corps. This ascription is in fact made in only a single manuscript of the group, that in the British Museum, the others being anonymous. To the D Group also belongs the chronicle composed by Muṣṭafā b. Ibrāhīm al-Maddāḥ al-Qīnalī, which Brockelmann lists as an independent work. Al-Qīnalī speaks of himself as "the retainer of the late *ağa* of *'Azeban* Ḥasan Damurdāshī". I have not yet discovered the relationship between the *Ağa* Ḥasan al-Damurdāshī and the *Kâhya* Aḥmad al-Damurdāshī.

I have examined the following D Group manuscripts:

(i) *Majmū' laṭīf* (DQ), the Qīnalī manuscript in the Nationalbibliothek, Vienna (MS. Hist. Osm. 38). This goes down to 1152/1739, and was brought from Egypt in 1829. It probably represents the primitive form of the narrative. (*GAL*, II, 299; *S.*, II, 419.)

(ii) *Kitāb* (*Majmū‘*) *al-durra al-munṣāna fī waqāī‘* [*sic*] *al-kināna* (DO). An anonymous manuscript in the Bodleian Library (MS. Bruce 43). It goes down to 1168/1754–5, and must have been written before 1773, when James Bruce, its purchaser, left Egypt. (Not in *GAL.*)

(iii) *Majmū‘ al-durra al-munṣāna fī waqāī‘* [*sic*] *al-kināna* (DC). An anonymous and incomplete manuscript in Cambridge University Library (MS. Add. 278[7]). Apart from slight verbal differences this is identical with DO, and does not require separate consideration in this article. (*GAL, S.*, II, 411.)

(iv) *Al-Durra al-muṣāna fī akhbār al-kināna* (DL). The manuscript, ascribed to Aḥmad al-Damurdāshī, is in the British Museum (MS. Or. 1073–4). It goes down to 1169/1756, and was copied in 1215/1800 from an earlier manuscript. It shows marked differences from DO/DC. (*GAL*, II, 300.)

4. *The Fāqariyya and Qāsimiyya in the D Group Chronicles and al-Jabartī*

Near the opening of each of the four D Group chronicles occur passages which exhibit a mutual resemblance, and also a resemblance to al-Jabartī's account of the Fāqariyya and Qāsimiyya (E):

(*a*) *The Account in DQ*

This is the simplest account, and runs as follows:

[3a] كانت اهل مصر من قديم الزمان فرقتين عساكر وعربان ورعية راية بيضا وراية حمرا البيضا تبعى والحمرا كليبى زغبى وهلالى قلاوونى وبيبرسى الى دولت [*sic*] ال عثمان نصرها الله تعالى فقارى سعد قاسمى حرام فرقتين فى بعضهم وعلى [two doubtful words] واحدة الفقارى يهوى الجراقات والقاسمى يهوى العمارات وكانت اهل مصر المحروسة يعرفون الفقارى والقاسمى فى المواكب اما الموكب المحفل الشريف واما موكب الباشا بالمزاريق المشالة قدام السناجق والاغاوات واختيارية الاوجاقات الفقارى مزراقه برمانة والقاسمى مزراقه بجلبة امر معروف بينهم

"From ancient times the people of Egypt, soldiery, Arabs, and civilians [*or* peasantry] were two parties: white flag and red flag.

The white was Tubbaʿī, and the red Kulaybī: Zughbī and Hilālī; Qalāwūnī and Baybarsī; until the time of the House of ʿUthmān (may God Most High grant it victory), when the two parties became Faqārī-Saʿd and Qāsimī-Ḥarām.[7] [Doubtful phrase] . . . The Faqārī loves retainers,[8] and the Qāsimī loves buildings. The people of Cairo would recognize the Faqārī and the Qāsimī in processions, whether the Pilgrimage procession or the procession of the Pasha, by the javelins borne in front of the beys, the *ağas*, and the senior officers of the Corps. The javelins of the Faqārī had a knob, and the javelins of the Qāsimī had a disc (?): the circumstance was known amongst them."

(b) The Account in DO and DC

These give a variant account of the factions as follows:

[DO: 2a; DC: 2b] كانت اهل مصر سناجق [صناجق :DC] واغاوات
والسبعة اجاقات فرقتين راية بيضا عن التبع اليمانى وراية حمرا عن كليب
اخوا [*sic*] الزير [DC: الوزير] سعد وحرام فقارى وقاسمى

"And the people of Egypt, beys, *ağas*, and the Seven Corps, were two factions: a white flag for the Yamānī Tubbaʿ, and a red flag for Kulayb, the brother of al-Zīr [DC: *al-wazīr*];[9] Saʿd and Ḥarām, Faqārī and Qāsimī."

In the lines that follow, the statement in DQ that "the Faqārī loves retainers, and the Qāsimī loves buildings" is replaced by the anecdote, too long to quote here, of the Feast of Zayn al-Faqār.[10] The gist of this anecdote is that Qāsim Bey the *Defterdar*, the eponym of the Qāsimiyya, lavished his wealth on building a great hall, and invited the *Amīr al-Ḥājj* Zayn al-Faqār Bey,[11] to a feast there. In due course Zayn al-Faqār invited Qāsim to a feast in his own house, and summoned all his retainers to attend. A great concourse of grandees was present when the two beys sat down to eat, and Qāsim wished to wait until they were also seated. But Zayn al-Faqār replied, "They will eat after us; they are all my *mamlūks*. When I die, they will remain to ask for mercy for me. Will your hall speak, and ask for mercy for you? Wealth is squandered in stone and mud."

The passage concludes with a description of the insignia of the two factions, similar to that in DQ:

[DO: 2b; DC: 4a] الكثرة والجودة عند الفقارية والمال والبخل عند
القاسمية وكنا نعرف الفقارى والقاسمى فى موكب الباشا او موكب
المحفل مزارق الفقارى برمانة ومزارق القاسمى بجلبة

"The Faqāriyya had numbers and generosity, and the Qāsimiyya had wealth and miserliness. We used to recognize the Faqārī and Qāsimī in the Pasha's procession or the Pilgrimage procession [because] the javelins of the Faqārī had a knob, and the javelins of the Qāsimī had a disc (?)."

The narrator then gives a list of the Faqārī and Qāsimī beys in the time of Ḥasan Pasha IV.

(*c*) *The Account in DL*

This resembles the expanded account given by DO/DC. It begins as follows:

[5a] وكانت فى ايامه دولة مصر فى فرقتين سعد وحرام تبعى وكليبى [supply حسينى] ويزيدى الحسينى رايته بيضا واليزيدى رايته حمرا واكرى [?] وقيسى وكنا نعرف سعد وحرام من المواكب رمانة سعد بجلبة مدورة ومزارق نصف حرام بجلبة من غير رمانة وما كان ظهر فقارى وقاسمى بمصر عسكر وعربان وقرى الا فى دولة آل عثمان

"And in his days [i.e. the viceroyalty of Baltajı Ḥasan Pasha III at the end of the eleventh *hijrī* century] the government of Egypt was in two factions, Sa'd and Ḥarām, Tubba'ī and Kulaybī, [*supply* Ḥusaynī] and Yazīdī; the Ḥusaynī's flag was white, and the Yazīdī's flag was red: and Akrī (?) and Qaysī. And we used to recognize Sa'd and Ḥarām in the processions: the knob of Sa'd had a circular disc (?), and the javelins of Niṣf Ḥarām had a disc (?) without a knob. And Faqārī and Qāsimī only appeared in Egypt among the soldiery, Arabs, and villages in the time of the House of 'Uthmān."

The narrator then tells the story of the Feast of Zayn al-Faqār, substantially as it is given in DO/DC, but with some difference of detail and considerable variations of phrasing. The passage concludes with an account of the insignia of the two factions, approximately repeating what has gone before:

[6a] وسمى من ذلك اليوم نصف سعد فقارى و سمى نصف حرام قاسمى وصرنا نعرف فى المواكب الفقارى والقاسمى من المزارق لان الفقارى المزارق الذى يكون قدامه اذا كان برمانة فهذا يكون فقارى واذا كان المزارق [6b] بجلبة من غير رمانة فيكون قاسمى

"And from the day [i.e. of the Feast of Zayn al-Faqār] Niṣf Sa'd was called Faqārī, and Niṣf Ḥarām Qāsimī. And we used to recognize the Faqārī and the Qāsimī in the processions from the javenlins; for the javelins that were in front of the Faqārī—if they had a knob, they were Faqārī, and if the javelins were with a disc (?) without a knob, they were Qāsimī."

The narrator then gives a list of the Faqārī and Qāsimī beys in the time of Ḥasan Pasha III.[12]

(d) Al-Jabartī's Prose Account

Now let us compare these accounts in the D Group with al-Jabartī's prose account (Passage E; p. 23, line 20–p. 24, line 4). He begins by stating that "the Qāsimiyya originate from Qāsim Bey the *Defterdar*, the retainer of Muṣṭafā Bey, and the origin of the Faqāriyya is from Dhu'l-Faqār Bey the Elder (*al-Kabīr*); and the first appearance of this was from the year 1050—and God knows best the truth!" He then proceeds to give the anecdote of the Feast of Dhu'l-Faqār Bey, concluding with the words:

وكانت الفقارية موصوفة بالكثرة والكرم والقاسمية بكثرة المال والبخل وكان الذى يتميز به احد الفرقتين من الآخر اذا ركبوا فى المواكب ان يكون بيرق الفقارى ابيض ومزاريقه برمانة وبيرق القاسمية احمر ومزاريقه بجلبة

"And the Faqāriyya were characterized by numbers and generosity, and the Qāsimiyya by abundance of wealth and meanness. The means of distinguishing one of the factions from the other, when they rode in processions, was that the Faqārī's flag was white, and his javelins had a knob, while the flag of Qāsimiyya was red, and his javelins had a disc (?)."

Al-Jabartī then gives a list of the Faqārī and Qāsimī beys at the beginning of the twelfth *hijrī* century.

From the preceding examination of passages in the D Group chronicles and al-Jabartī, the following inferences may be made:

(i) DQ represents the oldest form of the D Group chronicles, and the framework it supplied served as a basis for later augmented narrations or recensions.

(ii) DO/DC and DL are both derived from DQ, but are sufficiently different in their phraseology to represent distinct lines of development, or the versions of different oral narrators. Of the two, DL is more colloquial and corrupt than DO/DC.

(iii) Al-Jabartī's account was derived from one of the expanded narratives, which *prima facie* appears to be one in the DO/DC line of development. This is indicated by Al-Jabartī's contrast between the numbers and generosity of the Faqāriyya, and the wealth and meanness of the Qāsimiyya—a contrast found in DO/DC but not in DL. Furthermore, although the lists of beys in DL and al-Jabartī differ, the list given in DO/DC is identical with that in a British Museum manuscript of al-Jabartī.[13] On the other hand, al-Jabartī makes two statements which do not appear in the D Group narratives: that Qāsim Bey was the retainer of Muṣṭafā Bey, and that the Faqāriyya and Qāsimiyya originated from the year 1050/1640–1.[14]

We have now accounted for virtually all the prose passages in the portion of al-Jabartī's introduction dealing with Ottoman Egypt, and may summarize our conclusions, with reference to the analysis of the introduction on pp. 161–2 above as follows:

(A (*a*)) Authorities mentioned, but specific identification of sources not feasible.

(A (*b*)) Source probably al-Isḥāqī.

(C) Reproduced from al-Isḥāqī.

(E) Derived from a D Group chronicle, probably of the DO line.

Two further points may be added. First, it seems reasonable to equate the "quires written by some common soldiers", mentioned by al-Jabartī, with the D group chronicles. From al-Jabartī's phraseology, it is possible that he used more than one chronicle of this group. Secondly, al-Jabartī seems to have been influenced by the popular chronicles in starting his detailed narrative with the opening of the twelfth *hijrī* century, although a further influence may well have been the scope of al-Murādī's biographical dictionary.[15]

There remain for consideration the two passages in *saj*', B and D, to which we now turn.

5. *The* saj' *passages in al-Jabartī*

With regard to the first passage in *saj*', the eulogy of Sultan Süleyman and of the Ottoman rulers in the heyday of the Empire (*fī ṣadri dawlatihim*), no problem of the identification of sources arises, since this is, superficially at least, a conventional piece of panegyric.

Passage D is more complex. It contains al-Jabartī's first account of the appearance of the Faqāriyya and Qāsimiyya, which is prefaced (D(*b*)) with the following remarks:

> "And during the period of Ottoman rule, and their Egyptian viceroys and grandees, there appeared among the soldiery of Egypt a heathenish custom and devilish innovation[16] (*sunna jāhiliyya wa-bid'a shayṭāniyya*), which sowed worldliness (*nifāq*)[17] in them, and established contention among them. Therein they concurred with the base artisans, with their talk of Sa'd and Ḥarām. This was that the troops as a whole were divided into two divisions, and in their entirety became partisans of two parties, a faction called Faqāriyya, and another known as Qāsimiyya."

Al-Jabartī then gives a long story purporting to describe the origin of the two factions. This narrates that after Selim I had conquered Egypt, and proscribed the Circassians, he asked his courtiers if they knew of any survivors. Khayr (Khā'ir) Bey replied that there yet remained an aged *amīr* named Sūdūn, who had two sons, peerless champions in equestrian exercises. During the recent catastrophe, Sūdūn had shut himself up in his house with his two sons, and had taken no part in affairs. At once Selim rode to the house of Sūdūn, whom he found, surrounded by retainers, reading the Qur'ān. The sultan calmed the old man's fears, and asked him why he had separated himself from his people. Sūdūn replied that he had seen the disorder and oppression of the Mamluk sultanate, and so he had withdrawn himself and his sons from the evil. He then produced his two sons, whose appearance and speech pleased the sultan. After a feast and an exchange of gifts, Selim left Sūdūn.

On the next day, the sultan rode out into the wilderness, and summoned all his soldiery to appear. Among them were Sūdūn and his two sons, Qāsīm and Dhu'l-Faqār, who were bidden to perform their equestrian exercises. Their skill amazed the Turks, and Selim conferred on them both the rank of *amīr*, and extolled them.

When the next day came, the sultan again mustered his soldiery, and ordered them to divide into two groups, one led by Dhu'l-Faqār, the other by his brother, Qāsim. Dhu'l-Faqār was joined by most of the Ottoman champions, Qāsim by most of the Egyptian warriors. The Faqāriyya were distinguished by wearing white robes, and the Qāsimiyya red. A mock cavalry-battle then took place, which almost turned into serious warfare, but the two sides were ordered to separate.

The ancedote is followed by the words:

> "So from that day, the grandees (*umarā'*) of Egypt and her soldiery were separated into two factions, and divided by this exercise into two parties. Each continued to love the colour in which he had appeared, and hated the other colour in everything possible, even in the table implements and utensils for food and drink. The Faqāriyya inclined to Niṣf Sa'd and the Ottomans, and the Qāsimiyya were friendly only with Ḥarām and the Egyptians. This became an unbreakable principle with them, one not to be abandoned in any circumstances."

This anecdote is completely unhistorical: apart from its obvious characteristics as a folk-tale, there is nothing in Ibn Iyās's contemporary account of the Ottoman conquest to support it. I have been unable to find it in any earlier source, and am inclined to think that it may have been a popular story, set in *saj'* by al-Jabartī himself.

Nevertheless, in spite of its lack of historicity, it presents certain interesting features. The first of these is the attempt to trace back the factional rivalry of the seventeenth and eighteenth centuries to the time of the Ottoman conquest. This method of legitimatizing, so to speak, a new political situation by antedating its origin is not uncommon, particularly in the history of the Muslim Near East at this period. A notorious example, which has befogged a good deal of European writing on Ottoman Egypt, is the belief, widely held in the eighteenth century, that the contemporary constitution of Egypt, and especially the functions of the beys, had been established by Selim I or Süleyman I. Another instrument for legitimatizing the present by misrepresenting the past was the spurious genealogy, of which the forged pedigree of (89) Riḍwān Bey,[18] and the alleged Umayyad descent of the Funj kings of Sinnār, are seventeenth-century examples.[19]

The second feature of interest in this anecdote is the role played by Sultan Selim. In spite of the fact that Selim destroyed the Circassian Mamluk sultanate, legends began to gather around his name in Ottoman Egypt, and he seems to have appeared to the popular view (including that of neo-Mamluk military society) as a beneficent hero. The present anecdote is one of these legends. Another is the story of Selim's pardon of the Circassians. This is based on an historical incident, Selim's execution of Yūnus Pasha, but it is marked by a dramatization and a telescoping of events such as is characteristic of legend. It was, however, a legend with a purpose. In the context in which al-Isḥāqī gives it, it is said to form part of a *fatwā* delivered in 1031/1621–2 by a *muftī*, Shaykh Muḥammad Ḥijāzī al-Wā'iẓ al-Sha'rāwī al-Khalwatī, giving protection to *iltizāms* and *waqfs*. It is significant also that al-Sha'rāwī's own authority for the story was "our master, the historian . . . Shihāb al-Dīn Aḥmad al-Jarkāsī"—a Circassian, or of Circassian descent.[20]

The most striking of these hero-legends is one which is given by al-Isḥāqī[21] and by the seventeenth-century verse chronicler, al-Ghamrī.[22] The story tells how Sultan Bayezid II was warned by an astrologer that he would be overthrown by a son yet unborn. Bayezid thereupon ordered the court midwife to kill any male children born in the harem, but to spare the girls. When Selim was born, the midwife, struck with his beauty, decided to save him, and he was brought up among the daughters of the sultan, and called Selima. One day, when Bayezid was in the harem, he noticed the rough and masterful behaviour of Selima, which aroused his suspicions. On discovering the sex of the child, he summoned the midwife who had disobeyed his command. She declared that fear of God had restrained her from killing the sinless child. Thereupon Bayezid accepted the will of God, and permitted his son, henceforward called Selim, to live, until in due time the prophecy was fulfilled. The story is a typical example of that great class of legends which deal with the miraculous preservation of a hero in infancy, and also seek to explain the hero's name.[23]

6. *The Significance of al-Jabartī's Account of Early Ottoman Egypt*

Al-Jabartī's account of early Ottoman Egypt, which we have analysed above, is in marked contrast to the body of his history which follows immediately. The alternating blocks of annals and obituaries for the years following A.H. 1100 abound in precise historical data. They are written for the overwhelmingly greater part in ordinary prose, and legendary elements are practically absent.

How is this contrast to be explained? It is not enough to say that the earlier part is merely introductory, and that for an introduction a synopsis of events is adequate. For, as we have seen, al-Jabartī's introduction is not a synopsis of events, but in very large measure, an assemblage of anecdotal and legendary materials. Neither can we say that al-Jabartī was compelled to use these materials for lack of genuine historical data: he was acquainted with al-Isḥāqī's chronicle, and probably with a continuation of it, which would have provided him with precise and reasonably detailed information at least down to 1033/1623–4, and very likely for fifty years afterwards. Furthermore, the next portion of his chronicle provides indubitable proof that he had access to chronicles covering the whole of the Ottoman period until well into the twelfth/eighteenth century. Finally, we cannot assume that al-Jabartī wrote his introduction as he did through carelessness or indolence, since the whole of the main body of his work displays him as a most conscientious and devoted historian.

The conclusion then must be that al-Jabartī deliberately selected these legendary anecdotes, and composed the introduction in the way he did, of set purpose. Consideration will show that the whole passage, far from being a hodge-podge of stories assembled by a naïve and credulous chronicler, is a subtle piece of historical interpretation and criticism.

Instead of attempting to summarize the complicated political history of nearly two centuries of Ottoman Egypt, al-Jabartī picks out two main themes. These are the contrast between the splendour of the Ottoman Empire at its zenith, and its tragic decline after the time of Süleyman I; and the resurgence within Ottoman Egypt of the neo-Mamluk military *élite*, from its first beginnings during the reign of Selim I himself, to the eve of the twelfth *hijrī* century. He does not attempt to trace out these themes in detail, but indicates their significance through the legendary anecdotes, which have a parabolical quality.

Al-Jabartī's use of the legends therefore serves as an interpretation of the course of Ottoman Egyptian history. Their setting also forms a vehicle for criticism. He gives the story of Selim II and Shemsi Pasha, and shows the sultan indignantly refusing the temptation to corruption. But his real opinions on the decay which set in throughout the Empire at this juncture are conveyed in his concluding comments (D(*a*)):

> "But see, my brother, and reflect on the significance of this anecdote: and I say that thereafter my heart is burdened, and my tongue is not free. The state of affairs is not unknown, for the tongue to speak of it. Inability has rendered me dumb, and unable to open my mouth: does any but God desire wisdom?
> 'Formerly they were in health;
> Then the signs of sickness entered in them.' "

He then goes on (D(*b*)) to describe the "heathenish custom and devilish innovation" of the Faqārī-Qāsimī rivalry.

In a similar mood he reflects on the results of this rivalry after giving the legend of Selim I and the Mamluk brothers (D(*c*)). The legend itself is a deliberate piece of fine writing, implicitly exalting the qualities and ideals of the Mamluk chivalry. But the reader is carried on by the flow of the *saj*ʿ to these concluding remarks, which reflect a very different attitude:

> "The matter continued to spread and increase, and the masters and slaves (*al-ʿabīd*) transmitted it by inheritance, until it became serious, and grew, and blood was shed for it. How many villages were laid waste and dignitaries slain, houses thrown down and castles burnt, freemen made captives and noblemen constrained by force!
> 'God knows, the pleasure of an hour
> Has bequeathed a long-drawn war.' "

Why did al-Jabartī decide to follow his *saj*ʿ account of the origins of the Faqāriyya and Qāsimiyya with another one in prose? Here again the significance can be inferred from the contrast. The *saj*ʿ account is a romantic set-piece, glorifying the exploits of two young Mamluk heroes, and stressing their obedience and loyalty to the Ottoman sultan. The prose account reflects the darker days of the following century. There is no mention of the Ottoman suzerain, and the Mamluk protagonists are no longer young and chivalrous warriors, but wealthy grandees, one lavishing his substance in a costly hall, the other in building up a retinue permeating the whole military organization.

Qāsim and Dhu'l-Faqār are almost allegorical figures of Avarice and Ambition, struggling for domination over Egypt. Al-Jabartī is still employing legend, but legend with a harshly realistic significance. Finally, with the list of rival beys, we cross the bridge from legend to historical fact, and encounter the grandees whose struggles are to be the substance of Egyptian history in the new century.

NOTES

1 See above, pp. 153–4, 159.

2 David Ayalon, "The historian al-Jabartī and his background", *BSOAS*, XXIII, 2, 1960, p. 222, n. 3.

3 See above, pp. 154, 159.

4 Numbers prefixed to names of seventeenth-century beys refer to notices in "The beylicate in Ottoman Egypt during the seventeenth century". See pp. 192–217 below.

5 The criteria are:

(i) Al-Jabartī's use of the word خلخلة (p. 21, line 15), which corresponds to the reading in the 1286 version, as against the 1296 version, which reads خلل.

(ii) Al-Jabartī's phrase يا بادشاه لا تعجل (p. 21, line 21). Here the 1286 version reads يا بادشاهم لا تعجل, and the 1296 version لا تعجل ايهسا الملك.

It may further be noted that the turcicism بادشاهم is retained in a British Museum manuscript of al-Jabartī (MS. Add. 26042, Vol. I, f. 21a), thus bringing al-Jabartī's text still closer to that of the 1286 version of al-Isḥāqī.

6 See above, pp. 156–7, 159.

7 This list of factions and its counterparts in DO and DL are of interest. Combining the data given in the three sources, we get the following pedigree of the factions in Ottoman Egypt:

White flag: Tubbaʻī: Ḥusaynī: Zughbī: Qalāwūnī: Saʻd: Faqārī.
Red flag: Kulaybī: Yazīdī: Hilālī: Baybarsī: Ḥarām: Qāsimī.
White and Red were synonyms in Syria for the Yamanī and Qaysī factions respectively. Tubbaʻī is, as DO indicates, synonymous with Yamānī (i.e. Yamanī), *tubba*ʻ being the dynastic title given in Arabic sources to the pre-Islamic kings of the Yemen. Kulaybī represents Kilābī and is used as equivalent to Qaysī, Kilāb being a subdivision of Qays. Ḥusaynī and Yazīdī recall the conflict between al-Ḥusayn b. ʻAlī and Yazīd b. Muʻāwiya, the Umayyad caliph. Banū Zughba and Banū Hilāl were historical tribes (Zughba being a division of Hilāl) but the mention of Zughbī and Hilālī here relates to a clash between the two groups in the legendary saga, *Sīrat banī Hilāl* (cf. *EI*², III, 385–7, HILĀL (H. R. Idris, J. Schleifer)). Qalāwūnī and Baybarsī refer to the supplanting of the dynasty of Baybars by that of Qalāwūn in 678/1280. Sa'd and Ḥarām existed as factions of the Arabs of Egypt as late as the end of the eighteenth century: see General Reynier, *De l'Eypte après la bataille d'Héliopolis*, Paris, X/1802, 49:

"Outre les alliances entre les tribus, il existe encore chez les Arabes de grands partis ou ligues, dont les cheiks puissans sont les chefs; chaque famille et chaque tribu tiennent à l'une de ces ligues; celles qui sont du même parti se soutiennent réciproquement dans leurs guerres. Lorsqu'il s'élève une rixe entre deux tribus du même parti, celle qui n'est pas soutenue par le reste de la ligue passe momentanément dans le parti opposé. Je n'ai pu découvrir l'origine de ces ligues, elles sont très-anciennes et se retrouvent chez tous les Arabes. Dans la basse Egypte l'un des partis est nommé *Sath*, l'autre *Haran*; en Syrie, *Kiech* et *Yemani*: les familles de fellahs et les villages sont attachés à l'une ou à l'autre de ces ligues; les beys dans leurs dissentions s'en appuyaient lorsqu'il y avait deux partis principaux dans le gouvernement. A l'arivée de l'armée française, Ibrahim bey était Sath et Mourad bey, Haran; en général, le parti Sath était attaché au gouverneur du Kaire."

The pedigree of factions indicated by the D group chronicles does not signify that successive groups evolved from their predecessors, but rather shows the self-identification of factions in Ottoman Egypt with earlier historical or legendary parties.

8 The word translated "retainers" is *jirāqāt*. *Jirāq* and its variant *ishrāq* represent the Turkish *çirak/çirağ*. In an eighteenth-century source (the *Nizamname-i Mısır* of Aḥmad Pasha al-Jazzār, the term is used for free-born armed servants of the grandees, who at the end of their service were enrolled in the military corps and made partners of Jedda merchants: see S. J. Shaw (ed. and tr.), *Ottoman Egypt in the eighteenth century*, Cambridge, Mass., 1962; Turkish text, p. 8, line 8. In D. Ayalon, "Studies in al-Jabartī", *JESHO*, iii/3, 1960, 321–2, a rather different significance is deduced from data provided by al-Jabartī. See also below, p. 230, n. 13.

9 The text is corrupt in both DO and DC. Read (following DL) *Yazīd*.

10 The provenance of this anecdote is obscure. It is recounted in Le Mascrier, *Description de l'Égypte*, Paris, 1735, 176*–7* and so must have been in circulation by the end of the seventeenth century. Le Mascrier, however, does not give the names of the beys, which suggests that the story may have been a folk-tale, subsequently linked by the D Group chroniclers with the eponyms of the Faqāriyya and Qāsimiyya.

11 The form Zayn al-Faqār for Dhu'l-Faqār is found throughout these passages in the D Group chronicles. I am very doubtful whether the eponym Dhu'l-Faqār ever existed. The first bey of this name mentioned in the seventeenth-century chronicles is (22) Dhu'l-Faqār Bey, who flourished in 1071/1660, after the epithet al-Zulfiqārī/Faqārī had already been applied to (89) Riḍwān Bey (d. 1066/1656), who seems to have been the real founder of the Faqāriyya. Admittedly Muḥibbī (see below, p. 223) says that Riḍwān was a *mamlūk* of Dhu'l-Faqār, but Muḥibbī is an alien writer, whose statement is unsupported. Riḍwān may himself have borne the honorific name Dhu'l-Faqār, as an epithet of honour, the name of the sword of 'Alī b. Abī Ṭālib, indicating his link with the White flag—Sa'd faction, which, as we have seen had Ḥusaynī and hence 'Alid traditions.

12 Ḥasan Pasha III was the immediate predecessor of Ḥasan Pasha IV, whom DO mentions in the corresponding context. As one succeeded the other in 1099/1688, the divergence of the two chronicles here is unimportant. It will be noted that al-Jabartī seems to have been aware of a discrepancy, since he cautiously dates his list of the beys to the beginning of the twelfth *hijrī* century without naming a viceroy.

13 BM, MS. Add. 26042. Vol. I, f. 24a. In the printed text, two names have been dropped (Sulaymān Bey Dughri Jān and Ḥusayn Bey Abū Yadak).

Both DO and the manuscript of al-Jabartī state, erroneously, that there were nine Faqārī beys.

14 Neither of these statements is of much value historically. It is, however, possible that the eponym Qāsim may be identified with (84) Qāsim Bey, and his patron with (72) *Koja* Muṣṭafā Bey. The precise dating of 1050 for the emergence of the two factions is misleading, but the usage Faqāriyya-Qāsimiyya, superseding Sa'd-Ḥarām, seems to have crystallized about the middle decades of the eleventh *hijrī* century.

15 For the link between al-Jabartī and al-Murādī, see Ayalon, "The historian al-Jabartī and his background", *BSOAS*, XXIII, 2, 1960, 224–7.

16 "Innovation" (*bid'a*), not in the sense of a new development in Egyptian history (the same passage alludes to the older factions of Sa'd and Ḥarām), but a departure from the religiously approved norm of Muslim behaviour. The soldiery of Egypt were part of the Ottoman forces, the *ghāzīs* and soldiers of Islam *par excellence*, for whom civil war was a species of schism.

17 *Nifāq* is usually translated "hypocrisy" but its primary sense is the subordination of religion to political and worldly ends—the characteristic of the *Munāfiqūn* of Medina, who accepted the Prophet's call only with inner reservations.

18 See below, pp. 220–30.

19 See above, pp. 67, 68, 75.

20 It is possible that this person may be identical with another pseudo-historian of the neo-Mamluks, Shihāb al-Din Aḥmad al-Ṣafadī, who is cited as his chief source by the anonymous author of *Qahr al-wujūh*, a spurious genealogy of (89) Riḍwān Bey. The genealogist states that al-Ṣafadi was the *imām* of a mosque in Ak Şehir, and died in 980/1572–3. Al-Ṣafadī could have been the teacher of a man who was *muftī* in 1031/1621–2. See further, "The exalted lineage of Riḍwān Bey", p. 220.

21 In the printed edition of A.H. 1286, it appears on pp. 301–2; in that of 1296, on pp. 215–16.

22 Aḥmad b. Sa'd al-Dīn al-Ghamrī al-'Uthmānī, *Dhakhīrat al-i'lām* (BM. MS. Or 6377), ff. 123 a–b.

23 Selim (Salīm) = safe. Al-Ghamrī says: "Before him, not one of them [i.e. the Ottoman sultans] was called Selim before he was so called. I have found an anecdote in writing, and the reason why he was called by this name".

11

THE BEYLICATE IN OTTOMAN EGYPT DURING THE SEVENTEENTH CENTURY

Part I. Prolegomena

1. *Bibliographical Introduction*

The period of nearly three centuries which lies between Selim I's overthrow of the Mamluk sultanate in 1517, and Bonaparte's landing at Alexandria in 1798, is one of the most obscure in the history of Muslim Egypt. For the latter part of the period, from the early twelfth/eighteenth century, there are ample materials for the reconstruction of the political history in the famous chronicle by al-Jabartī.[1] The Ottoman invasion, and the years which immediately succeeded it, have also received some attention, thanks to the detailed information provided by the chronicler Ibn Iyās.[2] In contrast, there has been virtually no investigation of the last seventy-five years of the sixteenth century and the whole of the seventeenth.

This is not entirely due to lack of material. Admittedly the chronicles which purport to cover this period are very meagre on the events of the middle decades of the sixteenth century (their meagreness probably reflects a real absence of significant political developments in these years), but towards the end of the century their information becomes more copious. For the following century, although there is no historian of the stature of Ibn Iyās or al-Jabartī, there is a group of smaller chronicles, written in Arabic and Turkish, which are surprisingly full and detailed where the writers are dealing with events during their own lifetimes.

The present study is based on three of these chronicles. The first was composed by Shams al-Dīn Muḥammad b. Abi'l-Surūr al-Bakrī al-Ṣiddīqī,[3] and is extant in two forms. The shorter, which goes down to 1041/1632, is contained in his *al-Rawḍa al-zahiyya fī wulāt Miṣr w'al-Qāhira.*[4] The longer form, which appears to be textually identical with the shorter as far as the above date, continues the record of events down to 1062/1652, and forms a part of *al-Kawākib al-sā'ira fī akhbār Miṣr wa'l-Qāhira.*[5] The second chronicle is an anonymous, and apparently unique, manuscript in the British Museum, entitled *Zubdat ikhtiṣār ta'rīkh mulūk Miṣr al-maḥrūsa,*[6] hereafter shortly referred to as the *Zubda.* It ended originally in 1111/1699, but has a further note on 1113/1701–2. The third chronicle is an anonymous fragment preserved in the Bibliothèque Nationale in Paris, which breaks off abruptly in 1120/1708–9. It will be referred to as the Paris Fragment.[7] All these are far superior as sources of information to the one chronicle of this period which has been published, al-Isḥāqī's *Akhbār al-uwal fī man taṣarrafa fī Miṣr min arbāb al-duwal*;[8] a thin production, which in any case ends in 1033/1623–4. All these are literary chronicles of the "sultan-pasha" type.[9]

The value of these chronicles is naturally highest where the writers are describing the events of their own lifetimes. The point at which their works become contemporary or near-contemporary can be marked by noting the increasing abundance and detail of information. Ibn Abi'l-Surūr actually mentions a feast given by his father, in Rabīʻ I 1005/October–November 1696, apparently on the occasion of his birth. The *Zubda* becomes a detailed source from about the middle of the eleventh/seventeenth century, thus overlapping with the latter part of Ibn Abi'l-Surūr's chronicle. Much of its later data is clearly the jottings, almost the diary, of a contemporary. The effective scope of the Paris Fragment is similar to that of the *Zubda*, which it resembles and confirms. Details and language, however, show it to be an independent source.

The material in the two succeeding sections of this part is based primarily on the above chronicles, and on accounts by European travellers and residents in Egypt. The biographies in the second part are compiled from the chronicles. Part II includes notices of some beys who lived on into the twelfth/eighteenth century, but not those who receive obituaries in al-Jabartī, since a study of these would involve a preliminary examination of al-Jabartī's sources.

2. *The Political History of Ottoman Egypt in the Sixteenth and Seventeenth Centuries*

The evolution of the beylicate in Ottoman Egypt took place within the context of far-reaching political changes. Several main phases may be distinguished. The first of these, from the Ottoman conquest of 922/1517 to the viceroyalty of Ibrāhīm Pasha I in 931/1525, saw the overthrow of the Circassian Mamluk sultanate, and the establishment of a new order under the viceroy Khā'ir Bey (7 Shaʻbān 923–8 Dhu'l-Qaʻda 928/25 August 1517–29 September 1522). The new régime was by no means purely Ottoman. Sultan Selim I never attempted a detailed territorial conquest of Egypt: his more limited objective was to eradicate his opponents in the Mamluk *élite*, grouped around their last sultan, Ṭūmān Bāy, and the settlement under Khā'ir Bey was essentially a symbiosis of Ottoman and Mamluk elements. Khā'ir Bey was himself a member of the old

Mamluk high amirate, and during his viceroyalty many of his former colleagues emerged from hiding, and received favourable treatment. The garrison of Egypt was composed partly of Ottoman, partly of Mamluk forces, later consolidated in the historic Seven Corps, the establishment of which was ascribed by legend to Sultan Selim himself.[10]

The death of Selim in 926/1520, followed two years later by that of Khā'ir Bey, imperilled the stability of the new régime, which was challenged by the revolt of the Mamluk *amīrs*, Jānim al-Sayfī and Īnāl, *kāshifs* of Egyptian sub-provinces. This was suppressed, as was the attempt of the viceroy Aḥmad Pasha I (*Khā'in* Aḥmad) to make himself an independent sultan in Egypt. Ottoman suzerainty was reasserted by the viceroy Ibrāhīm Pasha I, who was responsible for the promulgation of the *Kanunname* of Egypt. This body of regulations formalized the fusion of Ottoman and Mamluk elements in the administration.

The succeeding period of about sixty years was one of almost total quiescence in Egypt, during which no viceroy faced a concerted or dangerous opposition. The legend that the viceroys were confined to the Citadel of Cairo during their terms of office finds no support in these years.[11] Two of them, Sulaymān (931–45/1525–38) and Sinān Pasha I (975–80/1567–73) used Egypt as a base for operations in the Indian Ocean and the Yemen respectively. Ibrāhīm Pasha II (appointed 991/1583) travelled throughout Egypt. During this period Ottoman suzerainty was extended over the lands neighbouring Egypt. The Yemen, over which the Mamluk sultanate had established its sway during its last years, was administered as a dependency of Ottoman Egypt. A Circassian Mamluk, Özdemir (Azdamur), who had come to Egypt before the Ottoman conquest, and who served in the Yemen, of which he was governor for several years from 956/1549, was authorized by Sultan Süleyman to recruit troops in Egypt for a campaign against Abyssinia. He went to Upper Egypt, thence to Suakin, perhaps conquering from the Funj the province of Lower Nubia (Berberistan).[12] Although he failed to conquer Abyssinia proper, he established the littoral province of Habeş (al-Ḥabasha) with its two ports of Suakin and Massawa. He died in 967/1559–60.[13]

The last years of the tenth/sixteenth century saw a rapid decline in the power and prestige of the Ottoman viceroys. The challenge came from the soldiery, especially, it seems, the *sipahis*, the three cavalry regiments whose principal functions were to assist the *kāshifs* to gather the taxes and maintain order in the petty provinces. The basic cause of their discontent was economic: the inflation resulting from the influx of silver into the Ottoman Empire, and the consequent depreciation of the currency.[14] From the time of Uways Pasha (995–9/1587–91) to that of Muḥammad Pasha IV (1016–20/1607–11) recurrent military revolts took place. In one of these a viceroy was himself attacked and killed—Ibrāhīm Pasha III (d. 1 Jumādā I 1013/25 September 1604) who appears in the lists of rulers with the ominous epithet *al-Maqtūl*, "the Slain".

The last and most menacing of these revolts, that of 1017/1609, was a general rising of the soldiery throughout the Delta. The rebels bound themselves by an oath at the shrine of *Sayyid* Aḥmad al-Badawī in Ṭanṭā, and appointed a sultan and vizier from among themselves. Confronted at al-Khānqa, on the road to Cairo, by loyal troops under (72) *Koja* Muṣṭafā Bey,[15] they suddenly lost heart, and were destroyed piecemeal. In a phrase which reflects the apprehension of the government rather than the magnitude of the military operations, the chronicler Ibn Abi'l-Surūr speaks of this incident as "in truth the second conquest of Egypt during the sacred Ottoman government".

During the period of the military revolts, the viceroys and the beys seem to have worked in alliance. Henceforward they were competing for predominance. Before the seventeenth century the beys had played no prominent part in events; now, in the middle years of the century, they were to display a steadily increasing power and audacity. In 1032/1623 they refused to accept a viceroy sent by the sultan, and insisted on the continuation in office of Muṣṭafā Pasha V. They acted still more boldly in 1040/1631, when they removed from power the viceroy Mūsā Pasha, who had killed one of their number, and successfully petitioned the sultan for his formal deposition; thereby setting a precedent which was to be followed in the next century.

The ascendancy of the beylicate was personified in (89) Riḍwān Bey al-Faqārī, who from 1040/1631 until his death in 1066/1656 was the dominant figure in Egyptian politics. Formally he held only the office of *amīr al-Ḥājj* on an annual tenure; in practice he was virtually irremovable, and his influence both within Egypt and at the imperial court frustrated the efforts of three viceroys to destroy his hegemony. Internally, Riḍwān's power lay in his position as head of a great political faction, the Faqāriyya,[16] which had its nucleus in his own Mamluk household. After his death, the position of the Faqāriyya was challenged by the rival faction of the Qāsimiyya, which centred around a group of Bosniaks. A petty quarrel in the countryside, involving questions of patronage, developed into a trial of strength between the two factions. The Qāsimiyya joined forces with the viceroy Muṣṭafā Pasha VIII, and the Faqāriyya grandees were driven out of Cairo and hunted down. Three of their beys, who had surrendered under a safe-conduct, were put to death at al-Ṭarrāna by their inveterate enemy, (7) Aḥmad Bey the Bosniak.[17] The power of the Faqāriyya was broken for a generation. It seemed at first as if a hegemony of the Qāsimiyya would be set up, but on 9 Dhu'l-Ḥijja 1072/26 July 1662 Aḥmad Bey was assassinated by the retinue of the viceroy Ibrāhīm Pasha V, called *Shayṭān* Ibrāhīm.

Bereft of their leaders, both the Faqāriyya and the Qāsimiyya lived in reasonable peace and subordination during the later years of the eleventh/seventeenth century. The rank of bey became less esteemed. In the middle years of the century, the viceroy could obtain a payment of twenty to thirty purses from an aspirant to the beylicate: by 1672 the *khidmat al-ṣanjaqiyya* had dropped to fifteen purses.[18] Not until the opening years of the twelfth century A.H. does factionalism revive with the attempt of the Faqārī, Ibrāhīm Bey b. Dhi'l-Faqār, to establish his ascendancy in Cairo at the expense of the Qāsimī, Ibrāhīm Bey *Abū Shanab*. A feature of this new phase of factionalism was the existence of close links between the beys and the regimental grandees, and the important role played by "bosses" controlling the Janissary headquarters, such as *Küçük* Muḥammad and *Afranj* Aḥmad. These developments, and their outcome in the great struggle of 1123/1711, lie beyond the scope of the present study.[19]

3. *The Beylicate in Ottoman Egypt*

The beys of Egypt bore an ancient Ottoman designation (*sancak beyi*) which was universal throughout the Empire. Nevertheless a distinction existed between the beys of Egypt and those of the other Ottoman provinces. The beys of the usual type held land-grants; they were in origin commanders of the provincial levies and, by a natural extension of their functions, governors of their provinces. Hence in standard Ottoman terminology *sancak* (Arabic *ṣanjaq*)[20] came to mean a province governed by a bey. By the sixteenth century, the status of the beys in the old Ottoman Empire had declined: the *sancaks*, or petty provinces, had been grouped into great provinces governed by *beylerbeyis*. Nevertheless, the principle remained that in the old Empire the title of *sancak beyi* implied the tenure of a post with definite administrative and military functions under a governor-general.

This was not true of the beys in Egypt. They were, in the first place, not holders of land-grants but recipients of an annual allowance (*saliyane*) which was a charge upon the treasury of Egypt. It is therefore possible to speak of a salaried Egyptian establishment of beys, distinct from the general Ottoman establishment. Secondly, although they were subordinate to the *beylerbeyi* (viceroy) of the great province of Egypt, they were not *ex officio* governors of the sub-provinces of which it was composed. Eighteenth-century European writers sometimes speak of the twenty-four beys governing the twenty-four provinces of Egypt; and this statement has been uncritically accepted by some later historians, but it is a myth, arising from the application to Egypt of Ottoman usages elsewhere.

In this connexion the idiomatic usage of *ṣanjaq* in Egyptian administrative terminology is significant. It never acquired any territorial significance whatsoever, but it (or the derivative *ṣanjaqiyya*) was regularly used to signify the rank of bey. Thus al-Jabartī frequently uses the formula *taqallad al-imāra wa'l-ṣanjaqiyya* to signify that a person was raised to the rank of bey. The plural *ṣanājiq* is invariably used by the chroniclers to mean "beys": *bak* or *bayk* is used in the singular only, the modern plural *bakawāt* never appearing.

It must be stressed that in Egyptian usage a bey was originally the holder of a rank, not of a specific office or function. The beylicate formed a group closely connected with the viceroy, who was theoretically the normal agent of their elevation and downfall. Those of them who were resident in Cairo formed part of the viceroy's court, although by virtue of their permanent Egyptian domicile they were an element distinct from the household officers who accompanied him during his tour of duty. Together with the high officers of the Seven Corps of the Ottoman garrison, they constituted the grandees who came increasingly to dominate Egyptian affairs in the seventeenth century.

Although the neat systematization of an Egypt divided into twenty-four provinces ruled by as many beys is a myth, there is this much of truth in it, that some beys were appointed to some provincial commands which were in effect military governorships. The sub-provinces of Egypt were styled, sometimes *iqlīm* (pl. *aqālim*), sometimes *kushūfiyya*, i.e. territory administered by a *kāshif*. But *kāshif* was a term unique in the Ottoman administrative vocabulary, and was in fact inherited from the old Mamluk sultanate. One finds in the seventeenth-century chronicles numerous references to the appointment of beys as *kāshifs* of sub-provinces, particularly when a territory was threatened by Arabs, and there are also examples of *kāshifs* who did not hold the rank of bey. There are also loose phrases such as "the bey of the Manūfiyya", "the governor of the Gharbiyya", but these are colloquialisms. A bey governed a sub-province, not by virtue of his rank as bey, but by virtue of his commission as *kāshif*. The *Kanunname* of Sultan Süleyman (1524), which states the norm of administrative practice in the early Ottoman period, has only two passing references to the beys, but lays down in considerable detail the functions of the *kāshifs* as provincial governors.

One provincial post that was to be of outstanding importance did not exist in the time of Süleyman: this was the governorship of Upper Egypt. Egypt south of al-Bahnasā and the Fayyūm seems (with the exception of the Khārja Oasis) to have lain outside the area of direct administration in the early Ottoman period, and was controlled by tribal chiefs (*mashāyikh al-ʿUrbān*, *umarā' al-Saʿīd*) belonging to Banū ʿUmar, the ruling clan of a fraction of Hawwāra who had been settled in Upper Egypt from the time of Barqūq in the late eighth/fourteenth century. Direct Ottoman rule was instituted in Dhu'l-Ḥijja 983/March 1576, when the governorship of Upper Egypt was conferred on Sulaymān Bey b. Qubād, a descendant of the Ramazanoğlu, the former ruling family of Karaman.[21] Vansleb, writing in the 1670's, postdates the event by fifty years, and the name he gives to the governor, Soliman-Gianballat (Sulaymān Jānbulād) does not occur in the literary sources, although it seems to have survived in local tradition as late as the nineteenth century.[22] The governor of the South (*ḥākim al-Ṣaʿīd*) or of Upper Egypt had his capital at Jirjā. From the middle of the seventeenth century, several of these governors of the South, or of Jirjā, played an important part in Egyptian history. They were invariably beys, and had authority over a number of *kāshifs*, administering districts on the banks of the Nile as far south as Lower Nubia (Berberistan).

Besides providing the governors of the South and, frequently at least, the *kāshifs* of the sub-provinces of Middle and Lower Egypt, the beylicate also furnished commanding officers for special expeditionary forces. Such forces might be summoned by the sultan to serve in Crete, eastern Europe, Syria, Iraq, or elsewhere, or by the viceroy for action in the Ḥijāz, Yemen, or Habeş, which were dependencies of Egypt, or within Egypt itself. They were composed partly of troops drawn from the Seven Corps, partly, no doubt, from the retainers of the grandees themselves, but their command was invariably committed to a bey, not to a regular officer of the regular Corps. Of a similar nature to these *ad hoc* appointments were two of a regular, annual character: the command of the treasure-convoy (*Khazna*), which took the tribute of Egypt overland to Istanbul; and the command of the Pilgrimage (*imārat al-Ḥajj*). The holder of the latter appointment was one of the great officers of state. He was responsible for the safe convoy of the pilgrims and the *maḥmal* to Mecca, and for the still more difficult management of their return. Although theoretically held on annual tenure only, this office was frequently retained by successful commanders for a series of years, notably by the great (89) Riḍwān Bey, who was *amīr al-Ḥājj* almost without interruption for a quarter of a century. His long tenure played an important part in establishing the prescriptive claim of the Faqāriyya to this office.

The annexation of the command of the Pilgrimage to the beylicate was essentially a resumption of the practice current under the Circassian Mamluk sultanate. Before the Ottoman conquest, this office had been an annual appointment held by an *amīr* of the highest rank.[23] No Pilgrimage caravan left Cairo in 922/1517, the troubled year of the actual conquest; and in the two succeeding seasons the post was held by a bureaucrat, not a military grandee. Thereafter there was a partial return to tradition: in 925/1519 the commander was a *mamlūk* of the viceroy Khā'ir Bey, and, in the three following years the post was held by a leading Mamluk notable who held office under the new regime, the *amīr* Jānim al-Sayfī, *kāshif* of al-Bahnasā and the Fayyūm.[24] Subsequently the command of the Pilgrimage may have been held by the *amīr* Jānim al-Ḥamzāwī, a man of Mamluk descent who played a now obscure but clearly influential role in the early years of the Ottoman suzerainty. When Jānim and his son Yūsuf were put to death by the viceroy Sulaymān Pasha at the end of Dhu'l-Ḥijja 944/May 1538, Yūsuf was *amīr al-Ḥājj.*[25] These men indubitably belonged to the military *élite*, but it is not clear whether they were members of the beylicate. The earliest unequivocal reference to a bey as commander of the Pilgrimage is to (80) Pīrī Bey in 1006/1597–8.[26]

A non-military office of considerable importance which also appears in the seventeenth century as a perquisite of the beylicate was that of treasurer (*defterdar*). On the evidence at present available, the date of its annexation by the beylicate is not clear. In 944/1537–8, the *defterdar* was a Circassian, hence a Mamluk, Muḥammad b. Sulaymān.[27] In Ḥijja 967/August–September 1560, the *defterdar* was a certain Ibrāhīm b. Taghrīwardī (a name suggesting Mamluk descent), who is referred to in one source as Ibrāhīm Bey.[28] His successor is called by one writer Muḥammad Bey (975/1567–8), by another Muḥammad Efendi.[29] From the second quarter of the seventeenth century at latest, the treasurership seems invariably to have been held by a bey.

Besides these permanent offices, a temporary position of great importance which came to be annexed to the beylicate during the seventeenth century was that of acting viceroy (*qā'im maqām*). The holder exercised full viceregal powers between the death or removal from office of one viceroy and the installation of the next. The earliest *qā'im maqām* to be noted is a certain Muṣṭafā Bey, who was installed in office by a resolution of the military *élite* (*al-'asākir al-manṣūra al-Miṣriyya*) on the death of Dā'ūd Pasha (13 Rabī' I 956/11 April

1549).[30] The next *qā'im maqām* to be noticed was a judge: the *qāḍī* Ḥusayn Efendi b. 'Abd al-Muḥsin on the death of 'Ālī Pasha II in 967/1560.[31] But in 1012/1603, (80) Pīrī Bey was appointed *qā'im maqām* by the outgoing viceroy, 'Ālī Pasha IV, and when Pīrī died in office, he was succeeded by another member of the beylicate, (101) 'Uthmān Bey, who was elected by his colleagues.[32] On the assassination of Ibrāhīm Pasha III in 1013/1604, the position of *qā'im maqām* was again offered to 'Uthmān Bey, but he refused it, and the military *élite* installed the *qāḍī* Muṣṭafā Efendi 'Azmīzāde.[33] This appears to have been the last occasion when the office was held by a member of the Religious Institution. Since the formal approval of the viceroy was necessary for some acts of state, the practice developed in the twelfth/eighteenth century of the removal of an obstructive viceroy by the dominant faction, and the installation of one of their own members as *qā'im maqām*: by this device a kind of constitutional sanction was given to acts of partisan policy. This development lies outside the period of the present study, but precedents were established in the eleventh/seventeenth century, when the grandees rejected the viceroy-elect 'Alī Pasha in 1032/1623, and removed the ruling viceroy, Mūsā Pasha in 1040/1631: on both occasions installing a bey as *qā'im maqām* until their acts received retrospective approval from the sultan.

The marked differences between the beys in Egypt and in the other Ottoman provinces suggest that the Egyptian establishment was not a genuine Ottoman institution, but the continuation or revival of the high amirate as it had existed under the Mamluk sultans. There are several indications which support this identification. Traditionally there were twenty-four beys, just as there had been twenty-four *amīrs* of the first class (*amīr mi'a*). Furthermore, there is a close resemblance between the functions discharged by the beys and those of the high *amīrs*. The command of the Pilgrimage is the clearest example, but the *defterdar* is the counterpart of the former *khāzindār kabīr*, and the *qā'im maqām* performed functions resembling those of the *nā'ib al-ghayba*. The governor of the South in Ottoman times corresponded to the *nā'ib al-wajh al-qiblī*, resident in Asyūṭ, under the Mamluk sultans. *Amīrs* of the first class were also appointed as *kāshifs*, just as were the beys.

If we grant that the beylicate represented the old high amirate with a thin Ottoman veneer, the question arises as to whether it was a continuation or a revival of the older institution. Against continuity, it may be urged that the term "bey" is not applied by Ibn Iyās to any grandee permanently domiciled in Egypt during the first few years after the Conquest. On the other hand, Ibn Iyās's terminology may be misleading: his indiscriminate use of the title *amīr* in these years may in some cases conceal the fact that its holder was a bey. More positive evidence of continuity is given by the *Kanunname* of 931/1524. Since a *kanun* was declaratory of existing practice, the provision which this ordinance makes for the payment of stipends to the beys[34] indicates that the beylicate was already established before the time of Sultan Süleyman. This indication is supported by later Mamluk tradition. Ḥusayn Efendi, writing at the end of the eighteenth century,[35] states that the beylicate was instituted by Sultan Selim I. That the sultan formally established the order may be doubted; no such act is recorded by Ibn Iyās either of Selim or of his viceroy Khā'ir Bey. The more probable sense of the tradition is that the high amirate was allowed to continue under the new regime and was assimilated in name to the Ottoman institution of the beylicate. There are other and earlier traditions which indicate Selim as the restorer (not, as might be expected, the destroyer) of Mamluk power and institutions, but these do not refer directly to the beylicate.[36]

The beylicate was, then, on the present hypothesis, a Mamluk and not an Ottoman institution. A further question now arises: to what extent were the beys of Egypt themselves *mamlūks*?[37]

The only direct evidence on this point would appear to be provided at the very end of the period of Mamluk hegemony by Ḥusayn Efendi. He divides the beys into two categories. The deputy-viceroy (*kâhya al-wazīr*), and the garrison-commanders (*qapudans*) of Alexandria, Damietta, and Suez, were all appointed from Istanbul. The remainder were "beys of Egypt".[38] Here it would seem that we have a distinction between Ottoman and Mamluk personnel in the beylicate. How far back this went is not easy to establish. The *qapudan* at Suez in 1041/1632 was (48) Muḥammad Bey b. Suwaydān: certainly not a first-generation *mamlūk*, but perhaps not an Ottoman either.

There are, however, some sporadic examples of Ottomans being appointed to the beylicate, although not to the specific offices mentioned by Ḥusayn Efendi. An example at the turn of the eleventh/seventeenth century was (66) Muḥammad Bey *Murjān Jūz*, who had been the *kahveci* of Sultan Mehemmed IV, and became *kāshif* of the Fayyūm.

A considerable number of members of the beylicate cannot in any case have been *mamlūks*, but must have been free-born Muslims. This must have been so with some at least of the Qāsimiyya beys in the eleventh/seventeenth century who are referred to as a *Bashāniqa*, i.e. Bosniaks. All bearers of the epithet *al-Bushnāq*, "the Bosniak", were not necessarily such—they may have been genuine *mamlūks* of a household founded by a Bosniak *ustādh*—but it is perhaps significant that at least three of them (7) Aḥmad Bey *bi-Qanāṭir al-Sibā'*, his brother (92) Sha'bān Bey, and the later 'Abdallāh Bey[39] are not spoken of as *mamlūks*. That (7) Aḥmad Bey stood outside the Mamluk system may be indicated by the incident in 1066/1656, when his appointment as *amīr al-Ḥājj* (after the death of (89) Riḍwān Bey al-Faqārī) was opposed by the Faqāriyya with the cry "How shall a foreigner take the place of our master?".[40]

A later Bosniak immigrant into Egypt was the man who later became famous as Aḥmad Pasha al-Jazzār, the governor of Acre at the time of Bonaparte's invasion of Syria. His career in Egypt is interesting, since al-Jabartī implies that he, a free-born Muslim, voluntarily affiliated himself to a Mamluk household: "He took service with 'Abdallāh Bey, the retainer of 'Ali Bey *Bulut Kapan*, and learnt horsemanship in the manner of the Egyptian military élite."[41]

Certain other beys who cannot have been *mamlūks* may be briefly noted. An obvious example is that of converts from Judaism. Two of these are recorded by al-Jabartī in the twelfth/eighteenth century. A number of beys are also noted by al-Jabartī and other chroniclers as having previously held office in the Seven Corps. This is suggestive of a non-*mamlūk* origin, but the evidence is admittedly inconclusive, and it is known that members of Mamluk households were appointed as officers in the Seven Corps.[42]

A special case was that of sons of *mamlūk* beys who succeeded their fathers in the beylicate. Technically, such men, as sons of Muslim fathers, were free-born Muslims. Practically, they formed a very important part of the Mamluk *élite* in the Ottoman period. This represented an important departure from the practice of the Mamluk sultanate, when the sons of Mamluks had not usually held military office. In contrast, such beys as (68) Muḥarram b. (44) Māmāy, (79) Özbek b. Riḍwān *Abi'l-Shawārib*, and, in the eighteenth century, the powerful Ismā'īl b. Īwāẓ,[43] were leading figures in the history of Ottoman Egypt.

A feature of the old Mamluk sultanate which reappeared in a new form during the Mamluk revival of the seventeenth century was inveterate factionalism within the military *élite*. Under the sultanate this had appeared in its most marked form as hostility between the *Julbān*, the household of the reigning sultan, and the *Qarānisa*, the survivors of earlier sultans' households. This polarization naturally ceased with the extinction of the Mamluk sultanate.

But already before that event signs of a new factionalism had appeared, between those Mamluks who were prepared to accept Ottoman suzerainty (admittedly with the intention of safeguarding their own positions), and those who were determined on resistance.

The protagonists of these two groups at the time of the conquest were Khā'ir Bey and Ṭūmān Bāy, although the latter was probably more moderate than the faction which supported him. With the defeat and execution of Ṭūmān Bāy, followed by the appointment of Khā'ir Bey as Selim's viceroy in Egypt, the party of collaboration seemed to have triumphed, but a nucleus of irreconcilables still remained. The revolt of Jānim and Īnāl in 929/1522–3, after the deaths of Selim I and Khā'ir Bey, showed that the Ottoman suzerainty was still not unchallenged. The attempt of the viceroy Aḥmad Pasha I in 930/1524 to establish himself as independent sultan of Egypt was backed by some survivors of the old regime. At this juncture, the collaborationist faction was headed by Jānim al-Ḥamzāwī, who with loyal Ottoman officers and troops crushed the revolt. Perhaps the last outburst of the resistance faction came in the great revolt of the provincial soldiery in 1017/1609.

After 1017/1609 there are no further attempts to throw off Ottoman rule, but as the seventeenth century moves on signs appear of a new factionalism in the beylicate. This is the famous division between the Faqāriyya and Qāsimiyya groups. Of the two eponyms, Dhu'l-Faqār Bey does not appear in the contemporary chronicles, but the founder of the Qāsimiyya may just possibly be (84) Qāsim Bey, who was an elderly man in 1040/1631. The strength, coherence, and duration of these two groups may be ascribed to their association with two already existing factions in Egypt, Sa'd and Ḥarām.[44]

To summarize the conclusions of this investigation. The time-honoured phrase, "the Mamluk beys" is a valid expression in so far as it relates to the institution of the beylicate being of Mamluk, not Ottoman, origin. It is incorrect if it is taken to mean that, in the Ottoman period, all the beys were *mamlūk* (i.e. slave) recruits, or specifically Circassians. Although the beylicate was probably derived without a break from the high amirate of the Mamluk sultanate, the seventeenth century seems to have witnessed an extension, or perhaps more truly a resumption, of its powers, so that in the eighteenth century it came to control the administration of Egypt. In this phase of its development, the beylicate reduced the viceroys, who had hitherto been significant political figures, to impotence, and completely overshadowed the high regimental officers, who in the late seventeenth century had been the peers of the beys. Although it became increasingly possible as time went on to describe the beys in terms of their functions,[45] the title was essentially one of rank and not one of office. One may indeed hazard the hypothesis that the lack of specific functions attached to the beylicate in the early Ottoman period assisted this group to strengthen its hold over the Egyptian administration during the decline of Ottoman power. But the rise of the beylicate created new problems. The events of 1032/1623 and 1040/1631 had demonstrated the power of the beys as against the viceroy, but the reduction of the viceroys to figureheads was followed by the appearance of factionalism within the beylicate itself. From this resulted the instability of Egyptian politics which is so marked a feature of the later seventeenth and the eighteenth centuries. This instability continued until Muḥammad 'Alī Pasha, in the abnormal circumstances of the early nineteenth century, succeeded in resuming viceregal powers which had long been in abeyance, and in annihilating the Mamluk military *élite*.

Appendix: Ottoman Viceroys of Egypt in the Eleventh/Seventeenth Century

The following date-list of the Ottoman viceroys of Egypt is based on the principal Arab chronicles used in the present study, viz. Ibn Abi'l-Surūr, *al-Rawḍa* and *al-Kawākib* down to Muḥammad Pasha XI; the *Zubda* thence to Muḥammad Pasha XIII; and the Paris Fragment for the remaining viceroys. The dates given by Hammer, presumably from Turkish chronicle sources, have been compared with these. Generally Hammer agrees with the Arabic chronicles, and these agree among themselves, as far as the month, although they may differ as to the day of the month. I have therefore given the dates of commencement and termination of the viceroyalties to the nearest month only, and have noted divergencies between Hammer and the Arabic sources. The Arabic chroniclers regard a viceroyalty as commencing effectively with the entry of the viceroy into the Citadel, and as terminating usually with the arrival of a messenger bearing news of deposition. The Turkish and Arabic sources distinguish the viceroys with a variety of patronymics and epithets, some of which are given in Hammer's lists. I have substituted simple enumeration for this cumbersome system.

Viceroy	*Commencement*	*Termination*
Muḥammad II	Shawwāl 1004/ June 1596	Dhu'l-Ḥijja 1006/July 1598
Khiḍr	Dhu'l-Ḥijja 1006/Aug. 1598	Muḥarram 1010/July 1601
'Alī IV	Ṣafar 1010/Aug. 1601	Rabī' II 1012/Sept. 1603
Ibrāhīm III	Dhu'l-Ḥijja 1012/May 1604	Jumādā I 1013[1]/Sept. 1604
Muḥammad III	Rajab 1013/Dec. 1604	Ṣafar 1014/July 1605
Ḥasan II	Rabī' I 1014/July 1605	Muḥarram 1016/May 1607
Muḥammad IV	Ṣafar 1016/June 1607	Jumādā II 1020[2]/Aug. 1611

Notes

[1] Assassinated: see (101) 'Uthmān *Khaṭṭāṭ*. Hammer gives his death date as Rabī' II, whereas the Egyptian chroniclers date the assassination 1 Jumādā I.

[2] Hammer: 1 Jumādā I 1020/12 July 1611.

Viceroy	*Commencement*	*Termination*
Muḥammad V	Sha'bān 1020/Oct. 1611	Rabī' I 1024/Apr. 1615.
Aḥmad III	Rabī' II 1024/May 1615	Ṣafar 1027/Feb. 1618
Muṣṭafā III	Jumādā I 1027/Apr. 1618	Dhu'l-Ḥijja 1027[1]/Dec. 1618
Ja'far	Rabī' I 1028/Feb. 1619	Sha'bān 1028/Aug. 1619
Muṣṭafā IV	Ramaḍān 1028/Sept. 1619	Ramaḍān 1029/Aug. 1620
Ḥusayn II	Ramaḍān 1029/Aug. 1620	Rabī' I 1031[2]/Feb. 1622
Muḥammad VI	Jumādā II 1031/Apr. 1622	Ramaḍān 1031/July 1622
Ibrāhīm IV	Ramaḍān 1031/July 1622	Ramaḍān 1032/July 1623
Muṣṭafā V[3]	Ramaḍān 1032/July 1623	Dhu'l-Ḥijja 1032/Oct. 1623
Muṣṭafā V[4]	Rabī' II 1033/Feb. 1624	Sha'bān 1035/May 1626
Bayram	Sha'bān 1035/May 1626	Muḥarram 1038/Sept. 1628
Muḥammad VII	Muḥarram 1038/Sept. 1628	Rabī' I 1040/Oct. 1630
Mūsā	Jumādā II 1040/Jan. 1631	Dhu'l-Ḥijja 1040[5]/July 1631
Khalīl	Rabī' I 1041/Oct. 1631	Ramaḍān 1042/Mar.–Apr. 1633
Aḥmad IV	Dhu'l-Qa'da 1042/May 1633	Jumādā I 1045/Oct.–Nov. 1635
Ḥusayn III	Rajab 1045/Dec. 1635	Jumādā II 1047[6]/Nov. 1637
Muḥammad VIII	Rajab 1047/Dec. 1637	Jumādā I 1050/Aug. 1640
Muṣṭafā VI	Jumādā II 1050/Sept. 1640	Rajab 1052/Oct. 1642
Maqṣūd	Sha'bān 1052/Nov. 1642	Dhu'l-Ḥijja 1053[7]/Mar. 1644
Ayyūb	Rabī' I 1054/May 1644	Ṣafar 1056/Mar.–Apr. 1646
Muḥammad IX	Jumādā I 1056/June 1646	Dhu'l-Qa'da 1057/Dec. 1647
Muḥammad X[8]	Ṣafar 1058/Mar. 1648	Ṣafar 1059/Mar. 1649
Aḥmad V	Rabī' II 1059[9]/Apr. 1649	Ṣafar 1061[10]/Jan. 1651
'Abd al-Raḥmān I	Rabī' II 1061/Apr. 1651	Shawwāl 1062/Sept. 1652
Muḥammad XI	Muḥarram 1063/Dec. 1652	Sha'bān 1066[11]/May 1656
Muṣṭafā VII	Shawwāl 1066/Aug. 1656	Shawwāl 1067[12]/July 1657
Muḥammad XII	Dhu'l-Qa'da 1067/Aug. 1657	Ramaḍān 1069[13]/June 1659
Muṣṭafā VIII	Dhu'l-Qa'da 1069/July 1659	Ramaḍān 1071[14]/May 1661

Notes

[1] Hammer: 13 Dhu'l-Qa'da 1027/21 November 1618.

[2] Hammer: 21 Rabī' II 1031/5 March 1622.

[3] First term.

[4] Second term. In the intervening period a certain 'Alī Pasha was appointed viceroy, and is so listed by Hammer. He was refused recognition by the beys, and never entered Cairo: see (36) 'Īsā.

[5] Deprived of office by the beys: see (86) Qayṭās *al-Kabīr*.

[6] Hammer: 15 Jumādā I 1047/5 October 1637.

[7] Hammer: 14 Ṣafar 1054/22 April 1644. The discrepancy is due to the fact that the beys deprived Maqṣūd Pasha of office on 21 Dhu'l-Ḥijja 1054/1 March 1644, but his formal deposition by the sultan did not arrive until later. See (92) Sha'bān.

[8] Hammer inserts a certain Muṣṭafā Pasha between Muḥammad Pasha IX and Muḥammad Pasha X, but his appointment was almost immediately revoked.

[9] Date from the Paris Fragment.

[10] Hammer: 16 Ṣafar 1060/18 February 1650.

[11] Date from Hammer. Month confirmed by the Paris Fragment.

[12] Hammer: 8 Ramaḍān 1067/20 June 1657.

[13] Hammer: Shawwāl 1070/June 1660.

[14] Date from Hammer. The Paris Fragment gives Shawwāl 1071.

Viceroy	*Commencement*	*Termination*
Ibrāhīm V	Shawwāl 1071/June 1661	Shawwāl 1074[1]/Apr. 1664
‘Umar	Dhu’l-Ḥijja 1074/July 1664	Sha‘bān 1077/Feb. 1667
Ibrāhīm VI	Shawwāl 1077/Apr. 1667	Jumādā II 1079[2]/Nov. 1668
‘Alī V	Dhu’l-Qa‘da 1079/Apr. 1669	Sha‘bān 1080[3]/Dec. 1669
Ibrāhīm VII	Muḥarram 1081/June 1670	Jumādā I 1084[4]/Sept. 1673
Ḥusayn IV	Shawwāl 1084/Jan.–Feb. 1674	Rajab 1086[5]/Sept. 1675
Aḥmad VI	Shawwāl 1086/Dec. 1675	Dhu’l-Ḥijja 1086[6]/Feb. 1676
‘Abd al-Raḥmān II	Jumādā I 1087/July 1676	Sha‘bān 1091[7]/Sept. 1680
‘Uthmān	Ramaḍān 1091/Sept. 1680	Ramaḍān 1094[8]/Sept. 1683
Ḥamza	Shawwāl 1094/Sept. 1683	Jumādā I 1098[9]/Mar. 1687
Ḥasan III[10]	——	Muḥarram 1099[11]/Nov. 1687
Ḥasan IV	Rabī‘ II 1099/Feb. 1688	Dhu’l-Ḥijja 1100[12]/Sept. 1689
Aḥmad VII	Muḥarram 1101/Oct. 1689	Jumādā II 1102[13]/Mar. 1691
‘Alī VI	Ramaḍān 1102/June 1691	Muḥarram 1107[14]/Sept. 1695
Ismā‘īl	Ṣafar 1107/Oct. 1695	Rabī‘ I 1109/Sept. 1697
Ḥusayn V	Rajab 1109/Feb. 1698	Rabī‘ I 1111[15]/Sept. 1699
Muḥammad XIII	Rabī‘ II 1111/Oct. 1699	Rajab 1116[16]/Oct.–Nov. 1704
Muḥammad XIV[17]	Sha‘bān 1116/Dec. 1704	Rajab 1118[18]/Oct. 1706
‘Alī VII	Sha‘bān 1118/Nov. 1706	Rajab 1119[19]/Sept. 1707

Notes

1 Hammer: 5 Ramaḍān 1074/1 April 1664.

2 Hammer: deposed, 9 Jumādā II 1079/14 November 1668. Both the *Zubda* and the Paris Fragment agree that he died in office: the former gives the date as 17 Jumādā I, the latter as 17 Jumādā II 1079/22 November 1668.

3 Hammer: deposed, 5 Sha‘bān 1080/29 December 1669. Both the *Zubda* and the Paris Fragment agree that he died in office. The former gives no date, the latter Sha‘bān 1080.

4 Date from the Paris Fragment. Hammer gives 23 Ṣafar 1084/9 June 1673.

5 Hammer: 5 Jumādā II 1086/27 August 1675.

6 Hammer: 27 Ṣafar 1087/11 May 1676. The viceroy was deprived of office by the beys in Ḥijja 1086. His formal deposition by the sultan followed later.

7 Hammer: 20 Jumādā I 1091/18 June 1680.

8 Hammer: Jumādā I 1094/May 1683.

9 Date from Hammer.

10 The events of the viceroyalties of Ḥamza Pasha and Ḥasan Pasha III are confused in the Arabic chronicles, and I have been unable to arrive at any certain date for the accession of the latter viceroy.

11 Date from Hammer.

12 Date from the *Zubda*: Hammer gives 1 Muḥarram 1101/15 October 1689.

13 The *Zubda* and the Paris Fragment agree that Aḥmad Pasha VII died in office on 12 Jumādā II 1102/13 March 1691. Hammer gives his death-date as 13 Rajab 1102/12 April 1691.

14 Hammer: Dhu’l-Qa‘da 1106/July 1695.

15 Hammer: 14 Rabī‘ II 1111/9 October 1699. The *Zubda* and Paris Fragment give this as the date of commencement of the viceroyalty of Muḥammad Pasha XIII.

16 Hammer: 1 Muḥarram 1116/6 May 1704.

17 Hammer inserts a certain Sulaymān Pasha between Muḥammad Pasha XIII and Muḥammad Pasha XIV. He did not take office.

18 Hammer: Jumādā I 1118/September 1706.

19 Hammer: Jumādā II 1119/September 1707.

Part II. Biographical Dictionary

The beys in the eleventh/seventeenth century

1. ʻAbdī

Appointed commander of 2,000 troops intended by Muḥammad Pasha IX to fight the Faqāriyya grandees, (13) ʻAlī Bey and (89) Riḍwān Bey: 13 Ramaḍān 1057/12 October 1647. He incited the grandees and the troops to refuse to obey the viceroy's order.

2. ʻĀbidīn

Amīr al-Ḥājj at some date before 1022/1613–14. In 1022 he brought about the submission of several thousand troops sent by the grand vizier Naṣūḥ Pasha to Cairo *en route* to the Yemen, who had blockaded themselves in the Bāb al-Naṣr quarter, and refused to leave. Probably identical with the ʻĀbidīn Bey who took part in the expedition to Mecca under the command of (84) Qāsim Bey (Shawwāl 1041/May 1632), and who died in the viceroyalty of Aḥmad Pasha IV.

3. ʻĀbidīn

Dragoman of Muṣṭafā Pasha VI, who appointed him *kâhya* of the *Çavuşan*, when these troops revolted in Shawwāl 1051/January 1641 against their former *kâhya*.

4. Aḥmad

Maternal nephew of (86) Qayṭās Bey. Raised to the beylicate by (81) Qānṣawh Bey, when the latter was appointed governor-general of the Yemen and Habeş, he took part in the expedition to the Yemen which left Egypt in Muḥarram 1039/August–September 1629. Possibly identical with the Aḥmad Bey who, in the viceroyalty of Muṣṭafā Pasha VI was given plenary powers to fill the state granaries and give the troops their arrears of rations, thereby averting a general revolt. The grain had been embezzled by the clerk of the Divan.

5. Aḥmad b. Qānṣawh

Probably son of (81) Qānṣawh Bey. Head of the mission sent with the sultan's orders, in Ramaḍān 1057/October 1647, reinstating the Faqāriyya grandees, (89) Riḍwān Bey and (13) ʻAlī Bey. Appointed commander of the *Khazna* by the victorious Faqāriyya after their revolt against Muḥammad Pasha XI in (? Shaʻbān) 1066/(? May) 1656.

6. AḤMAD *al-Qahwajī*

Raised to the beylicate by Aḥmad Pasha V. Possibly a member of the viceroy's suite; cf. (14) 'Alī *al-Tutunjī* and (53) Muḥammad.

7. AḤMAD *bi-Qanāṭir al-Sibā'*

A Bosniak, member of the Qāsimiyya faction. Possibly the *defterdar* Aḥmad Bey who served as *qā'im maqām* on the deposition of 'Abd al-Raḥmān Pasha I (Shawwāl 1062/September 1652). He commanded an expeditionary force to Habeş, which suppressed a revolt under a certain Darwīsh, and was absent from Cairo between Muḥarram or Rabī' II 1065/November 1654 or February 1655, and Ṣafar 1066/November 1655. His appointment as *amīr al-Ḥājj* by Muḥammad Pasha XI, after the death of (89) Riḍwān Bey, provoked the revolt of the Faqāriyya in 1066/1656. He was rusticated by the victorious Faqāriyya to the Qalyūbiyya, then to Alexandria. Muṣṭafā Pasha VII effected a reconciliation between Aḥmad Bey and the Faqāriyya. He is possibly identical with the Aḥmad Bey who left Cairo in Muḥarram 1065/October 1657 on a mission concerning the revenue of an estate: this person returned at the end of Jumādā I 1068/March 1658, and was invested as *defterdar* by order of the sultan. On the appearance in Cairo, in (? Jumādā I) 1069/ (? January–February) 1659, of the Faqārī governor of Jirjā, (54) Muḥammad Bey, with an army, an imperial order was obtained appointing Aḥmad Bey to the governorship of Jirjā. Muḥammad Bey's refusal to accept a transfer to Habeş resulted in his defeat and death. Aḥmad Bey did not apparently take up residence in Jirjā, as on the deposition of Muḥammad Pasha XII, shortly after the campaign against Muḥammad Bey, he served as *qā'im maqām*. In the great revolt of the Faqāriyya against Muṣṭafā Pasha VIII (Ṣafar 1071/October 1660), Aḥmad Bey played a leading part. He commanded some of the troops sent against the Faqāriyya, and was personally responsible for the breach of the safe-conduct and the execution of the Faqāriyya grandees at al-Ṭarrāna. He made a ceremonial entry into the Divan on 25 Ṣafar 1071/30 October 1660, and was honourably received by the viceroy. He accompanied the next viceroy, Ibrāhīm Pasha V, on his entry into Egypt, but was assassinated in the Divan by the same viceroy's orders on 9 Dhu'l-Ḥijja 1072/26 July 1662.

8. AḤMAD *bi-Suwayqa*

Transferred from the beylicate to a regimental post (?) after the revolt of the Faqāriyya in 1066/1656.

9. AḤMAD

Mamlūk (or *tābi'*) of (88) Qayṭās Bey *bi-Qanāṭir al-Sibā'*, a member of the Qāsimiyya faction. Joint commander of an expedition sent on 24 Rabī' I 1099/29 January 1688 by Ḥasan Pasha III against predatory Arabs in the province of al-Jīza. He was worsted in his engagements with the Arabs. He commanded the *Khazna* which was sent by sea in Ramaḍān 1099/July 1688. At the time of his death, shortly before 26 Ramaḍān 1101/3 July 1690, he was *kāshif* of the Manūfiyya. Mentioned by al-Jabartī (I, 24) as Aḥmad Bey of the Manūfiyya, one of the Qāsimiyya grandees at the opening of the twelfth century.

10. AḤMAD *Yāqūt*

One of the five grandees instructed to proceed with reinforcements to Upper Egypt, where Īwāẓ Bey[46] was on campaign against the predatory Arabs of Ibn Wāfī: 11 Rajab 1110/13 January 1699.

11. 'ALĪ B. AL-KHABĪR (*al-Khabīrī*)

A tribal notable, associated with (72) *Koja* Muṣṭafā Bey in the operations against the rebels in Dhu'l-Qa'da 1017/February 1609. Raised to the beylicate by (81) Qānṣawh Bey, when the latter was appointed governor-general of the Yemen and Habeş, he took part in the expedition to the Yemen of 1039/1629.

12. 'ALĪ

Defterdar before 1040/1630–1, when he took part in the events leading to the removal by the grandees of Mūsā Pasha: 11 Dhu'l-Ḥijja 1040/11 July 1631. Died during the viceroyalty of Aḥmad Pasha IV.

13. 'ALĪ

Member of the Faqāriyya faction: probably a *khushdāsh* of (89) Riḍwān Bey. He took a leading part in the events leading to the deposition of Mūsā Pasha (11 Dhu'l-Ḥijja 1040/11 July 1631). He was a member of the commission which subsequently assessed Mūsā Pasha's liability to the treasury for receipts during his viceroyalty. He was in the expedition to Mecca under (84) Qāsim Bey in Shawwāl 1041/May 1632. He and (89) Riḍwān Bey were alternatively designated by the sultan as commanders of a force to be levied in Egypt for service against the Safavids. They were excused this service on the grounds of their important functions in Egypt, Riḍwān being *amīr al-Ḥājj*, and 'Alī, as governor of Jirjā, being responsible for the supply of corn to Cairo: Sha'bān 1044/January

1635. Possibly identical with the 'Alī Bey whom Maqṣūd Pasha sought to have assassinated together with (44) Māmāy Bey in 1053/1643–4. When Muḥammad Pasha IX, acting on the advice of (82) Qānṣawh Bey, attempted to deprive him of the governorship of Jirjā, and (89) Riḍwān Bey of the command of the Pilgrimage, a serious revolt of the Faqāriyya ensued. Riḍwān and 'Alī received the sultan's sanction to proceed against their opponents. On 21 Jumādā I 1057/24 June 1647, 'Alī brought a numerous body of his troops to Cairo and imposed his will on the viceroy. The Qāsimiyya grandees were proscribed, Qānṣawh and others being killed. On 8 Ramaḍān/ 7 October, 'Alī withdrew from Cairo, in obedience to the viceroy's order. Two days later, Riḍwān, feeling himself threatened by the viceroy, fled to join 'Alī. The viceroy prepared a force to fight them, but the troops, instigated by (1) 'Abdī Bey, refused to proceed. In the meantime letters arrived from the sultan confirming Riḍwān and 'Alī in their respective commands for life, and 'Alī returned to Jirjā. Aḥmad Pasha V endeavoured to break the alliance between the two beys by obtaining an imperial order dismissing Riḍwān from the command of the Pilgrimage and conferring this office on 'Alī. 'Alī arrived in Cairo on 19 Muḥarram 1061/4 January 1651, and was invested as *amīr al-Ḥājj* four days later. Riḍwān, who at this time was absent from Cairo with the Pilgrimage, accepted his dismissal, but on 8 Ṣafar/23 January, he received news of the appointment of a new viceroy, 'Abd al-Raḥmān Pasha I. 'Alī made a declaration of his alliance with Riḍwān before an assembly of grandees, and reinvested Riḍwān with the command of the Pilgrimage. 'Alī continued to hold the governorship of Jirjā until his death in 1063/1652–3.

14. 'ALĪ *al-Tutunjī*

Raised to the beylicate by the viceroy Aḥmad Pasha V. Possibly a member of the viceroy's suite; cf. (6) Aḥmad al-Qahwajī and (53) Muḥammad.

15. *Küçük* 'ALĪ

A member of the Faqāriyya faction, who nevertheless served under the viceroy Muḥammad Pasha XII in the expedition against the rebel Faqārī governor of Jirjā, (54) Muḥammad Bey, in Jumādā II 1069/February–March 1659. He was one of the principal grandees implicated in the great revolt of the Faqāriyya (Ṣafar 1071/October 1660). At this time, although governor of the town of Damietta, he was resident in Cairo, and ignored the viceroy's order to return to his command. When the Faqāriyya grandees dispersed before the viceroy's forces, *Küçük* 'Alī, together with (28) Ḥasan Bey and

(41) Lājīn Bey made their way to the Buḥayra. Here with his colleagues he surrendered under a safe-conduct, but was put to death at al-Ṭarrāna by order of (7) Aḥmad Bey on the night of 23 Ṣafar 1071/27–8 October 1660. Al-Jabartī (I, 91) mentions him as 'Alī Bey *al-Ṣaghīr*, a member of the household of (89) Riḍwān Bey.

16. 'ALĪ

Multazim of al-Za'īra (-Dha'īra) in the Manūfiyya. Raised to the beylicate of (9) Aḥmad Bey on 26 Ramaḍān 1101/3 July 1690, after the latter's death: hence he presumably succeeded Aḥmad as *kāshif* of the Manūfiyya. At the end of Shawwāl 1103/14 July 1692, he was appointed *kāshif* of the Buḥayra, in place of Ibrāhīm Bey *Abū Shanab*, after troubles which had occurred during the previous year in this province and quarrels among the grandees in Cairo. He still held this province when he was appointed commander of the *Khazna*, but died on his way to take up his new command: 25 Dhu'l-Ḥijja 1106/6 August 1695.

17. *Kara* AYYŪB

Retainer (*tābi'*) of (54) Muḥammad Bey, the Faqārī governor of Jirjā; raised to the beylicate by Muṣṭafā Pasha VII: 16 Muḥarram 1067/4 November 1656. He was killed in the suppression of Muḥammad Bey's revolt: Jumādā II 1069/February–March 1659.

18. BĀYAZĪD

One of the grandees who were accompanying Ibrāhīm Pasha III when he was killed by rebel troops at Shubrā: 1 Jumādā I 1013/25 September 1604. Cf. (20) Darwīsh b. 'Uthmān Efendi.

19. BAYRAM

Qapudan at Damietta. Died during a great epidemic, which lasted from late Rabī' I to late Jumādā II 1028/March–June 1619.

20. DARWĪSH B. 'UTHMĀN Efendi

Son of a *qāḍī* in Cairo. One of the grandees who were accompanying Ibrāhīm Pasha III at the time of his assassination: 1 Jumādā I 1013/25 September 1604. Cf. (18) Bāyazīd.

21. DARWĪSH

Ağa of the *Çerakise*. Raised to the beylicate of (16) 'Alī Bey on the latter's death: 26 Dhu'l-Ḥijja 1106/7 August 1695.

22. DHU'L-FAQĀR

Appointed by Muṣṭafā Pasha VIII to the joint command of troops sent against the rebellious Faqāriyya: Ṣafar 1071/October 1660. On 22 Jumādā I 1076/30 November 1665, he escaped from prison, and made his way to Istanbul. Possibly identical with either (23) Dhu'l-Faqār Bey *al-Māhī*, or (24) Dhu'l-Faqār Bey *Abū Sa'da*.

23. DHU'L-FAQĀR *al-Māhī* (*-Māḥī*)
Summoned to Istanbul together with the *Rüznameci* Muṣṭafā Efendi b. Suhrāb: 16 Jumādā I 1075/5 December 1664. Mentioned by al-Jabartī (I, 91) as a Faqārī grandee of the household of (89) Riḍwān Bey, and a survivor of the cataclysm of 1071/1660.

24. DHU'L-FAQĀR *Abū Sa'da*
Appointed as deputy-governor (*nā'ib*) by (56) Muḥammad Bey, governor of Jirjā: 13 Jumādā I 1075/2 December 1664.

25. DILĀWAR
Commander of an expeditionary force levied in Egypt against the Safavids: 23 Dhu'l-Qa'da 1044/10 May 1635. He had previously been *amīr al-Khazna*.

26. ḤASAN
Defterdar: served as *qā'im maqām* on the deposition of Ḥusayn Pasha II: 19 Rabī' I 1031/1 February 1622. When the grandees refused to accept 'Alī Pasha as viceroy, and insisted on the continuance in office of Muṣṭafā Pasha V (Dhu'l-Ḥijja 1032/October 1623), the vital meeting was held at Ḥasan's house: it is not clear whether he had yet been raised to the beylicate. When the grandees deposed Mūsā Pasha in Dhu'l-Ḥijja 1040/July 1631, they appointed Ḥasan (now referred to as "bey") *qā'im maqām*. In Ṣafar 1043/August–September 1633, the sultan ordered an expeditionary force to be levied in Egypt for operations against the Druze *amīr* Fakhr al-Dīn Ma'n, and Ḥasan was given the command. On his suggestion, the viceroy Aḥmad Pasha IV wrote to the sultan for a supply of copper, because of the lack of small coins in Egypt. The arrival of this copper in Shawwāl 1043/April 1634 gave rise to further problems; cf. (73) Muṣṭafā. His great tent, which was erected with others by (89) Riḍwān Bey on the occasion of the state entry of Ḥusayn Pasha III (17 (?) Rajab 1045/27 December (?) 1635), was confiscated by the viceroy without compensation.

27. ḤASAN *Ṣahr Sinān Pasha* (? *Ṣahr al-Naqīb*)
Ḥasan Bey *Ṣahr Sinān Pasha* was made *qā'im maqām* on the deposition of Muḥammad Pasha IX in Dhu'l-Qa'da 1057/December 1647. He is probably identical with a Ḥasan Bey called in one source

Ṣahr al-Naqīb, whom Muḥammad Pasha IX had invested as *amīr al-Ḥājj* (12 Ramaḍān 1057/11 October 1647) in an attempt to weaken (89) Riḍwān Bey: the slip *Ṣahr al-Naqīb* for *Ṣahr Sinān Pasha* could arise from confusion with the later (109) Yūsuf Bey *Ṣahr al-Naqīb*.

28. Ḥasan

A member of the Faqāriyya faction; he is described by Jabartī (I, 91) as belonging to the household of (89) Riḍwān Bey. He accompanied Riḍwān, when the latter fled from Cairo on 12 Ramaḍān 1057/11 October 1647 to join (13) ʻAlī Bey. After the successful revolt of the Faqāriyya against Muḥammad Pasha XI and (7) Aḥmad Bey in 1066/1656, Ḥasan was appointed *amīr al-Ḥājj*. He played a leading part in the great revolt of the Faqāriyya in 1071/1660, and was one of the victims of (7) Aḥmad Bey at al-Ṭarrāna (23 Ṣafar 1071/27–8 October 1660).

29. Ḥaydar

A member of the commission which detained Ḥusayn Pasha III after his deposition (15 Jumādā II (?) 1047/4 November 1637) to settle his accounts with the treasury.

30. Ḥusayn

Mamlūk of (84) Qāsim Bey. He had been raised to the beylicate before 9 Dhu'l-Ḥijja 1040/9 July 1631. Probably identical with the Ḥusayn Bey who was exiled to Alexandria after the assassination of (7) Aḥmad Bey.

31. Ḥusayn

A member of the Faqāriyya faction. He played a leading part in the great revolt of the Faqāriyya in 1071/1660. When the Faqāriyya grandees dispersed before the viceroy's forces, Ḥusayn took a company by way of the oasis of al-Khārja to the Sudan, where he disappears from history. He may be identical with the Ḥamza Bey, not otherwise noted, who is stated by al-Jabartī (I, 91) to have been killed in the revolt of al-Ṭarrāna.

32. *Topal* Ḥusayn

Accompanied the expeditionary force sent to the Ḥijāz by Ibrāhīm Pasha VI to fight the rebellious *Sharīf* Ḥammūda: Shawwāl 1078/March–April 1668. Died Jumādā II 1107/January–February 1696.

33. Ibrāhīm

Died during the viceroyalty of Muḥammad Pasha VIII.

34. Ibrāhīm

Kâhya of (89) Riḍwān Bey: he was raised to the beylicate after the successful revolt of the Faqāriyya in 1066/1656. Probably identical with the Ibrāhīm Bey who was *amīr al-Ḥājj* for the Pilgrimage of 1070/1660: he returned to Cairo in Ṣafar 1071/October 1660, and supported the viceroy in his action to suppress the rebellious Faqāriyya grandees. He was exiled to Mecca with other grandees (? of the Faqāriyya faction) by Ibrāhīm Pasha V: 5 Dhu'l-Ḥijja 1072/22 July 1662.

35. Ibrāhīm

Formerly chief of police (*wālī, za'īm*) in Cairo, and hence a member of the Janissary Corps. Appointed to collect the loot taken from Arabs defeated in the province of al-Jīza: 17 Rajab 1110/19 January 1699.

36. 'Īsā

Appointed *qā'im maqām* at the time of the first (unsuccessful) deposition of Muṣṭafā Pasha V: Dhu'l-Ḥijja 1032/October 1623. He was confronted by the mutinous troops demanding a special payment (*taraqqī*) on the occasion of the change of viceroys. This situation gave rise to the refusal of the grandees to receive 'Alī Pasha, the newly nominated viceroy.

37. Ismā'īl

The maternal nephew of a *muftī* in Anatolia: this relationship led to his selection by the grandees to carry their petition to the sultan after they had deposed Mūsā Pasha in Dhu'l-Ḥijja 1040/July 1631. Died during the viceroyalty of Muḥammad Pasha VIII.

38. Ismā'īl

Died when an expeditionary force returning from Crete under his command was shipwrecked at Alexandria: 1 Ramaḍān 1080/23 January 1670.

39. 'Iwaḍ (Īwāẓ)

He was appointed *qā'im maqām* by Muṣṭafā Pasha VIII, when the viceroy left Cairo to suppress the great revolt of the Faqāriyya in Ṣafar 1071/October 1660. This appears to be the sole instance of the appointment of a *qā'im maqām* while a viceroy was in full exercise of his powers. He served as *qā'im maqām* in the customary fashion on the deposition of Ibrāhīm Pasha V: 24 Jumādā I 1074/24 December 1663. In Shawwāl 1086/December 1675–January 1676, he took command of an expeditionary force of 2,000 men for (?) Kamenets.

40. KAN'ĀN

He was present when (86) Qayṭās Bey was assassinated by order of Mūsā Pasha (9 Dhu'l-Ḥijja 1040/9 July 1631), and took part in the events leading to the deposition of Mūsā two days later. A leader of the grandees' opposition to Maqṣūd Pasha. He was invested as *qā'im maqām* by the dying viceroy 'Alī Pasha V (Sha'bān 1080/December 1669–January 1670), and in this capacity sent a relieving force to Alexandria, to help the troops who had been shipwrecked on their return from Crete: 17 Ramaḍān 1080/8 February 1670. The incoming viceroy Ibrāhīm Pasha VIII investigated his accounts, and sent him with the *Khazna* to Istanbul. After being held for a time, he was released, but died in Istanbul.

41. LĀJĪN (LĀCHĪN)

A member of the Faqāriyya faction; he is described by al-Jabartī (I, 91) as belonging to the household of (89) Riḍwān Bey. He accompanied Riḍwān when the latter fled from Cairo on 12 Ramaḍān 1057/11 October 1647 to join (13) 'Alī Bey. He took part in the expedition organized by Muḥammad Pasha XII against (54) Muḥammad Bey, the rebel Faqārī governor of Jirjā in Jumādā II 1069/February–March 1659. He was one of the ringleaders in the great revolt of the Faqāriyya in 1071/1669 and perished together with (15) *Küçük* 'Alī Bey and (28) Ḥasan Bey at al-Ṭarrāna: 23 Ṣafar 1071/27–8 October 1660. He had held the post of governor of the Gharbiyya.

42. MAḤMŪD B. RIḌWĀN *Abi'l-Shawārib*

Son of (90) Riḍwān Bey *Abu'l-Shawārib*. He was apparently raised to the beylicate during the viceroyalty of Muṣṭafā Pasha VI, on the death of (75) Muṣṭafā Bey b. 'Abd al-Nabī.

43. MAḤMŪD

He was sent in command of an expeditionary force of 1,000 men to the Morea: 28 Rabī' II 1098/13 March 1687. Possibly identical with the Maḥmūd Bey who was appointed governor of al-Bahnasā in Ṣafar 1109/August–September 1697.

44. MĀMĀY

Raised to the beylicate, and given command of the *Khazna* by Muḥammad Pasha VIII. On appointment he paid the viceroy a relief (*khidma*) of 15,000 gold pieces. Maqṣūd Pasha sought unsuccessfully to have him and (13) 'Alī Bey killed in the Divan: 1053/1643–4. He was an associate of (82) Qānṣawh Bey, the favourite of Muḥammad

Pasha IX. When Qānṣawh tried to obtain the transfer of the command of the Pilgrimage from (89) Riḍwan Bey to Māmāy, the Faqāriyya revolted. Māmāy and Qānṣawh were arrested on 27 Jumādā I 1057/30 June 1647, and put to death the next day. One account states that the executioners found Māmāy already dead in the attitude of prayer.

45. Muḥammad b. al-Ṭabbākh

The rebellious soldiers demanded his life from the viceroy Muḥammad Pasha II. He was intercepted on the way to the Citadel, and beheaded: 1 Rajab 1006/7 February 1598.

46. Muḥammad *Ḥājjī*

Served as *defterdar*. He was appointed *qā'im maqām* by Muḥammad Pasha IV on leaving Egypt: Jumādā I or II 1020/July–August 1611. He was subsequently governor-general of the Yemen.

47. Muḥammad *Cebeci*

Died in the great epidemic of 1028/1619; cf. (19) Bayram.

48. Muḥammad b. Suwaydān

Qapudan at Suez. Joint commander of the naval force which took part in the expedition under (84) Qāsim Bey to the Ḥijāz in Shawwāl 1041/May 1632. The force occupied Jedda without resistance. He died in the viceroyalty of Aḥmad Pasha IV.

49. Muḥammad

Formerly *ağa* of the *'Azeban*, he was raised to the beylicate by (81) Qānṣawh Bey, when the latter was appointed governor-general of the Yemen and Habeş. Qānṣawh appointed him his *qā'im maqām* in Habeş and he set out with a small force of about 200 men about the end of 1038/August 1629.

50. Muḥammad *Ash.k Sh.lān* (? *Eshek Chalan*)

Died in the viceroyalty of Aḥmad Pasha IV. His son took part in the expedition to Baghdad under (90) Riḍwān Bey *Abu'l-Shawārib*: 1048/1638.

51. Muḥammad b. al-M.k.s.ḥ (? *al-Mukassiḥ*)

An associate of (82) Qānṣawh Bey and (44) Māmāy Bey. Qānṣawh is said in one account to have endeavoured to make him governor of Jirjā in place of the Faqārī grandee, (13) 'Alī Bey. He lost his life in the proscription of the Qāsimiyya which followed the failure of this attempt: 1057/1647.

52. Muḥammad b. al-Muyūlī (? *al-Mawlā*)
Warden (*muḥāfiẓ*) of Sabīl 'Allān. Arrested and put to death during the proscription of the Qāsimiyya: 1057/1647.

53. Muḥammad *F.wālī* (*N.wālī*)
Raised to the beylicate by Aḥmad Pasha V; cf. (6) Aḥmad *al-Qahwajī* and (14) 'Alī *al-Tutunjī.*

54. Muḥammad
Mamlūk of (13) 'Alī Bey, whom he succeeded as governor of Jirjā (1063/1652–3); a member of the Faqāriyya faction. During the absence of the Faqārī *amīr al-Ḥājj*, (87) Qayṭās Bey, with the Pilgrimage of 1068/1658, Muḥammad marched on Cairo with a host including 400 armed *mamlūks* and 1,600 Circassian troops, as well as a vast number of Arab tribesmen. Muḥammad with his troops camped in the Qarāfa, and greeted with insults and blows a delegation of beys who had waited on him, to promise him their intercession with Muḥammad Pasha XII. Muḥammad Bey was clearly aware of a plot to remove him from the governorship of Jirjā, since at this juncture an imperial order arrived, transferring him to the province of Habeş and appointing (7) Aḥmad Bey to Jirjā. The viceroy duly invested Aḥmad with his new command, despatched a *musallim* to Jirjā with a token force of 70 men (ten from each of the Seven Corps), and sent a delegation to the camp of Muḥammad Bey, to invest him as governor-general of Habeş. Muḥammad refused to accept this transfer, which was tantamount to exile. The viceroy convoked the grandees and religious notables, and obtained a *fatwā* that Muḥammad might be punished as a rebellious subject. A punitive expedition was then organized under the command of the viceroy, which began its advance to the south on 7 Jumādā II 1069/2 March 1659. Qayṭās Bey had by this time returned from the Pilgrimage, and was sent with (41) Lājīn Bey, (15) *Küçük* 'Alī Bey, and others with an advance force against Muḥammad, who had withdrawn to Manfalūṭ. The rift between Muḥammad and his Faqāriyya colleagues was complete. The advance force routed some of Muḥammad's troops under his *kâhya*, Qānṣawh, and on receiving the news Muḥammad fled to the oasis at al-Khārja. Here he was defeated and captured by a force under Qayṭās Bey. He was taken to the viceroy's camp at Mallawī, where he was put to death on the night of 4 Rajab 1069/27–8 March 1659.

55. Muḥammad b. Afranj
Raised to the beylicate early in the viceroyalty of Muṣṭafā Pasha VIII; i.e. probably late 1069–70/late 1658–9.

56. MUḤAMMAD

Although probably a Faqārī, he supported Muṣṭafā Pasha VIII against the rebels in the great revolt of the Faqāriyya: 1071/1660. He is described at this time as governor of Jedda. Ibrāhīm Pasha V exiled him to Mecca: 5 Dhu'l-Ḥijja 1072/22 July 1662. He subsequently returned to Egypt, and was apparently appointed governor of Jirjā on 13 Jumādā I 1075/2 December 1664. During the viceroyalty of 'Umar Pasha he headed a disorderly company of soldiers (*ṭā'ifat al-zurab*) which caused damage and looting in Cairo. The viceroy ordered his assassination in the Divan. His associates shut themselves up in the Mu'ayyadī mosque, but were seized and for the most part put to death.

57. MUḤAMMAD

Possibly identical with (56) Muḥammad Bey. He took part in the operations against the rebels in the great revolt of the Faqāriyya 1071/1660.

58. MUḤAMMAD B. AL-BAYṬĀR

Raised to the beylicate in 1077/1666–7, he resigned his position in the following year and went to Mecca, where he remained until his death.

59. MUḤAMMAD *Abū Qūra*

He was the commander of an expeditionary force sent in Shawwāl 1078/March–April 1668 against the *Sharīf* Ḥammūda in the Ḥijāz. He was appointed governor of Jedda for the occasion.

60. MUḤAMMAD *Abu'l-Shawārib*

A Bosniak, raised to the beylicate at the end of Dhu'l-Qa'da 1079/ April–May 1669.

61. MUḤAMMAD *al-Jāwīsh*

Arrested on 26 Jumādā II 1080/17 April 1670; cf. (94) Shāwīsh Bey.

62. *Jundī* MUḤAMMAD

A member of the delegation sent to Istanbul on 10 Dhu'l-Ḥijja 1086/25 February 1686 to report on the deposition of Aḥmad Pasha VI. On his arrival there, he was exiled to the island of *L.mīh* (? Limni = Lemnos).

63. MUḤAMMAD *al-Ḥabashlī*

Formerly a *kâhya* of Janissaries. When *Küçük* Muḥammad seized control of the Janissary headquarters on 10 Jumādā II 1087/20

August 1676, he was raised to the beylicate. This was a device to evict him from the Janissary Corps. He subsequently resigned his position.

64. Muḥammad

Formerly *ağa* of Janissaries, he was raised to the beylicate on 1 Ṣafar 1098/17 December 1686, in accordance with an imperial order.

65. Muḥammad

Abkhaz (*Abāza*) by origin, he was raised to the beylicate and appointed governor of Jirjā in Jumādā II 1100/March–April 1689.

66. Muḥammad *Murjān Jūz* (*Kūz*)

Mentioned by al-Jabartī (I, 24) as a Faqārī grandee at the beginning of the twelfth century A.H. Al-Jabartī states that he was originally *kahveci* of Sultan Mehemmed [IV, 1058–99/1648–87]. He was appointed *kāshif* of the Fayyūm in Ṣafar 1109/August–September 1697.

67. Muḥarram

Died in the great epidemic of 1028/1619.

68. Muḥarram b. Māmāy

A certain Muḥarram *Çelebi* b. Māmāy was raised to the beylicate at the same time as (55) Muḥammad b. Afranj: probably late 1069–70/late 1658–9. A Muḥarram Bey, one of the *umarā al-Jarākisa* (i.e. not a *ṣanjaq bey*) is mentioned in the events leading to the great revolt of the Faqāriyya (1071/1660). Later in the same episode, it is stated that Muṣṭafā Pasha VIII raised Muḥarram *Çelebi* b. Māmāy Bey to the beylicate. All three notices probably refer to the same person, the son of (44) Māmāy Bey. Muḥarram died in Rabīʿ I 1075/September–October 1664.

69. Murād *al-S.k.rī*

One of the grandees whose lives were demanded by the provincial soldiery from Muḥammad Pasha II in the revolt of Rajab 1006/February 1598. He succeeded in escaping to Anatolia.

70. Murād

A member of the Faqāriyya faction, possibly governor of Jirjā. In 1067/1656–7, he came from the south to Old Cairo, where he was killed by one of his *mamlūks*.

71. MURĀD

A member of the Qāsimiyya faction, *mamlūk* of (79) Özbek Bey. He was raised to the beylicate in 1092/1681–2. He became *defterdar*. When the superintendence of four important *waqfs* was transferred from Janissary and *'Azeban* control to the beys, he received one of them: 8 Rabī' I 1103/29 November 1691. He ceased to be *defterdar* on 11 Shawwāl 1103/26 June 1692, perhaps in order to take command of an expeditionary force. He subsequently resumed the position of *defterdar*. On 13 Shawwāl 1106/27 May 1695, he summoned, on the order of 'Alī Pasha VI, a council of the grandees and *multazims* to deal with the effects of a serious shortage of grain in the imperial stores (*al-shuwan al-sharīfa*). The council's proposal to commute the troops' corn-rations for a money-payment produced a mutiny. The soldiers were pacified by the issue of their usual ration-coupons, which they then sold to the *multazims*. This satisfied both parties, since the soldiers received an inflated sum in lieu of corn, while the *multazims* were dispensed from the necessity of producing corn to the imperial stores. In 1107/1695–6, Murād was appointed *kāshif* of the Gharbiyya and the Manūfiyya, but on 11 Sha'bān 1107/16 March 1696 he was given command of an expeditionary force required by the sultan. His death on campaign was reported on 13 Rabī' I 1108/10 October 1696.

72. *Koja* MUṢṬAFĀ

Formerly *kâhya* of the *Çavuşan*, he was raised to the beylicate by Muḥammad Pasha IV (late Shawwāl 1017/January–February 1609) and put in command of the force sent against the rebellious provincial soldiery of the Delta, who were marching on Cairo. The rebels were defeated near al-Khānqa by 10 Dhu'l-Qa'da 1017/15 February 1609, and Muṣṭafā Bey made a triumphal entry into Cairo. He may probably be identified with the Muṣṭafā Bey who was implicated in the revolt of the soldiery against the retinue of Muṣṭafā Pasha III (7 Shawwāl 1027/27 September 1618), and with the Muṣṭafā Bey *al-B.q.j.lī* (*-B.q.j.h*) who was put to death by Muṣṭafā Pasha IV on 5 Muḥarram 1029/12 December 1619.

73. MUṢṬAFĀ

Defterdar before 1040/1630–1. He was appointed by Aḥmad Pasha IV on 5 Dhu'l-Ḥijja 1043/2 June 1634 to superintend the compulsory purchase of copper (originally sent by the sultan for the manufacture of coins; cf. (26) Ḥasan) by the people of Cairo. The sale of this copper to the artisans and *waqfs* began on 16 Dhu'l-Ḥijja 1043/13 June 1634, and the full price was not collected until the end of Sha'bān 1044/17 February 1635. He died at Qūṣ, on the way to Habeş, of which he had been appointed governor-general, in 1048/1638–9.

74. MUṢṬAFĀ

Governor of Jedda. He was killed in Sha'bān 1041/March 1632 during an invasion of the Ḥijāz, stirred up by a pretender to the amirate of Mecca.

75. MUṢṬAFĀ B. 'ABD AL-NABĪ

Raised to the beylicate by Muḥammad Pasha VIII, at the same time, and for the same expenditure, as (44) Māmāy. He died during the viceroyalty of Muṣṭafā Pasha VI. The troops at this time were in a mutinous condition owing to a lack of grain in the imperial stores: the discovery of 200,000 *ardabbs* of wheat among the effects of Muṣṭafā Bey helped to restore the situation.

76. MUṢṬAFĀ

Defterdar. He served as *qā'im maqām* after the deposition of Aḥmad Pasha V, and while holding this position, presided over the reconciliation between (89) Riḍwān Bey and (13) 'Alī Bey. In 1063/1652–3 he was appointed as commander of an expeditionary force to Crete. He is probably to be identified with Muṣṭafā Bey *al-Faqārī*, who acted as *qā'im maqām* before the arrival of Muṣṭafā Pasha VII in Shawwāl 1066/August 1656. This Muṣṭafā was, in 1071/1660, governor of Jirjā, but was in Cairo at the time of the great revolt of the Faqāriyya. He disobeyed the viceroy's order to return to Jirjā, and was deprived of both his rank and his province. When the Faqāriyya rebels dispersed before the viceroy's advance, he withdrew to Jirjā. He was arrested and sent to Cairo, where he was beheaded on the route of the triumphal procession of (7) Aḥmad Bey *bi-Qanāṭir al-Sibā'*: 25 Ṣafar 1071/30 October 1660.

77. MUṢṬAFĀ *Jād*

Like (63) Muḥammad *al-Ḥabashlī*, he was originally a *kâhya* of the Janissary Corps, and was raised to the beylicate in consequence of the *coup d'état* of *Küçük* Muḥammad in 1087/1676. He retained his position as bey until he died in Jedda.

78. MUṢṬAFĀ *Ṭ.kūz Kh.lāf* (? *Dokuz Khalāf*)

He commanded an expeditionary force of 2,000 men, sent to Adrianople: 1 Jumādā I 1100/21 February 1689; cf. al-Jabartī, I, 24.

79. Özbek b. Riḍwān *Abi'l-Shawārib*

A member of the Qāsimiyya faction, son of (90) Riḍwān Bey *Abu'l-Shawārib*. He was raised to the beylicate during the viceroyalty of Muḥammad Pasha IX. He was *amīr al-Ḥājj* for the Pilgrimage of 1077/1667, and while in Mecca promised to obtain the amirate of the city for the *Sharīf* Ḥammūda. The refusal of Ibrāhīm Pasha VI to concede this amirate led to the revolt of Ḥammūda. This was ultimately suppressed by an expeditionary force under (59) Muḥammad Bey *Abū Qūra*, which accompanied the Pilgrimage of 1078/1668 with Özbek again as *amīr al-Ḥājj*. On 17 Ramaḍān 1080/8 February 1670, he was sent by the *qā'im maqām* (40) Kan'ān Bey as the joint commander of a force to assist the troops who had been shipwrecked on returning from Crete.

80. Pīrī

Amīr al-Ḥājj. He was one of two grandees who attempted unsuccessfully to calm the mutinous soldiery during the revolt against Muḥammad Pasha II in Rajab 1006/February 1598. He was appointed *qā'im maqām* when 'Alī Pasha IV personally accompanied the *Khazna* to Istanbul (Rabī' II 1012/September 1603), but died in office on 15 Sha'bān 1012/18 January 1604.

81. Qānṣawh

Amīr al-Ḥājj. Because of his wealth, he was appointed on the suggestion of Muḥammad Pasha VII as governor-general of the Yemen, which was slipping from Ottoman control: early Jumādā I 1038/late December 1628. He was at the same time appointed governor-general of Habeş, to which he nominated (49) Muḥammad Bey as his *qā'im maqām*. He commanded a force composed partly of volunteers enrolled in Egypt, and partly of troops sent by the sultan. He set out in Muḥarram 1039/August–September 1629. The expedition failed. Some of the troops who had accompanied Qānṣawh were found in Mecca by the expedition which accompanied (84) Qāsim Bey in 1041/1631–2.

82. Qānṣawh *al-Ṣaghīr*

A member of the Qāsimiyya faction, *mamlūk* of (84) Qāsim Bey. He served as *qā'im maqām* on the deposition of Ayyūb Pasha: Rabī' I 1056/April–May 1646. The incoming viceroy, Muḥammad Pasha IX, made a favourite of Qānṣawh and allowed him to dominate his actions. Qānṣawh and his associate (44) Māmāy used their influence to weaken the powerful Faqāriyya grandees, the *amīr al-Ḥājj* (89) Riḍwān Bey, and the governor of Jirjā (13) 'Alī Bey.

A report was sent to Istanbul, laying the responsibility for a brawl in Cairo on 10 Rabīʿ I 1057/15 April 1647 on a gang stated to be retainers of Riḍwān and ʿAlī. The two beys were also accused of detaining the revenue due from them, and the viceroy requested the transfer of the command of the Pilgrimage and the government of Jirjā to Qānṣawh and his party. Riḍwān dispatched a counter-petition to Istanbul, and received imperial authority to investigate the question of the revenue. The arrival of ʿAlī Bey with an army from the south on 21 Jumādā I 1057/24 June 1647, strengthened his hand. Six days later a great assembly of the grandees and troops was held in the Rumayla, to which Qānṣawh and Māmāy were summoned. Qānṣawh wished to defend himself in his house against his adversaries, but was finally persuaded by Māmāy to attend the assembly. ʿAlī Bey accused them of detaining tribute, a charge which they denied. They were then summoned before the viceroy. Once again Qānṣawh wished to stand and fight, but was overborne by Māmāy who desired to avoid bloodshed. On arriving at the Citadel, they were arrested by the *ağa* of the Janissaries, and put in confinement. On the morning of Jumādā I/1 July, they were put to death by the attendants of (87) Qayṭās, the chief of police, Qānṣawh resisting to the end.

83. QĀNṢAWH *Fātiḥ Jarīd* (i.e. "the Conqueror of Crete")

He was commander of a force of 1,000 troops, levied on 13 Ramaḍān 1079/14 February 1669, for service in Crete, where the siege of Candia was then entering its final stage. He served as *qāʾim maqām* on the deposition of Ḥusayn Pasha IV: Rajab 1086/22 September 1675. In Jumādā II 1097/May 1686 he again led a force to Crete, where he died.

84. QĀSIM

Possibly the eponym of the Qāsimiyya faction, he is described as an elderly man in 1040/1631. After the assassination of (86) Qayṭās Bey in the Divan, by order of Mūsā Pasha (9 Dhu'l-Ḥijja 1040/9 July 1631), he took a leading part in the events leading to the deposition of the viceroy by the grandees. After the deposition, he, the *qāʾim maqām* (26) Ḥasan Bey, and (13) ʿAlī Bey formed a commission to investigate the accounts of Mūsā Pasha. He was commander of the expedition sent by Khalīl Pasha to the Ḥijāz in Shawwāl 1041/May 1632. The Yamanī troops, who had seized Mecca in the name of a pretender to the Sharifian amirate, offered no effective resistance, and Qāsim's forces occupied the city, and performed the Pilgrimage. After an engagement on the frontiers of Najd, the Arabs capitulated. Qāsim and his army left Mecca for Egypt in Ṣafar 1042/August–

September 1632. He died during the viceroyalty of Muḥammad Pasha VIII.

85. Qāsim

Qapudan at Damietta. Joint commander of the naval force which took part in the expedition under (84) Qāsim Bey to the Ḥijāz in Shawwāl 1041/May 1632; cf. (48) Muḥammad b. Suwaydān.

86. Qayṭās *al-Kabīr*

Maternal uncle of (4) Aḥmad Bey. In Sha'bān 1040/March–April 1631, the viceroy Mūsā Pasha received imperial orders to send an expeditionary force to fight against the Safavids. Qayṭās accepted the appointment of commander of this force, and paid the viceroy about 22 purses. After receiving this and about 100 purses levied on the Egyptians for the hire of camels, Mūsā Pasha cancelled the expedition, on the grounds that the treasury lacked sufficient funds to bear the expense. Qayṭās tried in vain to persuade the viceroy to let the expedition proceed. Mūsā now determined to rid himself of Qayṭās, who was assassinated in his presence on 9 Dhu'l-Ḥijja 1040/9 July 1631, at the end of the visit customarily paid by the beys to the viceroy on the Feast of the Sacrifice. This incident provoked a revolt of the grandees, culminating in their deposition of Mūsā Pasha. The estate of the dead bey was used to meet the expenses of a delegation sent to report the action of the grandees to Istanbul: cf. (37) Ismā'īl.

87. Qayṭās *al-Majnūn*

A member of the Faqāriyya faction, by origin a Circassian retainer (*tābi'*) of (89) Riḍwān Bey. As chief of police (*subaşı*), he was responsible for the execution of (82) Qānṣawh Bey and (44) Māmāy Bey when the Faqāriyya seized power in Jumādā I 1057/June–July 1647. He was probably raised to the beylicate about this time. He was appointed governor of Jedda, but in 1060/1650 a certain Ḥasan Pasha was sent from Istanbul to supersede him. Fighting broke out between Ḥasan and the *Sharīf* Zayd, the *amīr* of Mecca. Qayṭās supported Ḥasan, and bombarded the houses of the *Ashrāf* and the Ka'ba. The '*ulamā*' of Mecca reported his sacrilegious act to the sultan, who ordered the viceroy, Aḥmad Pasha V, to put him to death. At this time Aḥmad Pasha V was trying to break the power of the Faqāriyya, but the imperial orders which he intended to use against them lapsed with his deposition in Ṣafar 1061/January 1651, and Qayṭās returned to Cairo in safety. After the death of (89) Riḍwān Bey, he was invested as *amīr al-Ḥājj* for the Pilgrimage of 1068/1658. During his absence from Cairo, the revolt of the governor of Jirjā, (54) Muḥammad Bey, took place. Qayṭās took a leading part in the subsequent operations, and captured Muḥammad in the oasis of al-Khārja: Jumādā II 1069/March 1659. The death of Qayṭās himself occurred soon afterwards, in Dhu'l-Qa'da or Dhu'l-Ḥijja 1069/August–September 1658.

88. QAYṬĀS *al-Kabīr* (*bi-Qanāṭir al-Sibā'*)

A member of the Qāsimiyya faction, he was appointed *qā'im maqām* on the deposition of 'Abd al-Raḥmān Pasha II: 10 Sha'bān 1091/5 September 1680. On 12 Jumādā I 1097/6 April 1686, after serving as *defterdar*, he took command of an expeditionary force sent to the Morea: he was again appointed *qa'im maqām* on the deposition of Ḥasan Pasha IV: 5 Dhu'l-Ḥijja 1100/20 September 1689, when again he was *defterdar*. He died on 24 Rajab 1102/23 April 1691.

89. RIḌWĀN[47]

A Circassian; member of the Faqāriyya faction, of which he was the most outstanding representative in the eleventh/seventeenth century. He was *amīr al-Ḥājj* in the Pilgrimage of 1040/1631, and held this post almost uninterruptedly until his death, a quarter of a century later. He took part in (84) Qāsim Bey's expedition to Mecca in 1041/1632. His great influence as head of the Faqāriyya in Cairo led to several attempts by various viceroys and the Qāsimiyya faction to displace him. In Sha'bān 1044/January 1635 he and the other powerful Faqārī grandee, (13) 'Alī Bey, governor of Jirjā, were nominated by the sultan as alternative commanders of an expedition against the Safavids but succeeded in obtaining exemption from the viceroy Aḥmad Pasha IV. On the deposition of this viceroy in Jumādā I 1045/October–November 1635, Riḍwān served as *qā'im maqām*. His probity in this office was eulogized by his friend, the chronicler Shams al-Dīn Muḥammad b. Abi'l-Surūr. He spent over 100 purses of his personal wealth on the reception of the incoming viceroy, Ḥusayn Pasha III, who confiscated Riḍwān's great tent. Much distress was caused to the people of Cairo by the Druzes in Ḥusayn Pasha's retinue. When these attempted to extort an illicit levy from the shopkeepers at the end of Ramaḍān 1045/March 1636, under colour of gifts for the Feast, the tradesmen closed their shops and sought the mediation of Riḍwān. He induced the viceroy to prohibit the practice. He or (90) Riḍwān Bey *Abu'l-Shawārib* was a member of the commission which investigated Ḥusayn Pasha's accounts on his deposition in Jumādā II 1047/November 1637. With the next viceroy, Muḥammad Pasha VIII, Riḍwān's relations were hostile from the start. In 1048/1638–9 he was again appointed to command an expedition to Baghdad, but obtained exemption by paying the viceroy 40 purses. A disagreement between Muḥammad Pasha and Riḍwān occurred at the outset of the Pilgrimage of 1048/1639, and the viceroy took advantage of the death of (73) Muṣṭafā Bey to obtain the nomination of Riḍwān as governor-general of Habeş. At the same time he seized Riḍwān's effects for the sultan. The viceroy sent a messenger to Riḍwān, ordering him to hand over the temporary command of the Pilgrimage to a janissary officer at Jedda, and proceed at once to Habeş. (103) *Turk* Walī Bey was appointed as *amīr al-Ḥājj*, and set out for the Ḥijāz on 27 Dhu'l-Ḥijja 1048/1 May 1639. When the viceroy's messenger reached Riḍwān in Medina, he declared his obedience, but the janissary officer announced his own incompetence to take the temporary command of the Pilgrimage. Riḍwān therefore remained in command until he met Walī Bey at Wajh, when he surrendered his powers. Instead of going to Habeş, however, he fled to Istanbul, and sought the mediation of the *vezir* Muḥammad Pasha and the *muftī* Yaḥyā Efendi. Sultan Murad IV at first intended to have him put to death for disobedience in evading the command of the expedition to Baghdad, and in neglecting to proceed to Habeş. Finally he was placed under house-arrest. He obtained an amnesty a few days before Murad's death on 16 Shawwāl 1049/8 February 1640. The accession of Ibrahim I was followed by the appointment as viceroy of Muṣṭafā Pasha VI, in whose house Riḍwān had been detained. Riḍwān obtained the restoration of his previous position in Egypt, including the command of the Pilgrimage. The news of his return led to a dispute among the troops, as to whether he should be received, but on the advice of (44) Māmāy Bey, the grandees agreed that their intervention in the matter of his restoration would be *ultra vires*. Riḍwān reached Būlāq on 6 Rajab 1050/22 October 1640, and received a great welcome from the people of Cairo. In 1054/1644–5 Riḍwān mediated in a dispute between the ex-viceroy Maqṣūd Pasha, and his successor, Ayyūb Pasha, over the former's financial liabilities. Under Muḥammad Pasha IX, a very serious clash occurred between the viceroy in alliance with the Qāsimiyya, and the Faqāriyya headed by Riḍwān. The viceroy was guided by (82) Qānṣawh Bey, the mouthpiece of the Qāsimiyya. After a brawl in Cairo on 10 Rabī' I 1057/15 April 1647, the viceroy reported to Istanbul that the cause of the trouble was a gang of hooligans from the Yemen, who were retainers of Riḍwān and (13) 'Alī Bey. The two beys and their followers were further accused of detaining the revenue. The viceroy proposed to relieve them of their offices in favour of Qānṣawh and and Māmāy. The proposals were supported by numerous signatories, one of whom disclosed the scheme to Riḍwān. He immediately wrote to Istanbul, denying the accusations in advance, making counter-charges against Qānṣawh and Māmāy, and protesting his loyalty to the sultan. His version was favourably received, and he was instructed by the sultan to investigate the matter of the revenues, in association with ʻAlī Bey. On receipt of the imperial order, Riḍwān summoned ʻAlī Bey to Cairo, where he arrived on 21 Jumādā I 1057/24 June 1647, accompanied by a large army. Breaking all precedent, the viceroy went down from the Citadel to greet ʻAlī in Qarā Maydān. Six days later an assembly of the grandees and troops, now dominated by the Faqāriyya, was held in the Rumayla. A proscription of the Qāsimiyya followed, in which Qānṣawh and Māmāy were the first victims. When the killing was over, on 8 Ramaḍān 1057/7 October 1647, the viceroy instructed ʻAlī to return to Jirjā. The order was obeyed, but a fresh crisis between the viceroy and Riḍwān was already developing. On 12 Ramaḍān/11 October, Riḍwān, suspecting treachery, thrice refused an invitation to a banquet in the Citadel. The viceroy then appointed (27) Ḥasan Bey to the command of the Pilgrimage. This was an open breach, and Riḍwān fled with his friends from Cairo, to take refuge with ʻAlī Bey. The viceroy conferred the governorship of Jirjā on (107) Yūsuf Bey, and ordered an expeditionary force of 2,000 men to set out against ʻAlī and Riḍwān. (1) ʻAbdī Bey, who had been nominated as commander of this force was, however, a partisan of the Faqāriyya, and persuaded the grandees to discountenance the action. When the troops were paraded on 14 Ramaḍān/13 October, ʻAbdī announced their unwillingness to proceed, and the viceroy, conscious that he had become the pawn of contending and unstable factions, exploded with anger. At this juncture, Riḍwân's *kâhya* arrived from Istanbul with imperial orders granting Riḍwān and ʻAlī the tenure of their commands for life. A delegation was sent to the Faqāriyya grandees, and on 19 Ramaḍān/18 October, Riḍwān returned to Cairo. One further attempt was made to displace him, by Aḥmad Pasha V. Sultan Ibrahim I, who had favoured Riḍwān since his accession, had been deposed in 1058/1648, and the nominal sultan, Mehemmed IV, was a child. When Riḍwān left Cairo with the Pilgrimage in Shawwāl 1060/September–October 1650, the viceroy petitioned Istanbul for his removal from the command of the Pilgrimage, which was to be conferred on (13) ʻAlī Bey. This action, which was undertaken without ʻAlī's knowledge, was clearly an attempt to sow discord between the two Faqāriyya grandees. ʻAlī was summoned to Cairo, and invested as *amīr al-Ḥājj* on 23 Muḥarram 1061/8 January 1651. Riḍwān accepted his supersession equably. He was at this time on his return journey to Cairo, but on 8 Ṣafar/23 January the news arrived of the deposition of Aḥmad Pasha V, and the appointment of ʿAbd al-Raḥmān Pasha I as viceroy. With this, the transfer of the command of the Pilgrimage lapsed. Riḍwān made a triumphal entry into Cairo amid popular acclamation. He was reconciled with ʿAlī Bey, who on 10 Ṣafar/25 January, in the presence of the *qāʾim maqām* (76) Muṣṭafā Bey and the grandees, solemnly renounced the command of the Pilgrimage and invested Riḍwān with the official robes. Riḍwān Bey died on 23 Jumādā II 1066/18 April 1656. Riḍwān is briefly mentioned by al-Jabartī (I, 91), as the patron of one of the two households (the other being that of Balfīyya) from which most of the grandees of Egypt originated. He calls him *Ṣāḥib al-ʿImāra*.

90. Riḍwān *Abuʾl-Shawārib*

A member of the Qāsimiyya faction. He unsuccessfully opposed the deposition of Mūsā Pasha in Dhuʾl-Ḥijja 1040/July 1631. He accompanied (84) Qāsim Bey on the expedition to the Ḥijāz in Shawwāl 1041/May 1632. He was commander of the expedition sent to Baghdad in 1048/1638–9, in place of (89) Riḍwān Bey. A conspiracy of the grandees against Maqṣūd Pasha met on 12 Ramaḍān 1054/11 November 1644 at his house. Al-Jabartī states (I, 91) that after the death of (89) Riḍwān Bey (1066/1656) he formed a triumvirate with a certain Qāsim Bey Charkas (not otherwise known) and (7) Aḥmad Bey *bi-Qanāṭir al-Sibāʿ*, whom he predeceased by about seven months. This would place his death in *c.* Jumādā I 1072/December 1661–January 1662.

91. Ṣāliḥ

Amīr al-Ḥājj before Muḥarram 1025/January–February 1616, when he was appointed commander of an expeditionary force of 1,000 men, sent to Persia. He served as *qāʾim maqām* on the deposition of Ibrāhīm Pasha IV (7 Ramaḍān 1032/5 July 1623), and again on the deposition of Bayram Pasha (9 Muḥarram 1038/8 September 1628).

92. Shaʿbān

Defterdar in the time of Maqṣūd Pasha, who sought to dispose of him. He was apparently raised to the beylicate when the troops removed Maqṣūd (21 Ḥijja 1053/1 March 1644) and appointed him *qāʾim maqām*.

93. Shaʿbān

A Bosniak member of the Qāsimiyya faction, brother of (7) Aḥmad Bey *bi-Qanāṭir al-Sibāʿ*. He was raised to the beylicate by Muṣṭafā Pasha VII on 16 Muḥarram 1067/4 November 1656. During the great revolt of the Faqāriyya in 1071/1660, Muṣṭafā Pasha VIII invested him as governor of Jirjā, in place of the rebel Faqārī (76) Muṣṭafā Bey. In the operations against the Faqāriyya, he commanded the troops sent up the Nile in ships. He died on 10 Jumādā I 1076/18 November 1665 in Crete, where his tomb became an object of pilgrimage. He was a pious man.

94. SHĀWĪSH

Amīr al-Ḥājj. He was arrested on 26 Jumādā II 1080/17 April 1670 with (61) Muḥammad Bey *al-Jāwīsh*.

95. SULAYMĀN

A Bosniak; hence presumably a member of the Qāsimiyya faction. During the viceroyalty of Ḥusayn Pasha IV he was in command of an expeditionary force of 3,000 men sent to (?) Kamenets. He is probably to be identified with Sulaymān Bey *al-Daftardār* who took part in Dhu'l-Ḥijja 1097/October–November 1686 in an expedition against the Arab chief 'Abdallāh b. Wāfī. A Sulaymān Bey, probably the same, took part in a relief expedition sent to the province of al-Jīza, where (9) Aḥmad Bey had been worsted by the Arabs: Rabī' I 1099/February 1688. He is also perhaps to be identified with a Sulaymān Bey who was *kāshif* of the Manūfiyya in 1106/1694–5, and was sent to Istanbul with the *Khazna* at the end of that year. If, as seems probable, a further identification can be made with a Sulaymān Bey *tābi' Qayṭās Bey*, who took part in a relief force sent to assist Īwāẓ Bey[48] against the Arabs of al-Jīza on 11 Rajab 1110/13 January 1699, the subject of this notice was a *khushdāsh* of (9) Aḥmad Bey.

96. SULAYMĀN

Formerly *ağa* of the *Çerakise*, he was raised to the beylicate on 17 Ḥijja 1105/9 August 1694.

97. SULAYMĀN

A retainer (*tābi'*) of 'Alī *Ağa al-Khazindār*, he was appointed by the *qā'im maqām* Muṣṭafā Bey *Qizlār* (al-Jabartī, I, 114) as *kāshif* of the Manūfiyya, 14 Rabī' I 1109/30 September 1697.

98. 'UMAR

One of the commanders of the advance force sent by Muḥammad Pasha XII to fight the rebel Faqārī governor of Jirjā, (54) Muḥammad Bey, in Jumādā II 1069/March 1659.

99. 'UMAR

A retainer (*tābi'*) of Ramaḍān Bey,[49] he was transferred from his beylicate in Jumādā II 1091/June–July 1680, and made governor of Gaza. He was killed by nomad Arabs on 22 Rajab 1092/7 August 1681.

100. 'UMAR

He fled from Egypt on 3 Ṣafar 1105/4 October 1693 with Muṣṭafā Bey (?) *Qizlār* (Jabartī, I, 114) to Istanbul, to complain of the viceroy 'Alī Pasha VI.

101. 'UTHMĀN *Khaṭṭāṭ*

He was appointed *qā'im maqām* by the beys on the death of the *qā'im maqām* (80) Pīrī Bey: 15 Sha'bān 1012/18 January 1604. He held office until the arrival of Ibrāhim Pasha III in Dhu'l-Ḥijja 1012/May 1604. He was in the company of this viceroy when the latter was assassinated by mutinous troops on 1 Jumādā I 1013/25 September 1064. The rebels sought to reinstall him as *qā'im maqām*, but he refused, and the appointment was given to the judge Muṣṭafā Efendi 'Azmīzāde. He may perhaps be identified with the 'Uthmān Bey who died in the viceroyalty of Aḥmad Pasha IV.

102. UWAYS

A member of the Qāsimiyya faction, who was raised to the beylicate by Muṣṭafā Pasha VIII during the great revolt of the Faqāriyya in 1071/1660, in place of the rebel (76) Muṣṭafā Bey, governor of Jirjā. He was sent by the *qā'im maqām* (39) 'Iwaḍ Bey to Būlāq, to meet a party of the rebels who had decided to surrender. He subsequently became *defterdar*, but was killed during a rising of the Janissaries and '*Azeban* in the Rumayla: 19 Rabī' I 1075/10 October 1664. The mutineers claimed that he had killed one of his *mamlūks* who belonged to their regiment.

103. *Turk* WALĪ

He was appointed *amīr al-Ḥājj* in Dhu'l-Ḥijja 1048/May 1639, in place of (89) Riḍwān Bey, by Muḥammad Pasha VIII.

104. YŪSUF *al-Ghaṭṭās*

One of the grandees sent to parley with the rebel provincial soldiery in Dhu'l-Qa'da 1017/February 1609. His *kâhya* was a member of the delegation sent to Alexandria to induce the viceroy-designate, 'Alī Pasha, to leave Egypt: Dhu'l-Ḥijja 1032/October 1623. He is probably identical with the Yūsuf Bey who served as *qā'im maqām* when Muṣṭafā Pasha V was finally deposed in Sha'bān 1035/May 1625.

105. YŪSUF

Amīr al-Ḥājj. He fled from Egypt after the rising of 7 Shawwāl 1027/27 September 1618 against the retinue of Muṣṭafā Pasha III.

106. YŪSUF *Afranj*

Commander of the marine expedition which formed part of the force sent to the Ḥijāz in Shawwāl 1041/May 1632 under the general command of (84) Qāsim Bey. He may be identical with the Yūsuf Bey who died during the viceroyalty of Muḥammad Pasha VIII.

107. YŪSUF

Defterdar. He was appointed governor of Jirjā on 13 Ramaḍān 1057/12 October 1647 by Muḥammad Pasha IX, when the latter attempted unsuccessfully to oust (13) ʻAlī Bey. Probably identical with the Yūsuf Bey who was a leader of the opponents of Maqṣūd Pasha in Ramaḍān (?) 1053/(?) November–December 1643.

108. YŪSUF *bi-Darb al-Jamāmīz I*

Formerly clerk of the *Mutafarriqa* Corps, and *kâhya* of the *Çavuşan*. He was appointed *qā'im maqām* by the Faqāriyya, when they revolted and deposed Muḥammad Pasha XI in 1066/1656. He again served as *qā'im maqām* on the deposition of Muṣṭafā Pasha VII: Ramaḍān 1067/June 1657. He died at the end of Dhu'l-Qaʻda 1077/May 1667.

109. YŪSUF *Ṣahr al-Naqīb*

He took part in the operations against the Faqāriyya in the great revolt of 1071/1660. He was a member of the expeditionary force sent with (59) Muḥammad Bey *Abū Qūra* against the *Sharīf* Ḥammūda in the Ḥijāz after the defeat of (110) Yūsuf Bey: Shawwāl 1078/March–April 1668. On the death of Ibrāhīm Pasha VI (Jumādā I or II 1079/October–November 1668) he was appointed *qā'im maqām* in the Divan. He fell into disgrace during the viceroyalty of Ibrāhīm Pasha VI, in connexion with an investigation of the revenue, and his possessions were sold to liquidate his debt to the treasury: 1081–4/1670–3. He subsequently lived in poverty in Cairo.

110. YŪSUF

Appointed governor of Jedda and *Shaykh al-Ḥaram* by Ibrāhīm Pasha VI: 18 Rabīʻ I 1078/7 September 1667. He left Cairo with a force of 500 troops in late Jumādā II 1078/December 1667, but was defeated near Yanbuʻ by the *Sharīf* Ḥammūda, and died in captivity.

111. YŪSUF *bi-Darb al-Jamāmīz II*

Appointed commander of the *Khazna*: 15 Dhu'l-Ḥijja 1101/19 September 1690.

NOTES

1 'Abd al-Raḥmān al-Jabartī, *'Ajā'ib al-āthār fi'l-tarājim wa'l-akhbār*, Būlāq, 1297/1879–80—the edition used in this study. Later editions, both in Cairo, in 1302/1884–5 and 1322/1904–5.

2 Ibn Iyās, V.

3 See above, pp. 154–55, 159.

4 See Brockelmann, *GAL*, II, 383; *S*, II, 409. The manuscript cited in this article is Bodleian MS. Pocock. 80.

5 See Brockelmann, as above. The manuscript cited in this study is BM. MS. Add. 9973.

6 BM. MS. Add. 9972. See above, pp. 155, 159

7 Bibliothèque Nationale, MS. arabe 1855. See above, pp. 156, 159

8 See above, pp. 153–4, 159

9 See above, p. 162.

10 Of the Seven Corps, four (Janissaries, *'Azeban*, *Gönüllüyan* and *Tüfenkçiyan*) were originally formed from troops brought to Egypt by Selim. Two others (*Çavuşan* and *Çerakise*) first appear in the *Qanunname* of 931/1524, while the *Mutafarriqa* was constituted only in 962/1554–5. See further S. J. Shaw, *The financial and administrative organization and development of Ottoman Egypt 1517–1798*, Princeton, 1962, 189–97; idem, *Ottoman Egypt in the age of the French Revolution*, Cambridge, Mass., 1964, 82–95.

11 A belief has arisen that the viceroy of Egypt "could not leave Cairo, and was indeed confined to the Citadel by the *Kânûn-Nâma*" (H. A. R. Gibb and Harold Bowen, *Islamic society and the West*, I, Pt. I, London, 1950, 202, n. 4). Although it is substantially true that in the seventeenth and eighteenth centuries the viceroys were restricted to the Citadel, this was not so previously, nor was it in any case an administrative requirement. The *Kanunname* merely assigns the Citadel to the viceroy as his customary residence; cf. Ö. L. Barkan, *Osmanlı imparatorluğunda ziraî ekonominin hukukî ve malî esasları*, I, Istanbul, 1943, CV, "Mısır kanunnâmesi", 378. In 923/1517, Sultan Selim appointed a military governor of the Citadel, who was enjoined to remain there, and not to go down into the city (Ibn Iyās, V, 206). This person, an Ottoman named Khayr al-Dīn Pasha, was, however, quite distinct from the viceroy. Ibn Abi'l-Surūr, who copies Ibn Iyās's statement verbatim (*Kawākib*, f. 14b) indeed adds the gloss respecting this officer, "and now in our time he is called the *ağa* of Janissaries".

12 M. T. Petti Suma, "Il viaggio in Sudan di Evliyā Çelebī", *Annali dell' Istituto Orientale di Napoli*, n.s., XIV, 1964, 438. The date there given (935/1528–9) is impossibly early for Özdemir. See above, p. 83.

13 For the career of Özdemir, see Quṭb al-Dīn Muḥammad b. Aḥmad al-Nahrawālī al-Makkī, *al-Barq al-Yamānī fi'l-fatḥ al-'Uthmānī*, published as *Ghazawāt al-Jarākisa wa'l-Atrāk fī janūb al-Jazīra* (al-Riyāḍ, 1387/1968): hereafter indicated as *Ghazawāt/Barq*.

14 See Bernard Lewis, *The emergence of modern Turkey*, London, 1961, 28–31; also Halil Inalcık, "The heyday and decline of the Ottoman Empire" in P. M. Holt, Ann K. S. Lambton and Bernard Lewis (edd.), *The Cambridge history of Islam*, Cambridge, 1970, I, 344–5.

15 Numbers prefixed to the names of beys refer to the notices in the biographical dictionary in Part II of this study.

16 See *EI*², II, 233, DHU'L FAḲĀRIYYA (P. M. Holt).

17 This incident is mentioned, but not described, by al-Jabartī, I, 91. For a contemporary monograph on the subject, see Ibrāhīm b. Abī Bakr al-Ṣāliḥī, *Tarājim al-Ṣawā'iq fī waq'at al-ṣanājiq*, Bibliothèque Nationale, MS. arabe 1853.

18 P. Vansleb, *Nouvelle relation . . . d'un voyage fait en Egypte* (Paris, 1677), 93–4.

19 See "The career of Küçük Muḥammad (1676–94)", below, pp. 231–51, and André Raymond, "Une 'révolution' au Caire sous les Mamelouks—la crise de 1123/1711", *Annales Islamologiques*, VI, 1965, 95–120.

20 The form *ṣanjaq* is commoner in Egyptian sources than *sanjaq* or *sanjāq*, which are also found.

21 The text of an Arabic document formally notifying Sulaymān Bey's appointment to the judges and other functionaries of Upper Egypt is given in 'Alī Mubārak, *al-Khiṭaṭ al-jadīda*, X (Būlāq, 1305/1887–88), 54–5. A notice of Sulaymān's career is given by al-Ghazzī, *al-Kawākib al-sā'ira* (ed. Jibrā'īl S. Jabbūr), III (Beirut, 1958), 157–8, and other documents concerning him appear in Uriel Heyd, *Ottoman documents on Palestine 1552–1615*, Oxford, 1960, in one of which (p. 62), dated 18 Ṣafar 984/17 May 1576, he is described as "at present serving as sanjak-beg in Egypt". He was subsequently governor of Baghdad, Karaman and Damascus.

22 Vansleb, op. cit., 32, "Les Turcs chasserent il y a cinquante ans, ou environ, ces Princes Arabes, et mirent en leur place des Sangiac-Beys, qui estoient Turcs naturels, dont le premier s'appeloit *Soliman-Gianballat*". In the form "Ibn Janbalān", the name appears in a Nubian tradition transmitted by Shuqayr; see above, p. 82.

23 Cf. D. Ayalon, "Studies on the structure of the Mamluk army—II", *BSOAS*, XV, 3, 1953, 468.

24 Ibn Iyās, op. cit., 365, 389, 439.

25 *Ghazawāt/Barq*, 71–3.

26 *Kawākib*, f. 22b.

27 *Ghazawāt/Barq*, 78.

28 *Al-amīr* Ibrāhim b. Taghri (Bibliothèque Nationale, MS. arabe 1854, ff. 46a–49b); Ibrāhīm b. Taghrīwardī (Mar'ī b. Yūsuf, Bodleian, MS. D'Orville 544, unfoliated); Ibrāhīm Bey (*Kawākib*, f. 17a).

29 Bibliothèque Nationale, MS. arabe, 1854, f. 48a; *Kawākib*, f. 18b.

30 Paris Fragment, f. 31b.

31 *Kawākib*, f. 17a.

32 Paris Fragment, f. 37b; al-Isḥāqī, 169: confirmed by Ibn Abi'l-Surūr and the *Zubda.*

33 *Kawākib*, f. 25a. For Muṣṭafā 'Azmīzāde, see *EI*², I, 826, 'AZMĪ-ZĀDE, Muṣṭafā (F. Babinger).

34 *Kanunname* in Barkan, op. cit., 381.

35 Report of Ḥusayn Efendi to Estève, the French controller-general of the finances during Bonaparte's occupation of Egypt. Text in Shafiq Ghorbal, "Misr 'ind mafraq al-ṭuruq", *Bulletin of the Faculty of Arts of the University of Cairo*, IV, 1, 1936, 1–69. The report was translated (from a different manuscript) by Stanford J. Shaw, *Ottoman Egypt in the age of the French Revolution*, Cambridge, Mass., 1964. The passage referred to is at p. 36.

36 See above, p. 171.

37 The ethnic origins of the Mamluks have been discussed by Professor Ayalon in "Studies in al-Jabartī", *JESHO*, III, 3, 1960, 318–21. Since Ayalon's

underlying assumption is that the beys were necessarily *mamlūks*, his investigation overlaps with that pursued in the following paragraphs, which, however, query the assumption and reach rather different conclusions as far as the seventeenth century is concerned.

38 Ghorbal, "Miṣr", 14; Shaw, *Ottoman Egypt in the age of the French Revolution*, 36–8.

39 See al-Jabartī, I, 93.

40 Paris Fragment, f. 50b.

41 Al-Jabartī, III, 321.

42 One may note in passing a contrary process—the foundation of Mamluk households by officers of the Seven Corps. Such a regimental household, originating in the late seventeenth century, was established by Ḥasan Balfiyya, *ağa* of the Gönüllüyan (cf. al-Jabartī, I, 91). Another was founded in the middle of the eighteenth century by Ibrāhīm *Kâhya* (cf. al-Jabartī, I, 191–2, and note that neither Ibrāhīm nor his colleague, Riḍwān *Kâhya*, was a bey, as stated in Gibb and Bowen, op. cit., I, i, 227). These houses produced both beys and regimental officers.

43 See n. 46 below

44 See above, pp. 165–74.

45 Thus in Ḥusayn Efendi's late-eighteenth-century account four beys served as deputy-viceroy and *qapudans* of Alexandria, Damietta, and Suez (see above, p. 186), three held the great offices of state as *defterdar*, *amīr al-Ḥājj* and *amīr al-Khazna*, while five were the provincial governors of Upper Egypt, the Sharqiyya, the Gharbiyya, the Manūfiyya, and the Buhayra. The remaining twelve served in pairs on a monthly rota as commanders of the guard in Cairo. Here the definition of the term "bey" by function is complete, but it would be wrong to read this back into the more fluid conditions of the seventeenth century, and still more wrong to state, as Ḥusayn Efendi does, that a beylicate with these specific functions was instituted by Sultan Selim I.

46 Not (39) 'Iwaḍ/Īwāẓ Bey, but a later bey whose obituary is given by Jabartī, I, 94–5.

47 See below, pp. 220–30.

48 See n. 46 above.

49 See al-Jabartī, I, 93–4.

12

THE EXALTED LINEAGE OF RIḌWĀN BEY: SOME OBSERVATIONS ON A SEVENTEENTH-CENTURY MAMLUK GENEALOGY

1. *Description of the Genealogy*

The subject of this paper is a small work entitled *Qahr al-wujūh al-ʿābisa bi-dhikr nasab al-Jarākisa min Quraysh*, which might be rendered, "A cogent demonstration of the lineage of the Circassians from Quraysh". The work is anonymous but the style and language suggest that its author was an *ʿālim* who enjoyed the patronage of a Mamluk *amīr*, Riḍwān Bey. I have used the text printed in Cairo in 1316/1898–9 as the basis of my translation of passages. The two manuscripts I have seen, MS. Arabic 791 (711) in the John Rylands Library, Manchester, completed on 21 Rajab 1092/6 August 1681, and MS. Or. 3030 in the British Museum, dated in the colophon 21 Dhu'l-Ḥijja 1258/23 January 1843, have no differences of substance from the printed version, although there are variant spellings of outlandish names—and indeed these occur within the printed text itself. The Rylands manuscript gives an extended form of the title: *Qahr al-wujūh al-ʿābisa bi-dhikr nasab umarāʾ al-Jarākisa waʾttiṣālihi bi-Quraysh.* It states that the author completed the work on 1 Rajab 1041/23 January 1632.[1]

The author begins by saying that he carried out research into the descent of the Circassians from Quraysh by order of Riḍwān Bey, whom, after a long string of honorifics, he entitles "the Commander of the noble Flag, Bearer of the eminent Muhammadan *Maḥmal*,[2] trusting in the Powerful King, Riḍwān Bey al-Kabīr". He says that he came on an essay (*risāla*) by a certain Shihāb al-Dīn Aḥmad al-Ṣafadī, "an admirable, learned and judicious historian", the *imām* of a mosque in Ak Şehir, who died in 980/1572–3.[3] This provides him with the material for his genealogy.

He summarizes al-Ṣafadī's essay in an introduction, seven short chapters, and a long conclusion. The introduction deals with the universe before the creation of Adam, while the chapters relate the legendary history of the Kaʿba from Adam to the descendants of Ismāʿīl; the origin of Quraysh and their association with the Kaʿba, the mission of Muḥammad, and the dispersal of the tribes in the time of ʿUmar. This leads on in the seventh chapter to the real subject of interest, a legendary account of the ancestry of the Circassians, which runs as follows:

"There was a clan of Quraysh called Banū 'Āmir, whose chief was named Kisā'; he was their ruler and commander. He was the *amīr* Kisā' b. 'Ikrima b. 'Amr b. Wadd al-'Āmirī. It happened that they were exercising their horses at a feast when a palm-frond (alternatively, a reed) from the hand of the *amīr* Kisā' missed the mark and struck the eye of an Arab called Fuhayd, and put it out. They complained of him to the Caliph 'Umar, who wished to retaliate upon him for his adversary, according to the Law. So he fled by night (*sarā laylan*). When enquiry was made, it was said, '*Sarā*', and it was said, *Jarā*, i.e. 'He has gone with his people'. He came to the land of the Greeks, seeking safety for himself, and he was called Jāra Kisā' from that day. . . . This *amīr* Kisā' continued to pass from one locality to another until he came with his people to the land of Burṣa. His army was about 30,000 persons. If anyone of the land of the Greeks opposed him, he fought and slew him until the people feared him. This reached Qusṭanṭīn, so he gave him a safe-conduct and ordered him to pass beyond the channel of Constantinople and choose what land he would. So he passed beyond with his people and withdrew to the waste land between the east and the west of Constantinople. He found the country of al-'Abūbān,[4] known formerly as the land of al-Niyāriq,[5] in the land of Bulghār.[6] It was formerly in the possession of the Armenians and the Greeks (*al-Arwām*) overcame them. . . . In it he found the remainder of the Armenians in numerous groups. He fought and defeated them and made his home in their country. His kinsmen said to him, 'We wonder at the speed with which these territories submit to us', so he said to them, 'It is because of the strength of our courage' (*min quwwat ba'snā*). [They asked him, 'What shall we call this abode?' He said 'Bāsnā',][7] and it was so called and became a land of pleasant climate, abounding in soldiers, and now it is known as the land of the Jarākisa."[8]

The descendants of Kisā continued to live in this land, "ignorant of a revealed Scripture and not following a Holy Law, but their government [was] the government of the nomad Arabs, with submission to God Most High". Two other Arab tribes also fled from Muslim to Byzantine territory; the Banū Ghassān under Jabala b. al-Ayham,[9] whom al-Ṣafadī states to have been given fiefs by Qusṭanṭīn in Jabal Arnūd (presumably for Arna'uṭ, Albania), and the Umayyad Banū Mudlij. These last, he says, settled in Spain (*Bilād al-Andalus*) until they were overcome by the self-styled Fatimid, 'Ubaydallāh al-Mahdī!

The next topic is the return of the Banū 'Āmir to Islamic territory.

Some returned openly, such as the tribe of Ashrāf Banī 'Āmir in Sharqiyya and the 'Awāmir of Upper Egypt. Others returned obscurely and as individuals, such as the founder of the Circassian Mamluk sultanate in Egypt, al-Ẓāhir Barqūq b. Anaṣ.[10]

The account of Barqūq is interesting. He is shown as the thirteenth (or fourteenth) descendant of Kisā, all the intervening names except Anaṣ being Persian or Turkish. Emphasis is laid on his free origin, and two slightly variant accounts are given of the manner in which he was kidnapped into slavery. He was sold in Constantinople to the Mamluk *amīr* Ṭashtamur and brought to Egypt, where he became the *mamlūk* of Sultan al-Manṣūr 'Alī b. al-Ashraf Sha'bān.[11] In due course Barqūq himself became sultan; the phrase used, *intahat ilayhi al-riyāsa*, is that used in the seventeenth and eighteenth centuries of Mamluk grandees who acquired the supremacy over their colleagues—in this later period it preceded chronologically the use of the expression *shaykh al-balad*.[12]

The Circassian Mamluk sultans who followed Barqūq are then listed. A key position in the genealogy is given to al-Ashraf Barsbāy 825–42/1422–38), of whom it is said, "Barsbāy was at first a *mamlūk* of Barqūq; then it appeared that he was his kinsman (*walad 'ammihi*), so he emancipated him. Then he advanced him through the ranks and so he continued until the supremacy fell to him (*intahat ilayhi al-riyāsa*) and he sat upon the throne of the kingdom and administered Egypt".[13]

After speaking of the Ottoman conquest of Egypt by Selim, the genealogy gives an account of a supposed descendant of Barsbāy as follows:

"The Circassians dispersed to all parts, fearing lest they should be killed. Some returned to the country of Jarkas (alternatively, Sarkas). Among those Circassians who returned to seek concealment was the *amīr* Rustum[14] . . . and Rustum was at that time thirteen years old. When he returned to the country of his people, he joined his kinsmen and retainers (?) and married a girl of his kindred at his residence, Bāsnā. He had many children by her. Al-Khawājakī[15] al-Gharīqī al-Uṣaylī[16] Ḥasan b. al-Ṣabbāgh of the town of Tripoli has stated that he arrived to trade in the land of Jarkas and met this king Rustum. He saw him administering all those districts, aware of his worth and lineage from al-Malik al-Ashraf Barsbāy, the ruler of Egypt, which was confirmed and witnessed by all there. When Ḥasan b. al-Ṣabbāgh came to Egypt, he told this to the marshal Azdamur[17] the Elder [*al-Kabīr*], who confirmed it as true, for he was one of the Circassian *amīrs* and knew all that befell them. And when Rustum married his cousin, she bore him three sons and two daughters. The Grand *Vezir* Sinān Pasha,[18] Lord of the Black Sea, wrote for him to return to the Ottoman Porte. The letter reached him by the hand of Muḥammad *Ağa*, the Circassian. Having read it and understood its contents, he sent his reply in large Arabic script, and it is said that he sealed it with the seal of his ancestor, al-Ashraf. Its contents, after the opening, were as follows, 'Let it then be known, honourable Minister, that God Most High has recompensed us with all good and given us sons, thus and thus'. And he enumerated them, three sons, and specified their names, the eldest, Khān Faḍl; the middle one, Barsbayk; and the youngest, Jānbak 'Azīz.[19] This letter was found in the treasury of the Grand *Vezir* Sinān Pasha after his death (alternatively, before his death). This *amīr* Rustum never entered the gate of the city of Constantinople, out of fear for himself. He lived until the accession of Sultan Selīm the Younger, and the progeny of Rustum live in those parts until now."[20]

The remainder of the work recapitulates the genealogy. Rīdwān Bey is described as the son of Jānbak 'Azīz and the grandson of Rustum, whose ancestry is traced to Barsbāy, thence to Timurbughā, the grandfather of Barqūq,[21] thence to Kisā', 'Adnān, and Adam. The names are given of Riḍwān Bey's own sons, the *amīrs* Maḥmūd, Uzbak (Özbek), Muḥammad, Murād, Abū Yazīd, 'Āshūr, and Khūshqadam.

2. *Identification of the Subject of the Genealogy*

At the time when the genealogy was compiled, there were two prominent beys named Riḍwān, one of whom seems indisputably to be the subject of this genealogy.[22] A notice of him appears in al-Muḥibbī's biographical dictionary, where he is described as *amīr al-Ḥājj*, for which title the genealogist's *Hāmil al-Maḥmal al-Muḥammadī al-Sharīf* is a synonym.[23]

Al-Muḥibbī says that his subject, the *amīr* Riḍwān b. 'Abdallāh al-Ghaffārī, was a Georgian (*Kurjī*). At first he was a *mamlūk* of Dhu'l-Faqār, an *amīr* of Egypt. After his master's death, he had a lean time, but subsequently rose to eminence, four of his own *mamlūks* becoming beys like their master. He was a successful Commander of the Pilgrimage, and held this office for over 20 years. In the time of Muḥammad Pasha (i.e. Muḥammad Pasha VIII 1047–50/1637–40), he was dismissed from this command by the sultan, at the governor's request. He went to Istanbul, where he was imprisoned by Murad IV. Released by Sultan Ibrahim I (succeeded 1049/1640), he returned to Egypt, regained his lost possessions, and was recognized as premier bey (*in'aqada 'alayhi riyāsat Miṣr*). In the time of Aḥmad Pasha V (1059–61/1649–51), further troubles arose and he was again dismissed from the command of the Pilgrimage, which was conferred on 'Alī Bey, the governor of Jirjā. The supersession of Aḥmad Pasha by 'Abd al-Raḥmān Pasha I (1061–2/1651–2), however, nullified this further attempt to remove Riḍwān from power. He died in 1066/1655–6.

This identification is not completely free from difficulties. There is a serious divergence between the genealogy and al-Muḥibbī over the parentage and ethnic origin of Riḍwān. Al-Muḥibbī's statement that Riḍwān was a Georgian may be due to a failure to distinguish between two Caucasian peoples, the Georgians and Circassians, both of which furnished *mamlūks* to the Muslim world. His unexplained "al-Ghaffārī" is almost certainly an error for "al-Faqārī", perhaps the fault of a copyist or printer. The patronymic "Ibn 'Abdallāh" had been used by *mamlūks* in the time of the Mamluk sultanate. It was commonly used by *devşirme* recruits and implies non-Muslim parentage. Two alternative explanations of this divergence are possible: either that al-Muḥibbī was completely misinformed as to Riḍwān's origin, or that the pedigree given in the genealogy is wholly spurious. An examination of the motives behind the compilation of the genealogy may assist us to decide which is the more probable explanation.

Some other sources of information on the character and career of Riḍwān Bey may first be briefly noted. The most detailed are the chronicles which form part of two works by the seventeenth-century Çairene writer, Shams al-Dīn Muḥammad b. Abi'l-Surūr al-Bakrī al-Ṣiddīqī. The earlier of these is in *Al-Rawḍa al-zahiyya fī wulāt Miṣr wa'l-Qāhira.* It goes down to the year 1041/1631–2 and mentions a certain Riḍwān Bey al-Zulfiqārī (i.e. al-Faqārī) as Commander of the Pilgrimage in 1040 and 1041.[24] In the latter year, he took part in a military expedition to the Ḥijāz. The second of Ibn Abi'l-Surūr's chronicles, in *Al-Kawākib al-sā'ira* (or *al-siyāra*) *fī akhbār Miṣr wa'l-Qāhira*, transcribes the earlier chronicle to 1041 and then continues with a very detailed account of events to 1062/1651–2. Full information is given on the clashes, described by al-Muḥibbī, between Riḍwān Bey and the two governors, and in general al-Muḥibbī's account is supported. Between these two incidents, there was a serious struggle with Muḥammad Pasha IX in 1057/1647, which is not mentioned by al-Muḥibbī, but which Ibn Abī'l-Surūr recounts in much detail. It is clear from *Al-Kawākib al-sā'ira* that Ibn Abi'l-Surūr had close personal relations with Riḍwān, whom he regarded with respect.

A later chronicle, the anonymous *Zubdat ikhtiṣār ta'rīkh Miṣr*,[25] which ends in 1111/1699–1700, adds little to our information on Riḍwān Bey but gives the precise date of his death as 23 Jumādā II 1066/18 April 1656. Much later still is al-Jabartī's great history, which begins formally only with the twelfth *hijrī* century. It contains, however, a reference to this Riḍwān Bey, whom al-Jabartī distinguishes as *Ṣāḥib al-'Imāra*. Al-Jabartī's brief note is as follows:

"The majority of the *amīrs* of Egypt trace their origin to one of the two houses, the house of Balfiyya and the house of Riḍwān Bey *Ṣāḥib al-'Imāra*, who died in 1065 leaving no sons; but he left Ḥasan Bey, the Commander of the Pilgrimage, and [the names of nine other beys follow]. This Riḍwān Bey was greatly respected and of high authority. He held the command of the Pilgrimage for many years and was a pious man, observing the Fast, prayer, and the *dhikr*. He built the quarter known by his name[26] outside the Zuwayla Gate by his house, and he established a *waqf* for his freedmen and for pious and charitable objects."[27]

It will be noted that there is a slight discrepancy between al-Jabartī and the earlier writers over the date of Riḍwān's death. This is sufficiently explained by al-Jabartī's later date of writing and by the minor importance of the point to him. The fact that al-Muḥibbī mentions four, and al-Jabartī ten, beys of Riḍwān's household may perhaps be due to al-Muḥibbī enumerating only those created in Riḍwān's lifetime. Some difficulty is presented by al-Jabartī's explicit statement that Riḍwān Bey left no son, whereas the genealogy names seven; but the high mortality rate among the children of the Mamluks is well known and quite possibly all seven predeceased their father.

The other prominent Riḍwān Bey of this period is not mentioned by al-Muḥibbī, but appears in the other sources listed with the cognomen of *Abu'l-Shawārib*.[28] He belonged to the rival Mamluk group of the Qāsimiyya, and his identification with the subject of the genealogy is precluded by the fact that he was never Commander of the Pilgrimage. He became prominent after the death of the other Riḍwān. The junior status of Abu'l-Shawārib supports the identification of the subject of the genealogy with the Faqārī Riḍwān Bey, since the epithet *al-Kabīr*, applied by the genealogist, generally indicates seniority when used in Mamluk contexts.

3. *Purpose of the Genealogy*

The compiler of the genealogy seeks to establish two things: a connexion between his patron, Riḍwān Bey *al-Kabīr*, and the Circassian Mamluk sultanate; and a further connexion between the Circassians (and hence Riḍwān Bey) and Quraysh. His proof of a connexion between Riḍwān and the Circassian sultans is feeble in the extreme, resting on an assertion that Riḍwān was the son of Jānbak 'Azīz and the grandson of Rustum. It is noticeable that, in contrast to the abundant information given on Rustum, Jānbak

'Azīz is only known from a passing mention by Ibn al-Ṣabbāgh. Had Riḍwān been in fact the son of Jānbayk 'Azīz, one might have expected him to have furnished the genealogist with material about his father at least as copious as the information concerning Rustum. The absence of such material, as well as the fact that the account of Rustum himself is not derived from Riḍwān but from persons outside Rustum's family, strongly suggests that the genealogist arbitrarily derived Riḍwān from the family of a Circassian chief of whom he learnt from a literary source.

The account of Rustum and his career after the Ottoman conquest of Egypt is not inherently impossible but his descent from Barsbāy is asserted without any attempt at proof. In view of what is known about the exclusion of the sons of Mamluks from office under the Circassian sultanate, it is most unlikely that a descendant of a sultan should, in the fifth generation, emerge from the *awlād al-nās* and re-enter the privileged Mamluk military aristocracy. The principle of Mamluk society under the sultans was the superiority of the Mamluk household to the natural family. In the neo-Mamluk society of Ottoman Egypt, however, this principle was no longer rigorously maintained: the aristocratic clans which developed in the seventeenth and eighteenth centuries contained both hereditary and *mamlūk* members. The provision of a family tree for Rustum, linking him with two Mamluk sultans, appears as the natural anachronism of a genealogist familiar only with the neo-Mamluk period.

The anachronistic and spurious character of this genealogy itself bears witness to its compiler's determination to link Riḍwān Bey with the Circassian sultans. The period of its compilation was the time when Mamluk power revived in Egypt[29] after the century of Ottoman dominance which began with the suppression of Jānbirdī al-Ghazālī[30] and *Khā'in* Aḥmad.[31] One of the earliest figures of this Mamluk revival, the first whose career can be reconstructed in detail, was this Riḍwān Bey *amīr al-Ḥājj al-Sharīf*, and in the genealogy itself we may see a manifesto asserting the historical continuity of the Mamluk beys with the Mamluk sultans. The genealogy is a deliberate attempt to set the seventeenth-century resurgence of Mamluk power in the context of Egyptian history and thereby, in some degree, to legitimatize it. The use of spurious genealogy for such a purpose is not unprecedented: one recalls, for example, the official Ottoman tradition linking the dynasty with the Oghuz,[32] and, at the other pole of the Muslim world, the claim of the Funj sultans of Sinnār to be the descendants of the Umayyads.

The attempt of the genealogist to derive the Circassians from Quraysh thus appears to be something more serious than historical fantasy or servile flattery of an influential parvenu. The derivation of the Circassians from an Arab origin goes back to the period of the Mamluk sultanate. In connexion with his account of Barqūq, the first of the Circassian Mamluk sultans, Ibn Khaldūn mentions an assertion that "they [the Circassians] are the descendants of the Ghassānīs who entered the land of the Greeks [*bilād al-Rūm*] with their commander, Jabala b. al-Ayham, at the time of Heraclius's retreat from Syria".[33] This may conceivably have been propaganda intended to legitimize the usurpation of the sultanate by Barqūq from the Turk-descended house of Qalāwūn. While Ibn Khaldūn rejects this story, he gives some credence to the view that the Ghassānī immigrants and the Circassians became neighbours, and were bound by a pact of mutual defence. In the modified form of intermarriage, the legend appears in a panegyric of Sultan Ṭaṭar (824/1421),[34] and it was still current in Egypt at the time of the Ottoman conquest.[35]

Now, if Riḍwān's aim had simply been to obtain historical respectability, this tradition would have been sufficient. But this "established legend" is, as we have seen, deliberately rejected for a new fabrication which makes Banū Ghassān the ancestors of the Albanians, derives the Circassians from the Qaysī tribe of Quraysh, instead of the Yamanī tribe of Ghassān, and gives them for ancestor the Muslim Kisā' in place of the Christian Jabala.

The nature of these changes suggests the motive of the new fabrication. They were connected with Riḍwān's position as *amīr al-Ḥājj*. The command of the Pilgrimage was one of the great offices of state in Ottoman Egypt, as it had been under the Mamluk sultans. Although for the first two Pilgrimages after the Ottoman conquest, civilians were appointed as commanders, in 925/1519 the post was given to a Mamluk *amīr*, the secretary (*dawādār*) of the viceroy, Khā'ir Bey. In the three following years (926–8/1520–22) the appointment was held by another leading Mamluk *amīr*, Jānim al-Sayfī, the *kāshif* of the Fayyūm.[36] It is perhaps significant that Jānim, who, like Riḍwān in the following century, established a monopoly of the command of the Pilgrimage, rose in an unsuccessful revolt against Khā'ir Bey's successor as viceroy in the hope of throwing off Sultan Süleyman's rule over Egypt.[37] After this time information about the command of the Pilgrimage is sparse until the early seventeenth century, by which time the post was regularly held by a bey, although Riḍwān was perhaps the first to hold office over a long period of years.

His dignity as *amīr al-Ḥājj* made it expedient for his putative forefather to be a Muslim (even if a lapse had to be admitted after Kisā') and a Qurashī. The stress which the genealogist lays on the ancient association of Quraysh with the service of the Ka'ba is not a piece of pious antiquarianism but is intended to reflect glory upon the person and office of Riḍwān Bey.

At this point another consideration enters. The Ottoman conquest of Egypt and Syria brought little material profit to the sultanate, while it imposed a heavy burden on its strategy and military resources. The acquisition of these Arab provinces added only a single jewel to the sultan's regalia, but it was a jewel of unique and paramount importance to a Muslim ruler. From the defunct Circassian Mamluk sultanate (not, significantly, from the 'Abbasid puppet-caliphs of Cairo)[38] Selim and his successors had assumed the title of "Servant of the Two Noble Sanctuaries" (*Khādim al-Ḥaramayn al-Sharīfayn*) and with it the functions of provisioning the Ḥijāz, and of organizing and protecting the two great Pilgrimage-caravans of Cairo and Damascus. During the 300 years between Selim's conquest of Egypt and Muḥammad 'Alī Pasha's defeat of the Wahhābīs, concern to maintain this title by the proper discharge of its attendant obligations was a perennial consideration in Ottoman policy towards the Arab provinces. Recognition of the importance of this is a key to the understanding of the relations then subsisting among the authorities in Istanbul, Cairo, Damascus, and Mecca.

Seen in this light, the assertion by the genealogist that Riḍwān Bey *amīr al-Ḥājj* was descended both from the Mamluk sultans and from Quraysh was a twofold challenge to Ottoman authority. From the first, Selim and his successors had exercised their functions as Servants of the Two Noble Sanctuaries by delegation. During the reigns of the conqueror and of Süleyman the Magnificent, the subordination of these delegates had been clear, but in the years when Riḍwān Bey flourished, from 1040/1631 to 1066/1656 the situation, in Egypt at least, had changed. During his long tenure of the command of the Pilgrimage, Riḍwān was effectively and conspicuously fulfilling many of the sultan's duties towards the Two Noble Sanctuaries. The genealogy implies that Riḍwān Bey exercised his functions, not as a delegate of the remote Ottoman sultan, but by a species of hereditary right derived from Mamluk and Qurashī ancestors.

NOTES

1 See further Brockelmann, *GAL*, *S*, II, 406, where an earlier printed version (Būlāq, 1287/1870–1) is mentioned.

2 *Ḥaml al-Maḥmal al-Muḥammadī al-munīf*; Rylands 237a reads *Khādim al-Maḥmal*. The older (Rylands) reading may be a deliberate echo of the Ottoman sultan title, *Khādim al-Ḥaramayn al-Sharīfayn*. See below, p. 230, n. 2, and p. 228 above.

3 This writer is not mentioned by Brockelmann, *GAL*, nor by Babinger, *Geschichtsschreiber der Osmanen*. See above p. 176, n. 20.

4 Rylands, "al-Yūnān"; BM., "al-'Iyūyān".

5 Rylands, BM., "Alf Rāyiq".

6 For Bulghār, see below, n. 10. I have not succeeded in identifying the other place-names, which in this context are perhaps mythical. Qusṭanṭīn may be Constans II, the son of Heraclius.

7 The passage in square brackets is found in the Rylands MS.

8 Cairo 12–13. Rylands 249b–250b; BM 16b–17b.

9 The flight of the Ghassānī ruler, Jabala b. al-Ayham, is historical. For the legend that the Circassians themselves were of Ghassānī origin, see p. 227.

10 He is further styled *al-Jarkasī al-Bulghārī*. Rylands MS. adds *al-'Uthmānī*. Cf. his correct style as given by Ibn Taghrī Birdī (*Nujūm*, ed. Popper, V, 362; tr. Popper, *History of Egypt 1382–1469* A.D., I, 1): *al-'Uthmānī al-Yalbughāwī al-Jārkasī*. The genealogist's *al-Bulghārī* would seem to be an ignorant emendation of *al-Yalbughāwī* (i.e. the *mamlūk* of Yalbughā) and, in its turn, would account for the curious situation of "the land of the Bulghār" in Circassia (see above, p. 221). *Al-'Uthmānī* derives from the name of the slave-merchant ('Uthmān b. Musāfir) who imported Barqūq into Egypt. The genealogist's account of Barqūq's early career is muddled. He was never a *mamlūk* of Ṭashtamur, against whom he conspired. His father's name, given as Anaṣ by Ibn Taghrī Birdī, is arabicized to Anas in his funerary inscription (Max van Berchem, *Corpus inscriptionum arabicarum*, Paris, 1903, I, no. 189). No genealogy is provided for Anaṣ by either Ibn Taghrī Birdī or the funerary inscription.

11 Reigned 778–83/1377–81, the penultimate Turkish Mamluk sultan. He is, however, described in the genealogy as the twenty-third ruler of the Kurdish Ayyubids in Egypt.

12 Cf. the expression used by al-Muḥibbī of Riḍwān Bey, *in'aqada 'alayhi riyāsat Miṣr* (above, p. 223). It is interesting to note that Ibn Abi'l-Surūr says of Riḍwān, "He came to be called invariably in Cairo, 'the Shaykh Riḍwān'": *Al-Kawākib al-sā'ira*, BM. Add. 9973, f. 67a.

13 Cairo 16; Rylands 255b–256a; BM. 21b.

14 His genealogy is given for six generations back to Sultan al-Ashraf Barsbāy.

15 *Khawājakī* is an alternative form to *khawāja*. The plural, *khawājakīyya*, appears in texts of the Mamluk sultanate with the significance of "slave-merchants". See D. Ayalon, *L'esclavage du mamelouk* (Jerusalem, 1951), p. 37, n. 2. Ibn al-Sabbāgh was therefore presumably a sixteenth-century slave-merchant.

16 Thus in the Rylands MS. The BM. MS. reads "al-'Arīfī al-Uṣaylī", and the Cairo text (clearly corrupt) "al-'Arīfī al-aṣl".

17 Thus in the Rylands MS. The Cairo text, again corrupt, reads "Azdaman". Azdamur al-Kabīr is probably Özdemir, the conqueror of Habeş: see above, pp. 83, 179.

18 *Koja* Sinān Pasha, governor of Egypt in 1568, whence he conquered the Yemen, and 1574. He campaigned in Georgia (1580) and was appointed grand *vezir*, an office which he held five times in all. He planned to connect the Black Sea with the gulf of Nicomedia by a canal. D. 4 Sha'bān 1004/3 April 1596.

19 BM. "Jānbayk". Rylands (f. 262a) gives the variant Khānbayk.

20 Cairo 18–19. Rylands 261a–262b; BM. 26a–27a.

21 The fictitious nature of this section of the genealogy, which lists nine generations between Barsbāy and Timurbughā, is clear from the following considerations:

(i) Neither Barsbāy's own inscriptions nor the *Manhal ṣāfī* (Wiet, Cairo, 1932, p. 93, no. 644) give any indication of his parentage.

(ii) The reputed grandfather of Barqūq, Timurbughā, is not mentioned either by the *Manhal ṣāfī* (pp. 94–5, no. 650) or in the funerary inscription of Anaṣ, his alleged son.

22 See above, pp. 210–13, (89) Riḍwan.

23 Muḥammad al-Muḥibbī, *Khulāṣat al-athar fī a'yān al-qarn al-hādī 'ashar* (Būlāq, 1290/1873–4), II, 164–6.

24 His appointment was recent, since in Jumādā I 1038/Jan.–Feb. 1629 the Commander of the Pilgrimage had been a certain Qānṣawh, who was then appointed governor of the Yemen and Habeş.

25 See above, pp. 155, 159.

26 Hence presumably his cognomen, *Ṣāḥib al-'Imāra*, "The Master of the Building".

27 This information is given in the obituary of Ḥasan Aga Balfiyya; Al-Jabartī, *Ta'rīkh*, I, 91.

28 See above, p. 213 (90) Riḍwān *Abu'l-Shawārib*.

29 See above, pp. 178–81, and for more detail, P. M. Holt, *Egypt and the Fertile Crescent, 1516–1922* (London, 1966), 71–101.

30 Jānbirdī al-Ghazālī, a former Mamluk *amīr* appointed governor of Damascus by Selim, revolted against Süleyman and assumed in 1521 the title of *Sulṭān al-Ḥaramayn*, "the Sultan of the Two Sanctuaries". The significance of this title should be considered in the light of my remarks above (p. 228). See Muḥammad b. Ṭūlūn in H. Laoust, *Les gouverneurs de Damas* (Damascus, 1952), 158.

31 *Khā'in* Aḥmad Pasha, who claimed the sultanate of Egypt in 1523, was himself of Caucasian origin; in *EI*[2], I, 293, *s.v.* AḤMAD PASHA KHĀ'IN, Halil Inalcık states that he was a Georgian.

32 Cf. P. Wittek, *The rise of the Ottoman Empire* (London, 1938), 7–13.

33 Ibn Khaldūn, *Kitāb al-'ibar*, [Būlāq, 1867], V, 472.

34 Hans Ernst (ed.), *al-Rawḍ al-zāhir fī sīrat al-Malik al-Ẓāhir Ṭaṭar* (Cairo, 1962), 5.

35 Ibn Iyās, 197, V, 197, line 13.

36 Ibn Iyās, V, 218, 280, 317, 355, 407, 476.

37 See P. M. Holt, *Egypt and the Fertile Crescent*, 48. The source is the Continuation of al-Isḥāqī, ff. 52a–57a; see above, pp. 154, 159.

38 Ibn Iyās, V, 306.

13

THE CAREER OF KÜÇÜK MUḤAMMAD (1676–94)

KÜÇÜK MUḤAMMAD was a man of obscure origin who, in 1087/1676, seized control of the Janissary headquarters in Cairo. Twice ousted from this position, he regained power there finally in 1103/1692, after collusion with Ibrāhīm Bey b. Dhi'l-Faqār, a prominent grandee of the Faqāriyya faction, and Ḥasan Ağa Balfiyya, the influential commanding officer of the *Gönüllüyan* corps. During the following years he showed some of the characteristics of a tribune of the people, until his assassination in 1106/1694. His career is interesting in itself, and throws some light on the complexities of the struggle for power in Ottoman Egypt at the end of the seventeenth century.

1. *Sources of Information*

The most accessible account of Küçük Muḥammad's career is that given by al-Jabartī.[1] This is not, however, wholly reliable, since it is an amalgamation of several disparate sources. It is, moreover, scattered in several parts of the work. It is therefore necessary to go behind al-Jabartī to the older sources, including those which he himself used, as far as they can be ascertained.

The present study is based on six earlier chronicles, one of which is undoubtedly a source contemporary with Küçük Muḥammad himself. In a previous article (see pp. 162–5), I suggested that two types of Egyptian chronicle might be distinguished in the seventeenth and eighteenth centuries. The first type comprises the literary chronicles, in which the divisions of the narrative are usually provided by the reigns of the Ottoman sultans and the periods of office of their viceroys in Egypt. For the career of Küçük Muḥammad, three literary chronicles[2] are important:

(i) Anon., *Zubdat ikhtiṣār ta'rīkh mulūk Miṣr al-maḥrūsa* (British Museum, MS. Add. 9972), which ends in 1111/1699, with an additional note on 1113/1701–2. Short reference, Z (see above, pp. 155, 159).

(ii) Anon., the Paris Fragment (Bibliothèque Nationale, MS. arabe 1855), which breaks off in 1120/1708–9. The original length of the chronicle is unknown, but from the amount of detail in the last extant pages, the fragment is probably fairly far advanced. Short reference, PF (see pp. 156, 159).

(iii) Aḥmad Çelebi b. ʿAbd al-Ghanī, *Awdaḥ al-ishārāt fī man tawallā Miṣr al-Qāhira min al-wuzarāʾ waʾl-bāshāt* (Yale University Library, MS. Landberg 3), which ends in 1150/1737. This is the only work mentioned by name by al-Jabartī as a source for the part of his chronicle dealing with the early twelfth/eighteenth century. The question of its relationship to his chronicle will, however, be further investigated (p. 233 below). Short reference, AC (see pp. 156, 159).

The second type of historical writing in this period in Egypt comprises the popular chronicles, which, though not without value, are primarily narratives written for entertainment. Their diction is unashamedly colloquial; the "sultan-pasha" framework is attenuated to insignificance; they are constructed episodically around the deeds of the great military chiefs of Ottoman Egypt. As I noted in my previous article, the popular chronicles with which we are here concerned form a single family, the Damurdāshī Group (D Group). All open with the beginning of the twelfth *hijrī* century, but take their narrative down to different dates. In the present connexion, I have used three of these chronicles:

(i) Muṣṭafā b. Ibrāhīm al-Maddāḥ al-Qīnalī, *Majmūʿ laṭīf* (Nationalbibliothek, Vienna, MS. Hist. Osm. 38), which ends in 1152/1739. Short reference, DQ.

(ii) Anon., *K.* (*Majmūʿ*) *al-durra al-munṣāna fī waqāīʿ* [sic] *al-kināna* (Bodleian, MS. Bruce 43), which ends in 1168/1754–5. Short reference, DO.[3]

(iii) Aḥmad al-Damurdāshī, *kâhya* of ʿAzabān, *al-Durra al-muṣāna fī akhbār al-kināna* (British Museum, MS. Or. 1073–4), which ends in 1169/1756. Short reference, DL (see pp. 156–7, 159 above).

2. *Relationship of the Sources*

An analysis of the data provided by these six chronicles on the career of Küçük Muḥammad throws an interesting light on their relationships. Taking first the three literary chronicles, we find that the fullest account is given by Z, the earliest source. The coverage extends over nine principal incidents, from the revolt of the Janissaries in 1087/1676 (in which, however, Küçük Muḥammad's name is not mentioned) to his assassination in 1106/1694. The two other chronicles, PF and AC, agree on three points, on which they differ from Z: Küçük Muḥammad is specifically named in connexion with the revolt of 1087, while two of the nine incidents described in Z are ignored.

This agreement suggests a family relationship between PF and AC. To test this, I have compared their accounts of the viceroyalties of Ḥasan Pasha III, Ḥasan Pasha IV, Aḥmad Pasha VII, and ʿAlī

Pasha VI covering the *hijrī* years 1099 to 1106.[4] Both chronicles treat the same events in the same order; the only substantial differences are that AC inserts about four notices of events which are lacking in PF, and that there are several variations of dates. Such variations are frequent in manuscripts, and may chiefly be ascribed to copyists' errors.

The family resemblance of the two chronicles does not usually extend to phraseology, and at first sight one would be inclined to deny any close relationship between the two. But here al-Jabartī adds another element to the puzzle. His block of annals covering the *hijrī* years 1099–1120 (Jabartī, I, 24–35) is a very close reproduction of the corresponding portion at the end of PF. In a few places PF is summarized, and there are a few slight changes in phraseology, but in general and in detail the agreement of the two passages is very marked. Al-Jabartī, however, specifically mentions the work of Aḥmad Çelebi as known to him.[5] The implication would seem to be that al-Jabartī knew the chronicle of which we have only an anonymous fragment (PF) as the work of Aḥmad Çelebi. If this is so, PF and AC must be two members of a family of chronicles, related in structure but not in phraseology, rather like the D Group of popular chronicles, a phenomenon which may perhaps be explained by a common Turkish source.

Turning next to the three popular chronicles, we find, naturally, that they have no data on the career of Küçük Muḥammad before the beginning of the twelfth *hijrī* century, their starting-point. The information which they give may be broken down into ten main topics. These are found in all of them, but they differ in fullness of treatment and in the order of presentation. Although all except one of the incidents they describe appear in the literary chronicles, no reader could doubt that in the popular chronicles we have a different narrative tradition, and one common to all three, in spite of their variations in phraseology. Two differences from the literary chronicles suggest the entertainment motive which lay behind their composition. The incident which they all give, and which is not found in the literary chronicles, is the anecdote of Küçük Muḥammad and the jeweller. This is an oriental detective story, and may well have been a floating legend attached to Küçük Muḥammad after his death.[6] Furthermore, in their account of Küçük Muḥammad's final seizure of power in the Janissary headquarters (1103/1692) they reverse the order of events as given in the literary chronicles (see pp. 243–44).

Finally, we may consider the relationship of al-Jabartī's account to these older sources. His information about Küçük Muḥammad is to be found in four separate notices, the provenance of three of which is clearly identifiable. First, in his annals (Jabartī, I, 25) is a brief account of the capture of the Janissary headquarters in 1103. This is PF, slightly modified in an attempt to harmonize it with the D account.[7] A longer account of the incident of 1103 is given in the obituary of Ibrāhīm Bey b. Dhi'l-Faqār (I, 90). This is summarized from a D Group chronicle. An account of the assassination of Küçük Muḥammad is given in the obituary of Muṣṭafā *Kâhya* al-Qāzdughlī (I, 91–2). This again is derived from a D Group chronicle.[8] The sources of Küçük Muḥammad's own obituary (I, 92–3) are more problematic. It certainly contains data derived from a D Group chronicle, and probably some from PF, but it also draws on one, perhaps two, unidentified sources.[9]

3. *The Political Situation in Late Seventeenth-Century Egypt*

Although in the late seventeenth century Egypt was formally, as it had been since 1517, a province of the Ottoman Empire, administered by the sultan's viceroy, the realities of the political situation were very different. The viceroys were transient and almost impotent figures. In the eighteen years covered by this study, there were seven of them, and they seem to have played a passive role, as validating authorities for the execution of decisions made by others, although they may have had a hand in some of the conspiracies of the period.[10]

Wealth, influence, and power in Egypt were shared by several groups, whose members were either natives of, or permanently domiciled in, the country. Of native Egyptians, those of the greatest political significance were the religious notables and the tribal chiefs. The religious notables included not only the official hierarchy of the '*ulamā*' and the heads of the *ṭarīqas*, but also the members of the Bakrī family, who possessed great prestige as the descendants of the Caliph Abū Bakr al-Ṣiddīq. In the recurrent political crises of the seventeenth and eighteenth centuries, the religious notables acted as mediators and conciliators, and the habitual authority with which they assumed this part is in itself evidence of their standing and influence. Unlike other groups in Egypt, they did not conspire or fight to secure their position—because they had no need to. When in 1798 Bonaparte broke the power of the military grandees of Egypt, and sought the support of the religious notables, he was dealing with men who were neither politically naïve nor unused to the exercise of influence.

While the religious notables lay near the centre of the political structure of Egypt, the tribal chiefs were on its fringes. In Lower Egypt their power was an abiding threat to security: between them and the administration existed a long tradition of hostility, and indeed this very period of Egyptian history saw several military expeditions against the Arabs who pressed on the fertile land around the Delta, or ambushed the Pilgrimage Caravan. In Upper Egypt the situation was rather different. There, although Ottoman authority was represented by the governor of Upper Egypt (*ḥākim al-Ṣaʿīd*) at Jirjā, with his numerous subordinate *kāshifs* in the districts, a more permanent power was in the hands of the chiefs of Hawwāra, an arabized tribe of Berber origin, by this time sedentary, or partially so. The name of Humām seems to have become a patronymic for these chiefs, whose possession of the villages of Upper Egypt made them virtually monopolists of the corn supplies, and hence the chief source of the taxes in kind which filled the state granaries of Cairo.[11]

We have far less information than we should like about the political roles of the tribal chiefs. Egyptian historiography in the Ottoman period, as both before and since, was preoccupied to the almost total exclusion of any other interest with the course of events in Cairo, and in Cairo with the actions of the ruling military *élite*. Of the vicissitudes of the grandees, the factional struggles, and the *coups d'état*, we are therefore very fully informed, particularly for the seventeenth and eighteenth centuries, but the assumptions of the chroniclers often make it difficult for the modern student to understand the background of events, or to appreciate the real nature of the forces at work.

The military grandees became, with the decline of the viceroyalty, active competitors for political ascendancy in Egypt. These grandees were of two kinds. First were the senior officers of the Seven Corps of the Ottoman garrison in Egypt. The second order of grandees was the beylicate, whose members, the *sancak beyis*, stood outside the cadre of regimental grades, but held special commands, either of a recurrent nature, such as the command of the Pilgrimage (*imārat al-Ḥajj*) and of the Tribute-convoy (*imārat al-Khazna*) or *ad hoc* appointments to head expeditions within the borders of Egypt, or against the sultan's enemies abroad (see pp. 183–4 above).

In the years immediately following the Ottoman conquest, the garrison of Egypt was composed of troops recruited from both Mamluk and Ottoman sources. The garrison soon came to be organized in the Seven Corps, to which the chroniclers make frequent reference. But whereas the Mamluk system of recruitment continued uninterruptedly under Ottoman rule, the *devşirme* system, which had provided the Ottoman standing army at the time of the conquest, fell into disuse in the early seventeenth century. Thereupon a system developed in Egypt which seems to have had no parallel elsewhere in the Empire, and which was in fact a modification of the ancient Mamluk system extended to the recruitment of free-born Ottoman Muslims.

The characteristics of the Mamluk system as it survived the Ottoman conquest, may be briefly summarized.[12] The recruits, boys and youths of Caucasian origin, were imported into Egypt and purchased by masters (sing., *ustādh*), whose slaves (sing., *mamlūk*) they became. They were brought up as Muslims, given an equestrian and military training, and in due course were emancipated. After emancipation, some at least of the former slaves would establish Mamluk households of their own. The *mamlūk* or ex-*mamlūk* enjoyed the patronage of his master, by receiving appointments either to the master's domestic service (where the chief post was that of *khaznadār*, household treasurer), or to a commission in one of the Seven Corps, or to an administrative post, particularly that of *kāshif*, district officer. In popular usage, the Mamluks of the Ottoman period are always closely associated with the beylicate, of which they established a near-monopoly in the later eighteenth century. Earlier, however, the beylicate was by no means exclusively recruited from this source (see pp. 186–7 above).

Such was the stubborn vigour of the Mamluk system of recruitment and patronage, that its characteristics were impressed on the system by which free, Muslim immigrants were absorbed into the military society of Egypt. A detailed description of this is given in the *Nizamname-i Mısır* compiled by Aḥmad al-Jazzār, and probably based largely on his personal knowledge acquired between 1756 and 1768 (see note 11). The evidence of the *Nizamname* must be accepted with caution for the conditions of the last decades of the previous century, but there are indications in the contemporary chronicles and al-Jabartī that the system it describes already existed at that time, although it seems to have functioned less rigidly than in the time of al-Jazzār.

Briefly, the *Nizamname* describes the recruitment of *Rum uşağı* "youths of Rūm", i.e. immigrants from the old provinces of the Ottoman Empire. These by definition must have been freemen, in some cases Muslims born, in others converted *dhimmīs*. Like their *mamlūk* counterparts, they were first attached to the personal service of a master (*ağa*), in this case as personal guards (sing., *sarrāj*). There could be, of course, no change in their legal status, corresponding to the emancipation of a *mamlūk*, but after some years' service, the *sarrāj* also received his master's patronage. In al-Jazzār's account, this took the form of enrolment (as an ordinary soldier) in one of the Seven Corps, together with partnership with a wealthy member of the guild of Jedda merchants. Thus the ex-*sarrāj* (known as a *çirak*) was transferred from maintenance by his master to living on public funds, augmented by the profits of trade.[13]

As al-Jazzār describes the two systems of recruitment, the future prospects of the *mamlūk* and the *sarrāj* were widely different. On emancipation, the *mamlūk* could look forward to entering the military élite of Egypt, and becoming in time a bey or a high regimental officer. The *sarrāj*, by contrast, could only hope to become an ordinary soldier in the Seven Corps.[14] It is not surprising that al-Jazzār speaks of inveterate hostility between men so recruited and the *Mısırlu*, the military grandees. In the seventeenth and early eighteenth centuries, the discrimination seems to have been far less rigid. In the late seventeenth century several beys were Bosniaks, i.e. presumably *Rum uşağı*. The way to high regimental command was also still open to *Rum uşağı*; for example, two officers whom we shall meet later in this study, Ḥasan Balfiyya, *ağa* of the *Gönüllüyan*, and Muṣṭafā *Kâhya* al-Qāzdughlī, are both described by al-Jabartī as *Rūmī* by origin. It is significant that although Ḥasan was the master and patron of Muṣṭafā, al-Jabartī never speaks of the latter as a *mamlūk*. He uses instead the vaguer term *tābi'* (follower, retainer),[15] and proceeds to say that al-Qāzdughlī came to Egypt (implying a voluntary immigration) and took service with Ḥasan: *ḥaḍara ilā Miṣr wa-khadama 'ind Ḥasan aghā*.[16]

It appears, then, that the grandees of Egypt in the seventeenth and eighteenth centuries founded complex patronage-groups the members of which might be linked to the founder by any of three ties: that of servitude, as a *mamlūk*; that of maintenance, as a *sarrāj*; and that of natural kinship, since in some cases sons of grandees were also notables. Furthermore, since dependants in many cases became in course of time founders of their own patronage-groups, "clans" came to be formed which in times of crisis were transformed into political factions.

From about the mid-seventeenth to the mid-eighteenth century, there were two such factions, the Faqāriyya and the Qāsimiyya. Their original nuclei seem to have been two patronage-groups, of which the supposed eponyms, Dhu'l-Faqār Bey and Qāsim Bey, are shadowy and perhaps legendary figures.[17] The Faqāriyya were from the outset primarily a Mamluk household, recruiting from Circassians. In the Qāsimiyya, a Bosniak element is very noticeable, and the likelihood is that, during the seventeenth century, *Rum uşağı* provided many of its recruits. Both the Faqāriyya and the Qāsimiyya were thus originally patronage-groups which naturally expanded in time into "clans". The development of the Faqāriyya into a political faction was however aided, in the last decade or so of the seventeenth century, by the alliance of the original "clan" with another patronage-group, that of the regimental officer, Ḥasan *Ağa* Balfiyya. Balfiyya's retainer, Muṣṭafā al-Qāzdughlī, also a regimental officer, was the founder of the great "clan" of the Qāzdughliyya, which monopolized power in Egypt from about the middle of the eighteenth century until the overthrow of the old régime by the successive hammer-blows of Bonaparte's invasion and the rise of Muḥammad 'Alī Pasha.

The Seven Corps of Egypt consisted of the following.[18] First in precedence was the *Mutafarriqa*, a corps unique among the provincial forces of the Ottoman Empire, and bearing the same name as the sultan's own bodyguard. A second corps which was closely linked to the viceroy's court was that of the *Çavuşan*, which served as a body of pursuivants. There were three corps of cavalry (*sipahis*), the *Gönüllüyan*, whose original members had taken part in the Ottoman conquest of Egypt: the *Tüfenkciyan*, consisting of mounted musketeers; and the *Çerakise*, which, as the name indicates, was originally composed of Circassian Mamluks. Of greater military and political significance than any of these were the two infantry corps: the Janissaries (*Mustaḥfiẓan*) and their rivals, the *'Azeban*. These two corps were particularly well placed to dominate events, since they had their headquarters (sing., *bāb*) in the Citadel of Cairo.

The commanding officer of the Janissaries of Egypt bore, like his superior in Istanbul, the title of *ağa*. By the late seventeenth century, however, most of the actual routine administration of the corps seems to have devolved upon his lieutenant, the *vakit kâhyası* (Ar., *katkhudā al-waqt*), who held office for a year. During this time, the *vakit kâhyası* was the chief of the other officers of his rank, the *kâhyas*. The officers below the rank of *kâhya* bore the title of *çavuş* (not to be confused with the members of the corps of *Çavuşan*), with a *başçavuş* as their chief. There was a *cursus honorum*, by which officers passed through the grades of *çavuş* and *kâhya* to the position of *vakit kâhyası*. The senior officers (apparently after the completion of the *cursus honorum*) formed an influential group known as the *ikhtiyāriyya* ("veterans" or "elders"). Besides the senior officers, whose functions were related to the corps as a whole, there were junior officers heading the various companies (sing., *oda*), into which the corps was divided.[19] Each of these bore the title of *odabaşı*, and the chief of their grade was known as *başodabaşı*. There is, significantly, no evidence of a ladder of promotion from junior to senior officer status. There also existed the rank of *çorbacı*; elsewhere in the Ottoman Empire this was the title held by the head of a company of Janissaries. In Egypt, by this date, it had become purely honorary, presumably reflecting a displacement of the *çorbacıs* by the *odabaşıs*, who elsewhere were their subordinates.[20]

The middle decades of the seventeenth century had witnessed two important developments in the structure of Egyptian politics. The first of these was the temporary emergence of the beylicate as the dominant political group, its acquired authority being typified by the hegemony of Riḍwān Bey al-Faqārī between 1040/1631 and 1066/1656 (see above, pp. 210–13 and 220–30). The second was the development of hostility between the Faqāriyya and the Qāsimiyya. The first phase of this rivalry reached its height shortly after the death of Riḍwān Bey, and culminated in the proscription of the Faqāriyya by the viceroy in alliance with the Qāsimiyya in 1071/1660. The Qāsimiyya failed to substitute their ascendancy for that of the Faqāriyya, as the viceroy procured the assassination of their chief, Aḥmad Bey the Bosniak, in 1072/1662 (see p. 193). Thereafter there was a recession in the political pretensions of the beylicate, and a diminution of factional rivalry, until in 1103/1692, as we shall see, both issues were reopened by the ambitious Ibrāhīm Bey b. Dhi'l-Faqār (p. 244, below). It was during this period between the first and second ascendancies of the beylicate that a contender for political power arose outside the circle of the military grandees, in the person of Küçük Muḥammad the *başodabaşı*.

4. *The Early Career of Küçük Muḥammad*

The sources afford no information about the origins of Küçük Muḥammad. There is even some degree of uncertainty over the date when he first emerged into prominence. Z, our earliest source, first mentions him by name in 1091/1680, when his eviction from the Janissaries is described. PF and AC associate him with troubles in the corps of Janissaries as early as 1087/1676, an incident which is described in Z but without mention of Küçük Muḥammad's name. Al-Jabartī, the latest of our sources, goes back still further, asserting that Küçük Muḥammad was invested as *başodabaşı* in 1085/1674–5. The source of this statement has not yet been discovered, and al-Jabartī's dating for the rest of Küçük Muḥammad's career is so eccentric that it should be viewed with some suspicion. It seems reasonable, however, to accept the evidence of PF and AC that he had become *başodabaşı* by 1087, and had a hand in the troubles of that year.

The years from 1087/1676 to 1091/1680 were a time of recurrent troubles in the corps of Janissaries. On 20 Jumādā II 1087/30 August 1676, the Janissaries seized two of their senior officers, Muḥammad *Kâhya* al-Ḥabashlī and Muṣṭafā *Kâhya*, and imprisoned them. The viceroy, 'Abd al-Raḥmān Pasha II, then summoned the two *kâhyas*, and invested them as beys. Afterwards al-Ḥabashlī resigned his beylicate, but Muṣṭafā retained his until he died at Jedda. This is the account in Z. PF and AC agree in imputing the responsibility for the whole incident to Küçük Muḥammad.[21] The technique of procuring the elevation of opponents to the beylicate was one which he was to employ again: it was a treacherous honour for a Janissary officer, since it withdrew him from the protection and privileges of his corps. An appointment in Jedda, again, was a method of eliminating a rival, since it amounted to banishment from Egypt. According to AC, al-Ḥabashlī regained his former post of *kâhya*, but this is not confirmed in the other sources.[22]

Further revolts against the Janissary grandees ensued. On 12 Rabīʿ I 1088/15 May 1677, another Muṣṭafā, the *başçavuş*, was strangled by ʿAbd al-Raḥmān Pasha after a Janissary rising. Eleven other members of the corps were banished to Jirjā, amongst them a retainer of the *ağa*, named Muḥarram *Çavuş*. At the beginning of Dhu'l-Qaʿda 1089/15 December 1678, the same viceroy authorized measures against other Janissary officers, amongst them the *vakit kâhyası*, Dhu'l-Faqār, who fled to the tomb of *Sayyid* Aḥmad al-Badawī at Ṭanṭā. The sanctuary was not respected. At the viceroy's order, the *kāshif* of the Gharbiyya brought Dhu'l-Faqār out and beheaded him. The fullest account of these incidents is given by Z, who, however, again does not mention Küçük Muḥammad in connexion with them. Neither do PF and AC, but al-Jabartī inserts them in his rather garbled account of Küçük Muḥammad's career.[23] He states that the fall of Dhu'l-Faqār *Kâhya* and al-Sharīf Aḥmad *Çavuş*[24] was brought about by collusion between Küçük Muḥammad, who had temporarily left the Janissaries for another corps, and ʿĀbidī (i.e. ʿAbd al-Raḥmān) Pasha. The death of al-Sharīf "Aḥmad" is dated by al-Jabartī 5 Dhu'l-Ḥijja 1089/18 January 1679, and that of Dhu'l-Faqār ten days later. The telescoping of the two killings, and the dating, probably indicate that al-Jabartī has used a late and inaccurate source,[25] but the association of Küçük Muḥammad with these events is plausible.

Further evidence that the troubles of these years were due to Küçük Muḥammad is provided by the fact, on which all the early sources agree, that in the next Janissary revolt, he was himself the victim. The rising took place, according to Z, on 22 Rajab 1091/18 August 1680, and the Janissaries sought to kill him. He sought asylum with the *ʿAzeban*, but the viceroy ordered him to be banished to Cyprus, whither he set out under the protection of his new corps. The notices in PF and AC are less detailed, and indicate the place of his banishment more vaguely as *bilād al-Rūm*. They agree that his banishment was agreed upon to effect a reconciliation between the Janissaries and the *ʿAzeban*. While PF dates the rising 12 Rajab 1091 (not a serious difference), AC places it on 12 Rajab 1089, which would seem to be a dual error. Al-Jabartī, again, is eccentric in his dating. He places the banishment of Küçük Muḥammad in 1094/1682–3, which seems quite unsupported, but ascribes it to the victory of another Janissary faction-chief Sulaymān *Kâhya*. This, as we shall see, may have some truth in it.[26]

The return of Küçük Muḥammad from exile in Shawwāl 1097/ August–September 1686, was followed by another period of disturbance in the Janissary headquarters. The most detailed account is given by Z, but one or two details are added by the later sources. According to Z, followed by both PF and AC, Küçük Muḥammad, on his return, was received back into his old corps in the capacity of a simple Janissary.[27] However, on 25 Ramaḍān 1097/15 August 1686, he carried out a *coup* and took possession of the Janissary headquarters resuming his former post of *başodabaşı*. PF and AC, who do not give the date of the *coup*, state that it took place after the death of Sulaymān *Kâhya*, the rival faction-leader who had procured the banishment of Küçük Muḥammad in 1091/1680.

The opponents of Küçük Muḥammad did not give in without a struggle. Two of their leaders, Jirjī 'Alī and Jalab Khalīl, appealed to the viceroy's Divan, stating that they had not invited Küçük Muḥammad to be *başodabaşı* in their corps, and demanding that he be made a *çorbacı* or reduced to the ranks. Either alternative would have removed him from a position of power. Küçük Muḥammad rejected both, and, during the night which followed, turned the cannon of the Janissary headquarters in the direction of the Divan-hall. When the Divan met, on the next morning, to discuss the matter, they yielded to the accomplished fact, and accepted Küçük Muḥammad's offer to surrender the goods of his opponents. Following the custom in such circumstances, the plaintiffs, together with about seventy-five Janissaries, transferred themselves to the corps of *'Azeban*. PF, which gives no details of the *coup*, gives the number of dissidents as about ninety. In spite of his low official rank, Küçük Muḥammad was again the master of the Janissary headquarters, and the boss of the dominant gang in the corps.

His ascendancy was to be brief. On a date which appears to be 10 Shawwāl 1097/30 August 1686 a newly commissioned *ağa* of Janissaries arrived from Istanbul. After his installation, the Janissaries of Cairo assembled at headquarters and expelled Küçük Muḥammad from the corps. The rival gang had clearly triumphed, armed with the sanction of an imperial order. The whole incident throws some light on the alliances Küçük Muḥammad had established with the grandees. The *vakit kâhyası* at the time of his seizure of power was Muṣṭafā al-Qāzdughlī, whose patron, Ḥasan *Ağa* Balfiyya, the commanding officer of the *Gönüllüyan*, received Küçük Muḥammad when he was expelled by the Janissaries.[28]

Z alone is our source of information on the next episode. On 17 Dhu'l-Ḥijja 1099/13 October 1688, a group of Janissaries belonging to Küçük Muḥammad's faction, led by a certain Aḥmad Çelebi al-Bayraqdār and an *odabaşı* from Būlāq named Bunduq Khalīl, went to the headquarters, ostensibly to intercede for his readmission to the corps. Their real intention seems to have been to carry out a *coup*, for they found the headquarters almost deserted except for Küçük Muḥammad's old opponent, Jalab Khalīl.[29] He and his attendants succeeded, however, in routing their assailants, some of whom fled to the headquarters of the '*Azeban*. The dominant faction of the Janissaries felt that they had been betrayed. They deposed their *kâhya*, and imprisoned him. For three days and nights they remained mobilized in their headquarters, and they carried out a purge of their members.

The episode was concluded through the intervention of the viceroy and notables of Cairo. Küçük Muḥammad was rusticated on 20 Dhu'l-Ḥijja/16 October to the provincial town of al-Manṣūra in the Gharbiyya. The deposed *kâhya* was released but not restored. Four partisans of Aḥmad al-Bayraqdār were banished to the remote fortress of Ibrīm in Lower Nubia. Aḥmad himself and Bunduq Khalīl, in the meantime, were safe with the '*Azeban*, but their hosts were not anxious to become involved in a clash with Janissaries. A reconciliation was effected between the two corps, Aḥmad being sent to Banī Suwayf and Bunduq Khalīl to Rosetta.[30] For nearly four years more, Küçük Muḥammad remained an obscure *çorbacı* in the *Gönüllüyan*.

5. *The Coup d'état of 1103/1692*

Küçük Muḥammad emerged from obscurity, and regained power for the last time during a great *coup d'état* in 1103/1692. The events are noted in both the literary and D Group chronicles, but their accounts of the circumstances vary, making a comparative study necessary.

The earliest and fullest literary account is provided, as usual, by Z.[31] This states that on 13 Shawwāl 1103/28 June 1692, Jalab Khalīl, the *kâhya* of Janissaries, was seized and imprisoned by his corps. The *ağa* obtained a death-warrant from the viceroy, and the deposed *kâhya* was put to death. The Janissaries then plundered his property, and shut their headquarters for three days. While they were thus isolated, a faction proceeded to purge the corps. Eight *odabaşıs* were transferred to the honorary rank of *çorbacı*, but, since they would not accept this, they were rusticated. Meanwhile, four of the high officers and bureaucrats of the corps had sought refuge with the *Tüfenkçiyan*. They were summoned to return to Janissary headquarters, but refused to do so.

On 15 Shawwāl/30 June, the dominant faction in the Janissaries deposed the *ağa*, and appointed a new one. Two of the four fugitives were restored to favour, and recalled to their corps. The other two, Salīm *Efendi*, formerly the clerk of the corps, and Rajab *Kâhya*, were raised to the beylicate. The consequences of this ominous promotion were shortly to appear.

On 23 Shawwāl/8 July, Küçük Muḥammad made his reappearance, and seized the Janissary headquarters. Once again the headquarters was closed. He then summoned the senior officers of all the Seven Corps from the Divan. Such was the authority of the Janissary boss that they came at his bidding, and consented to the abrogation of certain dues (*ḥimāyāt*), which were thereupon formally abolished by a proclamation of the viceroy. The significance of this act will be examined subsequently (pp. 246–7). A week later, on 1 Dhu'l-Qa'da/15 July, the newly appointed Salīm Bey was wrongfully put to death, while his colleague, Rajab, was held in confinement for ten days, after which he was deprived of his rank and banished to Medina.

The account of the *coup d'état* in Z is substantially followed, although at much less length, by PF and AC.[32] Both these sources acribe the revolt of the Janissaries from its outset to Küçük Muḥammad. There are one or two discrepancies in dating; thus the elevation of Salīm and Rajab to the beylicate is dated 23 Shawwāl by PF, while AC places the killing of Jalab Khalīl on 27 Shawwāl. In effect, however, the three literary chronicles represent a single tradition.

On turning to the popular chronicles, one becomes conscious of a very different tradition. While the three versions, given respectively by DQ, DO, and DL,[33] differ among themselves in style and phraseology, they are in complete harmony in the structure of their narrative, and this differs in two main respects from the narrative of the literary chronicles. In the first place, the order of events is different: the killing of Jalab Khalīl follows the promotion and disgrace of Rajab and Salīm. In the second place, the revolt of the Janissaries is linked with an attempt of the Faqāriyya to re-establish their hegemony at the expense of the Qāsimiyya, and Küçük Muḥammad is shown as the ally and agent of Ibrāhīm Bey b. Dhi'l-Faqār.

We must, I think, reject the order of events as presented by these D Group chronicles, not only because they are of much later origin than the very full and circumstantial account of Z, but also because the D narrative shows marked signs of being heightened for dramatic effect. The popular chronicles give what purport to be the actual speeches of the participants, which the nearly contemporary Z does not attempt. The fates of Küçük Muḥammad's opponents are arranged, as it were, in a rising scale of tragedy: Rajab Bey escapes death, but is deprived of his rank and exiled; Salīm Bey is put to death in a private room; Jalab Khalīl is assassinated in his seat of office during a tumultuous assembly of his own comrades. Not only does this reverse the order of events in Z, but it alters the manner of the death of Jalab Khalīl, which, according to Z, was similar to that of Salīm.

More attention must be paid to the insistence of the D Group chronicles that the *coup* of 1103/1692 was an episode in the struggle of Faqāriyya and Qāsimiyya. The silence of the literary chronicles on this point need not be construed as evidence against it: indeed the cryptic remark in Z, that Küçük Muḥammad "took possession of the headquarters with the knowledge of God knows whom" (*malaka al-bāb bi-ma'rifat man ya'lamuhu Allāh*) implies an unwillingness to discuss the wider ramifications of the revolt of the Janissaries. While the dramatized presentation of the association between Küçük Muḥammad and the Faqāriyya may be dismissed as a narrative device, we may accept the basic account of the motives behind the *coup*.

The circumstances in which the *coup* took place are described as follows in DQ.[34] In 1104 [*sic*] Ibrāhīm Bey, the commander of the Pilgrimage, sought to obtain the supremacy (*ri'āsa*) in Cairo. The occasion was favourable to the Faqāriyya, since members of this faction held all the principal posts in the Divan and the provinces (except the Buḥayra, which was a Qāsimī stronghold), including the office of *defterdar*, until recently occupied by a Qāsimī bey. In the Janissary corps, however, the Faqāriyya were very weakly represented, so Ibrāhīm Bey's first aim was to install his partisan, Küçük Muḥammad, as *başodabaşı*, and to oust the leading Qāsimī officers, amongst whom were Rajab *Kâhya*, Salīm *Efendi*, and Jalab Khalīl. The plot was hatched amongst the leaders of the Faqāriyya, Ibrāhīm Bey himself, Ḥasan *Ağa* Balfiyya, Muṣṭafā *Kâhya* al-Qāzdughlī, and Ismā'īl Bey the *defterdar*, the last two of whom were respectively the *çirak* and the son-in-law of Ḥasan *Ağa*. Ibrāhīm Bey is shown throughout as the principal manager of the plot, who brings about the elevation and downfall of Rajab and Salīm, and who finally extends his protection to Rajab, and secures his banishment. The accounts in DO and DL are substantially the same as that in DQ. We are probably justified, therefore, in seeing the *coup d'état* of 1103 as a renewal of the prolonged struggle between the Faqāriyya and the Qāsimiyya.

6. *The Final Ascendancy of Küçük Muḥammad*

During the last two and a half years of Küçük Muḥammad's life, he was the real ruler of Cairo. As a successful faction-leader he was constantly threatened by the malice of his opponents. Chief amongst these was Aḥmad al-Baghdādlī, who had been *başodabaşı* before him. In Sha'bān 1104/April–May 1693, al-Baghdādlī made an unsuccessful attempt to shoot Küçük Muḥammad as he was passing along a lane in Cairo. The shot miscarried, and al-Baghdādlī fled. Although he was ordered to be banished from Egypt, he succeeded in absconding, and was never discovered. This incident is described by Z alone among the literary chronicles. The D Group chronicles also give this episode, with the usual dramatic touches, e.g. a pious speech by the intended victim.[35]

A more dangerous enemy was to be found among the Faqāriyya themselves. This was Muṣṭafā al-Qāzdughlī. For some reason he had fallen into disgrace after the *coup d'état* of 1103/1692, and was sent to the Ḥijāz, whence he returned with the Pilgrimage of 1104.[36] He bore Küçük Muḥammad a personal grudge for his fate, and began to plot against him. In this connexion, Z recounts an incident which is not found in any other source.[37] On 7 Dhu'l-Ḥijja 1105/30 July 1694, Muṣṭafā al-Qāzdughlī gave a feast to the Janissaries and their officers, at which a brawl arose between the son of Jalab Khalīl and Manaww [*sic*] Aḥmad, the son-in-law of Küçük Muḥammad. At the same time, an assembly of Küçük Muḥammad's partisans was meeting at his house, and leaguing themselves together.

Both parties were clearly building up their strength. Al-Qāzdughlī's next move was to betake himself and his friends to the headquarters of the '*Azeban*, thus revealing the schism in the Janissaries. Attempts were made at mediation between the two parties by the religious notables and the grandees, but Küçük Muḥammad refused to accept any change in his status. A proposal that the viceroy should give Küçük Muḥammad the rank of *çorbacı* failed because the viceroy refused to act. By now it was 9 Dhu'l-Ḥijja/1 August, the feast of *Yawm al-Waqfa*, and the viceroy ordered a suspension of the quarrel during the festival. Through the mediation of the religious notables, a temporary agreement was reached between the two factions.

The story suggests that by this time, the alliance between Küçük Muḥammad and the leaders of the Faqāriyya had broken down. He had, in fact, only a few more weeks to live. The account of his death, as given by Z,[38] is that on 23 Muḥarram 1106/13 September 1694, he was riding with a company of his men to the Janissary headquarters, as was his custom, when he was shot by a person sitting in the window of a mosque beside the street. The bullet passed through his chest, and he fell dead from his donkey. His followers scattered, only the donkey-boy remaining to carry his body home. The assassin remained unknown. The influence of his faction among the Janissaries collapsed at once. Manaww Aḥmad, his steward and son-in-law, and Köse Yūsuf, an *odabaşı* and one of his principal lieutenants, immediately transferred themselves, together with twenty-three of their associates, to the corps of *Çerakise*. The account in PF[39] makes possible the identification of the place where the murderer lay in wait: it was the Mu'ayyadī mosque "beside the '*Azeban* headquarters", in which, of course, al-Qāzdughlī and his friends had taken refuge. AC,[40] who dates the assassination ten days earlier, on 13 Muḥarram (although this is probably a copyist's error), adds some details about the hiring of the gunman. The D Group chronicles tell the same story, with the addition of one or two details. The assassin is described in DQ as "a soldier" (*wāḥid jundī*).[41] DO is more explicit: the killer was a mercenary (*sīmānī*)[42] belonging to the retinue of al-Qāzdughlī and living in the district of Ṭalkhā (?). After the murder, Köse Yūsuf tried in vain to catch the assassin, who was, however, killed on returning to Ṭalkhā by order of al-Qāzdughlī himself. DL, rather surprisingly, has only a brief account of the incident.[43] He does not name al-Qāzdughlī as the promoter of the assassination, but merely says that "one whom God Most High knows" instigated the domestic treasurer (*khāzindār*) of Salīm Bey to take vengeance for his late master upon Küçük Muḥammad. The picturesque details given by DO are omitted in this source.

7. *Küçük Muḥammad as a Tribune of the People*

There are some indications that the assassination of Küçük Muḥammad was not simply the outcome of personal jealousy, nor merely an incident in the gang-warfare of Cairo, but was at least partly procured by wealthy and influential speculators in grain, whose operations had been curtailed by the *başodabaşı*. Throughout the final phase of his career, there are signs that Küçük Muḥammad was executing a crude economic policy, designed to protect the middle and lower classes of Cairo and the other principal towns of Lower Egypt.

His accession to power in 1103/1692 was immediately followed by the abolition of the *ḥimāyāt*. This incident is described by Z as follows:

> "On 23 Shawwāl of that year [i.e. 8 July 1692] Küçük Muḥammad . . . sent to the senior officers [*ikhtiyāriyya*] of the Seven Corps, and they were in the Divan. So they came to him in the [Janissary] headquarters, and agreed with him that he should abrogate the *ḥimāyāt* entirely, and everything pertaining thereto connected with the corps of Janissaries, and the '*Azeban*, from the appointments in the ports of Damietta, Rosetta, Būlāq, and elsewhere."[44]

It is also mentioned a little lower that innovations in weighing-dues (*al-qabbāniyya al-muḥdatha*) were abolished. Both PF and AC have passages corresponding to the one cited above,[45] but it has no parallel in the D Group chronicles. These, at this point, represent Küçük Muḥammad as making certain stipulations to safeguard his personal authority on resuming office in the Janissaries.

What were the *ḥimāyāt*? The term *ḥimāya* has had various significances in Muslim history, but in Ottoman Egypt it meant an illegal levy made, in addition to legitimate taxes, by the holder of an office.[46] As time went on, some *ḥimāyāt* acquired a species of formal recognition in that the treasury drew off a proportion of them as revenue. The *ḥimāyāt* thus profited both the grandees, who levied them, and the Ottoman treasury; hence Küçük Muḥammad obtained their abolition by agreement of the grandees and proclamation of the viceroy. It is clear that the *ḥimāyāt* referred to in the passage quoted were connected with the trade and industry of the chief ports of Egypt. Their abolition would benefit the merchants and artisans, and would correspondingly injure the wealthy members of the ruling military *élite*. It need hardly be said that Küçük Muḥammad's abolition of the *ḥimāyāt* had only a transitory effect.

Shortly before Küçük Muḥammad's death, in Muḥarram 1106/August–September 1694, there was a disastrous failure of the Nile flood. This was in fact the beginning of the period of dearth which was to last for two years, producing misery for the people of Egypt, and a serious financial crisis for the administration. Although Z does not relate the onset of this dearth in any way to the circumstances of Küçük Muḥammad's death, such a connexion is made by each of the other five sources studied here.[47]

All agree that Küçük Muḥammad imposed a price ceiling for wheat on the middlemen of the corn trade in Būlāq. PF and AC, as well as DO and DL, state that an intolerable rise in wheat prices began immediately after his death, and this may also be implied by Z, who dates the beginning of the dearth on 1 Ṣafar. The fullest account of what happened is given, unusually, by AC, who writes as an eyewitness of the failure of the Nile. AC's narrative is somewhat confused and repetitive, in parts ungrammatical and difficult to read, but he describes the course of events as follows:

The failure of the Nile, at the beginning of Muḥarram 1106/22 August 1694, was followed by an immediate disappearance of bread from the market. On learning of the situation, Küçük Muḥammad rose to Būlāq, and summoned all those principally concerned in the handling of wheat, the *amīns*,[48] the official measurers, and the captains of the grain boats. He threatened them with unspecified consequences if the price per *ardabb* rose above that then current, 60 *niṣf fiḍḍa*. The agents of Hawwāra, and of the *multazims* (the tax-farmers who were in effect rural landlords), thereupon held a meeting. They offered Küçük Muḥammad an enormous bribe to be allowed to continue their profiteering. AC gives two versions of his reply: according to one, he threatened the agents with the destruction of their places if Hawwāra and *multazims* did not send wheat; according to the other, he upbraided his audience for their speedy forcing up of prices. Once again, he refused to allow a price in excess of 60 *niṣf fiḍḍa*. When, on the next day, he found the ships at Būlāq empty of corn, he stimulated the sluggish market by seizing three boat captains and two officials, and putting them to death. This stirred up the agents of Hawwāra to procure his own assassination, as has been described, on 23 Muḥarram 1106/13 September 1694.

In the D Group chronicles the episode is given with surprising economy, none of the picturesque details of Küçük Muḥammad's interview with the agents, or his killing of the officials and captains being given. Al-Jabartī's treatment of the episode has one unusual feature.[49] Although his account is very bare, he gives a brief anecdote not found elsewhere, that after Küçük Muḥammad had warned the profiteers of Būlāq, and (as in DO/DL) stationed two *kapıcıs* there, "he sent his donkey-boy every two or three days, with the donkey, to walk with it along the river-bank, and return. So they thought that Küçük Muḥammad was in Būlāq, and dared not increase the price of grain".

There remains one anecdote which is probably quite legendary, since no trace of it is found in the literary chronicles, but which is of some interest as conveying the popular idea of Küçük Muḥammad. This is the story of Küçük Muḥammad and the jeweller, found in the D Group chronicles, and taken over by al-Jabartī.[50] As he tells the story, it concerns a jeweller of Cairo, who went on Pilgrimage, leaving a chest of valuables with a friend named ʿAlī al-Fayyūmī. A year later he returned home, and went for his chest, but al-Fayyūmī denied all knowledge of him. In great distress, the jeweller laid the matter before Küçük Muḥammad, who concealed him, and sent for al-Fayyūmī. While they were speaking together, Küçük Muḥammad took al-Fayyūmī's rosary, and gave it to a servant, whom he ordered to go with al-Fayyūmī's servant to al-Fayyūmī's house for the chest. Deceived by the rosary and the presence of al-Fayyūmī's servant, the family handed over the chest. Meanwhile Küçük Muḥammad had asked al-Fayyūmī about the chest, and again al-Fayyūmī denied any knowledge of the matter. At that moment the chest was produced, and the jeweller was summoned to prove his ownership, which he did. He was sent home rejoicing, while his deceitful friend crept away, frightened almost to death.

As suggested above, this is essentially an oriental folk-tale of a genre known from biblical times onwards, and it may originally have had no connexion with Küçük Muḥammad at all. It is, however, interesting that later generations thought of Küçük Muḥammad in this way—as a wise and just judge, discovering fraud. Also, it is significant that the tale is set in bourgeois circles, for the other incidents studied in this section suggest that it was the interests of the urban middle and lower classes that Küçük Muḥammad sought to protect. He is indeed an almost unique figure in the history of Ottoman Egypt; a man outside the circles of the wealthy and powerful—the beys, the corps grandees, and the religious notables—who succeeded on repeated occasions in making himself a key-figure in politics, and imposing his will on the ruling groups. The conspiracies and violence by which he attained power were nothing unusual, and popular opinion in no way held these acts against him. Two of the chroniclers end their account of him with the words, "May the mercy of God be upon him; he was one of the people of good!"[51]

NOTES

1 'Abd al-Raḥmān al-Jabartī, *'Ajā'ib al-āthār fi'l-tarājim wa'l-akhbār*. Short reference, Jabartī. The edition used is the Būlāq edition, and all page-references in this article are to the first volume of this.

2 The term "literary chronicles" is used here to designate a genre of historical writing, and does not imply elevation of style or correctness of grammar. The three chronicles discussed here are late and debased specimens of the genre, and from a stylistic point of view are but little superior to the popular chronicles.

3 There also exists a fragmentary version (DC, i.e. Cambridge University Library, MS. Add. 278[7]) which is virtually identical with DO, and so does not demand separate consideration here.

4 For the viceroys of Egypt in the seventeenth century, see above, pp. 189–91.

5 Al-Jabartī, I, p. 6, ll. 22–5; p. 56, l. 8. Cf. David Ayalon, "The historian al-Jabartī and his background", *BSOAS*, XXIII, 2, 1960, 222.

6 For the possible appropriation of another floating legend by DO, DC, and DL (the Feast of Zayn al-Faqār) see above, pp. 166–7.

7 Al-Jabartī says that Rajab *Kâhya* absconded and then resigned his beylicate. PF says that he was arrested, and remained in the Citadel for ten days before being freed. The D Group chronicles all have a long account of Rajab *Kâhya* seeking asylum with Ibrāhīm Bey, and resigning the beylicate: they do not mention his imprisonment. This is a typical example of the dramatizing tendency of the D Group.

8 More specifically, in both cases, a chronicle of the DO sub-group, since al-Jabartī's notice contains information about Rajab *Kâhya*'s son, his house in Cairo, and the identity of Küçük Muḥammad's assassin, which is found in DO but not in DQ or DL.

9 The obituary may be broken down as follows:

p. 92, ll. 4–7: K.M.'s action during the dearth of 1106 (D Group).
7–8: Story of K.M.'s donkey (unidentified).
8–9: Rise in prices after K.M.'s death (? PF).

10–32: Story of K.M. and the merchant (D Group).
p. 92, l. 32–p. 93, l. 2: Al-Baghdādlī's attempt to kill K.M. (D Group).
p. 93, ll. 3–18: Outline of K.M.'s career. This bears some resemblance to PF, and is clearly derived from a literary chronicle, but the dates are impossible to harmonize with the known sources, and it contains some data not otherwise recorded.

10 The D Group chronicles make 'Ali Pasha VI a willing accomplice in the *coup d'état* of 1103/1692.

11 Cf. Aḥmad al-Jazzār, *Nizamname-i Mısır*, ed. and tr. Stanford J. Shaw, *Ottoman Egypt in the eighteenth century* (Cambridge, Mass., 1962): English text, pp. 44–6; Turkish text, pp. 15–16: short reference, *Nizamname*. Cf. also p. 247.

12 The best exposition is that by David Ayalon, "Studies in al-Jabartī", *JESHO*, III, 1960, 148–74, 275–325: short reference, "Studies". On p. 307, n. 1, the anonymous work referred to should be *Zubdat ikhtiṣār ta'rīkh mulūk Miṣr*.

13 *Nizamname*: Eng. text, pp. 23–6; Turkish text, pp. 7–8. There are two interesting points in al-Jazzār's description. The first is that when a master ended the personal service of his *sarrāj*, he allowed him to grow a beard. The growing of a beard similarly marked, in Ayalon's words, "a very important stage in the *mamlūk*'s career", either when he was emancipated, as European observers state, or on the eve of appointment to high office, as suggested by some passages in al-Jabartī. See Ayalon, "Studies", 322–3. The second is al-Jazzār's use of the term *çirak* for the ex-*sarrāj*. This term (in its arabicized form *ishrāq*) is of frequent occurrence in al-Jabartī. See note 8, p. 175.

14 *Nizamname*: Eng. text, pp. 24–6, 50; Turkish text, pp. 7–8, 10.

15 I cannot wholly accept Professor Ayalon's argument ("Studies", 282) that "*tābi'* and *mamlūk* of a certain patron are exactly the same in meaning". As with other terms (e.g. *ağa*, *çirak*), *tābi'* seems to have had a general and one or more specific meanings.

16 Al-Jabartī, I, p. 91, ll. 29–30.

17 See notes 11 and 14, p. 175, and also DHU'L-FAḲĀRIYYA, *EI*², II, 233.

18 For further information on the Seven Corps, see Stanford J. Shaw, *The financial and administrative development of Ottoman Egypt, 1517–1798* (Princeton, N.J., 1961), 189–97; short reference, *Ottoman Egypt*.

19 Richard Pococke, *A description of the East and some other countries* (London, 1743), I, 167.

20 Pococke, op. cit., I, 168–9: "In Constantinople they have Serbajees over every chamber; but here [sc. Egypt] a Serbajee is only an honorary thing, like a brevet-colonel. . . . Among the janizaries, when any one is made a Serbajee, 'tis laying him aside, and he is no further advanced". Cf. H. A. R. Gibb and H. Bowen, *Islamic society and the West*, I, 1 (London, 1950), 319. *Oda* superseded *orta* in Egyptian usage, to signify a company.

21 Z, f. 18a; PF, ff. 58a–b; 'AC, *sub* (66) Abd al-Raḥmān Pasha. The manuscript of AC is very sparsely foliated, and it is easier to refer to the viceroys who are numbered consecutively in the margin) and to the year. The incident is not mentioned in al-Jabartī.

22 A curious, and possibly significant fact, is that the two *kâhyas* bear names which may link them with Africa south of Egypt. *Al-Ḥabashlī* is, of course, arabicized Turkish for "the Abyssinian", perhaps indicating an origin in the Ottoman province of Habeş, i.e. the Red Sea littoral in the region of Suakin and Massawa. Muṣṭafā Kâhya is called in Z *Sīnār*, and in AC *Sh . nār*, possibly connecting him with the Funj sultanate of Sinnār.

23 Z, f. 18a; PF, f. 58b; AC, *sub* (66) 'Abd al-Raḥmān Pasha; Jabartī, I, 93.
24 PF and AC both call the *başçavuş* al-Sharīf Muṣṭafā. "Aḥmad" would seem to be a slip.
25 Another example of telescoping occurs in PF and AC, both of which link the killing of Muḥarram Çavuş in Jirjā with that of Dhu'l-Faqār Kâhya.
26 Z, f. 18a; PF, f. 58b; AC, *sub* (66) 'Abd al-Raḥmān Pasha; al-Jabartī, I, 93.
27 This would seem to be the significance of the expression *labbasūhu al-ẓulama* (Z), *albasūhu al-ḍulama* (PF, AC).
28 The sources for this episode in Küçük Muḥammad's career are Z, ff. 19a–b; PF, f. 59b; AC, *sub* (68) Ḥamza Pasha. Al-Jabartī, I, 93, ascribes the expulsion to Küçük Muḥammad's antagonism with Salīm Efendi and Rajab Kâhya, who appear in the earlier sources as his opponents in 1103/1692.
29 He is here called Jalab Khalīl *Sarrāj*; cf. above, p. 236.
30 The sole source of information on this episode is Z, f. 20b.
31 Z, ff, 24b–25a.
32 PF, ff. 63a–b; AC, *sub* (72) 'Alī Pasha.
33 DQ, ff. 4a–6a; DO, ff. 4a–5b; DL, ff. 9b–12a.
34 DQ, ff. 4a–b.
35 Z, f. 25b; DQ, f. 6a; DO, f. 8b; DL, f. 14a.
36 Z, f. 25a; DO, f. 7a; reason for his banishment not stated. DQ, f. 66; "he made an innovation against the *Qānūn*". DL, f. 12a; "he requested the increase" (*ṭalab al-zāyid*). The Group chronicles all state that Ḥasan Balfiyya brought about his return: DQ, f. 6b; DO, ff. 8b–9a; DL, f. 13b.
37 Z, ff. 26a–b.
38 Z, f. 27a.
39 PF, f. 64a.
40 AC, *sub* (72) 'Alī Pasha.
41 DQ, f. 8a. The term *jundī* had, however, the technical meaning of a Mamluk trooper: cf. *Nizamname*; Eng. text, p. 30; Turkish text, p. 10.
42 DO, f. 9a. *Sīmānī*, from Turkish *seğmen*, usually means in late Arabic contexts, a mercenary.
43 DL, f. 17a.
44 Z, f. 25a.
45 PF, f. 63a; AC, *sub* (72) 'Alī Pasha.
46 See Cl. Cahen, "Notes pour l'histoire de la *ḥimāya*", in *Mélanges Louis Massignon* (Damascus, 1956), 287–303; also Ḥimāya in *EI*², III, 394. For Ottoman Egypt, see Shaw, *Ottoman Egypt*, index ṣ.v. "*Mâl-ı Ḥımâye*" et seq.
47 The episode may be found in the following passages: PF, f. 64a; AC, *sub* (72) 'Alī Pasha; DQ, f. 7b; DO, f. 9a; DL, ff. 13b–14a.
48 *Amīn*, in this context, refers probably to the customs officers, but perhaps also to the *amīn al-baḥrayn*, the holder of a very profitable post at Būlāq and al-Fusṭāṭ. See Shaw, *Ottoman Egypt*, 103, 123–5, and also index, s.v. "*Emîn*", et seq.
49 Al-Jabartī, I, 92, ll. 4–9.
50 DQ, ff. 6b–7b; DO, ff. 7a–8b; DL, ff. 14a–17a; Jabartī, I, 92, ll. 10–32.
51 DQ, f. 8a; DL, f. 17a.

Index

(Please note that the Arabic article (al,' l) and the abbreviations b. for ībn and w. for walad have been disregarded in the alphabetical sequence)